THE FINDER LIBRARY

CARLA SPEED McNEIL

VOLUME 1

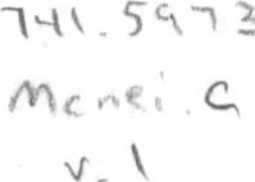

THE FINDER LIBRARY

CARLA SPEED McNEIL

VOLUME 1

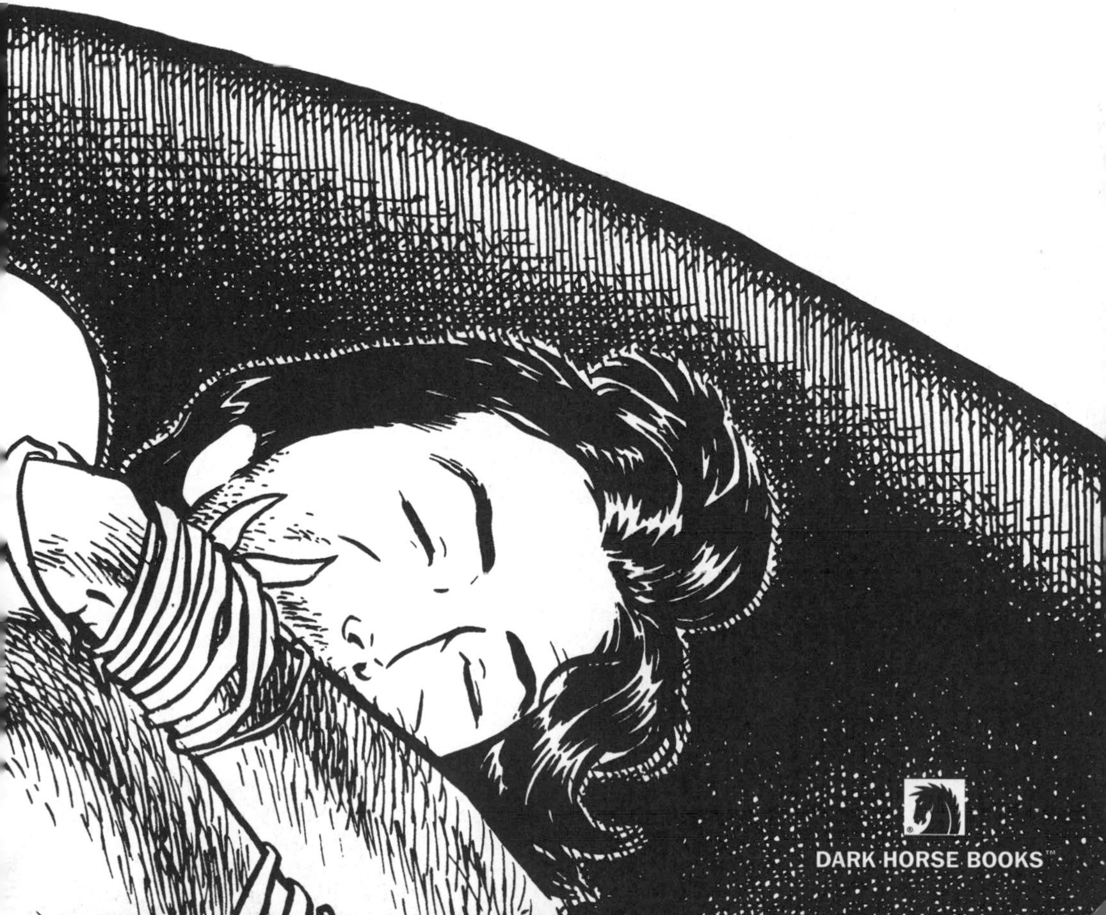

Publisher
MIKE RICHARDSON

Collection Editors
RACHEL EDIDIN and **KATIE MOODY**

Assistant Editors
JEMIAH JEFFERSON and **JOHN SCHORK**

Designer
JUSTIN COUCH

Special thanks to **CARY GRAZZINI**, **GARY GRINDE**, and **SUSAN TARDIF**.

This volume collects *Finder* #1–#22 and additional materials.

DARK HORSE BOOKS
A division of Dark Horse Comics, Inc.
10956 SE Main Street
Milwaukie, OR 97222

DarkHorse.com

To find a comic shop in your area, call the Comic Shop Locator Service:
(888) 266-4226

First Edition: March 2011

ISBN 978-1-59582-652-7

10 9 8 7 6 5 4 3 2 1

Printed by Transcontinental Gagné, Louiseville, QC, Canada.

Finder started in a little tiny apartment, and is now done in a much larger house. The series is dedicated to Michael. Love you.

Sin-Eater started with Cat Boy, who wanted to know what happened after that. And after that. And after that. Thanks, Kitty.

King of the Cats was inspired by the wildlife photography of Mitsuaki Iwago and the novel *Mind of My Mind* by Octavia Butler.

Talisman is for the kid with the book, wherever and everywhere.

INTRODUCTION

Carla Speed McNeil self-published *Finder* for fifteen years, including the stories that you, lucky person, are about to encounter. It took way too many of those years before I discovered it, but once I did, it became my stock answer to nearly anyone who asked me to recommend a comic that would satisfy their particular interests. You like crazy world-building science fiction? Have you tried *Finder*? Smart relationship dramas that acknowledge that relationships and sex are really complicated? Have a look at *Finder*. Adventure stories with stylistic flair and top-flight visual storytelling? Anthropological satire? Ultra-dense allusive responses to pop-culture overload? Comics that are, in a lot of ways, genuinely not like anything else you've ever read? Let me show you *Finder*. You can really start anywhere with it—the volumes are kind of modular—but maybe try *Talisman* if you're going to get just one.

I've lost track of how many times I slipped one *Finder* volume or another into a friend's hands, but more often than not I'd get a message a few days later that was something along the lines of "Wow. That was *really* not what I was expecting that story to be like. Where can I get more?" (The answer was "Well, if you can find a *really* well-stocked comic book store, you might find a volume or two around, or there's always mail-order." So three cheers to Dark Horse for making this stuff more widely available.)

McNeil is a cartoonist's cartoonist, the kind of artist that other comics professionals talk about with a little bit of awe. She's so much a master of character design that *Finder*'s premise involves multiple clusters of characters who look almost exactly like each other, and she still manages to make it clear who's who at a glance. Over the course of "Sin-Eater," you get to watch her alarm ingly rapid artistic evolution as she picks up cues from a handful of inspirations—Jaime and Gilbert Hernandez, Dave Sim and Gerhard, Hayao Miyazaki—tips her hat to them, then runs like wildfire into her own territory. She also thinks harder about storytelling than anybody else I've ever talked to, and as unusual as most of *Finder*'s story structures (and stories-within-stories) are, they've got rock-solid architecture. You just have to take the time to investigate them.

Which leads me to a bit of advice. If you're plunging into the world of *Finder* for the first time, the temptation is obviously to devour the book as fast as possible—to race through the book like a hellhound (or a Finder) is on your trail, flipping frantically between the story itself and the endnotes in which McNeil explains the dense web of invented and borrowed cultural traditions and extratextual references that make up the conceptual backdrop of almost every page. My advice is: don't. Don't even look at the endnotes your first time through. Read every page as slowly as you possibly can. This is a very big book—you really don't have to read it all in one sitting, or even three or four.

Finder plunks you down in a setting as alien as anything in our world, and a lot of the fun of it is the process of figuring out what's going on. McNeil's been known to describe the series as "Aboriginal Science Fiction," which is a good way of putting it. If you see a person or object or gesture whose significance you can't immediately identify, pause for a moment. File it away in your memory. You're likely to see something else later that makes it make more sense. If you don't, there are always the endnotes, but those can wait for a second or third re-reading. (Trust me: you'll be coming back for those.)

If, on the other hand, you're a veteran *Finder* reader, returning to the domed city of Anvard and the immaculately maintained attractions of Munkytown: welcome back. This brick of a volume is a good way to get a sense of the magnitude of what McNeil has invented. "Sin-Eater," in retrospect, is an introduction to the characters and themes of the whole *Finder* series—just not the way it seems to be on a first reading. (We see that in miniature in its interlude, "Fight Scene," originally written and drawn after the rest of this volume, and later expanded for its 2007 appearance in the *Sin-Eater* hardcover; it's about a conflict between a pair of badasses, but not the kind of tussle you'd expect.) "King of the Cats" is a pitch-black farce that moves away from the setting McNeil's established in the first story arc and makes *Finder*'s culture-clash theme more explicit.

And then there's "Talisman"—the section of this collection that I secretly wish were available as an oversized hardcover volume with hand-tooled leather covers and gilt edges, in part because it's great, in part because that would be formally appropriate, and in part because it would remind me that I really ought to keep it in my house. (I've lent way too many copies of the paperback to friends who appreciated it so much they never gave it back.) It's a story about a girl who falls in love with a book, and returns to it to find that it's something different from what she remembers. To say more would be too much for first-time readers.

But I'll say one more thing to those fortunate enough to be reading McNeil's work for the first time: *Finder* is another story you can fall into, a story not just to enjoy once but to explore. Whatever obstacles have kept it from you since it began in 1995, the last of them has just been removed. Turn the page, in fact, and Ganesha, the remover of obstacles, will introduce you to the unlikely hero sleeping in his bowl.

—Douglas Wolk

SIN-EATER

FOR MICHAEL:

WITHOUT WHOM, ETC.

PART ONE

CHAPTER ONE

SALUTATION

HAAAAHH...

AH A AOW!
SHIT!

PTCH!

WELL, SIR ...
I CAN'T MAKE YOU A PROPER OFFERING, 'CAUSE I DON'T KNOW WHAT YOUR PLEASURE IS.
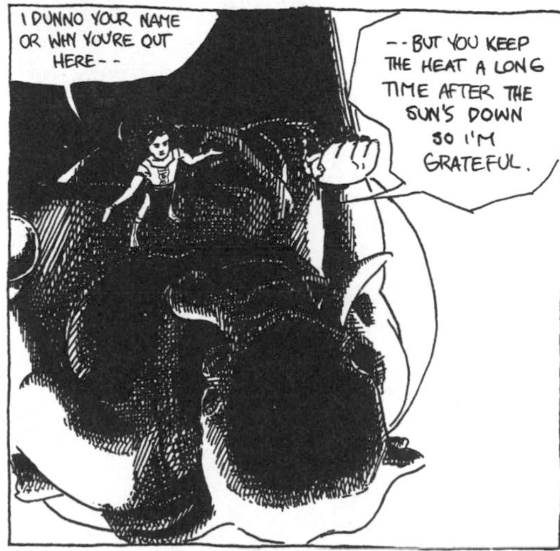
I DUNNO YOUR NAME OR WHY YOU'RE OUT HERE--
--BUT YOU KEEP THE HEAT A LONG TIME AFTER THE SUN'S DOWN SO I'M GRATEFUL.

—AH!—

USUALLY WHILE I WAS LIVING IN THE BADLANDS I WAS UP AND ABOUT ONLY AFTER DARK.

THE HEAT OF THE DAY IS INCREDIBLE, AND YOU LOSE MORE WATER THAN YOU'LL EVER FIND. AT NIGHT, THOUGH, THE DESERT TAKES ON A WEIRD NEON-BLUE GLOW AND EVERYTHING WAKES UP. **EVERYTHING.** BIGGER, NASTIER CREATURES THAN YOU'D THINK LIVE OUT HERE, AND MY OWN FOOLISH-NESS GOT ME TOO CLOSE TO ONE.

STILL, I **DID** GET MIGHTY CLOSE TO HER, AND THOUGH SHE GOT ME PRETTY GOOD, SHE DIDN'T KILL ME, SO IT WAS WORTH IT.

BUT I WAS A MESS, AND I'D STAYED SIX MONTHS INSTEAD OF SIX WEEKS AS I'D PLANNED. FELT LIKE TIME TO DO SOME-THING ELSE.

I FOUND MYSELF CLOSE TO THE NORTHERN FOOTHILLS AND SOMETHING SAID, "GO SEE EMMA," SO I WENT.

WARNING
NOTHING
NO SERVICES
NEXT
962m

HUH!
WELL, THERE HE IS.
PAY UP.

WELCOME TO
ANVARD
CYNOSURE
OF THE NORTH

WEIRD PLACE, IS ANVARD.
LIKE ANY CITY.

HER MAJESTY'S A PRETTY NICE GIRL, SOME DAY I'M GONNA MAKE 'ER MINE, OYEH — SOMEDAY I'M GONNA MAKE 'ER MINE —

HEY— 'ZAT YOU, BOB?
CLICK.

8 LOCATIONS MEGA
STRUMMER
BODES MUSIC CAFE AUTO PARTS CALL GIRLS
WHY WAIT!
NEWS HUTCH
STUFFED STUFF
السوق ◦ MARKET ◦ HA'ATYO ◦
GAP
KANG'S CRISPY THANGS
KANG'S

OOH! WHAT'S THIS?
THAT, M'DEAR, IS A SCALP.

SORRY, MY LADY. ONLY WHAT'S ON THE CLOTH'S FOR SALE.

YOU ARE ON THE CLOTH.
HA-HA...

THAT'S YOUR BEST OFFER? HELL, WHAT'S YOUR WORST?
HEY!
HEY, KID, WHATCHA WANT FOR THAT RON CHITIN ROOKIE CARD?

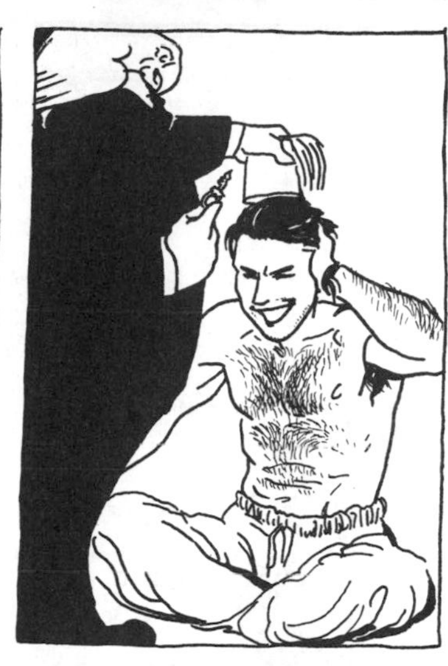

"NOTHING WRONG WITH THIS CITY THAT A GOOD PLAGUE WOULDN'T FIX," SEZEE.

"I'LL BE BACK WHEN THE CITY COUNCIL STRIPS DOWN AN' DANCES THE HULLY-GULLY AROUND THE BLACK ANGEL MONUMENT," SEZEE.
AMRIKI
WELL, EVVYBODDY, HEEE'S BACK, BIG AS LIFE AND TWICE AS NATURAL.

SO, ALL BILL COLLECTORS, REPO AGENTS, FORMAL VENDETTAS, AND ANGRY HUS-BANDS ARE DULY NOTIFIED. ANYTHING TO ADD, MR. JAEGER AYERS?
AHH, BITE ME, RUTHIE. O FIND YOURSELF SOME CE CAR-WRECK VICTIMS TO INTERVIEW, OKAY, KID?
CHANNEL 622
"THESE ARE THE PEOPLE IN YOUR NEIGHBORHOOD"

THANKEW, THANKEW!
MOVING RIGHT ALONG, WE BRING YOU TO JOSIE "JO-JO" JIMBROWSKI, FORMER CHILD STAR TURNED WRAX PUSHER.
WE'RE ALL HAPPY TO HEAR OF YOUR NEW OUTPATIENT STATUS, MS. JIMBROWSKI!
TEN FOR ONE, FIFTEEN FOR BOTH.

ALL RIGHT, FEZHEAD. PRESENT YOUR LICENSE AS REQUIRED BY LAW.
WARDEN
NOT HARDLY. I'M A FREE TRADER.

WHORESHIT. YOU'RE ABOUT AS INDIAN AS PRUNE POP-TARTS, YA TRENDY-ASS WANNA-BE WHITE BOY.
"WANNABE WHITE BOY..."

OOH, BOY! WE GOT OURSELVES A FINE, FINE EXAMPLE OF A CULTURE COP HERE! GONNA SPARE THESE NICE TOURISTS THE PAAIIN OF BUYIN' WHAT-EVER THEIR TRANSIENT LITTLE HEARTS DESIRE AND BE A NOBLE FRIEND TO THE DWELLERS IN THE WILDERNESS TOO?

O-KAY. YOU GOT IT, WISEASS-

WHO EVER TOLD YOU "HEY, YOU ARE THE ULTIMATE GOD-BOSS OF WHO LOOKS INDIAN ENOUGH TO BE ONE"? DIDJA EVER STOP TO THINK IT MIGHT NOT BE RIGHT FOR PEOPLE TO HAVE TO DRAG OUT SACRED CEREMONIAL CLOTHING OR DYE THEIR SKIN WITH ALL KINDS OF TOXIC CRAP JUST TO LOOK "INDIAN" ENOUGH TO PLEASE ASS-HOLES LIKE YOU WHO DON'T EVEN KNOW WHAT THEY'RE LOOKING AT?
WHAT'S UP?
FIGHT

HA!
CRUNK
POP
FUMP

CLAP CLAP CLAP
WHOOOOO
THAT'S FOR EVERY LITTLE OL' LADY WHO WASN'T WEARIN' ENOUGH TURQUOISE, YA GREASEBRAIN!
EEEEEE
CLAP CLAP CLAP
GUM-BALL~

CLAP CLAP
HA HA-HA HAHAHA~
CLAP CLAP CLAP
I'LL JUST SPEND IT ON GIN & CIGARETTES

HA HA HA~AWK HAK HAK
I'LL JUST SPEND IT ON GIN & CIGARETTES

C'MON, GRANDAD. GUESS I COULD GO FOR A DRINK AND A SMOKE MYSELF.
HOW 'BOUT IT? ANYBODY ELSE? ON ME.

AN' HOW ABOUT YOU, BLUEJAY? GOT TIME TO BLOW WITH YER OL' UNCLE AND A REEKING STRANGER?

~WHAT'S THE POINT O' WORKIN' HARD? WHAT'S THE POINT O' GAININ' RICHES? MONEY'S MEAN AN' BANKS ARE BITCHES— POVERTY'S ITS OWN REWARD—
HAMADA

TIMES GONE BY, WE'D A STUCK UP FOR THE WARDEN. NOW OL' GLAURIE, HE WAS A GOOD WARDEN~ DI'NT MESS WITH GOOD BIZNESS BUT KEPT MARKET RULES. BUT THIS NEW KID, HE SHITS ON EV'-BODDY NO MATTA' WHAT~ WHA' HAPP' TO OLD GLAURIE~ HE WASH OKAY~
WE DON'T KNOW, WHISKEY JACK. YER TH' ONLY ONE OL' ENOUGH TO KNOW WHO TH' HELL YER TALKIN' ABOUT!

WELL, WHAT I HEARD WAS HE'D STILL BE ALIVE AND WELL AND JUMPING OUT OF BEDROOM WINDOWS IF IT WASN'T FOR—
HEY!

YOU! YOU~YOU GET OUT OF HERE~ THIS AIN'T NO PLACE FOR YOU~GET BACK OUT OF THIS BURNT PLACE~ GET OUT-OUT~ OUT~
HEY, WHISKEY JACK—
JACK'S GOIN' OFF AGAIN~

IT'S NO PLACE FOR THE LIKES OF YOU, YOU HEAR?!
I'VE GOT BUSINESS HERE, YA CRAZY~
BUSINESS? HA! WHAT YOU MEAN? A WOMAN?

~I STILL KNOWS SOME STUFF~~~ OL' WISAKAJAC KNOWS~YOUR BLOOD'S FOLLOWING IN THE SECOND AIR, AND YOU DON'T HAVE A FUCKIN' CLUE~ GET OUT~YOU CAN SO YOU SHOULD—DON'T LISTEN WHEN ALL THAT'S TALKIN' IS YER DICK~~

SORRY, HON. JACK DOESN'T MEAN ANY HARM REALLY... HE'S BEEN GOING DOWNHILL EVER SINCE THAT FEY PLAGUE HIT HIM, BUT HE'S A GOOD OL' GUY USUALLY~
~FOX WENT OUT ON A SNOWY NIGHT~ HE PRAYED TO THE MOON TO GIVE HIM LIGHT~

HOW OFTEN DOES HE PROPHESY?
PFF! WHO CAN TELL?

BEHOLD, FRIENDS! SYMBOL OF OUR CITY OF ANVARD AND BELOVED CHILDREN'S FABLE HERE ELEGANTLY IMMORTALIZED! THE BLACK ANGEL!

HER SCULPTOR IS UNKNOWN, BUT IS NOW LARGELY BELIEVED TO HAVE BEEN RAEL UZENDERZO, THE LEGENDARY ICONOCLASSICIST. NOTE THAT HER HAIR AND FEATHERS ARE OF NATURALISTIC MATERIALS. OVER THE YEARS, THEY HAVE SUFFERED FROM EXPOSURE TO THE ELEMENTS—

HOW SO, YOU SAY? WITH THE CITY'S DOME TO PROTECT HER? WELL, FOLKS, THIS IS BECAUSE OUR ANGEL ACTUALLY PREDATES THE CONSTRUCTION OF THE DOME AND ITS SUPPORT STRUCTURE! YES, SHE'S THAT OLD!

BUT OLDER STILL IS THE COLUMN ON WHICH SHE STANDS, WHICH, ALONG WITH THE RUINS YOU'LL SEE LATER ON OUR TOUR AND THE FORTIFIED LOOKOUT ATOP MOUNT CINO YOU SAW WHEN YOU CAME IN SIGHT OF THE CITY, IS PREHISTORIC, AND NO CONCLUSIVE DATE OF CONSTRUCTION HAS EVER BEEN AGREED UPON.

NOT TO WORRY, FOLKS— SHE HAS THE FINEST RECONSTRUCTION CREW POSSIBLE TO SEE TO HER EVERY NEED, CHAIRED BY PROFESSOR BRIGID JAVENSEN, OF ANVARD'S PRESTIGIOUS DJURAS COLLEGE.

THINK
DON'T THINK
HAT A BUB BOBBA
BLABBA FLABBA
UB BUBBA BUB BL
CAUTION!

??
!
VIOLET
SENSITIVE

LOOK, YOU APE, I DON'T KNOW WHAT-

ZZZZZEEEEEEEE
EEEEEE
KANGG

NO POINT IN SCARING YOU, WAS THERE?

LADIES AND GENTLEMEN, WHAT A PIECE OF LUCK! OR RATHER, A PIECE OF OUR DOME! THE TECHNOLOGY THAT MADE OUR DOME AND ITS SUPPORT STRUCTURE IS NOW SADLY LOST. THE MATERIAL OF WHICH THE DOME IS MADE IS ENTIRELY UNKNOWN! ALTHOUGH IT ALLOWS VISIBLE LIGHT TO PENETRATE, IT APPEARS BLACK FROM ABOVE, AND IS OPAQUE TO ULTRAVIOLET AND CERTAIN OTHER FORMS OF RADIATION ——

ALTHOUGH IT IS WELL KNOWN TO BE HARDER THAN DIAMOND OR CRYSTAL CERAMIC -OUR MOST SOPHISTICATED TOOLS CANNOT EVEN SCRATCH IT! -AND HAS RESISTED EARTHQUAKES OF INCREDIBLE MAGNITUDE WITH NO SIGNS OF DAMAGE, FOR SOME INSCRUTABLE REASON A FEW VERY LARGE HOLES HAVE APPEARED, AND OCCASIONALLY SMALL PIECES DO BREAK OFF-
HSSSFFFF
FFHHSSSss

AS YOU SEE, OUR RESEARCHERS ARE EVER VIGILANT TO GLEAN WHATEVER DATA THEY CAN WHEN THIS HAPPENS - AND IT DOESN'T HAPPEN TWICE IN A YEAR, I ASSURE YOU!
OOP- AND THERE IT GOES! SORRY, BOYS, YOU MISSED IT!
DISSOLUTION AFTER APPROXIMATELY NINETY-SEVEN SECONDS.
RAPID RESEARCH
SCREEE
DEFINITE SIGNS OF REGROWTH ALONG LEADING EDGE.
FFFFFFFFFFFFFFHHHh....
ALL SAMPLES UNSTABLE.

UH~
I GUESS I OWE YOU AN APOLOGY.

NAH. YOU COULDA BEEN A LOT NASTIER ABOUT IT.

SEE THAT LITTLE BLACK-AND-WHITE BIRD CIRCLING UP THERE?
...YES?

THERE'S ONE NOW. A MINUTE AGO THERE WERE TWELVE.

WHATEVER THEY ARE, THEY AREN'T REAL BIRDS. THEY DON'T ACT RIGHT. I THINK THEY COME FROM THE DOME ITSELF.

THEY SEEM TO SHOW UP NEAR AREAS OF HIGH STRUCTURAL STRAIN. BUILDINGS WITH BAD FOUNDATIONS, OLD BRIDGES~ CARS WITH BAD FRAMES EVEN~
I SAW ONE ONCE CIRCLING A BASKETBALL PLAYER WITH A BAD KNEE ONCE!
HAHA.

SO WATCH FOR 'EM, YOU KNOW?
OH, I SURE WILL. LISTEN, I GOTTA RUN...THANKS!
MACE

FLEE!

HUH!

SO MUCH FOR "OH, MY HERO, HOW CAN I EVER REPAY YOU?"

OUR TOU AT THE BRID PROCEED D REACH T

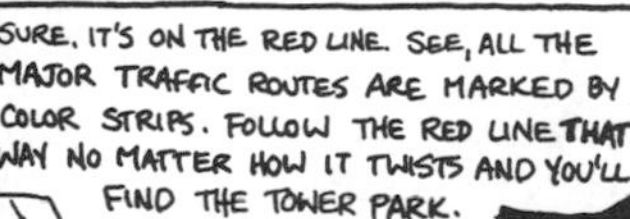
SURE, IT'S ON THE RED LINE. SEE, ALL THE MAJOR TRAFFIC ROUTES ARE MARKED BY COLOR STRIPS. FOLLOW THE RED LINE **THAT** WAY NO MATTER HOW IT TWISTS AND YOU'LL FIND THE TOWER PARK.

PEDESTRIAN RUSH-HOUR TRAFFIC IS MOVING RIGHT ALONG. ON TO VEHICULAR, HERE'S SPACEY KEN....

LAVEAU'S
BOOKS • MUSIC • MISCELLANY
LAVEAU'S
LAVEAU'S
OPEN
NO SMOKING

DING DING

SNIF?

HEL-LOO ?

Ho-**HO**!

WHERE'S YOUR LADY, COUSIN?

HAAAAHH~
OH!
HI. JAEGER!

HULGER, IT'S OKAY. HE'S OKAY. FRIEND, ALL RIGHT?
OGAY.

HI. ELLIE. WHAT'S WITH ALL THIS?
OH, WELL... WE'VE HAD A LOT OF... TROUBLE LATELY. HIS... OWNER, I GUESS, HIRED HIM OUT TO US AS A GUARD AND ANTITHEFT, YOU KNOW?

FAR CRY FROM THE USUAL BOOKSTORE CAT, HUH?
HA HA! YES, I GUESS... BUT HE'S BEEN SO SWEET. REALLY, HIS HANDLER'S A LOT SCARIER THAN HE IS!

SPEAKING OF WHICH, WHERE'S MAN-HANDLER?
NOW IF ONLY HE HAD FUR ...

EHHH ... IF YOU MEAN **ANN** HANDLER, THE HEAD HONCHA–
..RRRIGHT BEHIND ME.
WHERE ELSE?

BEST VANTAGE POINT THERE IS. MAKES YOU LOOK AS IF YOU'RE ALWAYS LEAVING.
OOOWW!
GIVE BLOOD
PLAY RUGBY

THEN I GUESS YOU WON'T WANT ME TO STAY LONG ENOUGH TO SHOW YOU THESE?
EEG–

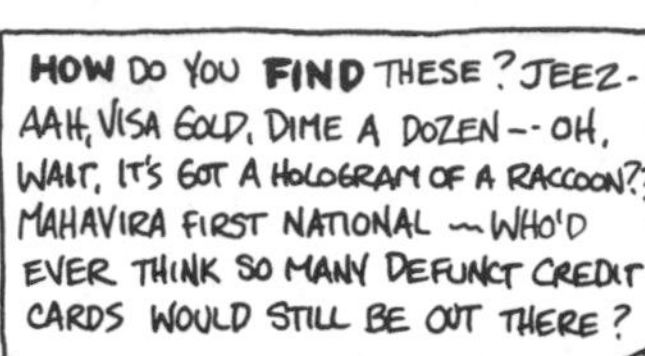
HOW DO YOU **FIND** THESE? JEEZ-AAH, VISA GOLD, DIME A DOZEN–- OH, WAIT, IT'S GOT A HOLOGRAM OF A RACCOON?? MAHAVIRA FIRST NATIONAL — WHO'D EVER THINK SO MANY DEFUNCT CREDIT CARDS WOULD STILL BE OUT THERE?

AHH, COLLECTOR'S MANIA ~

SO, YOUNGSTER. DID YOU HAVE A NICE WANDERING?
HEY, MISS LENNIE. I GOT YOUR ROCKS FOR YOU.

THAT'S LOVELY, DEAR. COME ON BACK INTO MY ROOM AND SHOW ME WHAT YOU'VE GOT.
OH, NOW, MISS LENNIE, I THOUGHT YOU'D NEVER ASK.

EEE HEE HEE! CHILD, YOU'D BETTER NOT BE ALL TALK WHEN I FINALLY CALL YOUR BLUFF!

YOU THINK I'M SCARED OF YOU BECAUSE YOU'RE NOT SEVENTEEN?

THAT WAS NICE, KID, BUT I'M STILL NOT CALLING YOUR BLUFF.

THAT'S THE GUY YOU'RE ALWAYS RAGGING ABOUT? HE DOESN'T SEEM SO BAD...

OH, HE CAN SLOP ON THE CHARM WHEN HE WANTS TO.
PSST— IT'S A PERSONALITY THING BETWEEN THEM. HER FAVORITE GAME IS "YOU CAN'T GET ONE UP ON ME" AND HIS IS "HOW MUCH CAN I GET AWAY WITH?"

IT'S WHAT MAKES HIM A MONSTER.
NOW, ANN...

I MEAN IT.
HE IS ARROGANT... HE IS SHAMELESS, IMMORAL, ANTI-SOCIAL, IRRESPONSIBLE... HE'S TOO SLICK. HE'S SO CHARMING, BUT HE'S CALLOUS, CUNNING, AND TOO SELF-ASSURED. HE IS DANGEROUS. HE HAS AN EXPLOSIVE TEMPER, AND SOMEDAY IT IS GOING TO GO OFF BIG TIME. HE'S A PSYCHOPATH WAITING TO HAPPEN, AND SOMEDAY EVERYBODY WILL KNOW--

AND THEN YOU'LL SAY YOU KNEW HIM WHEN, RIGHT?
OH, SHUT UP!

AH! WHAT A LOVELY PIECE OF AMBER!

IT'LL MAKE A FINE SUN STONE.
D'I DO OKAY?
WELL, A GOOD SET OF GYLEH STONES DEPENDS PARTLY ON HOW APPROPRIATE EACH STONE IS.
SO-TIGER'S EYE? THIS MUST BE MY MARS STONE. ACTIVE, AGGRESSIVE, SOMETIMES DESTRUCTIVE...
OBSIDIAN. NICELY POLISHED, TOO. SATURN FOR CERTAIN...
ENDINGS. DRAWING INWARD-

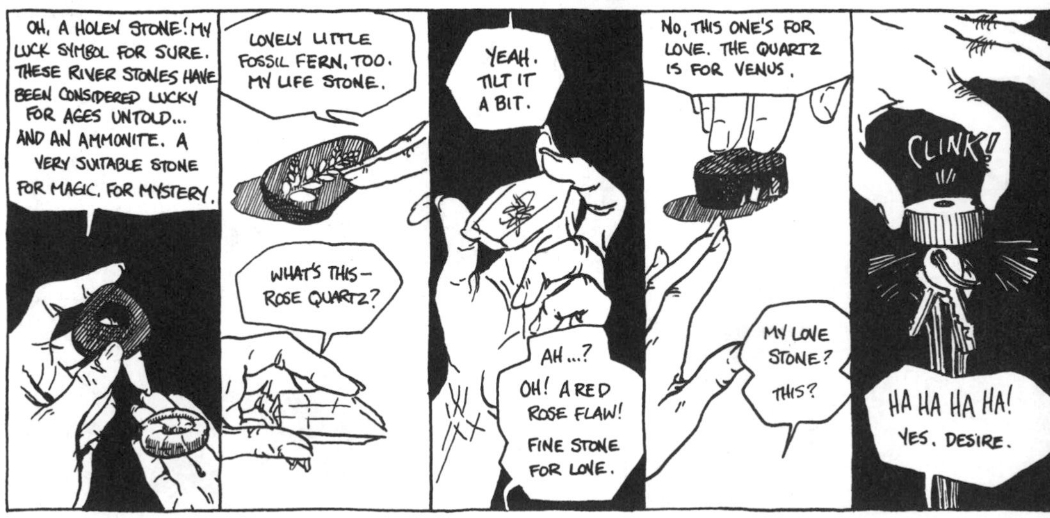
OH, A HOLEY STONE! MY LUCK SYMBOL FOR SURE. THESE RIVER STONES HAVE BEEN CONSIDERED LUCKY FOR AGES UNTOLD... AND AN AMMONITE. A VERY SUITABLE STONE FOR MAGIC. FOR MYSTERY.
LOVELY LITTLE FOSSIL FERN, TOO. MY LIFE STONE.
WHAT'S THIS-ROSE QUARTZ?
YEAH. TILT IT A BIT.
AH...?
OH! A RED ROSE FLAW!
FINE STONE FOR LOVE.
NO, THIS ONE'S FOR LOVE. THE QUARTZ IS FOR VENUS.
MY LOVE STONE?
THIS?
CLINK!
HA HA HA HA!
YES. DESIRE.

THESE TWO... WHICH IS MY MOON?
THIS IS A SILVER MARK OF THE OLD EMPIRE - SEEN BETTER DAYS —
WELL, SO HAS DAME MOON, THE HEMATITE?
THAT'S MERCURY.
THAT'LL DO. WHAT'S LEFT?
THREE.
JUPITER- THAT'S THIS BIG THREE-COLORED ONE -
NEWS - THIS DARK AND LIGHT STRIPY ONE.
BUT THIS ONE, YOU CAN'T LET ANYBODY GET, 'CAUSE GOD KNOWS WHERE I'D FIND ANOTHER ONE. IT'S THE SAME STUFF AS THE DOME, BUT IT'S STABLE.
MY HOME STONE, PRECIOUS BEYOND WORDS.
SO WHATTA YOU DO NOW?
DO?

PUT 'EM BACK INTO THEIR PRETTY LITTLE LEATHER BAG, WHICH I **DID** NOTICE THAT YOU WERE SWEET ENOUGH TO MAKE FOR THEM, AND SETTLE ON A PRICE.
BUT AREN'T YOU GONNA USE THEM? I THOUGHT WHEN I GOT 'EM ALL BACK TO YOU THAT AT LEAST I'D GET MY FORTUNE TOLD.

NOO, NO. PURE RESEARCH, ALL OF THIS. DON'T FRET, I WON'T SELL THEM. MY CUSTOMERS CAN MAKE DO WITH CLAY TILES.
C'MON, MISS LENNIE -

EVERY KIND OF FORTUNETELLING THERE IS, YOU'VE GOT A BOOK ON IT, AND THE STUFF IT TAKES TO DO IT. YOU TELLIN' ME YOU DON'T ACTUALLY **DO** ANY OF THIS STUFF?
TRYING TO TELL ME YOU'RE NOT A WITCH?

ETHNOFOLKLORIST, IF YOU PLEASE. THIS IS MY RESEARCH. IF CHARGING A FEE FOR DEMONSTRATING THE MANY FORMS OF DIVINATION FURTHERS THAT RESEARCH, THEN THAT'S WHAT I DO.
THE REST IS SETTING, LOOKS TO IMPRESS MY CUSTOMERS, WHO COME TO BUY YI-JING STRAWS, TAROT CARDS, LEAF TEA, LEAD...

I BELIEVE YOU.
SELENE.

SELENE - SELL-UH-NEE

NOW.
HOW DID YOU GUESS MY NAME?
THE SIGN OUTSIDE ...

"BOOKS, MUSIC, MISCELLANY." THERE'S A LOTTA MISCELLANEOUS STUFF IN HERE, BUT ONLY ONE MISS SELENE.
IT'S A HOLDOVER FROM WHEN IT WAS ILLEGAL, ISN'T IT? HIDING, PUTTING THINGS IN CODE.

WHAT YOU DO...
... WHAT YOU ARE...
... IS A FORM OF DIVINATION.
YOU'RE A GOOD TRACKE
A FINDER, AND THAT USE
TO MEAN A LOT MORE
THAN IT DOES TODAY.

IF YOU REALLY THINK HE'S SUCH A HORRIBLE PERSON, WHY DO YOU LET HIM HANG AROUND?
IF THERE'S A WASP IN THE ROOM, I WANT TO KEEP MY EYE ON IT.
GIVE BLOOD PLAY RUGBY

HEY, SO WHERE'S LYDIA? I FOUND A COPY OF THAT BOOK SHE WANTED.
SHE'S OFF TODAY.
WHAT BOOK?
FUMP!

"KNITTING WITH DOG HAIR." CAN I LEAVE IT HERE FOR 'ER?
SURE...
... IS THIS LEATHER?
GIVE BLOOD PLAY RUGBY

SIIGHH

NO, ACTUALLY, IT'S RAWHIDE, BUT YES, IT'S THE STOLEN FLESH OF ONE OF OUR ANIMAL BRETHREN, WHICH I NOT ONLY KILLED BUT ATE.
WHAT ABOUT IT?
KILLING ANIMALS IS ILLEGAL--.
NOW, GUYYS

DON'T FREAK OUT, GUYS. WHAT'S DONE IS DONE, RIGHT?

RETURN THE DEAD TO THE SOIL, RIGHT?
RIGHT.

SO....!
BEATS HELL OUT OF FLUSHING IT DOWN THE JANE TO RETURN IT TO THE SEA, DOESN'T IT?
"A NEEDLE PULLING THREAD ~"

CAUGHT YOUR ACT DOWN AT THE FREE MARKET. SIGN HERE.
TH' HELL IS IT?
GIVE
PLAY

IT'S AN ASSOCIATION FOR THE RIGHTS OF INDIGENOUS PEOPLE. I'M SURE YOU'LL WANT TO SHOW YOUR SUPPORT OF THEIR RECLAIMING THEIR LAND.

AIN'T NO SUCH THING AS INDIGENOUS. IT ALL COMES DOWN TO PUSH AND SHOVE OVER TERRITORY.

YOU'RE REALLY **NOT** TRIBAL, ARE YOU?
I'M TOLD YOU'VE BEEN PASSING YOURSELF OFF AS INDIAN FOR YEARS.

YEAH, WELL, **I'M** TOLD THAT THERE AIN'T A LESBIAN ALIVE WHO DOESN'T **REALLY** WANT TO SUCK COCK.
PLIK!

ONLY SO WE CAN BITE THEM OFF! GET BACK HERE
HEE HEE HEE ~ NOO, NO, CAN'T HIT A MEMBER OF THE FAIR SEX!
THUMP SMAT!
CLINK THUMPTHUMP CLINK THUMP CLINK THUMPTHUD THUMP CLINK THUMP!
YOU TWO OUGHTTA TAKE THIS ACT ON THE ROAD. SERIOUSLY.
WHAM!
NO! NO, ANN, NOT THE NEW COFFEE MUGS~
BESIDES, IF I BEAT T HELL OUT OF YOU NOW IT'LL BE WEEKS BEFOR I GET PAID FOR THAT PLASTIC, MAN-HANDLE
SKID
KRESH
TINK TINK
OH, AND BY THE WAY...
IT'S NOT THAT I'M SICK ON MY OWN. IT'S THIS PLACE THAT MAKES ME CRAZY.
AWAY FROM PEOPLE, I'M FINE.
THEN WHY THE HELL DID YOU COME BACK?
CLOSE
LIVE A LIDDE
CHECKPOINT 27 .... SELF-PACED WALKING TOUR
WALKING TOUR. F THE ELEVATED OU'LL FIND THAT PLUMMET!
MANY CITIZENS OF ANVARD TRAVERSE THE CITY ALL THEIR LIVES WITHOUT EVER TOUCHING THE GROUND. FOLLOW BLACK EARTH OVERPASS UP PAST THE MARICHARE BUILDING TO THE MAD RIVER OVERLOOK.

BEHOLD THE GREAT MAD RIVER! OR AT LEAST ITS IMAGE ON VIDEO, AS IT'S NOT ADVISED TO GET TOO CLOSE TO THE WATER. MANY RIVERS HAVE BEEN CALLED 'RED' BUT AS YOU CAN SURELY SEE, NONE HAVE EVER BEEN SO EMINENTLY QUALIFIED.

"HOW MANY RIVERS IN MYTH AND IN HISTORY HAVE BEEN SAID TO RUN RED WITH BLOOD? WITH WHOSE BLOOD DOES OUR MIGHTY DELTA RUN, TO GIVE IT SUCH A LIVID TINGE?"

"THE SEA'S A LOVELY LADY, IF YOU PLAY ***IN*** HER. IF YOU PLAY ***WITH*** HER, SHE IS A BITCH!"

—THIS IS PIRATE STATION 622 BRINGING YOU THE HOURLY NIGHTLIFE-HAZARD SPOT REPORT, COVERING ALL THIRTY-TWO BOROUGHS OF THE CITY.

UPPER AND LOWER AVENTINE ARE QUIET BUT TENSE— SNOB HILL'S JUST SLOPPIN' OVER WITH RENT-A-COPS LOOKIN' FOR RAISES—"

"—TOURIST JAM-PACK AT BAEDEKER'S, SO STEER CLEAR OR BY GOD BE PHOTOGRAPHED. EVER SINCE THIS CLUB WAS PUT ON THE CIVIC WALKING TOUR IT'S LOOKED LIKE THE METRO OUTTA TOWN ON GODZILLA TWO-FOR-ONE DAY— SHIT, LADY——"

"—PRETTY QUIET ALL THROUGH IMBRIUM. SLIGHT VEHICULAR DETOUR AROUND A GANG RUMBLE BETWEEN HARSKAE AND A GANG OF RUSALKAS NEW TO THE BOROUGH. COUPLE STREET FESTS WARMING UP FOR LAESKE RUNNING SEASON—"

—CHYERNY HAS AN UNUSUAL AMOUNT OF FOOT TRAFFIC TONIGHT, DIRECTLY RESULTING FROM HIGH TIDE IN SWINE LAGOON. BIG-TIME STANDING ON ALL MAJOR STREETS AND WALKWAYS, SO WE'RE WATCHIN' CLOSE FOR THE INEVITABLE RIOTING AS FUMES FROM THE RIVER DO WHAT THEY DO BEST—"

"—CHEMICAL SPILL FROM LOCAL FAST FOOD HAS EMPTIED OUT MOST OF JORAN. THE ARENA, HOWEVER, IS STILL GOIN' STRONG AS ALWAYS, SO IF YOU'VE GOT A SEAL SUIT OR THE CASH FOR A SURROGATE, COME ON DOWN!"

"—DOWN IN GULLAHINGLA WE HAVE A SPECTACULAR BAR FIGHT TAKING PLACE IN THE GODSFEAST TAVERN— IT'S PRESUMED TO BE OVER A WOMAN BUT THIS IS UNCONFIRMED —OVER THREE THOUSAND HOURS OF DAMAGE HAVE ALREADY BEEN DONE—"

AST
DANCING
R-RUTH — THAT'S —
SSHH!
SHUT UP, FOOL! WE'RE ON SIMULCAST! GIMME THE RIG—

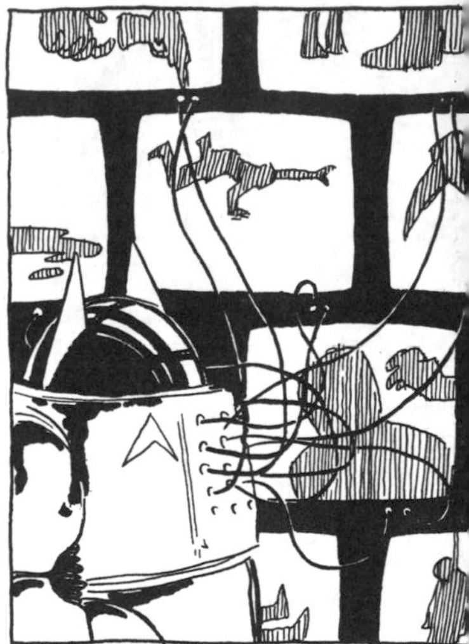

DON'T THINK THIS'LL SAVE YOU

I'LL JUST SPEND IT ON GIN &

SPANGG

SC BEEEEE BAM

FOR GODDESS'S SAKE, CHANGE THE CHANNEL. I CAN'T HANDLE ANY MORE CARNAGE TONIGHT.

BAMMAMA BAM BAM!
MRS. GROSVENOR~ MRS. GROSVENOR~~!

COME QUICK, COME QUICK ~ GOD, BE HOME, BE HOME! ~ THE MONSTER'S HURT BAD!
I'M NOT TH' PHEASANT PLUCKER, I'M TH' PLEASANT FUCKER'S SON ~

MARCIE -GO TO YOUR OWN BED NOW.
BUT~
MARCELLA. NOW.
'M ONLY FUCKIN' PLEASANTS TILL TH' PHEASANT PLUCKIN'S DONE ~

JUST PUT HIM DOWN- IN THE KITCHEN, SON, NOT ON THE CARPET~

CHRIST AND KRISHNA, KID. HOW DO YOU GET YOURSELF SCREWED UP LIKE THIS?
HI EM~- JUSH PASSHIN' BY AN' THOT I'D SHAY HELLOOO ~

CHAPTER TWO

FOLLOW THE PATH.

36

PIP!

36

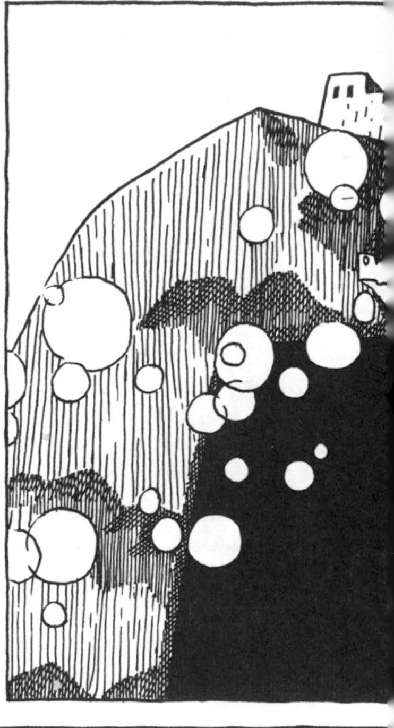

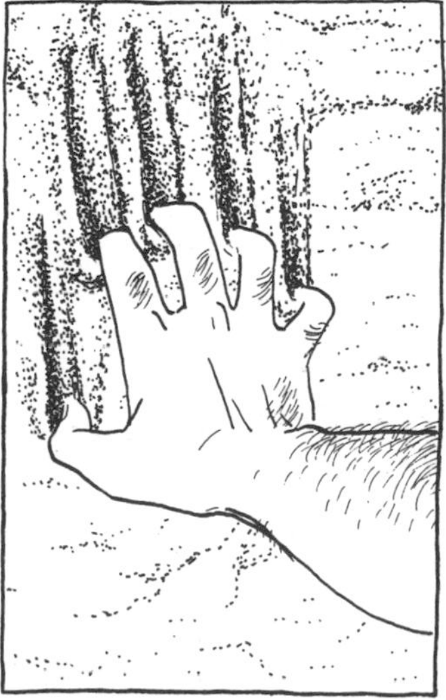

SO TRUSTING.

YAA—

=AAA=
FAPP
=AAA!

HEY-
-HA!

MARCIE, WHATSA MATTER?
GALLOW-GLASS... AYE TO DO MY BIDDING~ --
THERE GOES YOUR BACKUP.

ACK! NO! NO! I GIVE! UNCLE! UNCLE!
BOY, YOU THREE ARE FULLA RED PEPPER TODAY. AIN'T CHA?
GITCH GITCH

OOH, WELL, WHAT YA GONNA DO ABOUT IT? SPANK ME?
DAMN RIGHT I WOULD, IF I THOUGHT YOU NEEDED IT!

I THINK I NEED IT....

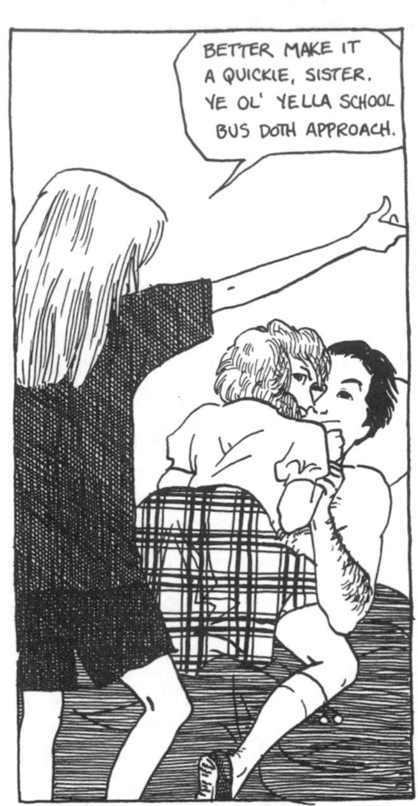
BETTER MAKE IT A QUICKIE, SISTER. YE OL' YELLA SCHOOL BUS DOTH APPROACH.

EXCUSE ME.
I MUST NOW KILL MY OWN FLESH AND BLOOD.

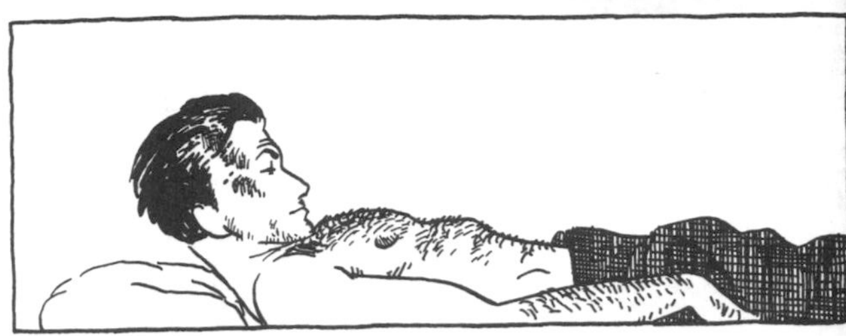

PHOO
GODDAMN HEARTBREAKER ....
TAPTAP TAP TAP

CAR, MOM. THINK WHEELS.
TUBE PASS, RACHEL. THINK CYLINDER.

mmf.

WELL, YOU LOOK MUCH BETTER TODAY.
YEAH... I ALWAYS DID BOUNCE BACK QUICK.

I DECLARE, IT'S AMAZING HOW A GOOD NIGHT'S SLEEP CAN BRING UP YOUR COLOR.

YOU'RE RAISING A DRAGON, EMMA.
HA HA HA HAA~

HEE HEE HEH!
SNORT!
NOO, NO. IT'S A PHASE. BELIEVE IT OR NOT, SHE'S STILL A VIRGIN, AND SHE'S TESTING THE WATERS. DOING "DANGEROUS" THINGS, YOU KNOW?

SHE'LL CALM DOWN.
NNGH~

SO ... BIG FIGHT OR LITTLE ONE?
EHH~ MIDDLING.

ANYBODY LOOKING FOR YOU?
I DON'T KNOW.

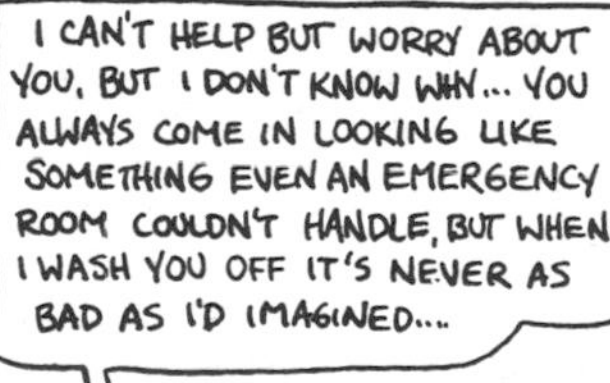
I CAN'T HELP BUT WORRY ABOUT YOU, BUT I DON'T KNOW WHY... YOU ALWAYS COME IN LOOKING LIKE SOMETHING EVEN AN EMERGENCY ROOM COULDN'T HANDLE, BUT WHEN I WASH YOU OFF IT'S NEVER AS BAD AS I'D IMAGINED...

MMF... STILL... I'D LIKE YOU TO STAY A... UM. FEW DAYS. HOWEVER LONG YOU WANT... REALLY... TILL I KNOW YOU'RE OKAY...

NOW **REALLY**. YA YOUNG FIRE HOSE - I GOTTA GO TO A SITE. WILL YOU BE OKAY WITH MARCIE HERE?

EMMA—
—I WOULDN'T THINK YOU'D HAVE THE NERVE TO LOOK SURPRISED YOU'D MISSED A FEW THINGS —
—EMMA—

...SIGH....
ALL RIGHT... ALL RIGHT.

SOMETIMES I'M JUST NOT SURE WHAT YOU NEED FROM US, LOVE.

....THURSDAY'S CIVIL-SERVANT DEATH TOLL INCLUDES LESTER ANTHONY SOFFIT, MARKET WARDEN OF MUNICIPAL FREE MARKET FIFTEEN. WARDEN SOFFIT WAS KILLED WHILE OFF DUTY IN A FIVE-LEVEL FALL FROM THE GODSFEAST TAVERN. HE WAS FIFTY-ONE — —
CLICK
CLICK!
IT'S TIME FOR "SAWING FOR TEENS

LAVEAU'S
BOOKS • MUSIC • MISCELLAN

AU'S

AVEAU'S

OF AN EVENING, SISTERS—
UM.
EVENING.

OOH.. WHOOZA SHWEETIE? BEEN EARNING YOUR KEEP? AMANNO HURAGA'AHE—
FULA AMA'HARAH— RAMALLAH NAAM AYO A'GOBAYEH—

HOW'S HE BEEN? PROVED USEFUL?
OH, UH, SURE—
WELL, YES AND NO.

OH?
YES, IN THAT EVERYONE'S ON THEIR BEST BEHAVIOR SINCE WE'VE HAD HIM. UNDERSTAND, IT WAS NEVER OUR CUSTOMERS WHO WERE THE PROBLEM—

ANN, HE'S CAUGHT EIGHT SHOPLIFTERS. FORMER REGULARS.
TRUE, BUT THE REAL PROBLEM WAS THE PERSISTENT HOLDUPS AND BREAK-INS.
AND HATE CRIMES.

IT ISN'T AS IF HE HASN'T PREVENTED THAT SORT OF THING. QUITE WELL, IN FACT. BUT SUCH A LARGE ANIMAL IS A CROWD DRAW. AND WE'VE HAD A LOT MORE FRINGE TYPES SINCE WE HIRED HIM.
...AND YOU CAN'T DENY THAT YOU YOURSELF ARE A SOURCE OF CURIOSITY.

COUPLE BIZARROS HAVE TRIED TO GET IN TOUCH WITH YOU THROUGH US.
SO?
I CAN'T BE BOTHERED WITH SUCH FOOLISHNESS. NOR, I PRESUME, CAN YOU. ARE YOU REFUSING HULGER'S HIRE?

=HAH=
NO, NOT YET. I'LL SWAP OLD WEIRDOS FOR NEW, FOR NOW.
GOOD. THE MONEY'S BEEN WELCOME. EVEN FULL SCHOLARSHIPS DON'T PROVIDE THAT MUCH FOOD MONEY.
NEVER UNDERESTIMATE THE ENTERTAINMENT VALUE OF ECCENTRICITY ~

HEY, WHO'S THIS LITTLE GUY? I DIDN'T KNOW YOU HAD TWO!
AH, THIS IS JINGKO. COME IN, SHY BOY.
THERE'S ALSO A THIRD, KOHUT. HE'S MY OTHER REASON FOR HIRING HULGER OUT. HULGER'S A RECENT ADDITION, AND THEY TWO HAVEN'T SETTLED WHO'S TO BE TOP CAT.
—OR DANGER~

HAS TO BE SETTLED. BUT AFTER FINALS.
THREE? GOOD GODDESS, THAT MUST BE EXPENSIVE!
WHY DO YOU, ANYWAY? REALLY, NOBILITY OR NOT, ISN'T IT SELF-INDULGENT TO KEEP SUCH EXTRAVAGANT PETS?

YOU MISUNDERSTAND US.
MY ULUHAKA - MY FOUR-LEGGED ONES - ARE NOT MY PETS. HULGER IS MY GRANDMOTHER'S BROTHER. KOHUT IS MY COUSIN. AND JINGKO ~
JINGKO IS MY SON.

SO.... THERE REALLY ARE — MALE NYIMA?

DON'T BE SILLY.

IF THOSE ARE THE MALES — UNCLE, COUSIN, SON—

—THEN WHO'S HER HUSBAND?

HEY, DEMON SEED.
MY-OH, WHAT A SHORT SCHOOL DAY.

OR IS IT JUST THAT YOU'RE SO BRILLIANT THAT YOU JUST SUCKED THE INSTITUTION DRY OF KNOWLEDGE IN HALF THE TIME AND NOW YOU'VE GOT NO REASON EVER TO GO BACK?
SO I HAD A FEW ERRANDS TO RUN.

YOU DON'T LOOK SO GOOD.
I DON'T FEEL SO GOOD.

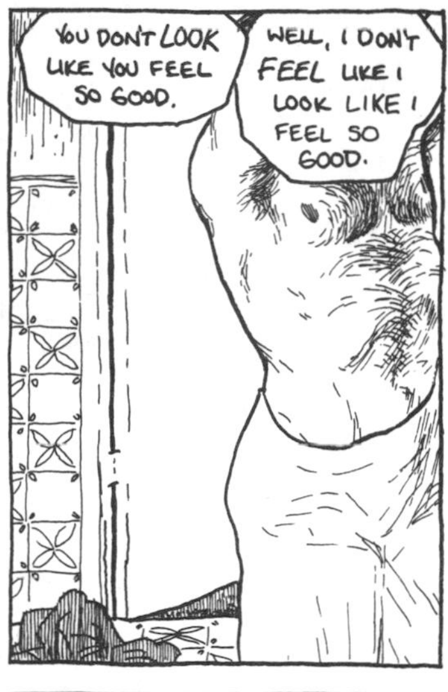
YOU DON'T LOOK LIKE YOU FEEL SO GOOD.
WELL, I DON'T FEEL LIKE I LOOK LIKE I FEEL SO GOOD.

YOU DON'T LOOK LIKE YOU FEEL LIKE YOU LOOK LIKE YOU FEEL SO GOOD.
YEAH, WELL, I DON'T FEEL LIKE I LOOK LIKE I FEEL LIKE I LOOK LIKE I FEEL SO GOOD.

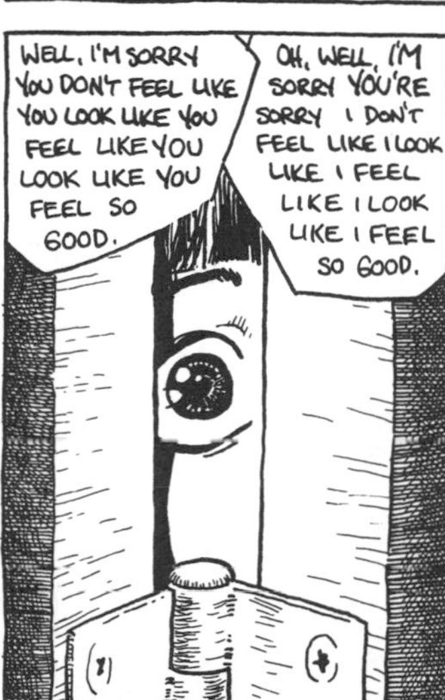
WELL, I'M SORRY YOU DON'T FEEL LIKE YOU LOOK LIKE YOU FEEL LIKE YOU LOOK LIKE YOU FEEL SO GOOD.
OH, WELL, I'M SORRY YOU'RE SORRY I DON'T FEEL LIKE I LOOK LIKE I FEEL LIKE I LOOK LIKE I FEEL SO GOOD.

I'M DEEPLY CONCERNED ABOUT YOUR SYMPATHY WITH MY EMPATHY OVER OUR COMMON PERCEPTION OF THE DETERIOR-ATION OF YOUR GENERAL APPEARANCE AND PRESUMABLY SIMILARLY DEFICIENT HEALTH! AAAGH!
HEY, LAY OFF THE HITTING! I DON'T FEEL SO GOOD.

YE HAVE ALL SINNED ~YEASS~ BUT WHICH ONE OF YOU CAN SAY AS I CAN SAY THAT YOU DROVE A GOOD MAN TO MURDER~OOGHH~'CAUSE I KEPT A-HOUNDIN' HIM FOR PERFUME AND CLOTHES AND FACE PAINT~OOOUHHH~ AN-AND HE SLEW TWO HUMAN BEINGS AND HE COME TO ME AND SAID TAKE THIS MONEY AND BUY YOURSELF THE CLOTHES AND THE PAINT ~BUT BRETHREN~BROTHERN~THAT'S WHERE THE LORD STEPPED IN~~

"NOW WEREN'T YOU AFRAID, LITTLE LAMBS, DOWN THERE IN ALL THAT DARK?"

KID... WHY IN THE HELL ARE WE WATCHING THIS MESS?
ARE YOU KIDDING? THIS IS A GREAT MOVIE.

NOW LEMME SEE IF I'VE GOT THIS STRAIGHT—
IT'S HARD TIMES. THESE TWO KIDS, THEIR DADDY GOT DESPERATE AND STOLE A BUNCHA MONEY. KNOWING HE COULDN'T GET AWAY, HE HIDES IT WITH HIS KIDS AND MAKES THEM SWEAR ON THEIR COMMON BLOOD NOT TO TELL.
LOVE

COPS COME AND TAKE HIM AWAY, AND HE'S TO DIE. WHILE HE'S IN JAIL THIS *OTHER* MAN, WHO PREY ON SAD LONELY WOMEN, FINDS OU ABOUT ALL THIS AND AS SOON AS THE DAD IS DEAD SETS OFF TO GET THAT MONEY.
NOW *THIS* MAN, HE'S A PREACHE BUT HE'S CRAZY—HE LOOKS AT A WOMAN, HE SEES A DEVIL. HE GOES TO THIS WOMAN, THE MOTHER, AND WORMS HIS WAY INTO HER, BUT MARRY HER OR NO HE WON'T TOUCH HER. HE JUST WOR ON HER, SHARPENS HER SORROW AND GUILT.
AND THE SON SEES THROUGH HIM, AND SO HE TURNS MOTHER AGAINS HER SON. THE LITTLE ONE, SHE'S TOO LITTLE TO SEE HIM FOR WHA HE IS. SHE WANTS A DADDY.

SO THE WOMAN COMES TO SEE THAT THE PREACHER MAN'S A RATTLE-SNAKE, AND HE KILLS HER AND IT'S CLEAR SHE THINKS SHE'S EARNED IT.
SO *NOW* THE BOY HAS TO RUN AWAY WITH HIS SISTER, NOW HIS ONLY BLOOD, DOWN THE RIVER ROAD. ALONE UNDER THAT BONE MOON, WITH THAT TWIST-HEAD RIGHT AFTER THEM?

NO, KID. UH-UH. I CAN'T WATCH THIS.
BIG OL' BUTCH THING LIKE YOU, AND YOU GET THE SQUEALS OVER A MOVIE—
WOULD IT HELP YOU TO KNOW THAT IT ALL ENDS IN A SICKENINGLY HAPPY, CATHARTIC WAY?

NO. SHIT LIKE THIS HAPPENS EVERY DAY. IF I CHANCE TO TRIP OVER IT, I CAN TRY TO *DO* SOMETHING ABOUT IT. I DON'T WANNA THINK ABOUT IT IF IT AIN'T REAL.
JUST MAKES ME TENSE.

NOW *HERE* WE GO.
"YOU'RE GONNA JUMP ON ME!"
"HUH?"
"YOU'RE GONNA JUMP ON ME! LIKE NERO JUMPED ON POPEIA!"
"WHO?!?"
HUH.
TEEK TOCK
TEEK TOCK
TEEK TOCK
....

"THIS TIME THE GROUND ITSELF HAD REARED UP AND DESTROYED WHAT WAS HIS.
'LOOKY HERE,' IT SAID. 'YOU AIN'T MORE'N A BUG T'ME... YOU GAVE UP MOST EVERYTHING T'GO A-ROVING ...HOME, FRIENDS, WIFELY COMFORTS, JUST TO BE FREE.
'WELL, NOW I'VE TOOK THE REST AND YOUR FREEDOM'S A DRUNKARD'S DREAM, 'CAUSE YOU BELONG T' **ME**.'
"SECH WERE THE THINGS THE GROUND WHISPERED TO HIM AND MACALUSTAIRE WAS INCLINED TO TAKE IT PERSONAL."

PSSH~
FUMP!

HEY, MARS --
WHAT'S WRONG, SIS?
'M SICK.

I KNOW, I MEAN WHAT'S THE MATTER?

MAMA SEES IT.
SHE **SEES** IT, BUT SHE DOESN'T BELIEVE IT. SHE JUST THINKS YOU WEREN'T EVER REALLY HURT BAD. BUT YOU **WERE**.

YES, KID.
I WAS.

IT'S JUST THE WAY I AM, MARCIE.

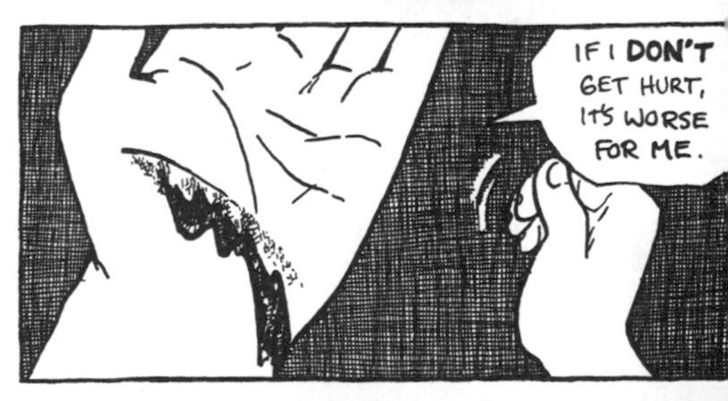
IF I **DON'T** GET HURT, IT'S WORSE FOR ME.

BUT I DON'T WANT YOU TO BE AFRAID OF ME.

THAT'S JUST WHAT DADDY USED TO SAY.
THAT HE DIDN'T WANT US TO BE SCARED.

BUT MAMA SAYS HE DID REALLY.

HOW VERY BRONTË ESQUE.
LITTLE SISTER IS DEVELOPING QUITE THE DRAMATIC FLAIR, NO?

THOUGH I'LL TELL YOU, I'LL TAKE HER DRAMAS OVER RRRACHEL'S ANY DAY.
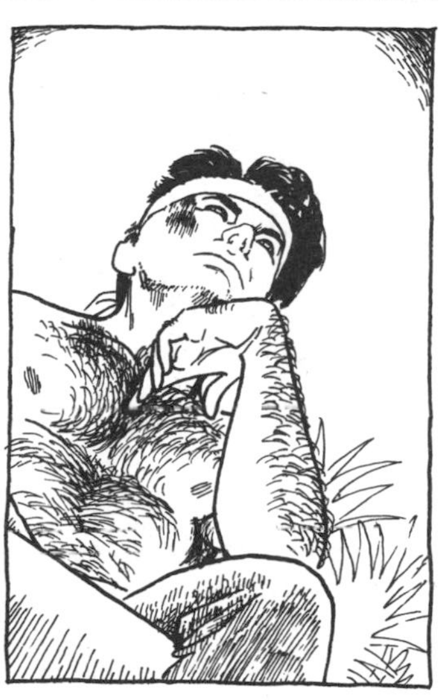

HOW'S THAT BROKEN COLLARBONE, BY THE WAY?
FINE.
CRACKED CHEEKBONE? CONCUSSION?
FINE.
NOT TO MENTION SOME CRACKED RIBS, MULTIPLE LACERATIONS, AND A FEW LOST TEETH?

WOULD YOU CARE IF I TOLD YOU I TOOK PICTURES OF YOU AFTER MOM WENT TO BED?
EASY ENOUGH TO TAKE MORE OF YOU AS YOU ARE TODAY FOR COMPARISON.
GIRL, THE FRICKIN' ARMY HAS TIME-LAPSE MOVIES OF ME DOING WHAT AIN'T ANYTHING SPECIAL TO ME. I'LL GO GET MY COPIES, WE'LL RUN 'EM BACKWARDS, LOADS O' LAUGHS.

STOMP
STOMP
STOMP
CLIC —
RATTLE RATTLE
CLUNK

WELP — MAIN FLOOR, EVERYBODY OFF —
MM.

GRRR~
SLAM
CLINKITY CLAK-

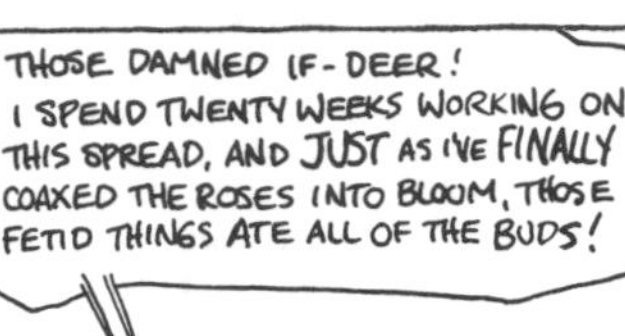
THOSE DAMNED IF-DEER! I SPEND TWENTY WEEKS WORKING ON THIS SPREAD, AND JUST AS I'VE FINALLY COAXED THE ROSES INTO BLOOM, THOSE FETID THINGS ATE ALL OF THE BUDS!

SO PUT TOBACCO WHEREVER YOU DON'T WANT THEM TO GO. ALL DEER HATE THAT.
OH, WELL. FINE! I HATE IT, TOO!

NO, NO, FRIZZIE. I MEAN LIVE TOBACCO PLANTS. WHO'D KNOW? JUST ANOTHER BIG BROAD-LEAFED ORNAMENTAL PLANT.
AND IT'S WHAT, DEER REPELLANT?
YUP.

THANKS, HONEY. NOW ALL I GOTTA DO IS FIND SOMEBODY WHO CAN SELL ME —
EMMA~ WHAT THE HELL DID BRIGHAM DO TO THAT KID TO MAKE HER SO FLINCHY?

IT WASN'T JUST TO HER.
IT'S JUST HARDER FOR MARCELLA TO LET GO OF, SINCE SHE WAS BORN TO IT. IT'S THE ONLY LIFE SHE KNEW.

"WE **WERE** LIVING IN A WAR ZONE. HE TOLD US THAT WE WERE IN DANGER... WHAT REASON DID I HAVE TO DISBELIEVE HIM?
"IT'S SO EASY TO BE AFRAID WHEN YOU HAVE CHILDREN.
"BRIGHAM...
"I'LL NEVER KNOW WHEN HE STARTED NEEDING OUR FEAR...
"FEEDING IT.
"HE WAS A CAPTAIN, AFTER ALL. HE KNEW WHAT WAS GOING ON. REALLY GOING ON. HE ALWAYS LET US KNOW WE WERE HEARING PRIVILEGED INFORMATION.
"BIT BY BIT HE WHITTLED AWAY OUR FREEDOM.
"FIRST IT'S DON'T GO OUT ALONE AT NIGHT, LOCK YOUR DOOR. THEN IT'S DON'T GO OUT AT NIGHT AT ALL. LOCK YOUR DOOR DURING THE DAY TOO.
"THEN IT'S SLEEP IN THE MARBLE BATHTUB, IN CASE SOMEONE SHOOTS THROUGH THE WALLS OF THE HOUSE. DON'T GO OUT EVEN IN DAYLIGHT WITHOUT AN ARMED ESCORT— BRIG, OF COURSE, SINCE HE DIDN'T TRUST THE OTHER SOLDIERS OR OFFICERS ANYMORE.
"BUT HE WOULDN'T TAKE US AWAY FROM THE DANGER.
"RACHEL... SUCH A LITTLE GIRL... MAKING CROWNS AND NECKLACES OUT OF SPENT SHELL CASINGS...
"HE NEVER HIT US.
"NEVER DID ANYTHING OVERTLY THREATENING.
"BUT EVERYTHING HE DID WAS CALCULATED TO MAKE US AFRAID, SO WE'D CLING TO OUR ONLY PROTECTOR.
"THE DANGER WAS REAL, AT FIRST... IT MUST HAVE BEEN, THAT BATTLE ZONE IS IN NEWS RECORDS... BUT BY THE TIME I LEFT HIM, I FOUND THAT THE FIGHTING HAD BEEN OVER FOR FOUR YEARS."

I'LL NOT FORGET MY TRIP OUT VERY SOON... OR MY LIFE WITH HIM.
EVEN NOW — WHEN YOU CAME IN HERE LAST NIGHT LOOKING HALF KILLED — EVEN THOUGH I KNOW HE'S IN A MILITARY PRISON I STILL THOUGHT IT MUST HAVE BEEN BRIG WHO'D BEATEN YOU SO TERRIBLY —

WHY DIDN'T YOU TELL ME, MOM?
YOU?
WHAT COULD YOU HAVE DONE? YOU WEREN'T AN OFFICER. YOU WERE JUST A KID, AND ON A CONVICT BILLET AT THAT.

BESIDES, YOU WERE IN THE VA HOSPITAL FOR SO LONG, WE NEVER EVEN KNEW WHEN YOU GOT OUT.
AND THEN, HOW COULD WE HAVE FOUND YOU?
OKAY, OKAY...

WHEN DID YOU WAKE UP, ANYWAY?
OH, MOM —

WHAT ARE YOU DOING HOME THIS TIME?
NORMALLY I'D NEVER BLOW MY COVER, BUT MARCIE ISN'T BREATHING.

ADMI TANCE
SAINT PODKAYNE GENERAL

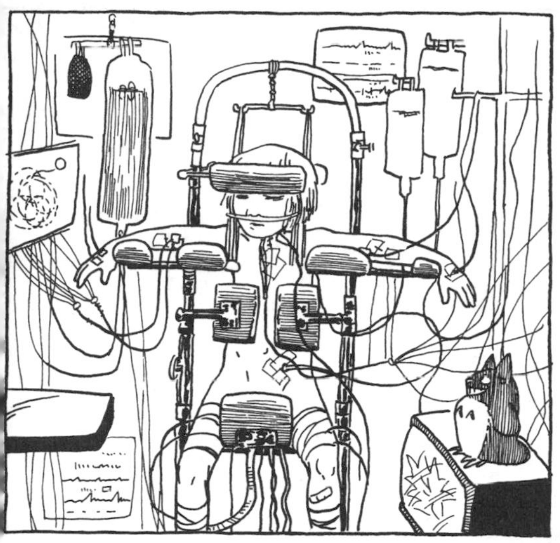

IF YOU'RE GOING TO BE SICK, GO BACK TO THE WAITING ROOM.

BORETUM
I KNOW THESE ANGEL FRAMES DON'T LOOK GOOD, SIR, BUT BELIEVE ME, IT'S THE BEST THING FOR YOUR LITTLE GIRL~
PLEASE HAVE AS MANY FORMS OF ID AS HUMANLY POSSIBLE READY AT ALL TIMES

HUL
URGH
HUK-HUK
BLAAH
ULK
EGH UHHH
BUICK! BUICK! BUICK!
MOANN

HAAHH

GOD. THAT HOSPITAL SMELL---
OH, WELL, THE AROMA OUT HERE IS MUCH IMPROVED.

CONFESS, MY LAD. PURGE THE SOUL AS WELL AS THE BODY. WHY DO YOU SO HATE HOSPITALS? IT'S NOT AS IF YOU HAVE ANY USE FOR THEM.

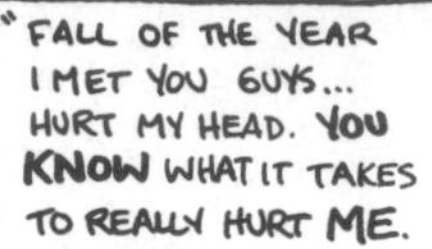
"FALL OF THE YEAR I MET YOU GUYS... HURT MY HEAD. YOU KNOW WHAT IT TAKES TO REALLY HURT ME.
I DON'T KNOW WHY, BUT I DIDN'T COME BACK OUT OF IT. THE DAMAGE HEALED. BUT I DIDN'T WAKE UP.
GODDAMN ARMY DOCTORS...."

"HOW LONG WERE YOU COMATOSE?"
"ELEVEN MONTHS. MAYBE IT WAS ALL THE JUNK THEY MUST'VE BEEN PUTTING INTO ME, I DON'T KNOW."
"BUT ARMY HOSPITALS DON'T KEEP SERVICE-MEN ON LIFE SUPPORT MORE THAN SIX WEEKS."

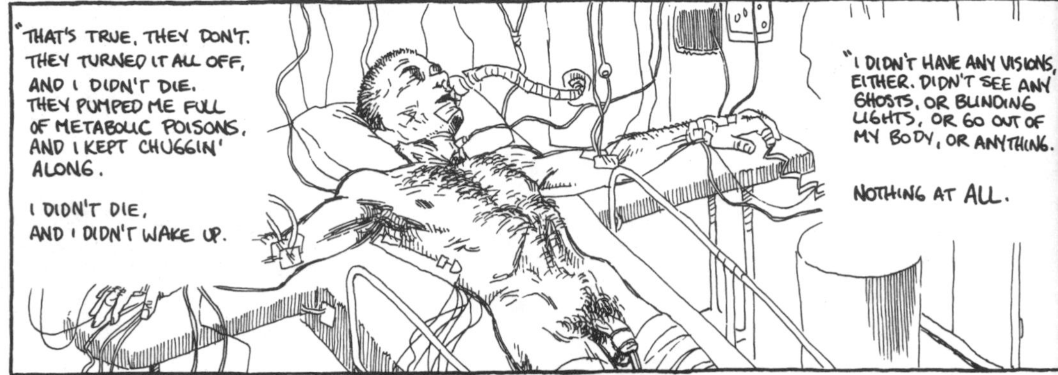
"THAT'S TRUE, THEY DON'T. THEY TURNED IT ALL OFF, AND I DIDN'T DIE. THEY PUMPED ME FULL OF METABOLIC POISONS, AND I KEPT CHUGGIN' ALONG.
I DIDN'T DIE, AND I DIDN'T WAKE UP.
"I DIDN'T HAVE ANY VISIONS, EITHER. DIDN'T SEE ANY GHOSTS, OR BLINDING LIGHTS, OR GO OUT OF MY BODY, OR ANYTHING.
NOTHING AT ALL.

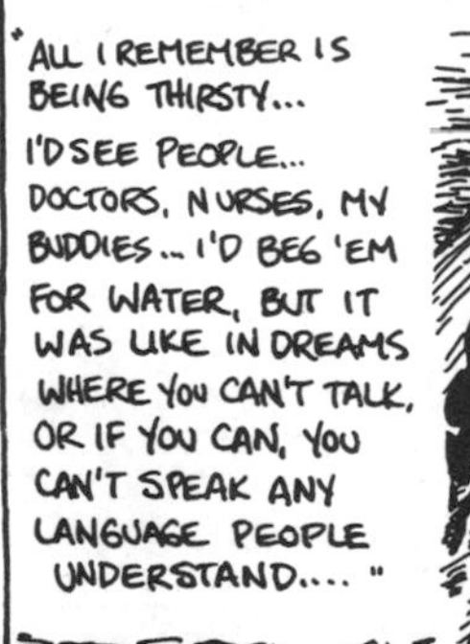
"ALL I REMEMBER IS BEING THIRSTY...
I'D SEE PEOPLE... DOCTORS, NURSES, MY BUDDIES... I'D BEG 'EM FOR WATER, BUT IT WAS LIKE IN DREAMS WHERE YOU CAN'T TALK, OR IF YOU CAN, YOU CAN'T SPEAK ANY LANGUAGE PEOPLE UNDERSTAND...."

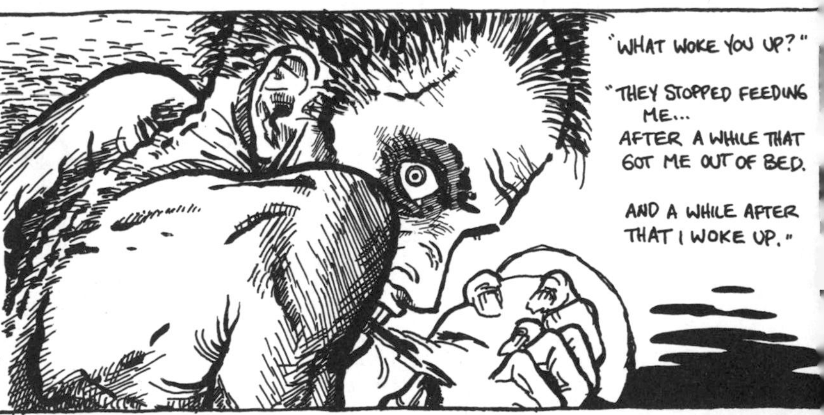
"WHAT WOKE YOU UP?"
"THEY STOPPED FEEDING ME...
AFTER A WHILE THAT GOT ME OUT OF BED.
AND A WHILE AFTER THAT I WOKE UP."

I HATE NOT KNOWING WHAT TO DO NEXT, GIRL.
I'M GOING NOW.

CHAPTER THREE

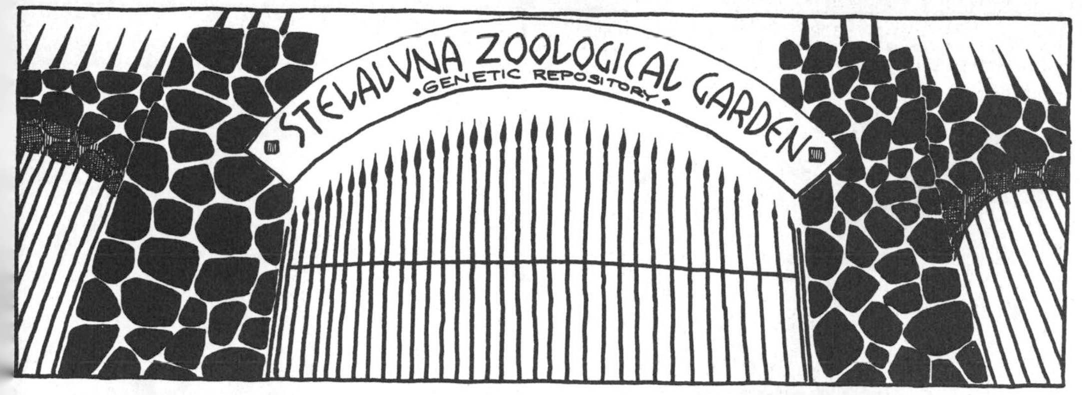
STELALUNA ZOOLOGICAL GARDEN
•GENETIC REPOSITORY•

YAHHN
SNIFF

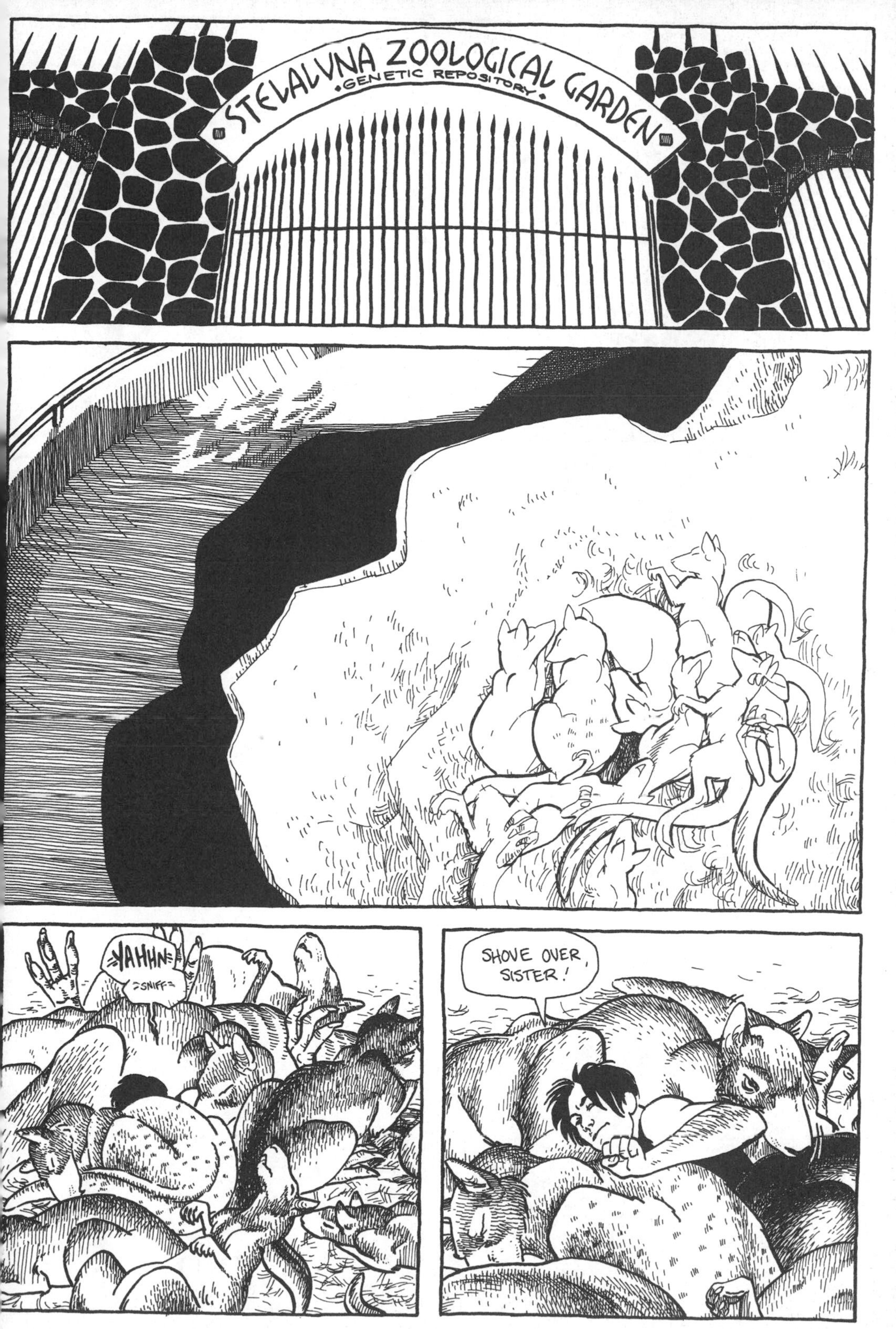

SHOVE OVER, SISTER!

YAHHH

YAHHHH

HEY!

GET THE **FUCK** **OUT** OF THERE!!
WHIK!

J-JUS' WAIT- DON'T PANIC! KEEP STILL -I'LL GET HELP!

OH SHIT OH SHIT
HEY, PAL—
100W LARGE PREDATORCH
100W LARGE
100W LARGE
100W LARGE

RELAX, MAN. I'M OUT.
LEGGED
TWO-LEGGED
NO-LEGGED
MULTIPLE
CONCESSION
GREATER NORTHERN BLANKET HOG

LOOK, JERKY, I DON'T KNOW WHAT KINDA CRAZED INSURANCE SCAM YER TRYIN' A PULL HERE, BUT YOU STAY TH' GODDAMNED HELL AWAY FROM MY ANIMALS!

YOU DON'T SEEM TO REALIZE THESE ARE REAL PREDATORS! HAVE YOU EVER SEEN AN ANIMAL MAULING?
NO, OF COURSE YOU HAVEN'T - PROBABLY NEVER EVEN SET FOOT OUT OF THIS NICE SAFE LITTLE CITY -

BUSTER, YOU DON'T SEEM TO REALIZE THAT THERE'S A BIIIG DIFFERENCE BETWEEN WILD ANIMALS AND THESE BORED, FAT ZOO-BRED VEGETABLES.
THAT'S ANOTHER THING!

YOU COULD BE CARRYING GOD KNOWS WHAT VIRUSES! THOSE ANIMALS ARE RARE AND HARD TO BREED, AND VERY SUSCEPTIBLE ~
HEY, MAN, MAKE UP YOUR MIND --

ARE THEY A DANGER TO ME, OR AM I A DANGER TO THEM?
IT DOESN'T MATTER - THE ZOO'S CLOSED, YOU'RE OUTTA LINE, AND YOU'RE OUT!

OKAY, OKAY, FINE. BUT MAN, YOU'VE GOT TO REALIZE THAT THOSE ARE NOT REAL PREDATORS.
HELL THEY'RE NOT!

NO, THEY'RE NOT. THEY'RE BORED SUBURBANITES.
ATTITUDES LIKE YOURS GET PEOPLE KILLED EVERY DAY!
JUST YESTERDAY SOME GADDAMN TOURIST GOT THE CRAP STOMPED OUT OF 'ER WALKIN' UP TO A RAY-DEER -
- TRYIN'A TAKE A PICTURE WITH IT FER CHRISSAKES - SO INSTEAD OF TELLIN' HER SHE'S A MORON WHO GOT OFF LIGHT WITH JUST STITCHES AN' A CONCUSSION, THE CITY'S GOTTA HUNT THE ANIMAL DOWN AND KILL IT! LIKE THEY'LL ACTUALLY FIND THE EXACT SAME DEER -

HEY, I NEVER SAID SUBURBANITES CAN'T FIGHT BACK. I WOULDN'T GET BETWEEN THEM 'N' THEIR REMOTE CONTROLS.
LEMME GET THAT FOR YA -
100W LARGE PREDATOR CHOW

WHAT I'M SAYIN' IS, IT TAKES MORE THAN CLAWS, TEETH, OR EVEN INSTINCT TO MAKE A PREDATOR.

REAL PREDATORS ARE OPPORTUNISTS. CAN'T AFFORD TO MISS A CHANCE.
CLANG!
HEY!
ZOO AND GENETIC REPOSITORY
100W LARGE PREDATOR CHOW

¡IG!
CRAK! GRUNCH
CRUNCH

CRIK
CRUK

HAVIN' TROUBLE?
UH — YEAH. WON'T START, AND I'M LATE.

AN' LOOKS LIKE YER GONNA BE LATER. LEMME TAKE A LOOK - I USETA WORK ON THESE THINGS.
HERE'S YOUR PROBLEM— REACH IN HERE —
WHERE?

WAY THE HELL DOWN IN THERE. IT'S A LOOSE WIRE. GOT IT?
YEAH ... YEAH, I GOT IT!

DAMNEDEST THING, TOO— THIS HEAP STARTED UP JUST **FINE** WHEN I DROVE IT HERE YESTERDAY.

WAIT—

WHAM!

SCHMUCK!
YOU'RE **LUCKY** I DON'T RUN YOU OVER FOR GOOD MEASURE!
BLPH=

HOW **COULD** YOU BE SO **STUPID**?
AAYYY-.
=GUH=

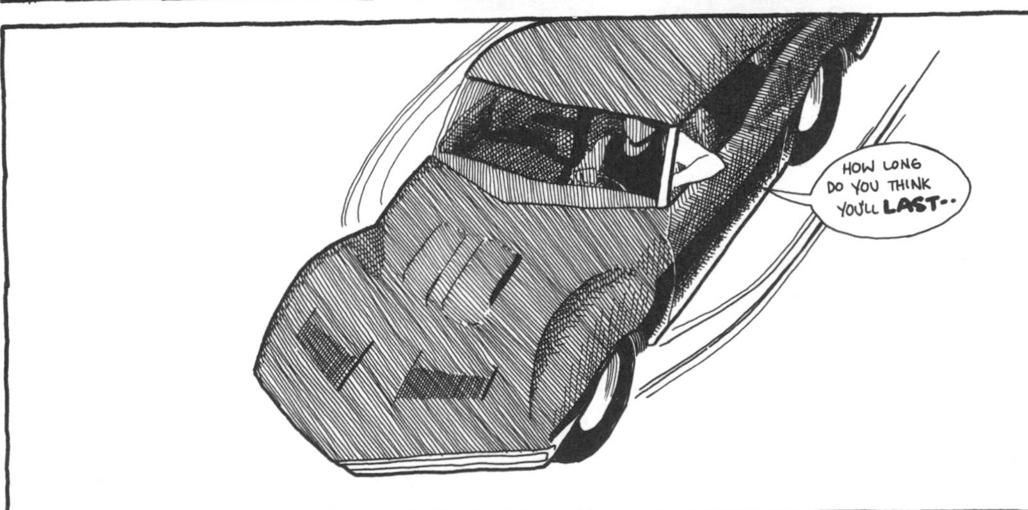
HOW LONG DO YOU THINK YOU'LL **LAST**-.

CLICK!
A-LONE WITH MY THOUGHTS THIS EVE-NING I WALKED ON THE BANKS OF TYNE — I WONDERED HOW I COULD WIN YOU — OR IF I COULD MAKE YOU MINE —

AARG.
CLIK
SHOT AND KILLED A WOMAN AND CHILD WHO STRONGLY RESEMBLED HIS OWN FAMILY. CURIOUSLY, HER OLDER SON WAS UNHARMED. IN THE STALKER'S OWN WORDS—"ARE YOU CRAZY? I HAVE NO SON!"

CLIK
I AM NO LADY NOBLE ~ AND MY YOUTH'S SWEET DAYS HAVE RUN ~ BUT I AM A WOMAN WRONGED, AND I NEED A CHAM-PI-ON ~

CLIK
RES-CUE MEE — AN' TAKE ME IN YO' ARMS, RESCUE ME — CAN'T YOU SEE — THAT I'M LONE-LY
AWW, A-REE-THA —

I MEAN WHAT THE HELL AM I SUPPOSED TO DO ABOUT IT ??
WHEN THE HELL DID THIS BECOME MY PROBLEM?
CHEEPS
PIYO

HELL, IT'S HER LIFE!
MAYBE SHE WANTS TO SOLVE HER OWN DAMN PROBLEMS.... NOT MY FAULT SHE DON'T EVEN KNOW SHE'S IN DANGER...
SIGH
IF SHE IS!
WHAT THE HELL AM I SUPPOSED TO DO ABOUT IT?

KILL HIM?
WHO ARE YOU TALKING TO?

POOF

KKHRISST-.

CRACKIN' UP ALREADY, EH, MATEY? Y' BETTER HEAD BACK UP THE HIGH COUNTRY!
G'WAN! GIT!

WASHIS
SCREE=
HEY!
SWERVE=
EEK!
SCREET=
VAROOOM=

ERT!
NO PARKING EVER EVER EVER

CULTURAL GALLERY 216
PAINWRIGHT

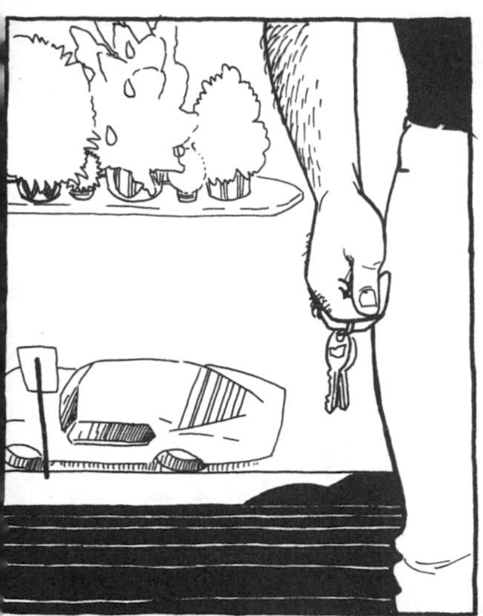

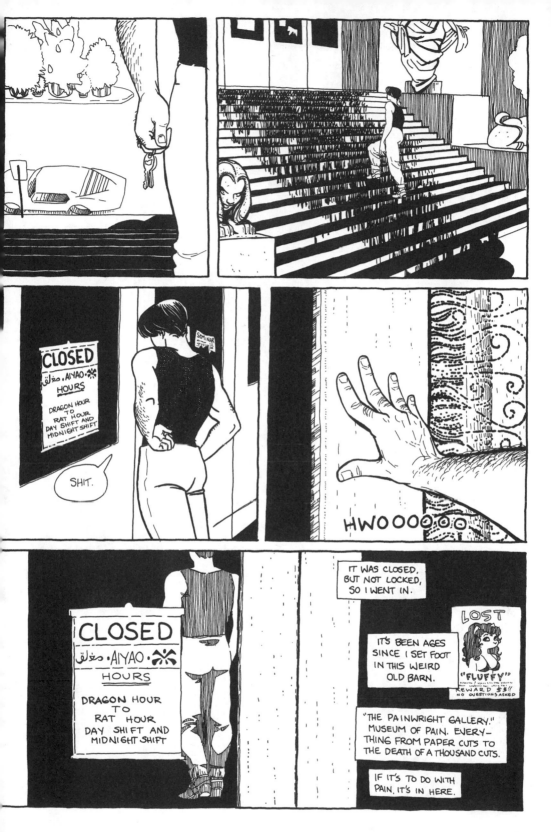

CLOSED
مغلق • AIYAO •
HOURS
DRAGON HOUR TO RAT HOUR DAY SHIFT AND MIDNIGHT SHIFT
SEMINAR
SHIT.

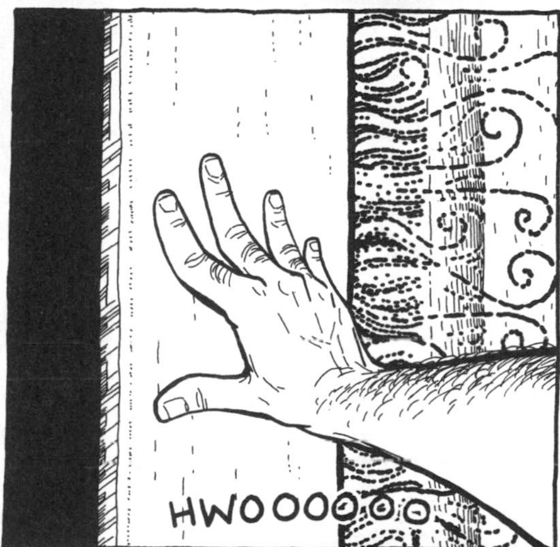

HWOOOOOOO

IT WAS CLOSED, BUT NOT LOCKED, SO I WENT IN.
CLOSED
مغلق • AIYAO •
HOURS
DRAGON HOUR TO RAT HOUR DAY SHIFT AND MIDNIGHT SHIFT
IT'S BEEN AGES SINCE I SET FOOT IN THIS WEIRD OLD BARN.
"THE PAINWRIGHT GALLERY." MUSEUM OF PAIN. EVERY-THING FROM PAPER CUTS TO THE DEATH OF A THOUSAND CUTS.
IF IT'S TO DO WITH PAIN, IT'S IN HERE.

LOST
"FLUFFY"
REWARD $$!!
NO QUESTIONS ASKED

...I CAME SO CLOSE ...
WHY ME, I ASK MYSELF ...
INADVERTENT
MALICIOUS
GRAND
CLANK
CLANK
FWEEEE
FWEE
TIK
TIC
HHHHSSSSSS
...YOU THINK YOU KNOW SOME-ONE
IMPERSONAL / BUREAUCRATIC
PERSON AL – FAMILY/FRIENDS
WHY DIDN'T ANYBODY STOP ME?
...ALL ALONE IN HIS HOTEL ROOM .....
...BUT WHEN I WOKE UP SHE WAS DEAD. NOW! ...
JUST MADE IT LOOK LIKE THEY WERE ...
BUT WHAT SHOULD I HAVE DONE?
WHY IS THIS SO HARD TO FACE ...
...IF I HAD PUT OUT MY HAND I COULD HAVE TOUCHED MY SISTER'S BRAINS ...
DON'T YOU MAKE ME HURT THAT ....
I JUST FEEL SO STUPID ...SO UGLY AND
I DON'T MIND THAT SO MUCH ...
BUT NOBODY CAME
MY PROBLEMS ARE SO SMALL
AUDITORIUM
I DON'T HAVE TO BE TOLD THIS ISN'T NORMAL ...
TEN THOUSAND SLAIN
I JUST COULDN'T STOP

≡HHAAHH≡
I HAVE A QUESTION.
FLIK!

FIRST I WANT TO SEE THE TESTAMENT OF EMMA MARLENA GROSVENOR.

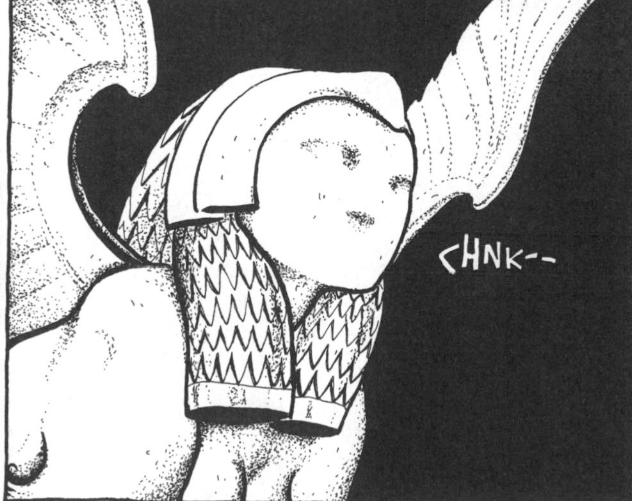

CHNK--

NO PARKING EVER EVER EVER

INFORMATION IS OUR CURRENCY.
YOU KNOW OUR PRICE.

ALL RIGHT.
FINE.
THE WORST THING THAT EVER HAPPENED TO ME, AND THE THING I'M MOST AFRAID OF.

THE DEATH OF MY FATHER.
I'M **SURE** HE WAS MY FATHER.
CRIK

FILE CROSS REF PARENT
SHOOP!
UHH!
YEAH, THAT'S HIM.
HE WAS NOT MUCH FOR TALK EVEN WHEN HE WASN'T DRUNK, AND I FOR MY PART DIDN'T ASK HIM QUESTIONS.
FILE CROSS REF FRIEND/ASSOC.
SHOOP!
IF I EVER HAD STARTED ASKING, I WOULDN'T HAVE BEEN ABLE TO STOP.
PLUS I DIDN'T KNOW WHERE TO START SO...
I JUST DIDN'T.
FILE NOT FOUND
CROSS REF
FILE SPEC CROSS REF
HIMASHA RESEARCH STATION
RUINS
SETTLEMENT ST CLAIR
IKHNATKO RIVER
WIMAMAKO RIVER
UNINHABITED WILD LAND
TRAVEL ADVISORY
THERE WERE ABOUT A MILLION LITTLE WARS WAITING TO HAPPEN BETWEEN ME AND MY FATHER.
I AT LEAST KNEW THAT IF EITHER OF US EVER LET ONE HARSH WORD SLIP OR RAISED A HAND IN ANGER THAT THE BOMB WOULD GO OFF AND ONE OF US WOULD END UP DEAD.
THE OLDER I GOT THE LESS LIKELY IT SEEMED THAT IT WOULD BE ME.
IT WAS ALMOST LIKE MUTUAL RESPECT.
I USED THE LAST NAME AYERS ALL THROUGH SCHOOL AND THE MILITARY 'CAUSE THAT'S THE NAME THAT SHOWED UP ON MY FATHER'S MAIL MOST OFTEN.
MY MOTHER... HE TOLD ME SHE DIED.
DIDN'T SAY HOW.
I THINK I KILLED HER. DIED OF CHILDBIRTH.
I GUESS A SCREAMIN' BRAT WASN'T MUCH OF A TRADE FOR A WIFE.
EARLY
MILITARY SERVICE
SHOOP
FILE CROSS REF PARENT
SHOOOOOP
THE OLDER I GOT THE MORE TIME I SPENT IN THE WOODS.
ONE WINTER I WAS GONE ABOUT FOUR MONTHS. WHEN I GOT BACK HE WAS ALREADY BURIED.
UP TILL THEN SOMEHOW I STILL BELIEVED THAT SOMEDAY HE'D TELL ME EVERYTHING.
I WAS WAITING... I HARDLY KNEW WHAT FOR.
TO GROW UP?
FOR HIM TO TALK--
FOR HIM TO DIE?
I JUST THOUGHT IT'D BE IN THAT ORDER.
WHAT IS OUR NAME?
WHO WAS MY MOTHER?
WAS IT ME HE WAS HIDING?
WHERE DID HIS MONEY COME FROM?

DO I HAVE OTHER FAMILY?
WHY AM I THE WAY I AM?

BUT THE ROTTEN OLD FUCK DIED, AND I GOT NOBODY ELSE TO ASK.

NOW.
EMMA.

FSSK!

NO PARKING EVER EVER EVER

I'M HERE BECAUSE I'VE BEEN TOLD THAT THERE ARE ONLY TWO THERAPIES FOR-- FOR ME.
I CAN'T AFFORD MASSAGE, SO I'M TELLING MY STORY.
MY STORY WASN'T SUPPOSED TO BE LIKE THIS ...

OH, SHE'UZ A SWEET ONE-
GOT PURTIER EVERY DAY-
MEBBE WARN'T SUCH A GOOD GAL ALLA TIME BUT CAIN'T BLAME 'ER-
ALL INNA BLOOD, Y'KNOW.
NAW, I WARN'T REALLY NO BLOOD KIN, BUT WHY TELL HER THAT?
ALL BE THE SAME INNA HUNDERD YEARS ....

SHE'S A BITCH.
YEAH.
YEAH.

TALKING ABOUT M, RIGHT? SOME PEOPLE ARE SO AMAZING ALL THEY NEED IS ONE NAME, RIGHT? M'S ACTUALLY DOWN TO ONE LETTER.
SHE'S WASTED ON ONE LITTLE MILITARY MAN, NO MATTER HOW LOUD HE IS-
HELL, HER TITS ALONE COULD RUN THIS WORLD BETTER!

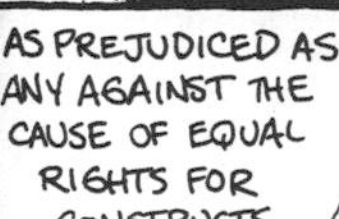

AS PREJUDICED AS ANY AGAINST THE CAUSE OF EQUAL RIGHTS FOR CONSTRUCTS.
WHAT'S THAT DUMB JOCK SKINJOB GOT THAT I HAVEN'T GOT?
LIPS.
FUCK YOU!

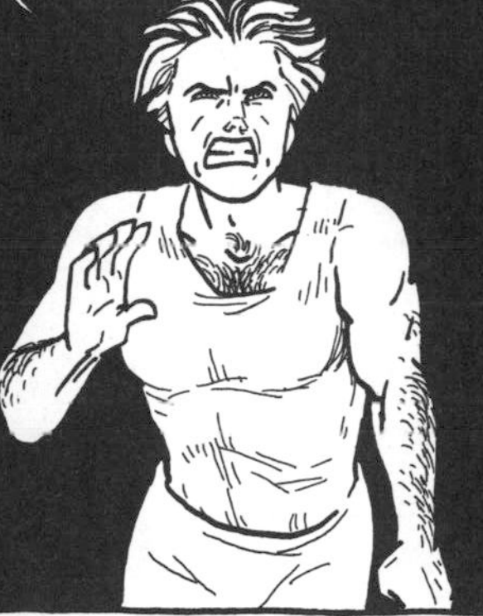

NO!
NOT ALL THESE OTHER IDIOTS— SHOW ME EMMA!

I AM PSYCHOLOGICALLY DIVERGENT.
I SUFFER— IF THAT IS THE CORRECT TERM —FROM "PRINCESS" PSYCHOSIS.

WITHIN MY MIND IS A DOOR TO ANOTHER PLACE, GAN GARIDAN. IT IS FAR MORE REAL TO ME THAN THIS, THE BAD WORLD. IT HAS ITS OWN DEITIES, A DISCRETE AND SUBTLE LANGUAGE, GEOGRAPHY, AND PHYSICS, AND WITHIN IT, I AM QUEEN.

WHEN THE BAD WORLD PUSHES ME OUT, I GO HOME. I WALK IN SHINING FORESTS. I SPEAK IN GLORY. I JOIN THE SINGING THRONGS IN THE STONE STREETS.
AT SUCH TIMES, MY "MIRROR IMAGE" GOES ABOUT MY DAILY LIFE. IT SAYS NOTHING OF THIS- FOR IT CAN'T - AND NO ONE'S THE WISER.

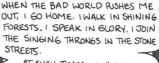

BUT I MISS MY CHILDREN. I CAN'T TAKE THEM WITH ME TO MY HOME. I OFTEN WISH TO COME BACK AND CAN'T. AT THE WORST OF THE FEARS MY HUSBAND PUT ON ME, I LOST TWO YEARS OF MY BABIES' LIVES. I KNOW WHAT HAPPENED, BUT I FELT NONE OF IT...

MY DAUGHTER RACHEL IS MYSELF, YOUNG, BEFORE BRIGHAM.
SHE TELLS ME THAT THE DOOR TO EO OPENED BECAUSE OF BRIGHAM'S ABUSE.
HOW CAN I DOUBT HER?
THE ONLY REASON I AM FREE TO ROAM THE BAD WORLD AT WILL IS THE FACT THAT BRIG IS FAR FROM HERE. CONTAINED.
IT'S HARD TO PICTURE.
YOU WANT TO KNOW MY WORST FEAR?
HORAGOROSI. THAT'S MY END OF THE WORLD, MY RAGNAROK. FOR BRIGHAM TO GET OUT. THAT WOULD BE THE WORST THING.

HE WAS MY PLATOON LIEU-TENANT WHILE I WAS IN THE BELLY OF THE BEAST.

HE GOT PROMOTED AWAY AND I HARDLY SAW HIM ANYMORE ... BUT I'D STILL GO SEE M AND THE KIDS.
HE NEVER SEEMED TO BE THERE, EITHER ....

THEN I GOT HURT AND WAS DISCHARGED - DIDN'T SEE ANY OF 'EM FOR AGES--
EMMA POPS UP IN ANVARD WITH NO BRIGHAM - I'D GO SEE 'EM, BUT WHAT BUSINESS OF MINE WAS ALL OF THAT?

AND STILL I NEVER KNEW WHAT SHE'D BEEN THROUGH.
LIKE WITH MY FATHER. I FELT LIKE I WAS ~ KEEPING AN UNSPOKEN AGREEMENT -
HEYA, CHOAD SMOKER!

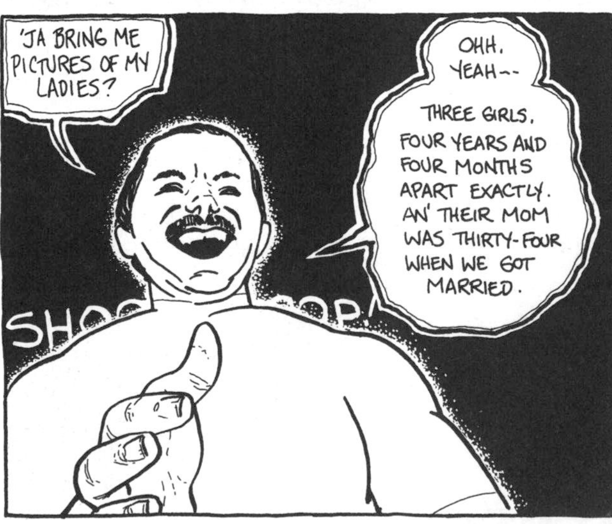

'JA BRING ME PICTURES OF MY LADIES?
OHH. YEAH--
THREE GIRLS. FOUR YEARS AND FOUR MONTHS APART EXACTLY. AN' THEIR MOM WAS THIRTY-FOUR WHEN WE GOT MARRIED.

HOWZAT FOR PRECISION, RECRUIT!
worst thing... worst.. ...
HE'S HERE IN THIS CITY.
AND EMMA DOESN'T KNOW.
BUT HE KNOWS JUST WHERE THEY ARE... ALWAYS HAS.... THANKS TO ME.

HE SAID.... SHE'D JUST UPPED AND LEFT HIM.... TOOK THE KIDS... SAID HE WANTED 'EM BACK... SAID HE... KNEW HOW ...TO WORK ON 'EM...
THANKS, BUDDY. I TRULY CAN'T THANK YOU ENOUGH.

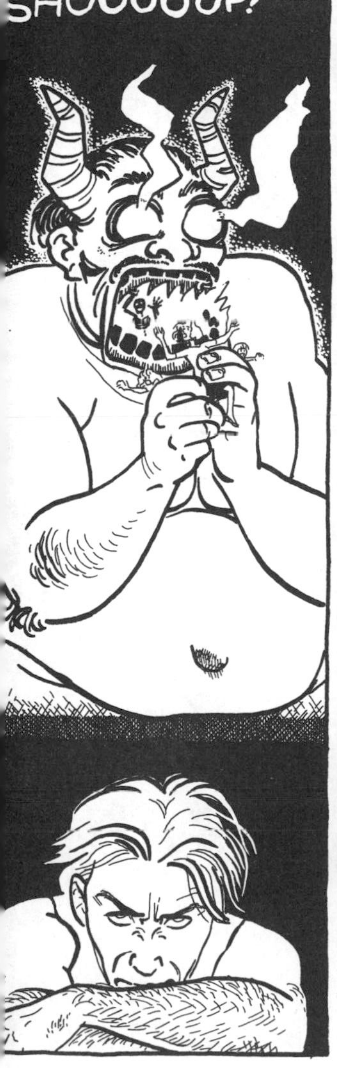
SHOOOOOP!

HOW COULD YOU?

MMY HHERO....
HHOW CCAN I EVER RREPAYY YYOU?

WELL.
NOW
WHAT?

I CAN'T FEEL WHERE THE DOOR IS.
THIS ROOM SWALLOWS UP SOUND AND SCENT.

IT COULD BE ANYWHERE OR NOWHERE.
THIS ROOM COULD BE ANY SHAPE AT ALL.

LET ME OUT!

PAYMENT IS DUE. IN FULL.
FUU--UCK--.

OKAY. OKAY.
THE THING I'M MOST AFRAID OF.

I HAVE A DISEASE.
AT LEAST THAT'S WHAT I THINK IT IS.
SEEMS LIKE, EVERY TIME I FIND A PLACE TO SETTLE, BACK IT COMES, ALL SMILEY.
AND IT GETS WORSE AND WORSE UNTIL I GET MOVING AND STIR SOME MORE SHIT UP.
IT NEVER GETS TO WHERE I FEEL LIKE I'LL DIE.
I JUST **WANT** TO.
IT DOESN'T MAKE SENSE ....
I CAN HANDLE **ANYTHING EXCEPT** PEACE AND QUIET?
AND I THINK, WHAT IF IT GETS WORSE? WHAT WILL I HAVE TO DO TO GET RID OF IT **NEXT** TIME?

WHRUMM

THANKS FOR THE SOUR PERSIMMONS, COUSIN.

SHOULD'VE KNOWN BETTER THAN TO GO TO THEM.
NO PARKING EVER EVER EVER

ANYTHING THEY TELL ME CAN'T HELP BUT BE WORST-CASE SCENARIOS.
AND THEY ALWAYS END UP TAKING MORE THAN THEY GIVE.
NO PARKING EVER EVER EVER

WHATTA YOU GONNA DO?? YOU GOT TO DO SOMETHING AND SO
YOU'S ALL SHE'S GOT! ... SHIT WHAT REASONS HE HAD?
THERE'S NO EXCUSE FOR WHAT HE'S DONE AND YOU KNOW
HE AIN'T DONE WITH THEM!! WHAT THE HELL ELSE YOU GOOD FOR ANYW

HEY, CAP. WE GOT A SITUATION HERE.
LOVELY. WHAT?
VRIIII... VR

WE WERE TURNING OUT ALL THE PICKUPS FROM THAT STREET PARTY— THIS ONE SAYS HIS CAR GOT TOWED FROM IN FRONT OF THE PAINWRIGHT GALLERY.
NOW HE WANTS TO PAY UP AND TAKE IT.
YEAH- BUT?
VRIIII.... VRIIII... VRIIII...

WELL, HIS STORY CHECKS OUT FINE, BUT HIS CAR DOESN'T. IT DID GET TICKET-AND-TOWED, IT DID GET CHECKED INTO THE LOT. BUT IT AIN'T THERE NOW.
SO WHERE **IS** IT?

.... NO CLUE.
COULD BE ONE OF THOSE TOW-TRUCK WEASELS BAGGED IT BACK OUT, AND IT'S IN A CHOP SHOP BY NOW. NICE CAR, LOTSA GOODIES.
SWELL.
JUST FAT SWELL.

WHAT ABOUT HIM?
TYPICAL BROWNWAYS TYPE. NO RECORD, BUT NO ID EITHER, EXCEPT FOR LICENSE AND PROOF OF OWNERSHIP ON HIS BUGGY.
MAGNIFICATION 300
RUNAWAY
LOST
WANT
LIKE YOU COULD EVEN **LOOK** AT A CAR THAT HOT WITHOUT A PAPER TRAIL TEN MILES LONG!

SIGH ....
ALL RIGHT, I'VE GOT IT.

OKAY, MR. LENNOX. YOU GOT US. YOU'RE HERE, AND YOUR CAR'S NOT.
NOW THIS HAS HAPPENED A HUNDRED TIMES IN THE LAST SIX MONTHS, AND FRANKLY I DON'T FEEL LIKE GOING THROUGH THE WHOLE SCRIPT.

YOUR CAR'S NOT GOING TO TURN UP. AT LEAST NOT INTACT.
I SUPPOSE YOU GOTTA HAVE CASH, RIGHT? NO BANK ACCOUNT OR CREDIT ID, RIGHT?
RIGHT.

HERE.
DON'T MAKE THIS WORSE BY COUNTING IT.

I SUPPOSE THIS MIGHT BE MISINTERPRETED AS A CHARITABLE ACT. TAKES NO GREAT BRAIN TO SEE THAT THE FIRST FAMILIES' WAYS MAKE IT HARD FOR YOU MIXED-BLOOD BROWNWAYS TYPES TO MAKE A DECENT LIVING. BUT I'D JUST AS SOON NOT HAVE MY NOSE RUBBED IN IT.
UNDERSTAND?

YOU'RE A CYNICAL MAN, CAPTAIN ASIAK.
AND YOU'RE A TWO-BIT SCAM ARTIST. GET OUTTA HERE AND STAY OUT OF MY SIGHT.

STOP!
1 2 3 4
LESS THAN FIVE?
SEEK LEGAL COUNSEL
MEDAWAR
THE FAC
OF SAFET
SUPPOR
LOCA

PETE?
SURE, I GOT IT.
OH, AND THANKS **SO MUCH** FOR SENDING ME OUT ON A JOB SO STALE THE COPS KNOW ALL ABOUT IT.

I DON'T **GIVE** TWO FARTS IN A HURRICANE THAT THEY CAN'T DO ANYTHING TO ME.
I DON'T **EE**-VEN CARE WHAT YOU HAD TO DO TO GET JERRY LOCKWOOD'S TOWING COMPANY IN ON THIS.

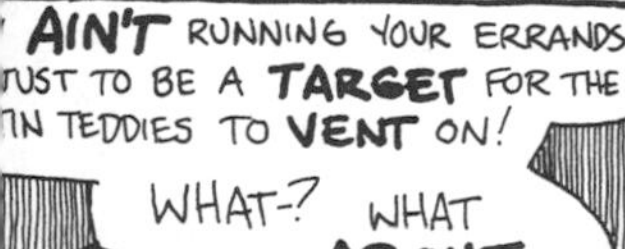
AIN'T RUNNING YOUR ERRANDS JUST TO BE A **TARGET** FOR THE TIN TEDDIES TO **VENT** ON!
WHAT-? WHAT **ABOUT LEMONS?**

WHA'TH' **FUCK** ARE YOU **TAKING**, YOU GOAT RAPER??

SHIT!
K'KLANGG!
AT **LEAST** IN THE WOODS ALL THE PREDATORS ARE AFTER IS YOUR BODY, NOT YOUR SANITY!

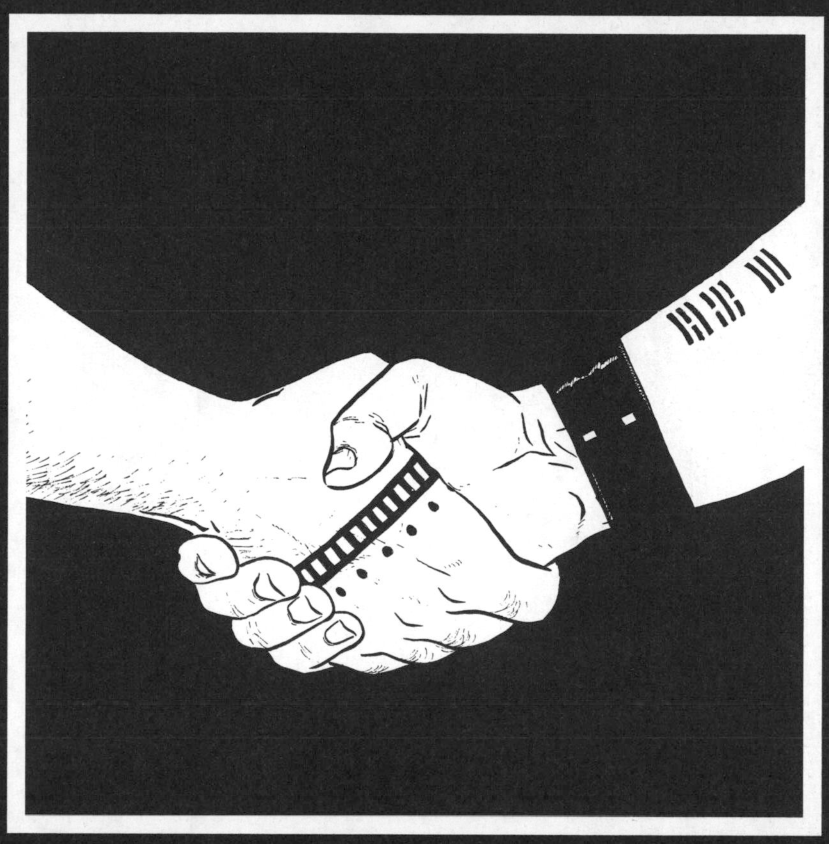

CHAPTER FOUR

THE FINDERS ARE NOW MAINLY FORGOTTEN.
THEY WERE HUNTERS, AND TRACKERS, AND MORE.
THEY LIVED SECRET LIVES.
MOST PEOPLE DIDN'T KNOW WHO HAD OR HADN'T BEEN ACCEPTED INTO THEIR SECRET SOCIETY.
THEIR SKILLS WERE HONED TO ARTISTRY.
TO CATCH THE SLIGHTEST GLIMPSE OF ONE AGAINST HIS INTENT WAS RARE INDEED, AND BROUGHT GREAT CENSURE FROM HIS BRETHREN.

SOME LIVED AS ORDINARY PEOPLE; OTHERS UNDERTOOK GREAT MISSIONS, TRAVELING VAST DISTANCES ALONE AND UNKNOWN.
IT WAS THE WAY OF THE FINDER TO HELP HIS PEOPLE BY STANDING APART FROM THEM, SEEING THEM AS ONLY AN OUTSIDER CAN.
BUT FOR THOSE WHO NEEDED TO ASK FOR HELP DIRECTLY, THERE **WERE** WAYS TO SPEAK TO THE FINDERS. THOSE CUSTOMS STILL LINGER, ALTHOUGH THE REASONS ARE ALSO MAINLY FORGOTTEN.
AND CUSTOMS CHANGE. FOR A WHILE, FINDERS EVEN WORE THE SIGNAL PATTERN OPENLY, SECURE IN THE KNOWLEDGE THAT ONLY OTHER FINDERS KNEW WHAT IT MEANT.
EVERY YEAR, I FIND SOMEBODY TO TATTOO IT BACK ON FOR ME.
BBBZZZZZzz BBBZZZZZZZZZZZ
Y'SURE YOU DON'T WANT ME TO JAZZ IT UP SOME? I GOT SOME **GREAT** LINE PATTERNS—
NAH. JUST LIKE THAT.

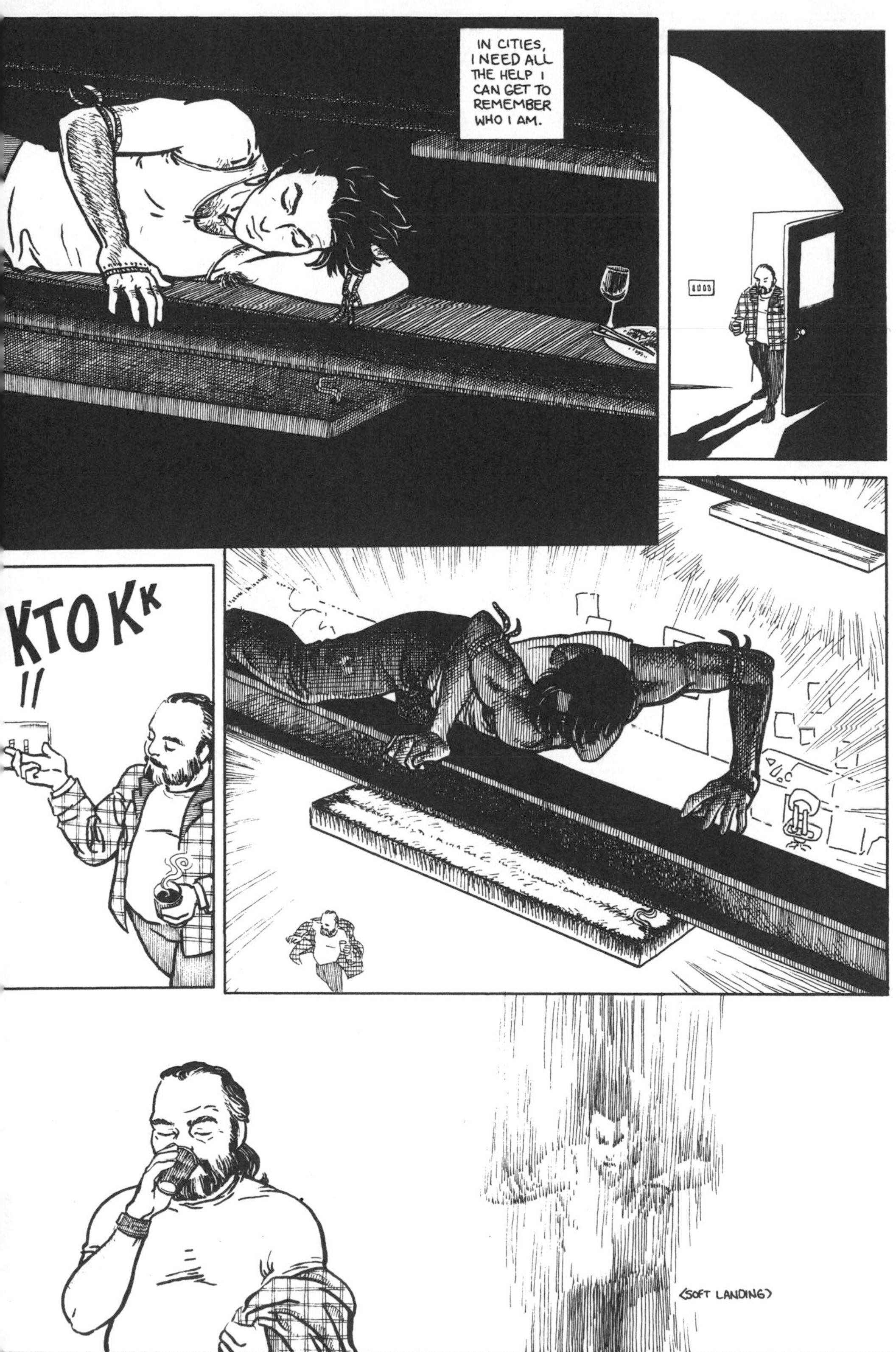
IN CITIES, I NEED ALL THE HELP I CAN GET TO REMEMBER WHO I AM.
KTOKK !!
<SOFT LANDING>

HELLO, BRIGHAM.
HOW'S THE WIFE AND KIDS?
YOU TELL ME, MAN.
AIN'T THAT WHAT I PAY YOU THE BIG BUCKS TO FIND OUT?
SO? GIVE!
OHH, YEAH.
HI, BABY.
OH, GOD. IT'S SO GOOD TO SEE YOU.
MY BEAUTIFUL BABIES.
YOIK!

KTAKKATAKKA TAKATAK TAK TAK TAKKAKATAKA TAK TAK TAKKA TAK TAK TAK
KUAI HUA
VITAL SIGNS MONITOR

AKKA TAK TAKKAKATAKA TAKKATAK TIK TIK TAKKATA TAKTK TAKTAK TAK TAKKA TAK TAKTIK TAKKA TAK TAK TAK TAKKA
VITAL SIGNS MONITOR
MODIFY
KUAI HUA
VITAL SIGNS MONITOR
LYNNE!

WHY CAN'T YOU LEAVE HER ALONE?
SHE MIGHT JUST GET WELL IF YOU DID, YOU KNOW!

THAT REGULATOR IS A DOCTOR'S TOOL!
I KNOW BEING A GENIUS GIVES YOU THE DIVINE RIGHT TO SCREW AROUND WITH ANYTHING YOU CAN GET YOUR HANDS ON, BUT DON'T YOU EVER STOP TO WONDER IF YOU SHOULD??
AND PUT THAT THING OUT!
HUA
MONITOR

THIS IS ONE OF HER FAVORITE DRESSES, YOU KNOW!
IF YOU REALLY CARED ABOUT HER, YOU'D CARE ABOUT WHAT SHE WANTS!

> OPEN CONNECTION
IMD PROTOCOL ENABLED
....CONNECTION ESTABLISHED
$ CHKCONFIG DIAGMODE ON
OK
$ CHKCONFIG DEBUG ON
OK
$ CAT /dev /kmem >/dev /console

whoami
root

OPEN INTERFACE 2: MARCIE
DOCTOR TO PATIENT CONNECTION
......ESTABLISHED

#_

WHAT'RE YOU DOING HERE, BRIG? SECURITY?
UNH? OH YEAH.
SPIRIT SCULPTURE, YOU KNOW.
PRIESTS AND SUCHLIKE DON'T GET ALONG SO WELL, AND FRANKLY, THE SCULPTORS WANT SOMEBODY HERE ALL THE TIME. THEY JUST BUZZ IN AND OUT. O' COURSE...
... AHHHHTEESTS.
THAT'S BLIND EXI, RIGHT?
YEAH, SAMA-EL. GOD OF HOLY WAR. GOD OF JUSTICE.
EHNH: IT REIGNS ON THE JUST AND UNJUST ALIKE.
HUH?
NOTHING.

BRIGHAM.... ALL THIS TIME YOU'VE BEEN IN STIR, I BEEN LOOKIN' IN ON YOUR FAMILY FOR YOU.
HAVE THEY EVER SO MUCH AS SENT YA A TIE ON FATHER'S DAY? A PHONE CALL? A GANG-RAPE GET-WELL CARD?
ANYTHING?
WHAT'S IT TO YOU?
THOUGHT NOT.
WHY DID EMMA LEAVE YOU?
WHAT'S SHE BEEN TELLING YOU?
WHATEVER IT IS, IT AIN'T THE WHOLE STORY.
FINE.
SO?
DAMMIT, YOU'VE GOT NO RIGHT TO GET BETWEEN ME AND MY FAMILY! THIS IS NONE OF YOUR BUSINESS!!
NONE OF MY BUSINESS?? JEEZUS, BRIGHAM!
THREE YEARS YOU'VE BEEN BEGGIN' ME— "C'MON, C'MON, JUST CHECK UP ON 'EM~ SO I'LL KNOW THEY'RE OKAY, 'CAUSE I'M SO ALOOOONE, DO IT FOR MEEEE, MAN!"
SHIT!

I THINK IF I'M BETWEEN YOU AND YOUR FAMILY, YOU PUT ME THERE.
YEAH.
ALLL RIGHT.
O-KAY.
SO.
ASK.
WHAT BULLSHIT OF EMMA'S DO YOU WANT CONFIRMED OR DENIED?
WHY DID EMMA LEAVE YOU?
I DON'T KNOW. TOPS MY LIST OF QUESTIONS, TOO.
WELL, WHAT'S YOUR BEST GUESS?
OH, NOW LET'S SEE ... I WAS AN ASSHOLE, AND SHE JUST DIDN'T LIKE ME ANYMORE.
PROB'LY I WAS SUPPRESSING HER PERSONAL GROWTH.
THE THRILL WAS GONE...
I DELIBERATELY LEFT THE SEAT UP.
I GOT A SNORE THAT SHOWS UP ON A SEISMOGRAPH.
I COMPULSIVELY COMPARED HER TO MY OLD GIRLFRIENDS!
SHE FINALLY REALIZED I CLASHED WITH THE DRAPES!
MAYBE SHE JUST RAN OUT OF MASCARA AND JUST GOT LOST ON HER WAY BACK FROM THE STORE!
I DON'T KNOW, GOD DAMMIT! HOW SHOULD I KNOW? SHE LEFT ME!

YEAH, AND I KNOW WHAT FREEHOLDS ARE LIKE, TOO — IT AIN'T ANY DIFFERENT FROM LIVING IN A CITY.

IN FACT, IT AIN'T ALL THAT DIFFERENT FROM LIVIN' ON THE MOON!
FILTERED AIR, FILTERED WATER, SCREWED-UP TEMPERATURE, PLASTIC FOOD ~ THAT WAS WORTH DESERTING FOR?

IT'S PART OF THE DEAL FOR OFFICERS - WHY ELSE D'YOU THINK I WANTED A COMMISSION?
THAT'S WHAT THE FREE TRADERS' PACT IS FOR - NOT JUST SO THOSE DAMN INDIANS AND GYPSIES AND SHIT YOU LOVE SO MUCH CAN BUY AND SELL WITHOUT CITIZENSHIPS!
I FINALLY GOT SENT INTO A BATTLE ZONE WORTH SETTLING WITH ENOUGH RANK TO DO IT, SO I DID!
LAND FOR PEACE!
AIN'T NOTHING ILLEGAL ABOUT IT!
NO, NOT TO YOU.
SO HOW COME EMMA DIDN'T KNOW ABOUT THIS?
-NO, SHE DIDN'T.
YEAH... WELL, THAT'S EMMA.
SHE PUTS UP A GOOD FRONT, BUT SHE'S NOT OKAY. HOW CAN YOU TELL HER EVERYTHING IF YOU NEVER KNOW WHAT'LL SET HER OFF?
YOU END UP TELLING HER NOTHING.
YEAH ....
YEAH, I GUESS I DID KNOW THAT.

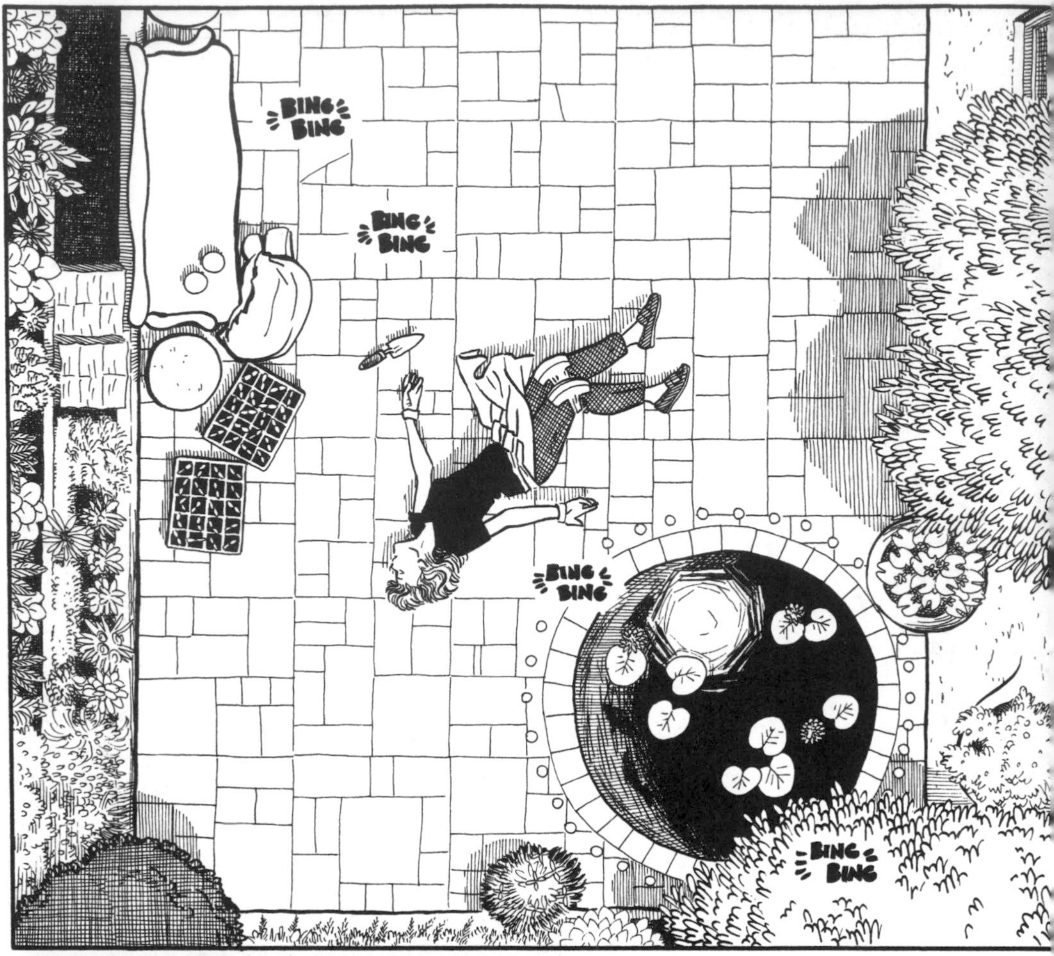

BING
BING

BING
BING

BING
BING

BING
BING

BING
BING

BING
BING

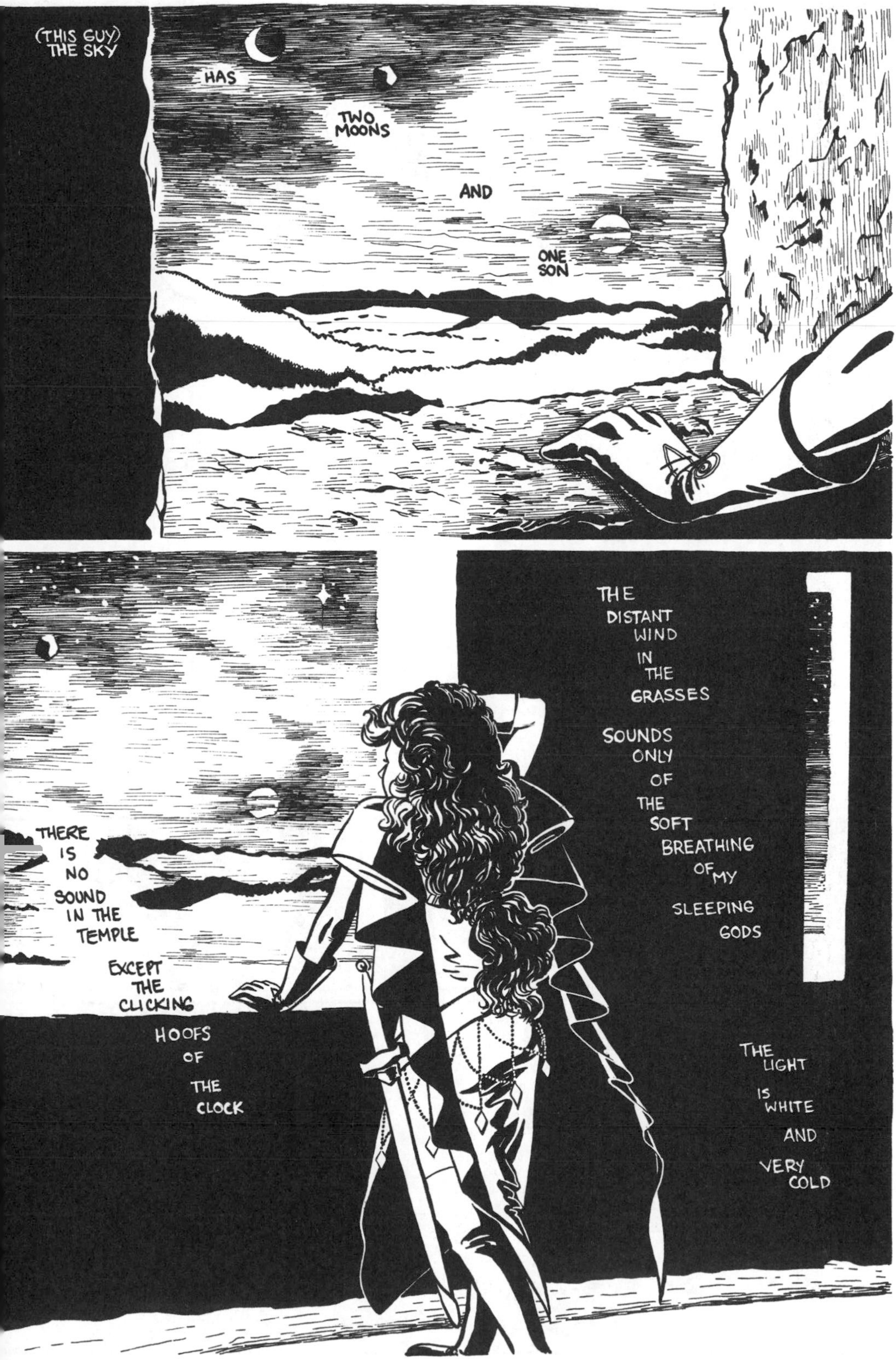

(THIS GUY)
THE SKY
HAS
TWO MOONS
AND
ONE SON

THE DISTANT WIND IN THE GRASSES
SOUNDS ONLY OF THE SOFT BREATHING OF MY SLEEPING GODS

THERE IS NO SOUND IN THE TEMPLE
EXCEPT THE CLICKING
HOOFS OF THE CLOCK

THE LIGHT IS WHITE AND VERY COLD

BING BING
BING BING
BING BING
SNFF
BING
CLIC-POP
YE K
KOFF!
YES, BLYTHE?
PARDONNEZ-MOI, MADAME. ZERE EES A CALL EENCOMING.
BRZZSSTT!
OHH...TAKE A MESSAGE, BLYTHE.
OUI, MADAME.
THAAT's A GOOD ARTIFICIAL INTELLIGENCE.
M'SIEU DANCENY SAYS 'E 'AS FOUND ZE TOBACCO PLANTS YOU WANT; ZEY ARE VER' EXSPENSEEVE B'CAUSE OF ZE DRUG BAN. 'OWEVER, 'E S'INKS ZAT 'E CAN FIND ANUZZER WAY AROUND ZE REGULASSIONS. 'E BID YOU GOOD DAY AN' 'E SEEM VER' 'URT ZAT YOU WEEL NOT SPEAK WIS HEEM.
hmm...POOR VILLIAN. I'LL MAKE IT UP TO HIM.

REMIND ME, WON'T YOU, BLYTHE? I'M JUST... HAVING ONE OF MY DAYS...
BIEN SÛR, MADAME. DOES MADAME WEESH ZAT ALL 'ER CALLS BE 'ELD TODAY?
JUST CAN'T SEEM TO GET IT TOGETHER...
MADAME~ oOOT!?
EH... PAUVRE MADAME EMMA! STRAHNJ DAYS, INDEED!
EH?
... I LEFT A NOTE... ...ON HIS DRESSER... WITH MY OLD.... ...WEDDING RING....
PING!
BLYTHE! BAD PROGRAM! NEVER LISTEN IN UNINVITED!
WITH THESE FEW... GOODBYE WORDS... ...HOW CAN... I SING...? ...GOODBYE, OLD SLEEPYHEAD... ...I'M PACKIN' YOU IN... TAKE CARE... ...OF EVERYTHING...
BUTT OUT! THIS COULD BE IMPORTANT!
BUT MADAME'S PRIVACY~
PING!
YEAH, YEAH, BUT MADAME'S THERAPY!
(HUMMING EDITH PIAF)
...I'M LEAVING MY WEDDING RING... ...DON'T LOOK FOR ME.....
...I'LL GET AHEAD.... ...REMEMBER, DARLING... ...DON'T SMOKE.... ...IN BED...
STHENO
TIKATIKATIKTIK TIKKATIK TIK TIK TIK TIKKA TIK

SO... WHAT ABOUT THE GIRLS?
WHAT ABOUT 'EM?
IF EMMA'S GONE CRACKERS, HOW DO YOU KNOW THEY HAVEN'T TOO? THEY WENT THROUGH THE SAME-
THEY AIN'T NOTHING WRONG WITH MY KIDS. RACHEL MAY LOOK LIKE EMMA'S CLAN, BUT SHE'S MEDAWAR TO THE BONE. SHE'LL FIGURE THAT OUT SOON ENOUGH.
HEY HO WHO IS THERE
NO ONE BUT ME MY DEAR
PLEASE COME SAY HOW DO
THE THINGS I'LL GIVE TO YOU
A STROKE AS GENTLE AS A FEATHER
HEY HO I AM HERE
AM I NOT YOUNG AND FAIR
PLEEASE COME SAY HOW DO
WOULD YOU HAVE A WONDROUS SIGHT?
MIDDAY SUN AT MIDNIGHT
FAIR MAID WHITE AND RED
COMB YOU SMOOTH AND STROKE YOUR HEAD
CHUG CHUG CHUG CHUG
SIGH
LINT
WE! CARRY! DEATH! OUT! OF THE VILLAGE!
WE! CARRY! DEATH! OUT! OF THE VILLAGE!

WE! CARRY! DEATH! OUT! OF THE VILLAGE!
WE! CARRY! DEATH! OUT! OF THE VILLAGE!
WE! CARRY! DEATH! OUT! OF THE VILLAGE!
WE! CARRY! DEATH! OUT! OF THE VILLAGE!
WE! CARRY! DEATH! OUT! OF THE VILLAGE!
TSK
THEY COULD AT LEAST MAKE HER WALK AT THE BITTER END.
BRIG JUST NEVER SHOULDA MARRIED THAT LLAVERAC WOMAN. IT'S THE END FOR HIS CAREER.
NOW, NOW... RACHEL'S A VERY SWEET AND RESPECT-FUL GIRL.
-PEG-
-AND HER MOTHER'S THE BEST BOTANIST WE'VE EVER HAD.
THEY PULL THEIR WEIGHT, SO SAVE THE CLAN SNOBBERY.
BESIDES, SHE'S JUST A KID. AND IT'S SPRING FESTIVAL, SO DON'T YOU TWO BUMS SPOIL EVERYBODY'S FUN. WORRY ABOUT RACHEL WHEN SHE'S OLD ENOUGH TO BE TROUBLE.

WHAT ABOUT MARCIE? THAT KID'S SICK MORE THAN SHE'S WELL.
YEAH? SO WHAT'S THAT PROVE BUT THAT EMMA AIN'T TAKING GOOD CARE OF HER?
=SIGH= IT'S NOT JUST THAT, BRIG.
YOU KNOW, SHE'S THE ONLY ONE I WAS THERE FOR. WHEN SHE WAS BORN, I MEAN. SHE'S MY~
YEAH, COURSE YOU WERE! SHE WAS BORN WHEN YOU HAD 'EM LOCKED UP IN THAT DUNGEON YOU BUILT FOR 'EM!
NO WONDER THEY'RE ALL HALF-NUTS NOW! LOCKED AWAY IN A "FREE" HOLD... THAT'S RICH~
DADDY DON'T FIGHT
HALF-NUTS? YOU MEAN MARCIE? NO, MAN, NO~ MEDAWAR GIRLS ARE ALWAYS QUIET AT HER AGE!
YEAH, COMATOSE KIDS ARE PRETTY QUIET, AT THAT.
WELL, WHAT ABOUT LYNNE? THAT KID'S DEVIOUS, AND I DON'T MEAN LITTLE-KID DEVIOUS, EITHER. YOU COULDN'T PUT A LEASH ON HER EVEN WHEN SHE WAS A BABY, AND NOW~
THAT ONE. THAT LITTLE GIRL CAN DAMN WELL TAKE CARE OF--HER SELF.

BRIG, SHE'S **TEN!** YOU DON'T TOSS A TEN-YEAR-OLD OUT TO FEND FOR HERSELF-
OH, NO? HOW OLD WERE **YOU** WHEN YOU LEFT **YOUR** FATHER'S HOUSE?

JAEGER, YOU DON'T **REALLY** WANT TO **STAY** IN THE MIDDLE OF THIS, DO YA?
NOT REALLY YOUR **STYLE.**
WHERE THEY AT?

MY SOUNDTRACK MUSTA BEEN WORKING OVERTIME, 'CAUSE ALL I COULD THINK OF WAS A LINE FROM A SONG I'D HEARD A MILLION TIMES A DAY DURING MY STINT IN THE ARMY:

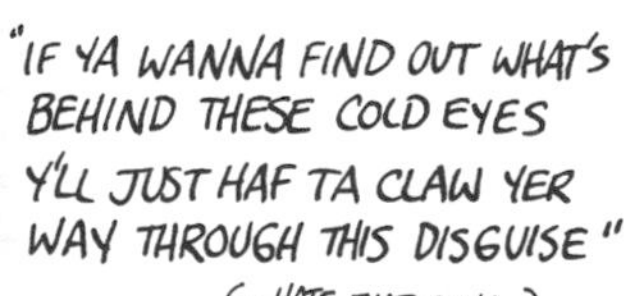
"IF YA WANNA FIND OUT WHAT'S BEHIND THESE COLD EYES
Y'LL JUST HAF TA CLAW YER WAY THROUGH THIS DISGUISE"
(....HATE THAT SONG...)

WOULD HE FLIP OUT AND ATTACK ME IF I SAID NO?
SHOULD I JUST PISS HIM OFF AND **MAKE** HIM TRY FOR ME?
(GET IT OVER WITH)

HIS PULSE IS HIGH, HIS PUPILS BIG AS EGGS.
HE'S AFRAID. HE'S ANGRY.
WHAT **ELSE** IS HE?

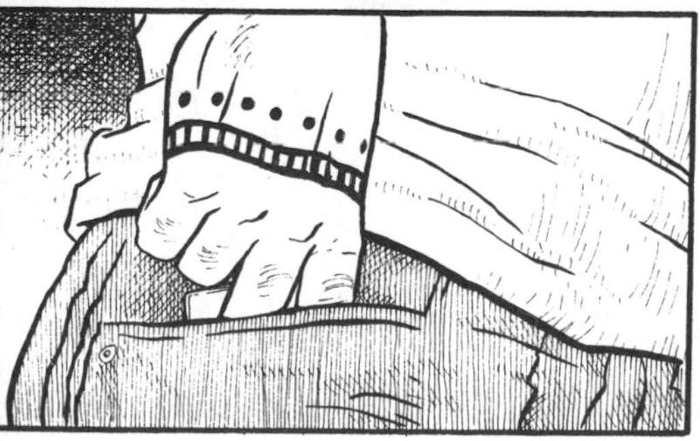

SECRET GARDENS
LANDSCAPING & GARDEN DESIGN
EMMA GROSVENOR
10100 RISING RD E ANVARD
8220-2706-8787-02AT
BRIGHAM... LOOK, IF SHE'S SICK, SHE DOESN'T NEED MORE TROUBLE. GO SLOW, OKAY?
I'VE BEEN LOOKING FOR EMMA ALL MY LIFE. EVERY WOMAN I'VE EVER KNOWN HAS ONLY BEEN A PART OF HER.
I'M NOT GONNA LOSE HER NOW FOR LACK O' TRYING.
BROTHER. THIS IS A LIFE DEBT.
YOU'VE GIVEN ME BACK MY LIFE.
AT LEAST NOW I KNOW WHAT I WANT TO DO.
I WILL WATCH HOW YOU RUN.
AND I WILL PURSUE YOU.
IN THE BLACK
4-21-97
CARLA SPEED MCNEIL

CHAPTER FIVE

WELCOWELCOME TO CHECKPOINT THIRTY-TWO OF ANVARD'S SELF-GUIDED WALKING TOUR! YOU ARE NOW AT THE GROUND LEVEL OF ANVARD, ON THE OUTSKIRTS OF THE OLD CITY!
ANVARD
FROM HERE, YOU MAY GO DIRECTLY TO POINT THIRTY-THREE AT THE HELIOMANCY BUTTERFLY GARDENS, OR TAKE THE LONG WAY ON ONE OF OUR "RED PATHS" ESPECIALLY DESIGNED FOR THE MORE ADVENTUROUS SIGHTSEER!
IF YOU WANT A RATHER MORE VIVID EXPERIENCE, THE RED PATHS ARE FOR YOU!
THEY ARE NOT RECOMMENDED FOR CHILDREN UNDER TWENTY, PREGNANT WOMEN, ANYONE NOT ON A STRICT REGIMEN OF CARDIOVASCULAR TRAINING, OR ANYONE WHO ABSTAINED FROM SIGNING THE CIVIC INDEMNITY WAIVER BEFORE COMMENCING THIS TOUR.
HOWEVER! FOR THOSE WHO ESCHEW THE SHALLOW NATURE OF TOURISM=
=FOR THOSE WHO TRULY WISH TO EXPERIENCE THE HEART OF THE LOWER CITY IN ALL ITS FORMS, THIS TRIP UP MILLINARIE ROAD WILL CERTAINLY PUT THE STAMP OF THE SINCERE STUDENT OF HUMAN EXPERIENCE UPON YOU!
AL'S ALLEY PAWN SHOP
QUESTIONS ASKED
NOW "SHOWING"!
ELIOT MESS
THIS SIDE
101
ENCRUSTATIO
WATS
Z
CARNAL TRI
THEATER
PLEASE CHECK WEAPON
BEFORE ENTERING
THE OLD CITY IS A PLACE OF GREAT VITALITY AND FREEDOM!
OF NECESSITY, THE TOUR NOW ASSUMES A MORE CHALLENGING ASPECT. YOU MAY HAVE TO LOOK HARD FOR THE NEXT CHECKPOINT INFO SITE!
REMEMBER, IF YOU MISS ONE, YOU WON'T KNOW HOW TO GET TO THE NEXT ONE!
CARPE DIEM!
(AND CAVEAT EMPTOR!)

UHH
(OH BABY)
UHH
UHH
(OH BABY)
UHH
DRUSILLA
JANKO
1962-1966
BILL
EAGAN
ASH
ZHENKO
UHH
UHH
UHH
(OH BABY)
OH YEAH
OH YEAH
UH!
OHH GOD
(OH YEAH BABY I LOVE YOU)
(NOW ROLL OVER)
GHASP
OAHH

NGH!
NAA HA HA HA HA HA
SIN-EATER!
SCAVENGER, DRIFTER, SHIT-GOBBLIN' PARASITE!
"WHERE HE LIES AND HOW HE FARES, NOBODY KNOWS AND NOBODY CARES!" REST IN PEACE!
HAW HAW HAW HAW HAW HAW!
NYAAA HAA HA!
BAM!
WHUMP! WHUMP! WHUMP!
WHUH-- FUH-?
NUH-NO --- PLEE'-- PLEE' GAW'---- NO--
PANT PANT
PANT
SHIT!
SORRY.
WHINE

I CLEANED THAT POOR OL' FART UP AND GAVE 'IM TWELVE BUCKS AND JUST LIKE THAT WE'RE BUDDY PALS.
BUT I STILL FELT LIKE A TOTAL BONEHEAD AND I HAD TO DO SOMETHING TO AVOID GOING INTO A FUNK.
DISPOSABLE SOCIETY, LTD.
CATHARTIC KICK-STARTS
WHITE ELEPHANTS EXTERMINATED
PSYCHOLOGICAL BAGGAGE LOST
THANKS, MAN. YOU GOT A GREAT THING GOING HERE!
HEAR ye, HEAR ye! PEOPLE of ANVARD, ye are SLAVES!
SLAVES, yes, SLAVES to "NEW AND IMPROVED" and "HIGHER UPGRADE"! WETWARE, HARDWARE, SOFTWARE!
HOW MANY TIMES HAVE YOU SCRAPED and SAVED and GONE WITHOUT FOR SOMETHING YOU REALLY COULDN'T AFFORD?
didja LOSE SLEEP WISHIN' YOU HAD it? QUESTION the VERY FABRIC OF YOUR EXISTENCE because YOU DON'T MAKE ENOUGH TO HAVE it RIGHT NOW?

DIDJA BY GOD FEEL YOUR OWN MORTALITY PRESSIN' HARD ON YA??
"OH, GOD! WHAT IF I JUST DON'T LIVE LONG ENOUGH TO HAVE ALL THE SHIT I CRAVE??"

WELL, IT'S JUST LIKE THIS CONCENTRATION ENHANCER I BOUGHT LAST YEAR-- IT'S TOP OF THE LINE, BUT THE EXTRA FEATURES SCREW UP THE STANDARD ONES!
WELL DAMN.
AND IT'S GOT AN EVEN SHORTER WARRANTY THAN THE LAST ONE DID AND I JUST CAN'T FACE WARRANTY COURT AGAIN..
AWWWWW TSK-TSK-TSK.
IT'S JUST SO FRUSTRATING! YOU SPEND SO MUCH IT OUGHT TO WORK RIGHT!
IT COST SO MUCH... I JUST WANTED TO, YOU KNOW, TREAT MYSELF...
DIDJA EVEN TRY TO GET THE SHOP TO TAKE IT BACK?
HUH (?)
OH~ UH- IT'S SO EMBARRAS- I~
NEVER MIND-
SISTAH, THE WAR CRY "LET'S GO SHOPPING" is the CALL of THE DOOMED! STEP RIGHT UP and FIND the ANSWER!
GRUNT
whimper
REMEMBER, SIS. THE HARDEST CHAINS TO BREAK ARE THE VELVET ONES.
SCRIIIIEE
BRSSZZZZ
HELLO♪! I AM YOUR PERSONALIZABLE ARTIFICIAL INTELLIGENCE- PLEASE SUBMIT THE FOLLOWING PERSONAL INFORMATION TO OBTAIN YOUR PASS WORD!

OTHERWISE, YOU'RE STUCK WITH ME!
hee hee hee
EEEK!

FREEP!
BLANG!

DIE FUCKER! DIE FUCKER! DIE
WATER FASHIO

I JUST NEVER COULD'VE TAKEN THAT FIRST SWING!
NOT A PROBLEM. THAT'S WHAT I'M HERE FOR.

JUST PISSIN' IN THE OCEAN, MAN.
I'M FREE, FREE! I CAN BUY A GOOD ONE NOW!
ASHION
TOAST MASTER GENERAL
DISPOSABLE SOCIETY, LTD
WELL, I GUESS THAT OCEAN HAD TO COME FROM SOMEWHERE.

HEY, PETE. JAEGER. I GOT ANOTHER LOAD FOR YA.
YEAH, YOU'RE **FUNNY.** WHATTA YOU **DO** WITH ALL THIS BUSTED-UP ELECTRONIC CRAP?

YEAHYEAH, QUICK MIKE MELTS IT DOWN. THAR'S GOLD ON THEM THAR CIRCUIT BOARDS, YA IGN'RANT HICK. CRYSTALS IN THE POWER SUPPLY TOO.
SHIT, YOU BELIEVE IN RECYCLING, DON'TCHA?

YEAHYEAH, SURE YA DO. THOSE FOLKS KNOW THAT SHIT'S THERE. THEY'RE JUST LAZY. WE'S JUST AVAILIN' OURSELVES OF GOOD OPPORTUNITY.
CORNER OF FIFTH AND ROYLE? SURE THING, YEAHYEAH.

ONLY **HE** COULD PULL OFF A SCAM LIKE **THAT** ONE. IT'S RI**DIC**ULOUS.
'S CUZ HE REALLY B'LIEVES THAT ANTICOMMERCIAL CRAPOLA.
SO, HE'S KINDA CRACKERS. **ALL** THEM TREE HANGERS ARE. HE'S A GOOD EARNER. =HURRGRETCH=

SONNY SITS BY HIS WINDOW AND THINKS TO HIMSELF

HOW IT'S STRANGE THAT SOME ROOMS ARE LIKE CAGES

SONNY'S YEARBOOK FROM HIGH SCHOOL IS DOWN FROM THE SHELF
AND HE IDLY THUMBS THROUGH THE PAGES
SOME HAVE DIED SOME HAVE FLED FROM THEMSELVES
OR STRUGGLED FROM HERE TO GET THERE

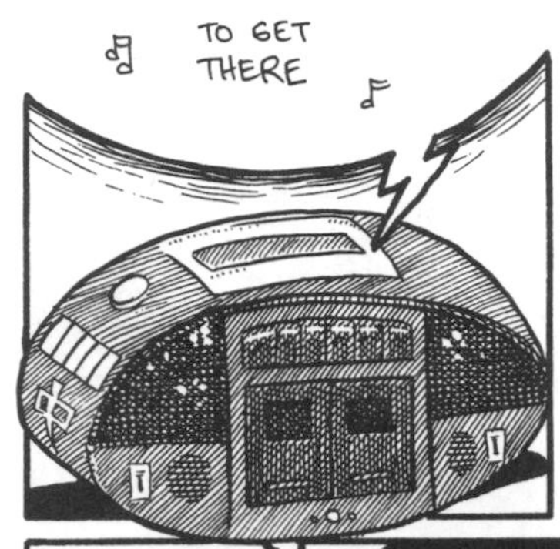

SONNY WANDERS BEYOND HIS INTERIOR WALLS
RUNS HIS HANDS THROUGH HIS THINNING BROWN HAIR
WELL I'M ACC
RRRIP
AND THAT'S ENOUGH A THAT! WELCOME TO ECLECTIC RADIO, WHERE WE NEVER WAIT TILL THE SONG'S OVER TO START TALKING!

THAT WAS SOMETHING OR OTHER BY SOME DEAD SOMEBODY WHO WAS JUST REMEMBERED BY THOSE FINE FINE PEOPLE AT THE PASTWATCH INSTITUTE FOR ALL YOU EVERYBODIES WHO CLING DESPERATELY TO THE CULTURE OF THE PAST RATHER THAN DISTILLING ANYTHING NEW OUT OF THE PRESENT.
MMWAH!

THE INSTITUTE HAS ALSO RECENTLY REINTRODUCED THESE BLASTS FROM THE PAST: FREEZE-DRIED ICE CREAM, WINE IN A BOX, COCAINE IN GREEN GLASS BOTTLES, AND PAINFUL CORSETRY.
BOY-OH, WEREN'T THE PEOPLE OF THE ANCIENT WORLD GENIUSES. HOP ON DOWN TO THE CORNER STORE AND CONSUME, CONSUME, CONSUME!
WOW, WHAT A BORING SUMMER. WE HAVEN'T EVEN TURNED UP A GOOD SERIAL KILLER. C'MON, G
'RF OUT HERE, WE LOO
LIKE YOUR MOTHE
ND WE STILL
THINK YOU'R
OSERS.

WELL, TEN SECONDS TO KILL, HO HO HO; DOES ANYBODY REMEMBER "CONJUNCTION JUNCTION"? NO? TOO BAD...

WE NOW RETURN TO OUR SEGMENT ON LIFE IN THE MILITARY! TODAY WE'RE TAKING A LOOK AT RELIGION! IT'S WELL KNOWN THAT THE REALITIE OF LIVING IN FEAR FOR ONE'S LIFE...

... CAN INSPIRE RELIGIOUS FERVOR IN THE MOST UNLIKELY PERSON.

BASH!
LEVITATE

STAND TO, STAND TO, DIPSHITS! GO GO GO GO!
LEAP
BOUND
SPROING
VAULT
BASHA BASHA BASH!

IN spec SHUN!
OOO
OH MY GOD!

OH GOD PLEASE I WANNA DIE NOW!
OKAY, NOW!

NOW! NOW!

IS DAT FOR MEE?
NO SIR IT'S FOR YOUR DAUGHTER SIR!

KEEP GOIN', IRON MAN! EIGHTY-SIX! EIGHTY-SEVE EIGHTY-EIGH
THANK YOU GOD! THANK YOU GOD! THANK YOU GOD!

WHIZZZ

GYAAH!
IS DAT FOR MEE?

=GASP -SHIT- =WHEEZ -FUCK-

GOD DAMMIT, JAEGER!
HOW DO YOU DO THAT SHIT??

IT AIN'T SO TOUGH TO LEARN IF YOU PUT YOUR MIND TO IT.

WELL, C'MON, WEASEL. PITCH IN, THIS OL' GAL'S FAMILY'LL BE BACK TOMORROW.
UHH-HUH. SIT IN YOUR OWN WET SPOT, BRIGHAM.

WHAAT?
YOU THINK I KILLED HER?
AND YOU THINK I'M TRYING TO COVER IT UP NOW.
SSHIT!
HUH-HUH-HUH
HUH-HUH-HEH HEH HEH-HEH HEHH
YOU COME IN HERE LOOKIN' ALL UGLY LIKE YOU THINK YOU KNOW SOMETHIN' ~I GUESS SINCE YOU AIN'T A KID ANYMORE, YER EYES MUSTA GONE BAD! WHATSA MATTER, YOU FINDERS PEAK OUT EARLY LIKE LITTLE-GIRL GYMNASTS OR SOMETHING ?

ALL RIGHT.
6

LYING IS LIKE ALCOHOLISM.
RECOVERING FROM IT IS A LIFETIME THING. YOU EITHER DIE **DOING** IT OR TRYING **NOT** TO DO IT.

BAJARE FAMILY
NOT HARD TO TELL BRIGHAM'S FALLEN OFF THE WAGON. NOT TO ME, ANYWAY.

THE QUESTION IS NOT **WHETHER** HE'LL LIE TO ME BUT HOW **WELL** HE'LL LIE.

SNF

AHH— DAMN!

JUTCHA
SWUTCHA
SWUTCHA
SWUTCHA
SWUTCHA

SWUT~-.

WELL?

THE COPS WERE HERE. THEY TOOK HER AWAY. THEY DIDN'T EXAMINE THE PLACE VERY THOROUGHLY, AS IF THEY DIDN'T THINK THERE WAS ANYTHING TO FIND.

NEAT, ORDERLY WOMAN. DIGNIFIED AND SELF-POSSESSED AS A CAT. RICH. PROSPEROUS, WELL PLACED IN HER CLAN, LOVELY IN HER YOUTH.
WELL, **WHAT?**

SHE RECENTLY CONTRACTED HEROD'S EVIL, PROBABLY IN JAVECEK. SHE LIKED TRAVELING, NOW THAT HER HUSBAND'S DEAD.
MM, NASTY ILLNESS.

I ALWAYS **SAID** THEM DAMN JAVECEKI WERE NO GOOD.
NASTY, PAINFUL, UNDIGNIFIED. NO CURE, BUT **LOTS** OF TREATMENTS.
SIGH
SHE DID IT THIS WAY RATHER THAN PAUPER HER HEIRS ON THE WAY TO DEATH.
SWUTCHA
SWUTCHA

WELL, THAT'S THE HONORABLE WAY OUT.
COPS DON'T TELL ME **SHIT.** I WOULDA AT **LEAST** WORN GLOVES.
I DOUBT IF THEY KNEW. SHE WAS CAREFUL. I'M SURE SHE SET IT UP SOMEHOW; THAT'S A TOUGH ONE EVEN FOR A DOCTOR TO SPOT—AT LEAST, IN ITS NONCONTAGIOUS STAGE.
SWUTCHA
SWUTCHA
SWUTCHA

SO— WHAT AM I DOING HERE?
ENGAGING IN A WEIRD FETISH.
SWUTCHA SWUTCHA
JERKASS!
THIS IS SORTA MY DAY JOB. PAYS WELL, BUT IT'S SPORADIC.
SMAK!
LOCAL COPS ARE MEDAWARS. THEY MAY BE PIGS, BUT THEY'RE FAMILY.
SEE, COPS JUST RUN DOWN CRIME SCENES. WHAT HAPPENS AFTER? THE FAMILY HAS TO SCRUB THEIR BLOOD KIN OFF THE CEILING. FIGURE OUT HOW TO GET IT OUT OF THE SOFA. BAD, BAD NEWS. PEOPLE DOING THIS KIND OF CLEANUP WORK SPARES THE FAMILY SOME PAIN.
... YEAH.
SOP!
SO.... WHATCHA DOIN' FOR MONEY THESE DAYS?
FINDER'S FEES... PROB'LY GET SOME WORK FROM THE ARCHAEOLOGY COLLEGE WHEN DIG SEASON BEGINS.
NO, MAN, I MEAN A J-O-B. YOU KNOW, CONTRIBUTING-MEMBER-OF-SOCIETY KIND OF THING?
AHH, BRIG, WHATYA DO, GET YER SOCIAL WORKER'S LICENSE IN THE PRISON REHAB PROGRAM?
KEE-REIST! YOU PISS ME OFF, YOU KNOW THAT??

EVERYBODY TELLS ME, DO WHAT YOU LOVE, THE MONEY WILL FOLLOW.
WELL, SOMEDAY SOON YOU'RE GONNA BE SOME KINDA RICH FUCKER!
BUT JAEGER– SHIT! YOU GOT EVERYTHING YOU NEED TO MAKE IT. TO BE AN EXAMPLE. TO BETTER YOUR KIND!

MY KIND.

WELL GODDAMMIT. SO YOU WEREN'T BORN INTO A CLAN! SO DAMN MANY OF YOU MIXED BLOODS JUST GIVE UP! JUST DRIFT THROUGH LIFE!

YOU GOT BRAINS, LOOKS, SPINE, AND YOU'RE JUST GONNA BE A SCAVENGER ALL YOUR LIFE? COME ON, KID!

STICK WITH ME, JAEGER.
I'LL GET YOU HONEST WORK.

I NOTICED ALSO THAT THIS LADY'S NAME WAS EMMA.
HUH?
NAW. DAVIS. HELLENA DAVIS. BAJARE CLAN.
HELLENA'S HER SECOND NAME. EMMA HELLENA DAVIS.

WELL–
–IT'S A COMMON-ENOUGH NAME.

WEYLL– GLAD OF THE HELP, BUD. YOU THINK ABOUT WHAT I SAID. I IMAGINE YOU CAN FIND YOUR OWN WAY OUT, HUH?
EMMA HELLENA DAVIS
I GOT TO GET MOVIN'–THINGS TO GO, PEOPLE TO DO.

SO YOU HAVE, BRIG.
SO YOU HAVE.

WRIIIINNNNGGG!
LLAVERAC CLAN HOME HIGH SCHOOL
FUCK YOU FUCK YOU FUCK YOU FUCK YOU

SNICKER
GIGGLE

TSK-TSK-TSK... NICE MEN DON'T HANG AROUND SCHOOL YARDS.
SSCRITTTCH

I'M JUST PICKING UP MY SIS ~ MY SISTER'S KID.
UH-HUH.

WOOYAH...GOOD THING THEY DON'T ALL SMELL ALIKE.
JAEGER!

MMFF

MMM POP!

HELL, BABY, DON'T STOP NOW!
SO NICE TO SEE AN UNFAMILIAR FACE!

DAMN BUT IT WAS WORTH THE MARCHIN' PARTY TO SEE THE LOOK ON THAT BASTID'S FACE!
HAHA
HAHAHAHA HA
HAHAHA HA
HA HAHA HAHA
NICE OF YOU
WALK ME HOME!
AND THOSE ROTTEN
LE JERKS WILL JU
PEA GREEN IF
START SHOWING
EVERY DAY
+ 6 YEARS
=
JUST FORGET IT
"NO SIR IT'S FOR YOUR DAUGHTER SIR!"
PPWAAHAHAHAHAHAHA
TOO BAD SHE'S ONLY EIGHT! AAH, SHE'LL GROW!
I MEAN, YOU'RE A GUY. GUYS ARE SUCH HORRIBLE FLIRTS, THEY'LL SAY JUST ABOUT ANY ~
..... THING.
CREAK
OHMYGAW
KID~
WE'VE BEEN WE'VE BEEN
MOM!
BAM!
MARCIE!
WHOA!
K!
RIGHT RIGHT RIGHT, YOU SHOULD GO FIRST, I-I-I~
IT'S OKAY. RAE. CALM DOWN.
THAT'S IT, HONEY. QUIET MIND.
YOU'RE RIGHT, YOU'RE RIGHT. CALM, CALM.
IT CANNOT POSSIBLY BE HIM, MY FAMILY HAS NOT LEFT ME BEHIND, AND I CAN TAKE CARE OF MYSELF....
RAE~-RAE, IT'S OKAY....
I DID IT.

HUH?
I DID IT. IT WAS ME.

YOU KICKED OUR DOOR DOWN??
YEAH, SO IT'S OKAY. OKAY?

IT'S NOT OKAY! WHY DID YOU DO IT??

I HAD TO GET IN. WHY ELSE?
WHAT WAS IN HERE THAT WAS SO IMPORTANT YOU COULDN'T WAIT!?

WHAT DIFFERENCE DOES IT MAKE?
WHAT DIFF-- WHAT DOES THAT MEAN??
IF YOU DON'T MIND MY BEING IN HERE WHEN YOU ARE HOME, WHY SHOULD YOU CARE IF I'M IN HERE WHEN YOU'RE NOT?
THAT'S RIDIC-- AAGH! JUST BECAUSE WE TRUST YOU ENOUGH TO --TO --TO -- THAT DOESN'T GIVE YOU THE RIGHT TO BUST THE PLACE UP!

DOOR WAS LOCKED. I NEEDED TO GET IN. REAL SIMPLE.
IT'S NOT SIMPLE!

LOOK. I'M FIXIN' IT, AIN'T I? IT WAS A CHEAP SHITTY DOOR FRAME. I GOT YA A GOOD ONE. NOT THAT IT MATTERS MUCH NOW.

WHAT ARE YOU TALKING ABOUT?? AND WHAT ABOUT MY MOM AND MY SISTERS?
I DUNNO. GO ASK 'EM.

HUH?
HI SWEETIE, GO GET CHANGED! BUSY, BUSY, BUSY!

MOM, DID YOU KNOW HE KICKED THE DOOR DOWN?
HEH! YES–LOST MY KEYS SOMEWHERE–DUMB LUCK, THAT–

YOU ASKED HIM TO DO IT?
NOOOOO–BUT IT WAS EFFECTIVE, WASN'T IT?

AND THIS DOESN'T BOTHER YOU?
OHH, BABY, TODAY NOTHING BOTHERS ME!
STUFF

LADIES AND GENTLEMEN, TODAY NOTHING BOTHERS EMMA GROSVENOR. SO WHAT'S THE STORY?
WE GOT THE GRASS HOUSE!

REALLY?!?
YES!
STUFF

OHH, FOURTEEN MONTHS ON THE WAITING LIST, ENDLESS FIGHTS WITH THE AGENTS, ALL THAT MONEY, BUT MY DREAM HOUSE IS MINE!!
LIKE MAGIC, THEY CALLED, AND THE DEAL'S ALL SET!
VRRRR!

SO GO GET CHANGED, BABY. WE GOTTA GET OUTTA THIS MOUSEHOLE NOW! THE LEASE IS UP IN TWO DAYS. THANK GOODNESS I DI... SIGN IT EARLY ~

CRINNKK
CREAK–
–SNAP–!

DAMMIT, YOU BITCH! COME OUT OF THERE! YER COMIN' OUT IF I GOTTA SNAP YOU IN HALF!
CLANK
CRINK!
CREEINK
CSM JULY 97

CHAPTER SIX

THERE IS NO SKY IN ANVARD.

ONE LOOKS UP AT BUILDINGS COLLAGED TOGETHER, GABLED AND BUTTRESSED AND GROWN INTO ONE ANOTHER LIKE SUGAR CRYSTALS.

NO STARS. NO MOON. NO WIND OR MISTS OR SNOW.

WHAT THERE IS ~ ARE~ ARE ROOMS. OOMS WITHIN ROOMS IKE A HOLY CAVERN. FROM THE VAULTED ATHEDRAL HALLS OF HE GREAT HIGHWAYS O THE VAST ARENAS DECORATED WITH STALAGMITES AND ALACTITES MADE NOT OF STONE BUT OF ONCRETE AND BRICK, STEEL AND GLASS.

LOOK DOWN AND OU SEE BOTTOMLESS PITS. THE CITY ESCENDS FAR BELOW HE SURFACE OF THE LAND IT SITS ON.

WINDOWS SPARKLE N THE GLOOM OF THE SUN GLOBES.

IT'S A SUNLIGHT HAT NEVER MOVES ITH THE HOURS OR HE SEASONS. NEVER BRIGHT OR DARK.

NO RAIN CLEANS UT THE DUSTY CORNERS.

ALL THE TREES IN OTS AND CAREFULLY ENDED GARDENS.

NETWORKS OF OPEN AQUEDUCTS SUFFICE FOR SUBTERRANEAN RIVERS, FEEDING LAKES AND POOLS ON EVERY LEVEL.

THE BURIAL CANOES THE CIMARGUE INDIANS PASS THROUGH ALL HIS CHAOS LARGELY NTROUBLED, BORNE BY THE POISONOUS RED RIVER.

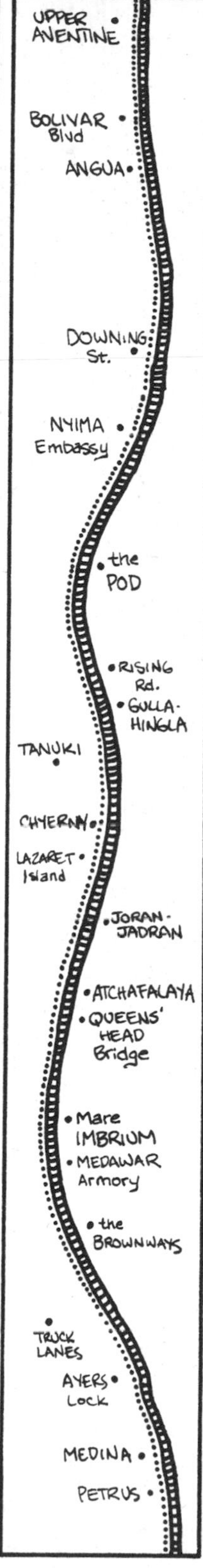

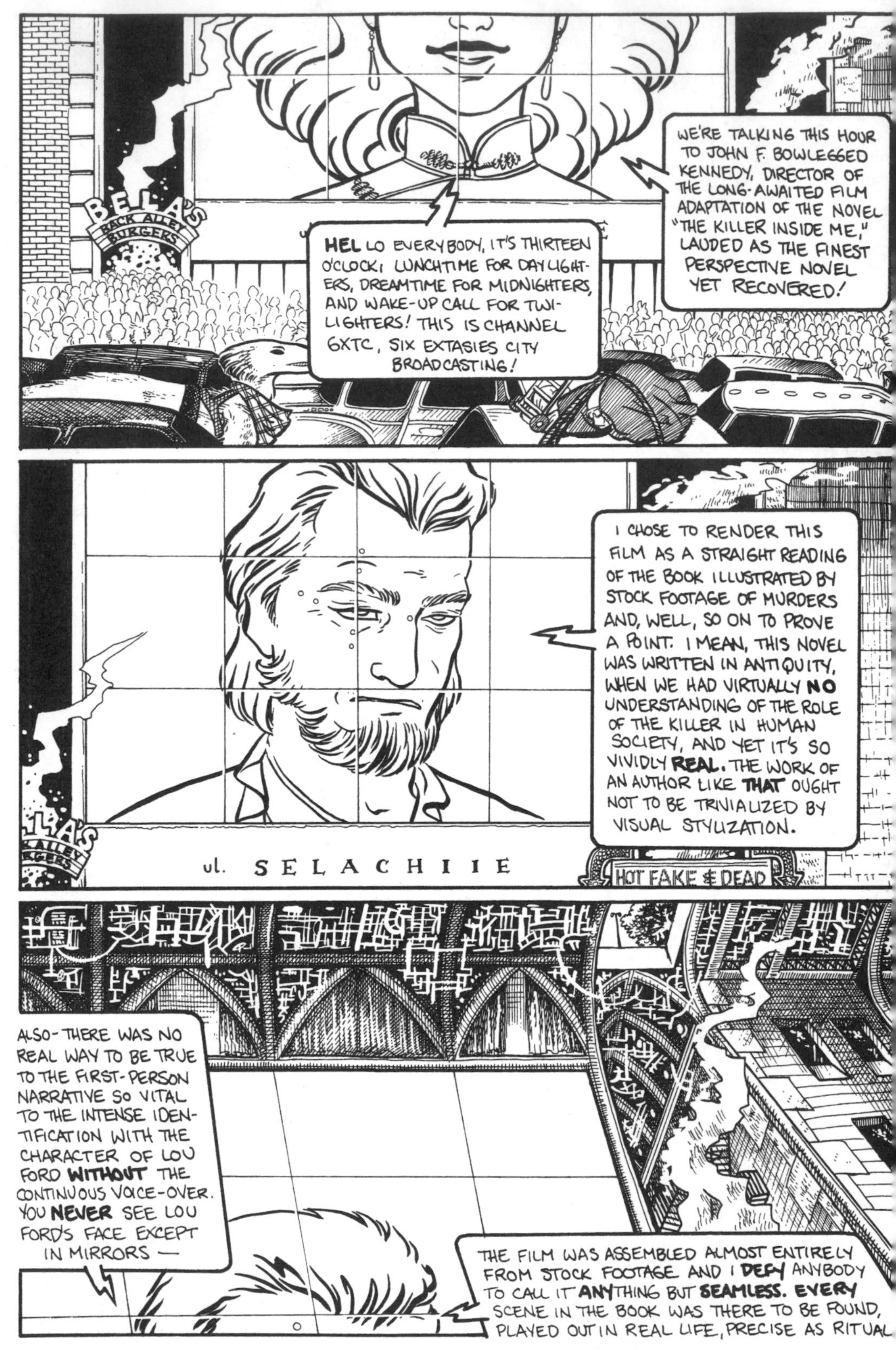
BELA'S BACK ALLEY BURGERS
HELLO EVERYBODY, IT'S THIRTEEN O'CLOCK: LUNCHTIME FOR DAYLIGHTERS, DREAMTIME FOR MIDNIGHTERS, AND WAKE-UP CALL FOR TWILIGHTERS! THIS IS CHANNEL 6XTC, SIX EXTASIES CITY BROADCASTING!
WE'RE TALKING THIS HOUR TO JOHN F. BOWLEGGED KENNEDY, DIRECTOR OF THE LONG-AWAITED FILM ADAPTATION OF THE NOVEL "THE KILLER INSIDE ME," LAUDED AS THE FINEST PERSPECTIVE NOVEL YET RECOVERED!
I CHOSE TO RENDER THIS FILM AS A STRAIGHT READING OF THE BOOK ILLUSTRATED BY STOCK FOOTAGE OF MURDERS AND, WELL, SO ON TO PROVE A POINT. I MEAN, THIS NOVEL WAS WRITTEN IN ANTIQUITY, WHEN WE HAD VIRTUALLY **NO** UNDERSTANDING OF THE ROLE OF THE KILLER IN HUMAN SOCIETY, AND YET IT'S SO VIVIDLY **REAL.** THE WORK OF AN AUTHOR LIKE **THAT** OUGHT NOT TO BE TRIVIALIZED BY VISUAL STYLIZATION.
ul. SELACHIIE
HOT FAKE & DEAD
ALSO- THERE WAS NO REAL WAY TO BE TRUE TO THE FIRST-PERSON NARRATIVE SO VITAL TO THE INTENSE IDENTIFICATION WITH THE CHARACTER OF LOU FORD **WITHOUT** THE CONTINUOUS VOICE-OVER. YOU **NEVER** SEE LOU FORD'S FACE EXCEPT IN MIRRORS —
THE FILM WAS ASSEMBLED ALMOST ENTIRELY FROM STOCK FOOTAGE AND I **DEFY** ANYBODY TO CALL IT **ANY**THING BUT **SEAMLESS. EVERY** SCENE IN THE BOOK WAS THERE TO BE FOUND, PLAYED OUT IN REAL LIFE, PRECISE AS RITUAL.

IT'S NICE, LIVING IN A CITY.
HE KILLER INSIDE E" WILL PREMIERE GHT HERE IN JUST EVEN HOURS—AND ILL REPLAY FOR ALL HREE LIFECYCLES— OTHER ENTERTAIN-ENT NEWS. BLAH LAH WAH WAHHWA AHH WAHHH—

NO RAIN, NO SNOW, NO COLD WIND. NO HOT SUMMER. NO THREE DIFF-ERENT WARDROBES TO KEEP UP WITH. AIR SCRUBBERS ON EVERY CORNER, AND ALL THE SUN YOU WANT FROM THE STREET LAMPS.
BLAHBLAH YACKADA YAPPITY FLAPPITY YABBA FLABBA
BIP

NO BUGS IN YOUR FOOD AND NO RATS IN YOUR WALLS AND NO BIG CRIME SURGE AFTER DARK BECAUSE THERE **ISN'T** ANY DARK. JUST SHUT OFF YOUR WINDOWS WHEN YOU DECIDE YOU'VE HAD ENOUGH.

HOURS AND **DAYS** AND **EEKS.** NICE, NEAT, AND EPENDABLE, AND TONS F THINGS GOING ON TO LL THOSE HOURS UP, ND A NICE QUIET NEST O RETREAT BACK TO. O MORE NEIGHBORHOODS JT IN THE OPEN WITH BIG WALLS AROUND HEM AND RAZOR WIRE AND BROKEN GLASS ON TOP OF 'EM. NO MORE ARMED GUARDS ND GUNFIRE AT NIGHT. O MORE LIVING IN A GLORIFIED ROOT ELLAR BECAUSE WE'RE O AFRAID TO LIVE IN THE HOUSE ITSELF. EVERYTHING ABOVE GROUND AND I **DON'T** JST MEAN THE BUILDINGS.

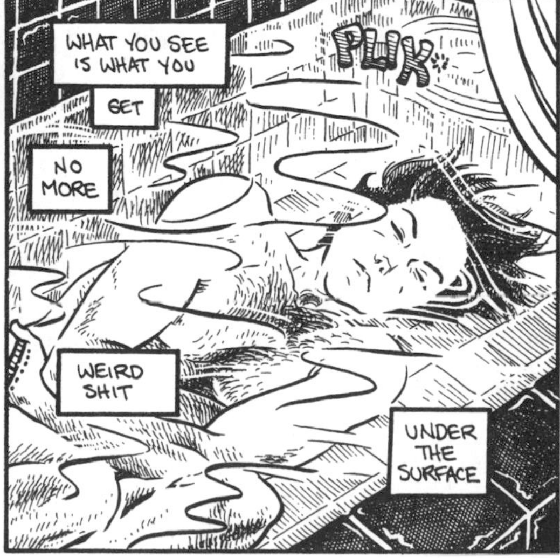

JUST SCHOOL. AND HOME. AND BOOKS AND MOVIES AND A HOT BATH ANYTIME I WANT ONE(!).
NO MORE WORRYING ABOUT WHETHER IT'S THE WORLD OUTSIDE THAT'S INSANE AND DANGEROUS, OR MY FATHER INSIDE THE BASEMENT WITH US.

AND HELP FOR MY LITTLE SISTER MARCIE AND ROOM TO RUN AND SCREAM FOR LYNNE~

AND PEACE AND QUIET AND GOOD MONEY FOR MOM-

WHAT YOU SEE IS WHAT YOU

UNDER THE SURFACE

SPLAGASSH!

OHGOD OHGOD
HOOPF!
SLOSSH

WHAWAWHAT, KID, WHAT?? WHASSA MATTA?!?
UH-AH-A-WAH-WHAT'S GOING ON? ARE YOU HURT?

ARE YOU CRAZY?? ALL I KNOW IS I COME IN HERE AND YOU DID IT ON PURPOSE TO SCARE ME YOU ASS~~-
CRACK WHACK SMACKA
RAE, RAE! CHILL OUT!!

RACHEL, IT'S NOTHING! IT'S JUST SOMETHING I LEARNED A LONG TIME AGO, FROM SOME PEOPLE WHO LIVE WAY OUT IN THE OCEAN, OKAY? THAT'S HOW THEY SLEEP– THEY COME UP FOR AIR EVERY FIFTEEN MINUTES OR SO. IT'S RELAXING, OKAY?
ANYBODY CAN LEARN TO DO IT, ALL RIGHT?

IT'S OKAY, STOP QUIVERIN'. I'M ALL RIGHT. I GUESS I SHOULDA LOCKED THE DOOR, BUT I DIDN'T THINK ANYBODY'D BE AWAKE.

AW~ JEEZ~ YOU'RE GETTING ME ALL W~~-

~WHA??
—OH.

WHOOPS.
~HEHH HEH~
STILL A KID AFTER ALL.

THIS IS NOT A DOG.
IT'S A

DAMN THING

THERE WAS A TIME WHEN I MEANT TO GIVE THE DAMN THING A NAME BUT THERE'S SOMETHING ABOUT THE DAMN THING THAT OFTEN PRECLUDES EVEN THE USE OF PRONOUNS, LET ALONE NAMES.
I DON'T REALLY LIKE HITTING THE DAMN THING. THERE JUST DOESN'T SEEM TO BE ANY OTHER WAY TO GET ITS ATTENTION!

ANYBODY'D SAY, START WITH A CUB, RAISE IT UP RIGHT, AND YOU'LL NEVER HAVE A PROBLEM, BUT **HELL**, THIS **IS** A CUB!

MY RAPPORT WITH THE DAMN THING IS NECESSARY TO MY SURVIVAL.

I DON'T KNOW HOW OR WHY EXACTLY.

I'VE HAD THIS DREAM THOUSANDS OF TIMES. IT COMES UPON ME NOW SOMETIMES EVEN WHEN I'M AWAKE.

GULP ULP SCARF SMACK

THE DAMN THING'S LIKE A CROSS BETWEEN A JUNKIE AND A TWO-YEAR-OLD, IN A DOG'S SKIN, WITH A CAT'S WAYWARDNESS .... AND A PIG'S PUNGENT REEK!

I SAID, NO BEG.

I'VE TRAINED **DOGS. BIG**, AGGRESSIVE DOGS, LITTLE YIP-YIP DOGS, EXOTIC DOGS WITH THREE HEADS AND POISON FANGS. **ALL** OF THEM WERE TRACTABLE AND EASY COMPARED TO THIS **DAMN THING!**

I SAID **NO, DAMMIT!**

YOU **CAN'T** TIE IT UP OR EVEN SHUT A **DOOR** ON IT. WHAT IT CAN'T UNTIE OR CHEW THROUGH IT'LL BREAK DOWN. IT CHEWED DOWN A FUCKIN' **TREE** TO GET AT FOOD I HUNG FROM A BRANCH!

A CHOKE CHAIN'S NO GOOD. I'M NOT STRONG ENOUGH.

YANK YANK YANK

ITS **BREATH** SMELLS **MOST** DELIGHTFUL FROM ITS FEASTING ON ITS OWN FECES, WHICH I'M TOLD IS NECESSARY TO ITS DIGESTION.

SHLORK SHLORK SHLOP SHLURPP

I DON'T SEE WHY THIS MAKES YOU SO CRAZY.

I DON'T SEE HOW A MER ANIMAL CAN BE AS DISRUPTIVE AS YOU SA

WHY **CAN'T** YOU CONTROL IT?

WHY CAN'T YOU JUS LET IT HAVE ITS W AND RELAX?

WHO'S TRAININ' **WHO** HERE?

HAH HAH HAH HAH HAH

OH, I LET IT HAVE ITS WAY, ALL RIGHT. IT AIN'T AS IF I HAVE MUCH **CHOICE** -
-BUT AS FOR **RELAXING**--
AS IN, LEARNING TO **LIKE** IT-

--**THEY** DON'T KNOW WHAT I HAVE TO FACE AT NIGHT.

NO **LOCK** WILL CONFOUND IT. NO **DOOR** WILL KEEP IT OUT FOR LONG. NO THREAT AFFECTS IT ONCE MY EYES CLOSE.

IT DOESN'T **JUST** INSIST UPON LAYING NEXT TO ME WHILE I'M ASLEEP.

T **LICKS** ME. WHEREVER T CAN GET TO SKIN-AND T RASPED OFF MY LEATHER OVERCOAT TO GET **AT** ME ONCE --

-- IT---

-ITS TONGUE IS HUGE AND FLABBY AND STICKY-WET LIKE A GIANT **SNAIL.**

T DOES THIS ALMOST **EVERY** NIGHT - IT BACKS OFF **ONLY** WHEN I WAKE UP AND **HIT** T.

I WANNA ASK OTHER PEOPLE **HOW** TO MAKE THE DAMN THING **STOP** BUT I HEARD OF A GUY WHO **NO SHIT** WENT TO **JAIL** FOR "ABUSING" ONE OF THESE THINGS --

AND **THAT** WAS JUST FOR **HITTING IT,** NOT FOR **KILLING** IT.

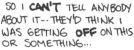

SO I **CAN'T** TELL ANYBODY ABOUT IT-- THEY'D THINK I WAS GETTING **OFF** ON THIS OR SOMETHING...

AFTER ALL, **I'M** THE **MAN;** **IT'S** JUST AN ANIMAL.

-- A **DAMN THING**--

I'M SICK ALL THE TIME FROM LIVING WITH THIS DAMN THING.

I CAN'T SLEEP, I CAN'T THINK, I CAN'T GET CONTROL OF IT.

TOUGH AS IT IS, I'M STILL AFRAID OF INJURING IT.

MY LITTLE HANDBOOK TELLS ME **WHAT** I'M SUPPOSED TO TEACH THE DAMN THING TO DO, BUT IT DOESN'T TELL ME **WHY** DOING THIS IS SO **VITAL** TO MY **SURVIVAL.**

I **CAN'T** RISK SOMEBODY **STEALING** IT. I **NEED** IT.

BUT BEFORE **GOD** I WISH I KNEW **WHY.**

I GUESS I **KNEW** THAT EVENTUALLY THE DAMN THING WOULD GET INTO THE STORE HOUSE. **HELL,** WHY **WOULDN'T** IT?

ALL THE FOOD. THE **ONLY** FOOD. ALL I HAD TO GET ME THROUGH THE WINTER. IT ATE **ALL** THE FOOD AND LEFT THIS ONE CONTINUOUS SHIT ON THE STORE-HOUSE FLOOR. (**THAT** ONE, IT DECLINED TO EAT.)

SO. NOW I HAD COME TO THE END. I WAS GOING TO STARVE TO DEATH. AND THE DAMN THING WAS GOING TO LIVE.

IT'D HANG AROUND AND BADGER ME; YOWL FOR FOOD, WATCH ME DIE, AND EAT MY BODY WHEN I DID.

I WAS SO RELIEVED I SAT DOWN AND CRIED LIKE A DAMN BABY.

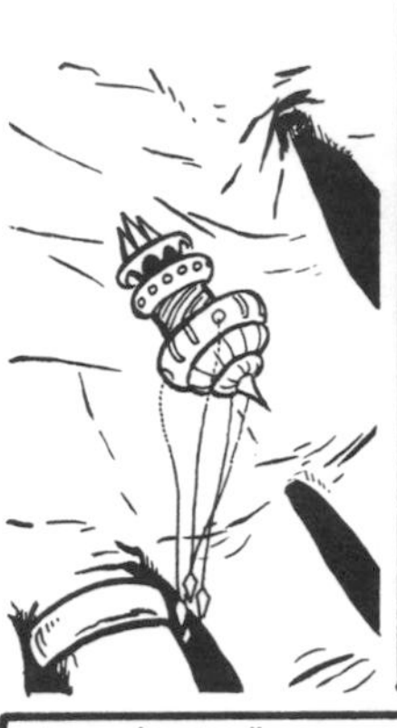
SO I WENT TO MY SHOP IN THE BACK AND BUILT A SMALL DEVICE.

I CAME UPON THE DAMN THING SLEEPING AND JAMMED THE DEVICE INTO ITS LEFT EAR.

IT KICKED AROUND SOME AS THE DEVICE DRILLED THROUGH BONE AND SETTLED PROBES INTO THAT LONG-NEGLECTED AND ATROPHIED PAIN CENTER OF ITS BRAIN. BUT WITH A GOOD SHAKE AND A RESONANT FART IT COMPOSED ITSELF.

THE "STICK" IS A TRANSMITTER, A SIMPLE DESIGN MADE FROM A LENGTH OF CAST-IRON PIPE.
NOW, THEN.
SIT.
SIT.
YEAH, YOU KNOW WHAT I'M SAYING.
THAT'S TWO.
SIT.
MAGIC NUMBER.

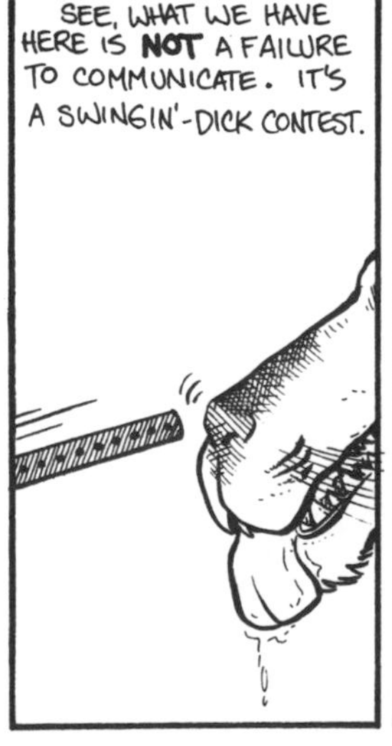
SEE, WHAT WE HAVE HERE IS NOT A FAILURE TO COMMUNICATE. IT'S A SWINGIN'-DICK CONTEST.

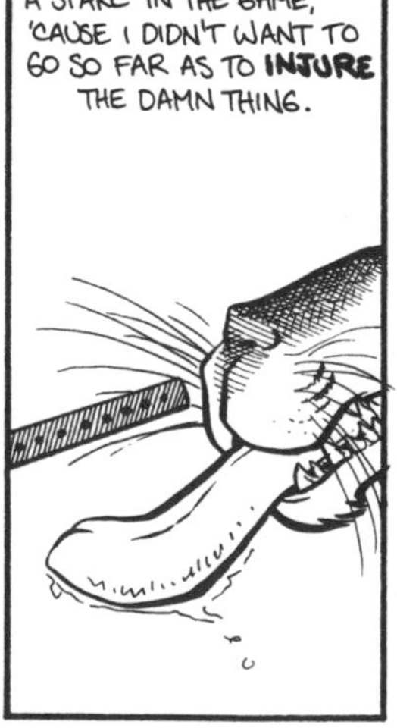
UP TILL NOW, I HAVEN'T HAD A STAKE IN THE GAME, 'CAUSE I DIDN'T WANT TO GO SO FAR AS TO INJURE THE DAMN THING.

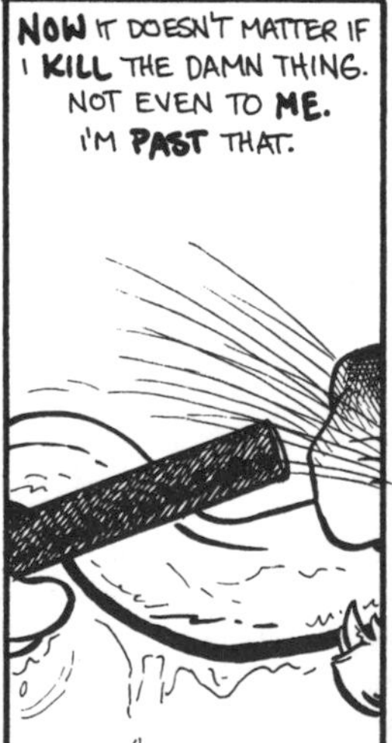
NOW IT DOESN'T MATTER IF I KILL THE DAMN THING. NOT EVEN TO ME. I'M PAST THAT.

THAT'S ALL THAT MATTERS NOW.

AH WHAT A GLOOOORIOUS SOUND~
~THAN A BEAUTIFUL WOMAN SAY SHE'S MINE--
LET'S~ JUST START OVER, SHALL WE?
NOW~THAT WE~ UNDERSTAND EACH OTHER~
I WOULD RATHER HEAR THIS DAMNED THING HOWL IN PAIN~-
WHO'S TRAININ' WHO NOW, YOU WHORE?
...KEEP THAT IN MIND, BRIG, AND I WOULDN'T WORRY ABOUT EMMA TAKIN' YOU BACK.
FINALLY I FOUND A WAY TO HURT YOU.
CZECHER CABS
SORRY, JAEGER... I DON'T FOLLOW. WHAT WERE WE TALKIN' ABOUT?
WHAAT?
MAN, YOU'RE A PREOCCUPIED MUTHA FUCKA, AIN'TCHEW?

LYNNE GONE OF COURSE, MOM "MEDITATING" OF COURSE, THE BABY STILL GETTING OVER BEING SICK OF COURSE, AND YOU DISAPPEAR ON ME, OF COURSE!!!

YOU COME, YOU GO, YOU DO ALL THIS WEIRD SHIT! YOU LOOK ALL WOUNDED WHEN I SAY MAYBE I DON'T TRUST TOTALLY A GUY WHO THINKS NOTHIN' OF BREAKIN' DOWN THE FRICK'N FRONT DOOR! AND ALL I DO IS SIT AROUND AND WAIT LIKE A --

OH..... HI, MRS. RENSIE... NO, NO, WE'RE NOT READY FOR EXIT INSPECTION YET....

YES, UH, IF WE COULD RESCHEDULE AGAIN THAT WOULD JUST BE GREAT...

UH, NO, MOM'S REALLY, REALLY, REALLY, UH, BUSY.

SIX O' CLOCK? -- SHURE. SIX O' CLOCK SHARP. YUP. NO PROBLEM. CLEAN AS A WHISTLE.

YUP. YES MA'AM.

THANK YOU MA'AM. THANK YOU FOR BEING SOO PATIENT.

I KNOW.

THANKS.

REALLY.

UH-HUH.

NICE DAY.

THERE COMES A TIME WHEN DULL PANIC OVERCOMES HOT PANIC. HOT PANIC IS USEFUL. YOU CAN LEAP TALL BUILDINGS IN A SINGLE BOUND IN HOT PANIC. DULL PANIC MAKES YOU SLOW. THE HOT LEAD IN YOUR VEINS TURNS COLD AND DRAGS YOU DOWN.

ONLY ONE THING TO DO.

ORDER A PIZZA.

HEY!
WHERE YOU HEADED, JAEGER? THERE'S THIS WILD NEW FAD CALLED "SHARING A CAB"--
...AAH. TECHNOPHOBE.

...AND HAVING DONE THE PIZZA THING, THE SPELL WAS BROKEN, AND I WENT BACK TO THE BATHROOM AND PACKED UP **EVERYTHING** IN IT, AND SHUT THE DOOR FIRMLY.

ONE ROOM DOWN, AND I WASN'T EVEN THINKING "THIS IS THE LAST TIME I'LL USE THIS ROOM" ANY-MORE. A BREAKTHROUGH!

KNOCK KNOCK

"OH, **HI**, JAEGER, YOU'RE **JUST** IN TIME TO DO A **LOT** OF HEAVY LIFTING"--

GOOD EVENING, MISS. ARE YOU RACHEL LOCKHART?
UH-- **GROSVENOR.** RACHEL GROSVENOR.
AH YES. THAT'S WHAT I'D LIKE TO SPEAK TO YOU ABOUT.
EXCUSE ME?
IS YOUR MOTHER EMMA LOCKHART ALSO AVAILABLE? I'D LIKE TO SPEAK TO HER AS WELL.

WELL, LADY, I GOTTA ADMIT, I CAN'T FIGURE OUT **WHAT** YOU'RE SELLING.
I BEG YOUR PARDON, MISS. I AM YOUR FATHER'S AUNT.

MISS?

MY FA-- UH
I AM YOUR **FATHER'S** AUNT.
BUT THAT MAKES YOU **MY**--

WHAT I AM TO YOU IS PRECISELY WHAT I WISH TO DISCUSS. MAY I COME IN?

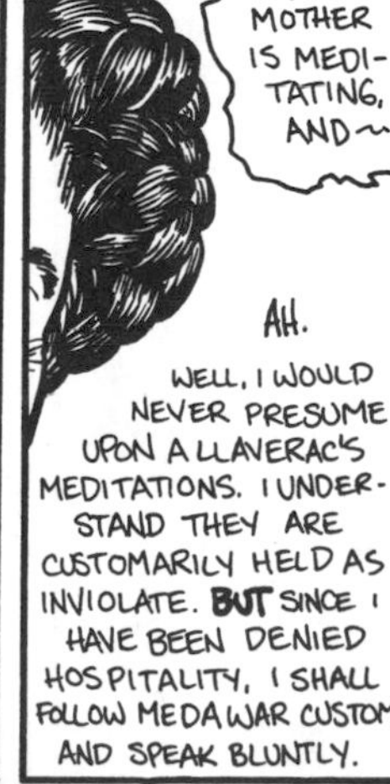
UH--AH, **NO**, MY MOTHER IS MEDI-TATING, AND--
AH.
WELL, I WOULD NEVER PRESUME UPON A LLAVERAC'S MEDITATIONS. I UNDER-STAND THEY ARE CUSTOMARILY HELD AS INVIOLATE. **BUT** SINCE I HAVE BEEN DENIED HOSPITALITY, I SHALL FOLLOW MEDAWAR CUSTOM AND SPEAK BLUNTLY.

WE -- I AM SPEAKING FOR THE GROSVENOR FAMILY SPECIFICALLY -- WE WISH **YOU** AND YOUR MOTHER AND YOUR SIBLINGS TO REASSUME YOUR MOTHER'S FAMILY NAME OF LOCKHART.

WHAT?
WHY?

WE PRESUME THAT YOU FOUR HAVE NO INTENTION OF ACCEPTING BRIGHAM GROSVENOR AS HEAD OF THE HOUSEHOLD, HUSBAND AND FATHER, **SHOULD** HE WISH TO REASSUME THIS ROLE UPON HIS RELEASE FROM PRISON?
WELL - I-I HADN'T -- THOUGHT ABOUT-

IF THAT IS THE **CASE**, THERE IS **NO** ADVANTAGE TO YOU IN RETAINING OUR NAME.
NOR TO HIM.
NOR TO **US.**

IN **FACT**, IF I MAY BE **BOLD** AS WELL AS BLUNT, **YOU** IN PARTICULAR ARE **FAR** BETTER OFF UNDER YOUR MOTHER'S NAME. YOU RESEMBLE YOUR MOTHER'S CLAN VERY STRONGLY INDEED.
YOU SHOULD HAVE QUITE A GOOD CHANCE OF BEING ACCEPTED BY THEM. YOU'D HAVE A BRIGHT FUTURE AHEAD OF YOU. WE'D **ALL** HAVE A BETTER CHANCE OF PUTTING ASIDE ...YOUR PARENTS' FOLLY.

MY PARENTS **WEREN'T--**
STOP.
THINK OF THE PAIN IT HAS CAUSED TO THEM. TO **YOU**.

YOUR LIFE **CAN'T** HAVE BEEN EASY. IT IS TIME NOW TO SMOOTH IT OVER. IF YOU WILL.
GOOD NIGHT.

UH!

NEVER EVEN TOLD ME HER **NAME**....
CLOSED **MY** FRONT DOOR **HERSELF**....

DOWNING
STREET
NEXT

SKO

HERE YA GO, BUD;
TWELVE FIFTY AND
YOU'RE A FREE MAN.

Smudko's
SURE YOU DON'T WANT ME TO STICK AROUND? THIS BEIN' A CLAN NEIGHBORHOOD, AND NOT **YOUR** CLAN, I MEAN --

I DON'T RECALL ASKIN' **YOU** A **GOD-DAMN THING!**

OKAY, OKAY-- COP-FACE **JERK!**
"IT DOESN'T REALLY TASTE GOOD UNLESS YOU'RE AFRAID IT MIGHT KILL YOU"
SKOPTS

CLAN OR **NO** CLAN.
NONE OF 'EM CAN COMPARE TO MY EMMA.

I SHOULD **WOR**-RY I SHOULD **CARE** I SHOULD **MAR**-RY A **MILL**-ION-AIRE
HE SHOULD **DIE** **I** SHOULD **CRY** **I** SHOULD **MAR**-RY A**NOTH**ER **GUY**

SIGH

I LOOK LIKE A LLAVERAC UNTIL I SMILE.

MY FATHER WAS ~ IS- A MEDAWAR. MILITARY MAN, LIKE MOST OF 'EM.
I GREW UP IN A MEDAWAR TOWN. THEY NEVER LIKED ME AND I CAN'T SAY I EVER LIKED THEM.

MY MOTHER IS, OR WAS, A LLAVERAC.
I ALWAYS PICTURED THEM AS THESE GAUZY ROMANTIC PRINCESSES AND THAT MY MOM AND I WOULD GO LIVE WITH THEM SOMEDAY AND LIFE WOULD BE GREAT.

NOW IN SPITE OF THE FACT THAT THAT BUBBLE WAS WELL AND TRULY POPPED, OUR WHOLE FUTURE DEPENDS ON MY GETTING INTO THE LLAVERACS WHEN I'M TWENTY-ONE. SHE'D BE ABSOLVED. MY KID SISTERS COULD GO TO COLLEGE.

I'D BE ON EASY STREET.
SKRIKK

WE CAME HERE, WHERE THE ENTIRE CITY GUARD ARE MEDAWARS- BECAUSE IT'S ALSO THE LLAVERAC CLAN HOME.
BUT EVERY ONCE IN A WHILE I SEE ONE OF THEM WHO SOMEHOW LOOKS MORE LIKE HIM THAN ALL THE OTHERS.

AND I WANT TO GO UP TO HIM AND SAY, MISTER, MY DADDY WAS A MEDAWAR, AND HE'S IN PRISON NOW, AND I KIND OF HOPE HE STAYS THERE, BUT IF HE WAS HERE RIGHT NOW I'D PROBABLY FORGIVE HIM FOR ALL THE THINGS HE DID TO US, AND COULD I JUST HOLD YOUR HAND AND CRY JUST A LITTLE BIT?

IT'S NOT LIKE I DON'T KNOW THAT'S A LOONY IDEA.
I KNOW WHAT WOULD HAPPEN IF I DID.

HE'D LOOK ME UP AND DOWN WITH THAT AWFUL STONE FACE THEY GET AND THINK I WAS JUST SOME HISTRIONIC LLAVERAC HAVING A FIT-.

-OR TRYING TO ROB HIM
R HIT ON HIM OR WHO
NOWS WHAT --

--HE'D JUST GET THAT SMIRK AND TURN AWAY WITH A SCORNFUL SNORT--

--AND I'D JUST WANT TO SMASH HIS TEETH IN--

--BUT JUST AS I GET REALLY STEAMED (WHICH DOESN'T FEEL THAT MUCH BETTER THAN PINING BUT I'LL TAKE IT)--

--THIS LITTLE TRICKLE OF FEAR STOPS ME COLD AND I THINK...

MAYBE IT'S REALLY HIM AND HE'S ONLY PRETENDING NOT TO KNOW ME.

MAYBE HE'S BEEN FOLLOWING ME, TRYING TO FIND OUT WHERE WE LIVE.

HE'S SUPPOSED TO BE IN PRISON FOR YEARS YET, A LOOONG, LONG WAY AWAY FROM HERE.

BUT IF HE GOT OUT EARLY, WOULD HIS FAMILY TELL US?

MAYBE, I THINK, MAYBE HE DOESN'T KNOW ME. I LOOK LIKE A LLAVERAC. MY BEST HOPE IS TO STICK WITH MY MOTHER'S PEOPLE (EVEN THOUGH I LOATHE THEM). USE MY NATURAL CAMOUFLAGE.

AND WIPE THAT SMILE OFF MY FACE.

KNOCK
KNOCK

DRRRRGH!

AAH, TURN BLUE. I GOT WORK TO DO.

KNOCK-
KNOCK
WHIMPER
SSHH, MARCIE. HE'LL HEAR YOU.

HE'LL HEAR
HE'LL
HE'LL

KNOCK
KNOCK
BOUND

MOM!
MOM!
STUDIO KEEP OUT
TAP TAP

LET'S RUB NOSES LIKE THE ES-KI-MO-SES

DON'T CHA KNOW THAT'S ES-KI-MO FOR "I LOVE YOU"
TYPE TYPE

KEEP OUT

KNOCK-KNOC

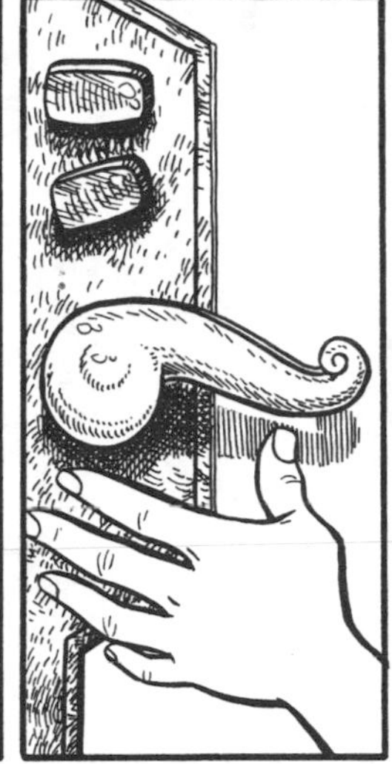

NOT TO MENTION THE DUMPSTER LOAD ALL THAT JUNK YOUR MAMA FINALLY AGREED TO LET GO OF?

RISING RD

MISC.
MISC.

SECRET GARDENS
LANDSCAPING &
GARDEN DESIGN
MA GROSVENOR
010110 RISING RD E
20-2706-8787-02A1

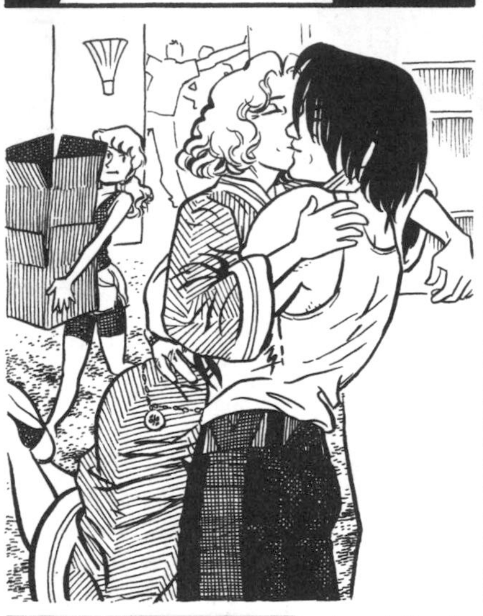

010110
GROSVENOR

MIS

SE
9
CS

OH, MY EMMA... YOU DO STILL WANT ME. I KNOW YOU DO NOW.
I THOUGHT THERE WAS NOTHING OF ME HERE. THAT YOU HAD CUT ME OUT OF YOUR LIFE.
THERE'S NOTHING HERE TO SHOW THERE EVER WAS A FATHER.
NONE OF THE OLD FURNITURE, NOT EVEN THE STUFF I WORKED BY HAND. NONE OF THE STUFF WE HAD FROM BEFORE, WHEN WE LIVED TOGETHER.
(COURSE, EMMA WAS TRAVELIN' PRETTY LIGHT WHEN SHE TOOK HER LEAVE OF ME.)
BUT I KNOW ALL OUR STUFF GOT SHIPPED TO HER WHEN I WAS SENT INSIDE.
STILL, THIS IS AN ANONYMOUS APARTMENT THAT COULD BE ANYBODY'S, FULL OF UNFAMILIAR SIGHTS AND SMELLS, THE HOUSE OF A WOMAN AND THREE KIDS THAT WENT ON WITHOUT ME.
EXCEPT HERE.
...IN THE LEFT-HAND CLOSET OF THE BIG BEDROOM ....ARE ALL MY OLD CLOTHES. UNIFORMS AND CIVVIES ALIKE.
OH EMMA. YOU WOULDN'T HAVE KEPT THESE. NOT WHEN YOU DIDN'T KEEP ANYTHING ELSE. NOT LIKE THIS - YOU WOULDA AT LEAST BOXED THEM UP OR SOMETHING.
OH EMMA... DO YOU OPEN THIS CLOSET SOMETIMES AND RUN YOUR HANDS OVER MY OLD CLOTHES THAT I HAVEN'T WORN IN YEARS AND THINK OF ME?

GHOD, THAT FEELS SO GOOD... WHAT A HOMECOMING....

NOW I CAN SEE WHAT I COULDN'T BEFORE.

I WAS SO PARANOID, ALL I COULD THINK WAS HOW ALL THIS COULD'VE BEEN FAKED UP SOMEHOW.

BUT NOW I CAN SEE THAT THERE ARE THINGS HERE THAT COULDN'T BE ANYBODY ELSE'S.

THANK GOD FOR THE KIDS. THEIR FACES SHOW SIGNS OF MINE THAT CAN'T EVER BE ERASED OR DENIED.

PROVE WHAT?
BRIGHAM, I LOVE YOU– DON'T TRY SO HARD!

WELL, I GOT TO TRY HARD NOW. DAMN HARD.

HELL, WHAT WOMAN'D WASTE HER TIME BELIEVIN' THAT OLD "OH, IT'S ALL DIFFERENT NOW, I'M A CHANGED MAN, TAKE ME BACK" CRAP?

WHAT MAN'D RESPECT HER IF SHE DID?

HELL'S BELLS, I GOTTA CLEAN THIS PLACE UP!

SHIT, I HOPE I DIDN'T BREAK ANYTHING SHE REALLY LIKED...

I'M SORRY, I'M SORRY EMMA, IT WAS ONLY 'CAUSE I WAS REALLY TENSE...

TALK'S NOT GONNA CONVINCE HER. I GOT TO SHOW HER I'M IN A GOOD GROOVE NOW, THAT I CAN GET BETTER, THAT EVERYTHING CAN BE FIXED....

HOW HOW HOW...

EMMA, I NEVER THOUGHT THIS WOULD BE **EASY.** I NEVER **WANTED** IT TO BE EASY.

I **BELIEVE** IN REDEMPTION. I **KNOW** DESPITE EVERYTHING THAT IT'S POSSIBLE.

RISING Rd E

010110

SO RAKE ME OVER THE COALS, BABY. I **WANT** IT.

MOM– I THINK I FOUND THE LAST OF DAD'S OLD CRUD!
OH?
–SORRY, AVERY—
RACHEL, JUST– Y'KNOW– DEFENESTRATE.
I'M HERE, AVE –YOU SURE YOU GUYS NEED SO BIG A TRUCK? I REALLY WANT TO GET RID OF A LOT MORE...
MISC

AI~YA~YAAHH... JUST LIKE THAT?
I, I, I LIKE IT!

ALL THIS CRAP WE'VE BEEN CARTIN' AROUND LIKE A DEATH SENTENCE ALL THESE YEARS...

...GONE, GONE, GONE!

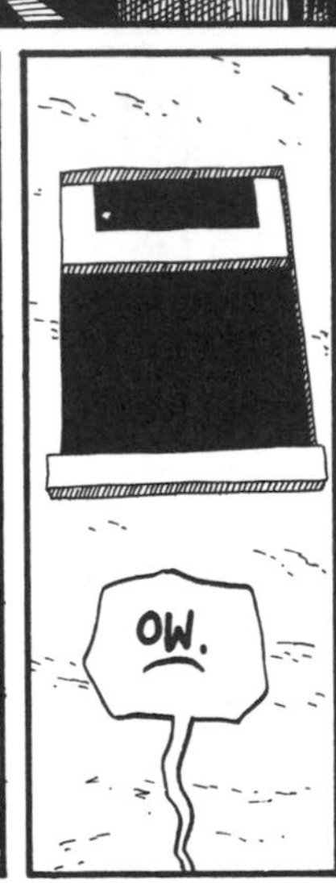
OW.

JAEGER?
WHAT THE HECK ARE YOU DOING IN THERE, MONSTER MAN??

JUS' TAKIN' A BREAK IS ALL.
IN THE DUMPSTER?
PERF'CLY COMFORTABLE.

YEAH, AS LONG AS I'M NOT THROWIN' AWAY ANYTHING NASTY!
YEAH, IT'S OKAY TO THROW OUT PERFECTLY GOOD SOCKET-WRENCH SETS?

IT'S HIS, ISN'T IT?
OKAY, KID.

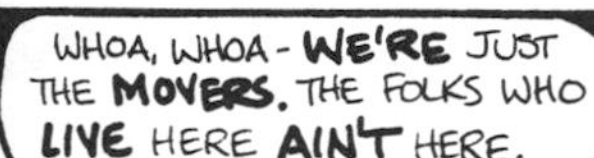

OH YEAH. THAT'S THE LITTLE GODSFEAST TAVERN.

SHEE-**YIT,** THEY **STILL** AIN'T GOT THAT BIG WINDOW FIXED.

YOU'RE FAMILIAR WITH THE PLACE?

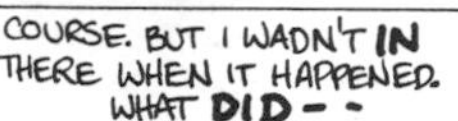

YEP. NOW, **ALL** FILM BELONGS IN THE PUBLIC DOMAIN FOR ITS FIRST MONTH OF EXISTENCE. THAT TIME'S ALMOST UP NOW, AND OWNERSHIP WILL REVERT TO THE PEOPLE DEPICTED AND TO WHOEVER SHOT THE FILM. FIRST CHURCH WANTS TO BUY IT FROM THEM FOR THEIR STOCK-FOOTAGE LIBRARY.

BUT YOU SEE, THEY CAN'T FIND **THIS** MAN. TO OBTAIN HIS PERMISSION TO USE HIS LIKENESS.

SHEE - IT'S SIX STORIES DOWN ON **THAT** SIDE. YOU **AIN'T** GONNA FIND 'IM.

HUH! NOT OUTSIDE A **DUMPSTER,** ANYWAY.

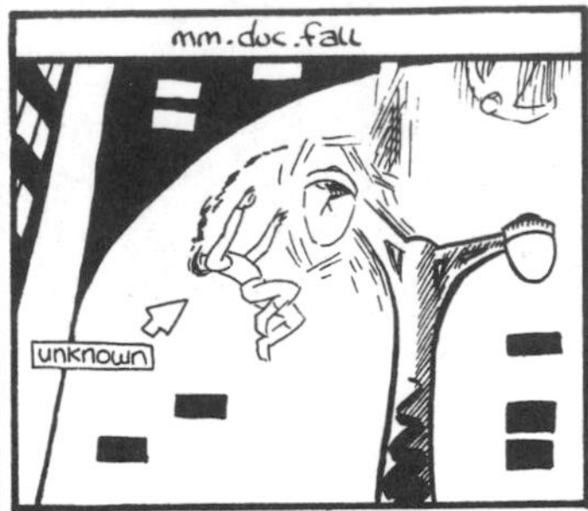

AAOW! MAN!
AW, HE'S **TOAST.**
mm.doc.fall
unknown
WELL, THE **OTHER** MEN INVOLVED IN THE ACCIDENT **DID** DIE ON IMPACT. BUT **THEY'VE** ALL BEEN IDENTIFIED AND THEIR FAMILIES' CONSENT OBTAINED.

SORRY WE DON'T HAVE A BETTER HEAD SHOT THAN **THIS.**
mm.doc.fall
enhance600+
THIS MAN VANISHED FROM THE SCENE WITHIN MINUTES OF HITTING LOCH RAVEN FREEWAY. NO IDEA **HOW,** WHERE **TO,** OR WITH WHOSE **HELP.**

ANY INFORMATION THAT LEADS TO OUR FINDING THIS GUY OR WHOEVER SHOT THIS FILM WILL BE **WELL** PAID FOR BY THE FIRST CHURCH OF HUITZILO-POCHTLI RELEASING COMPANY.

SORRY MAN, CAN'T HELP YA.
I BET 'E'S **GONE.** Y'ALL MIGHT AS WELL GO ON 'N' MAKE YOUR MOVIE.
HEH! WISH WE COULD, BUT IT'S NOT ORTHODOX.
HMM- WELL, IF HE'S **NOT** DEAD, I DOUBT **SERIOUSLY** HE STILL LOOKS LIKE **THAT!** SO YOU CAN SELL HIS **OLD** LIKENESS. NO PROBLEM!

WELL, THANKS ANY WAY. OH- THE FAMILY THAT LIVES HERE, HAVE YOU GOT A FORWARDING ADDRESS?
HUH?
OH. SURE.

THERE YA GO.
SECRET GARDENS
LANDSCAPING & GARDEN DESIGN
GROSVENOR
01010 RISING RD E
8220-2706-8787-02 AI

HEY!
WHAT?
ONLY
REFUSE

WELL, MONSTER MAN, LOOKS LIKE YOU **OWE** US ONE!
OH, YEAH? OWE YOU ONE **WHAT?**
REFUS
TURE
OH ~ **JUST** A **BEER.**

OH. JUST A BEER. NO PROBLEM.

SO, JAEGER MONSTER.
I B'LIEVE I NEED SOME PERSPECTIVE.
WHAT'S THE STORY HERE?
GREENTREE APTS.
fountainbleu apts.
ASILOMAR ACRES
VISTA VILLES
Dunroami

NO STORY **TO** IT. JUST HELPIN' OUT A LADY.
=SNIFFK=

YOU SURE ABOUT THE **LADY** PART? SHE **IS** LLAVERAC CLAN, ISN'T SHE?
HA! **SURE.** WELL, SHE'S A LADY WHERE IT **COUNTS,** THAT'S ALL.
HEH!

SO. SHE'S **YOUR** LADY THEN.
OH, I DUNNO. KIND OF UP TO **HER,** AIN'T IT?
UH-HUH. AND HOW 'BOUT THE LITTLE ONE?

RACHEL? SHE'S A **KID.**
HAW HAWHAW! NOT IN **MY** NEIGHBORHOOD!

NOT IN YOUR NEIGHBORHOOD, EITHER, FROM WHAT I UNDERSTAND. AIN'T IT "OLD ENOUGH TO BLEED IS OLD ENOUGH TO BREED"?
YOU'RE A PIG, CYN.

WE-E-E-LL, TRUTH BE TOLD, ONCE A KID THAT AGE MAKES UP HER MIND, YOU KNOW YOU CAN'T TELL HER A DAMN THING.
HA HAHA HA~ OHH YEAH!

BUT CITY KIDS ARE KINDA STUPID THAT WAY. OH NO. I BEEN DOWN THAT ROAD. I DON'T WANT ANY MORE OF THAT CRAZY SHIT.
SLAM!
HI, GUYS! WE'RE BACK!
SNFF

OH, THE NEW PLACE IS SO GORGEOUS!
SSCRRIIIIIITJ

HEY, LOOK HOW MUCH ROOM THERE IS IN HERE WITH ALL OUR JUNK OUT OF IT! WOW!

RAE! C'MERE AND HELP ME A MINUTE!
COMING, MOM!
SNICCKK
SNRK

WAHAHAHAHAHA
HAWHAH
STILL DON'T WANNA GET ANY MORE O' THAT??
HAAHA

DOES THAT MEAN YOU DON'T LIKE ME?

WHAT? OF COURSE NOT, MARCIE. I LOVE YOU.
BUT YOU SAID YOU LIKE GUYS MORE THAN GIRLS, AND I'M A GIRL.

IT'S NOT QUITE LIKE THAT, SIS. IT'S A WEIRD GROWN-UP THING. WHAT I MEAN IS, I FEEL MORE AT HOME WITH MEN THAN WITH WOMEN.

GUYS ARE.... MORE HONEST, SOMEHOW.
ALTHOUGH YEAH, A LOT OF THEM DO LIE TO GET WHAT THEY WANT...
I DUNNO, IT'S HARD TO EXPLAIN.

NO MATTER HOW MUCH THEY CUSS AND DRINK AND SPIT AND SCRATCH THEM-SELVES, I STILL LIKE 'EM BETTER THAN ♪LLLLADIES♪
WHO ARE JUST AS MEAN AND UNLOVELY, BUT THEY GET ALL PIOUS IF YOU CALL THEM ON IT.

WHAT?
YOU USED TO BE A LOT MORE LIKE A BOY YOURSELF. YOU AND LYNNE USED TO BE FRIENDS.

NOW YOU WEAR A DRESS AND MAKE-UP PRACTICALLY EVERY DAY.
HOW COME, IF YOU DON'T LIKE LADIES?

PROBABLY BECAUSE I CAN'T BE A GUY MY-SELF, AND THE OLDER YOU GET, THE LESS GUYS KNOW WHAT TO SAY TO YOU IF YOU DON'T—...
≡SIGH≡
OHH. I DON'T KNOW, BABY. I WISH I DID.

HEY, WHO SPRUNG FOR THE HOT DEAD BIRD?
OH FOR CRYING OUT LOUD
YEARS OF ENJOYMENT
GROTESQUE IMAGE
YOU'LL GIVE THE KIDS COMPLEXES.
OH IT'S A HARMLESS TREAT REALLY
HUH! IF ONLY IT WAS REAL MEAT.
I THINK YOU STREET CRAWLERS WOULD BE WAY BETTER OFF IF YOU ATE SOME THING BESIDES THIS FAKE

SHEEP DOG? "OH, KETTLE, THOU ART SO BLACK!" THE POT EXCLAIMS!

WE-HELL, LOOK WHO IT IS?!
GOOD TIMING. LYNNE, WE'RE OUTTA HERE AND YOU DIDN'T HAVE TO LIFT ANYTHIN

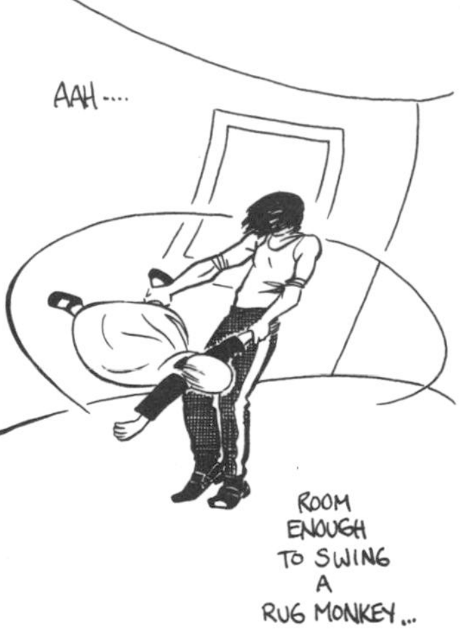
AAH....
ROOM ENOUGH TO SWING A RUG MONKEY...

DON'T YOU THINK THOSE GANGSTERS SCARE ME, EMMA GROSVENOR, YOU ARROGANT FULLBLOOD YOU'RE STILL NOT GETTING YOUR SECURITY DEPOSIT BACK OR
OH, KEEP IT, LUDIE, DO. BUY YOURSELF A LIFE.
FLIK!

OKAY, SAY "BYE, MOUSE HOLE"!
ASILOMAR ACRES

WHAT A PERFECT DAY!
SNITH

AAAAAA!!

OH MARCIE-
OH HONEY--
=SIGH=
WHAT THE HELL ARE YOU DOING TO THAT KID?
MARCIE, WHAT'S-
AAAA AAAP
OHH-- MOVING UPSETS HER, AND SHE'S BEEN SO SICK. OH HONEY, DON'T GO DOWN THERE, IT'S SO DIRTY--
AW, LET HER IF SHE WANTS TO.
U-ROB
Mad Aunt's Attic
SHEE-YIKES, I NEVER KNEW A KID THAT SIZE COULD SCREAM THAT LOUD.
BABY, PLEASE.
YEAH, I THOUGHT I HAD PIERCED EARS ALREADY.
I KNEW I SHOULDN'T LET HER HAVE THAT CANDY. SH CRASHING NOW.
YEAH, PROBABLY.
AAH
IT GETS HOT DOWN THERE THOUGH.
ALL RIGHT, BABY.
Y'KNOW, I USED TO DO THAT WHEN I WAS A KID.
OH, THAT'S JUST WITH THE OLD ENGINES WITH THE DRIVE SHAFT DOWN THE--
YEAH, DON'T WORRY, MARS. NO SUCH THING AS A PERFECT DAY. AFTER ALL, BIG SISTER RACHEL'S GOT THE HOTS FOR MOM'S KNOWN-FELON BOYFRIEND.
MISC.
MISC.
SO, HOW 'BOUT THEM JAGS?

NE KULTURNY. IT'S "I WENT TO THE WOODS BECAUSE I WANTED TO LIVE DELIBERATELY.
"I WANTED TO LIVE DEEP AND SUCK OUT ALL THE MARROW OF LIFE.

"TO PUT TO ROUT ALL THAT WAS NOT LIFE.

"AND NOT, WHEN I CAME TO DIE, DISCOVER THAT I HAD NOT LIVED."

HOT
HOT
TOO HOT.
ROUGH CLOTH.
SQUEAK-SQUEAK-SQUEAK-SQUEAK-SQUEAK
SMELL OF SWEAT AND SPOILED FOOD.
SILVER BARS PAINFULLY BRIGHT
WHINING, COMPLAINING VOICES
MOTHER'S VOICE STRANGE, HIGH AND FLUTING.
NOT COMPLETELY SOOTHING.
DUST AND SAND.

THEN COLD
WARM WIND
SILVER BARS NOW TOO COLD TO TOUCH.
STARS TOO NEAR
MOON TOO BRIGHT.
HISSING SOUND RISES TO A ROAR
SMELL OF BURNING GRASS
TASTE OF STALE WATER
HIGH WHINE OF INSECTS, RISING AND FALLING
GOING ON, AND ON, AND ON, AND ON, AND ON.

PSSST!

MARS.

IT'S OKAY THIS TIME. THIS TIME WE'VE GOT SOME WHERE TO GO.

WHOOPS.
WHAT? -OH.
WELL, ROLL UP YOUR WINDOWS, FOLKS.
AIR QUALITY REDUCED
SEAL VEHICLES
MAINTAIN MAXIMUM SAFE SPEED
EGHH... I HATE CANNED AIR.
SMELLS GET WAY TOO STRONG, WAY TOO FAST IN AN ENCLOSED SPACE.
MY DAMN NOSE ALREADY FEELS LIKE IT'S BEEN CORED OUT WITH SANDPAPER.
AIR-SCRUBBERS MUST BE DOWN ALL OVER HAIMOPHAGUS FOR THE FLAG BOYS TO BE OUT.
ALWAYS HAPPENS JUST AS YOU'RE THINKIN' HOW GOOD A CIGARETTE WOULD TASTE, DUDN' IT?
YEAHHP.
SIX KINDS OF PLASTIC.
SWEAT SOAKED INTO VINYL.
=UUUALKHH= SHEEZ, IT'S ALMOST WORTH GOING UP IN SOME MASSIVE FIREBALL.
CHALK DUST AND A BROWNING APPLE CORE.
GREASE AND SALT ON FAST-FOOD BAGS.
CLEAN SKIN.
TALCUM AND DEODORANT.
AND OTHER, MORE PUNGENT GIRL SMELLS THAT CUT RIGHT THROUGH THE PROTECTIVE LAYER OF TAR ON MY TONGUE.
DAMMIT, I AM NOT GOING TO START DROOLING.

mmf.
JUST LET ME OUT HERE.

OKAY.
"OUT"?
ON THE STREET?
IN THIS?

SURE. I GOT THINGS TO DO.
BUT THERE'S A NICE SEALED GARAGE AT THE NEW PLACE. WHY DO YOU HAVE TO GET OUT HERE?
MARCIE, STAY DOWN, HONEY. I'M JUST MOVING OVER.

AAH, IT AIN'T GONNA KILL YA.
OUUGHH! CLOSE THAT REEKHOLE!
AWGH!
ACTUALLY, THESE FOGS DO KILL PEOPLE-

-BUT-.
OH, LET HIM, LET HIM. GO ON, AVERY, DRIVE.
O-bee-KAY-bee...

FROM THE GUT.
sniFFFFFFFFF
VRRRMM

HAAAAHHH
THUMPA THUMPA THUMPA

SNERFF OH YEAH.

CINNAMON AND CANNABIS
DRIFTING IN THE HAZE
CONSIDER THE SENSE OF SMELL.
A LITTLE BROWNSKIN GIRL HE'D HAD, A LONG TIME AGO, BUT NOT LONG ENOUGH AGO...
SWEET TINKLY LAUGH
GREEDY LITTLE THING....
GASOLINE GARLIC AND VINEGAR
SMELLS ARE HOTLINES TO MEMORY, DIRECTLY GALVANIZING THE OLDEST PARTS OF THE VERTEBRATE BRAIN.
A TERRIBLE HUNT; KILLING WILD DOGS FOR MONEY NOT A GOOD ENOUGH REASON BUT FOR SOMETHING THAT HAPPENED TO HIM AS A BOY AND HE NEVER
EVEN THE WEAK HUMAN NOSE CAN DISCERN THE CHEMICAL SIGNATURES OF HOME, FAMILY, AND SUITABLE MATE; OF FEAR, DISEASE, AND DEATH.
HOT WATER WARM MILK AND COPPERY BLOOD
TO CREATURES MORE DEFINITIVELY RULED BY THE SENSE OF SMELL, AN OVER-WHELMING STEW OF ODORS IS A POWER-FUL INTOXICANT.
HOME WITH FATHER ALIVE AND MARTHA HAPPY
PROMPTING ACTION WITHOUT THOUGHT, BODIES JOLTING AND HYPERREACTIVE.

SULFUR, DARK COFFEE AND RANK HORSE SWEAT
THE AIR OF THE DOME CITY OF ANVARD (WHICH IS NOT SO MUCH ENCLOSED BY ITS DOME AS RESTRAINED AND SHAPED BY IT) IS POISONOUSLY RICH.
OUT ON THE STEPPES. BITTERLY COLD. MOST OF THE SOLDIERS FROZE TO DEATH AND HE COULDN'T UNDERSTAND WHY
THE EXHALATIONS OF BUSINESS AND MANUFACTORY AND HUNDREDS OF THOUSANDS OF PEOPLE SIMMER INTO A RICH POLYATMOS.
RANCID GREASE, AMMONIA, A GOATY SMELL THAT ISN'T GOAT
MACHINES SCRUB THIS CHEMICAL STAIN INTO A FAINT RESIDUE, MEANT FOR LESS ROBUST PALATES.
PRISON
CHIPPED PAINT
OLD STEEL
STALE WATER
THE RESULTING DISTILLATE IS OF COURSE DUMPED INTO THE RIVER, WHICH FLUSHES THE OCEAN VIVIDLY RED FOR MILES BEYOND THE RIVER'S MOUTH. IT IS NOT EXACTLY POISONOUS BY THEN.
JAEGER TRAVELS, CURIOUSLY SPLIT BETWEEN DELIRIUM AND CLARITY.
HE KNOWS EXACTLY WHERE HE IS GOING.

(DREAMILY)
AS HE
FALLS

(SEVERAL HUNDRED YARDS)

HE IS
SUDDENLY
STRUCK BY
A THOUGHT

(THIS RIVER BETTER BE AS
DEEP AS I REMEMBER IT)

CITY PEOPLE SAY
PINK OR BLUE TO
DESIGNATE INFANTS
AS FEMALE OR
MALE.

PEOPLE OF THE BARRENS
USE RED OR WHITE

BUT ONLY IN ADULTHOOD:
THE GENDERS OF CHILDREN
MATTER LITTLE TO THEM.

HE FALLS

FROM WHITE

INTO

RED.

WHERE IS HE? IT'S BEEN HOURS! DO YOU THINK HE'S OKAY?
REALLY, RACHEL. HE'LL TURN UP. ALWAYS WHEN YOU LEAST EXPECT HIM.
♪ HE WILL NOT AL-WAYS SAY.. ♪ WHAT YOU WOULD HAVE ... HIM SAY... STILL, NOW AND THEN HE'LL SAY... SOME-THING.. WON-DER-FUL... ♪
RAPPA RAP RAP
AH!

DON'T LOOK AT ME! DON'T LOOK AT ME! I'M HIDEOUS, OLD AND DECREPIT!!
OH... HI, GRANDAD ....
ZOOMMK

HELLO, DARLING.
HI, GRAM...
♪ HAP-PY BIRTHDAY, DEAR DAD-DEE ... ♪
WAIL!

HIS HAIR IS DRY, AND CRUMBLES UNDER HIS HANDS.
HIS CLOTHES ARE ROTTING OFF HIS BODY, FALLING AS HE ASCENDS.
BUT HIS SKIN GLOWS WITH HEALTH, HIS HEAD IS CLEAR, HIS ACHES AND PAINS ARE GONE.
HE HAS A DAY'S CLIMB AHEAD OF HIM.
HE RESISTS THE URGE TO WHISTLE.

OH, I'M WRETCHED, PERFECTLY WRETCHED. SAY SOMETHING SWEET TO ME, DEAR.
DADDY, DARLING.
AH, EMMA. PEARL OF MY MISSPENT YOUTH.
RESIDENTS NEAR THE RIVER ARE ACCUSTOMED NOT TO OPEN THEIR WINDOWS, IF THEY HAVE THEM.
IN MOST TOWNS, FEW PEOPLE LOOK UP. NEAR THIS RIVER, FEW PEOPLE LOOK OUT.
THE COURSE IS STRANGE, AS ALWAYS. DANGER LIES IN BOREDOM AND CERTAINTY.
WHAT'S THIS? PINING AWAY AFTER MOTHER'S PRETTY YOUNG THING?
SWEET RACHEL.
HOW ALIKE WE ARE, WE THREE.
PASSING THE MAIN WINDOWS OF THE "GOLDEN FRITILLARY," HE FINDS HIMSELF WONDERING WHY IT SEEMS SO EASY TO MOVE WITHOUT BEING SEEN.
AS ALWAYS, THE THOUGHT DISCONCERTS HIM, AND HE SHIFTS HIS COURSE TO A MORE DIFFICULT ONE.
OH, RACHEL. THERE'S NO POINT IN YOUR TYING YOURSELF UP IN KNOTS OVER JAEGER. YOU KNOW HE ONLY STAYS AWAY LONG ENOUGH TO MAKE YOU MAD.
SO YOU'RE SAYING, IF I DON'T GET MAD, HE'LL STOP GOING AWAY? COME ON--
"NO. IF YOU DON'T GET MAD, SOONER OR LATER HE'LL STOP COMING BACK.
"BUT THE WHOLE THING'LL HURT CONSIDERABLY LESS.
"AFTER ALL, HE'S A FREE MAN, ISN'T HE? DON'T YOU FIND YOU PREFER HIM THAT WAY?"

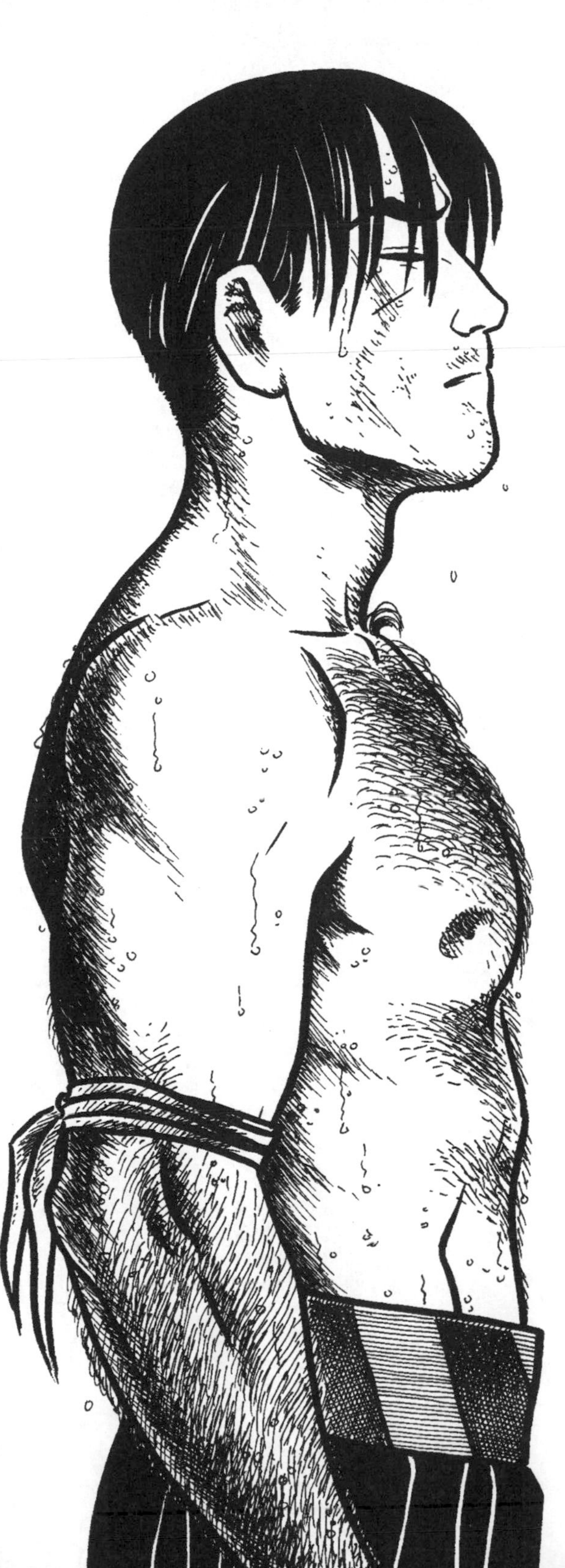

INTERLUDE

FIGHT SCENE

"HOW MANY FIGHTS HAVE I BEEN IN?
"HELL. I DON'T KNOW.
"IT'S NOT LIKE THEY'RE ALL THAT *IMPORTANT*.
"THE IMPORTANT ONES ARE THE ONES THAT *DIDN'T* HAPPEN.

"WHY DON'T I JUST MIND MY OWN BUSINESS?
"HUH!
"THERE *AIN'T* NO SUCH THING.

"*MINDING MY OWN BUSINESS* HAS GOTTEN ME INTO MORE TROUBLE THAN DAMN NEAR *ANYTHING* ELSE.
SNIFF

"YOU CAN'T CHANGE HOW PEOPLE ARE WIRED UP. AND YOU SHOULDN'T BLOW IT OFF, EITHER."
TSK!

"I MOVE AROUND A LOT. I'M ALWAYS THE NEW GUY.

"WHENEVER THERE'S A NEW GUY, THE OTHER GUYS HAVE TO KNOW WHERE HE FITS IN."
ASSHOLES?

"IS THE NEW GUY A DICK, GONNA RUIN EVERYBODY'S GOOD TIME? OR IS HE ALL RIGHT?
THINK WE'RE

"IT'S PERFECTLY NORMAL TO TRY THE NEW GUY OUT."
ZAT *RIGHT*, PRETTY BOY?
POKE

"IT'S **ALSO** NORMAL FOR THE NEW GUY TO TRY TO SHOW EVERYBODY HOW THINGS ARE.
"THERE ARE *MORE* AND LESS CIVILIZED WAYS OF DOING **BOTH** THINGS.

"SEE-- GROWING UP, I WAS ALWAYS THE WEIRD KID.
"I WASN'T THE ONLY HALF-ASCIAN KID, BUT I LOOKED MORE ASCIAN. MY DAD WOULDN'T CUT MY HAIR.
"IT WAS A COMPANY TOWN, THE PLACE I GREW UP IN.
"THAT MEANS MOST OF THE PEOPLE-- ALMOST ALL OF THE KIDS -- WEREN'T MUCH ABOVE SLAVES.
"BUT THEY GOT ISSUED NICE CLOTHES AND BIG HOUSES, SO THEY DIDN'T KNOW THEY WERE PROPERTY. THE KIDS DIDN'T, ANYWAY."
THIRTY-- SIX--
"AND EVERY TIME I GOT INTO A FIGHT-- WIN OR LOSE-- I'D GET MY ASS BEAT BY THE SCHOOL DRIVERS FOR 'WILLFUL PROPERTY DAMAGE.'
"THE COMPANY KIDS, Y'SEE. THEY WERE VALUABLE PROPERTY.
"THEY'D PICK FIGHTS WITH ME JUST TO SEE ME GET MY WHIPPIN' AFTERWARD.
"I NEVER SAW A FIGHT COMING BACK THEN.
"IT WAS JUST LIKE THE WEATHER."

SO I'D CUT SCHOOL AND LIVE IN THE WOODS FOR A FEW DAYS.
THEN I'D GO HOME AND MY DAD WOULD SHINE MY ASS FOR ME, FOR CUTTING.
WHAT?
I KNOW I SAID MY FATHER NEVER HIT ME IN ANGER. HE DIDN'T.
KUH
COME ON, THERE'S A HUGE DIFFERENCE BETWEEN A WHIPPIN' AND A BEATING.
MY DAD WASN'T MAD.
THAT? THAT WAS JUST THE PRICE I HAD TO PAY FOR A FEW DAYS OF PEACE AND QUIET.
LOOK, OKAY, MY IDEA OF WHAT IS A BEATING IS DIFFERENT FROM MOST PEOPLE'S, OKAY?
OKAY.
I WENT TO SCHOOL.
I GOT INTO FIGHTS.
I GOT INTO FIGHTS BECAUSE I HAD A SMART MOUTH.
I GOT INTO FIGHTS BECAUSE I WOULDN'T TALK AT ALL.
I GOT INTO FIGHTS BECAUSE I WOULDN'T PLAY SPORTS.
I GOT INTO FIGHTS BECAUSE I SHOWED 'EM I COULD HIT A BALL A COUNTRY MILE, BUT I STILL WOULDN'T PLAY.
I NEVER BACKED DOWN. BUT I NEVER UNDERSTOOD A THING.

"I'D TAKE MY WHIPPIN' FROM THE DRIVERS AS USUAL, AND ALSO AS USUAL MY FATHER WOULD GET CALLED IN.
"SOMETIMES HE EVEN SHOWED UP.
"THE OLD MAN DIDN'T DO MUCH. HUNT, FISH, SMOKE, DRINK.
HE HAD A FACE LIKE A HATCHET AND HARDLY EVER TALKED WHEN A GRUNT WOULD SUFFICE."
--AND I SAY AGAIN, MR. AYERS. THAT CHILD'S HAIR MUST BE CUT.
IT'S UNHYGIENIC. IT'S NOT FAIR OR HEALTHY FOR THE OTHER BOYS. IT'S CONTRIBUTING TO THIS ONE'S ALREADY UNHEALTHY EGO THAT HE STANDS OUT LIKE THIS.
HIS HAIR MUST BE CUT.
NAW.
NAW.
HIS MAMA WOULDN'T LIKE IT.

"HE
NEVER
NEVER
TALKED ABOUT MY MOTHER.
"HE HAD A GIRLFRIEND WITH TWO KIDS, BUT I'M SURE I WASN'T HERS."

HENRY, THAT'S A GOOD KID YOU'VE GOT.
GOOD LOOKING, TOO.

A COLT NEEDS BREAKING, THOUGH. ELSE HE'LL NEVER BE A GOOD HORSE.

"IT WAS LIKE HE WAS WAITING FOR SOMETHING.

"THE SILENCE IN THE HOUSE MADE MY EARS RING. LIKE BEING UNDERWATER, WAY OUT OF REACH OF THE SUNLIGHT.

"I WAS JUST A KID. I DIDN'T KNOW SHIT. HOW COULD I EVEN TRY TO BREAK THAT TERRIBLE SILENCE?

BBZZZZZ
BZZTT!
CRUNCH
CRUNCH
BZZZZZ

"I'D GO AND STAY GONE. STAY GONE TILL I DIDN'T KNOW WHAT DAY IT WAS. I *HAD* TO.

PARTLY BECAUSE I NEEDED SOME PEACE AND QUIET...
"PARTLY BECAUSE I WANTED TO RESPECT MY FATHER'S SILENCE.

"BUT THE LONGER IT TOOK ME TO CLEAR THE FLIES OUT OF MY HEAD, THE FASTER I'D RUN TO GET BACK HOME.

"--'CAUSE IF I STAYED GONE *TOO* LONG--"
LOSE YOUR KEYS?
THAT'S NORMAL.
LOSE YOUR JOB?
EH; IT HAPPENS.
BUT HENRY, *YOU* LOST A WHOLE *KID*.
NOW *THAT'S* CARELESSNESS IN *MY* BOOK.
--*SHIT*--

WE HEAR HE'S KIND OF A HELL DEVIL. MAYBE YOU'RE THINKIN' HE'S A BAD APPLE NOT WORTH SHININ', HUH?
YOU CAN'T SHINE SHIT, RIGHT?
THAT IS A PROVEN SCIENTIFIC FACT.
"--THESE WEIRD REGULATORS WOULD SHOW UP AT THE HOUSE--

"THEY IGNORED MARTHA. IGNORED HER KIDS."
MAYBE YOU'D RATHER RUN THIS KID OFF THAN FARM HIM OUT TO A RELATIVE.
AH, BUT WE ARE FORGETTIN MR. ANGIERS HE HAS NO RELATIV DO YA, HENRY?
YES, HENRY AVERRE JUST DROPPED OFF A TREE.
BLEW I ON A COL BREEZ
A POD PERSON.

MAYBE YOU'D RATHER MAKE A BUCK OFF YOUR LITTLE WOODS COLT, HAH?
"MARTHA SAID THEY WERE ONLY TRUANT OFFICERS. COMPANY MEN. PROTECTING THE COMPANY'S INVESTMENT."

MAYBE SELL HIM TO SOME ASCIAN CULL KEEPER?
MAYBE TO UTCHER.
"OTHER KIDS' PARENTS HAD TO TAKE SHIT WITHOUT END OFF OF SCHOOL DRIVERS, WORK BOSSES, ALL KINDS OF REGULATORS.
"BUT NOT FROM GUYS IN BLUR CAMOUFLAGE.

"BLUR CAMO'S EXPENSIVE.
"THAT'S WHAT SCARED ME. THE THOUGHT THAT WHATEVER WAS GOING ON, IT WAS WORTH A HUGE SHITLOAD OF MONEY. TO SOMEBODY.

"WHO?
"IF THEY WERE COMPANY MEN, WHAT COMPANY WAS FUNDING THEM?

"AND FOR WHAT? IF THEY WERE PROTECTING THEIR INVESTMENT, WHAT WAS THAT INVESTMENT?
"I'D COME BACK. THEY'D LEAVE. USUALLY WITHOUT ANOTHER WORD.

"I'D DREAM OF KILLING THEM FOR HURTING MY FATHER.
"AND THEN HE'D TELL ME EVERYTHING.

"BUT *WHY* DID HE **TAKE** THAT SHIT FROM THE BLURS?

"**HE** WAS NO COMPANY MAN. HE WAS THE LOCAL JAEGER.

"THAT'S LIKE A GAME WARDEN OR PARK RANGER, BUT MORE SO."

WHOKK

WHOKK
CREEK
WHOKK
CREEEK
WHOKK
CREEK
I AM THE LORAX. I SPEAK FOR THE TREES. I SPEAK FOR THE TREES FOR THE TREES HAVE NO TONS--
TONGUES.
TONGUES--

"IT'S A HOLDOVER FROM OLD TIMES. FROM BEFORE THE COMPANY. EACH PAR OF THE WOODS HAD A GU WHO LOOKED AFTER IT.

"IF YOU WANTED TO HUNT, YOU ASKED THE JAEGER FOR PERMISSION. IF HE DIDN'T GIVE IT, YOU DIDN HUNT. IF YOU HUNTED *WITHOU* HIS PERMISSION, YOU WER A POACHER AND HE COULD **KILL** YOUR ASS.

"IF ANYBODY GOT LOST IN THE WOODS, *HE'D* GO GET 'EM HE ALWAYS KNEW WHERE TO LOOK FOR 'EM.

"IF THE TOWNIES NEEDED MEAT, HE PROVIDED IT. THERE'S ***NOTHING*** ABOUT HI PATCH OF WOODS THAT TH JAEGER DOESN'T KNO

"IN TOWN THEY CALLED HIM 'THE LORD OF THE WOOD' AND SAID IT WITH A SNEER BECAUSE HE WAS A DRUNK.

UT HE COULD SEND ME TO SCHOOL --
(GOD KNOWS WHAT KIND OF DEAL THAT WAS)
AND STILL BLOW OFF THE DRIVERS' AUTHORITY.

"FOR EXAMPLE --
WHEN THE OTHER KIDS FOUGHT AMONG THEMSELVES,
THEY DIDN'T GET WHIPPED FOR IT.

"THE KIDS DIDN'T. BUT THEIR PARENTS DID.

"SAME HUMILIATING SHIT THEY DID TO ME. BUT NOT BEHIND CLOSED DOORS--IN FRONT OF THE SCHOOL.
MERCY
"PEOPLE WALKIN' BY AN' SHIT, KIDS GIGGLIN'.

"FUCK. TRY THAT WITH MY OLD MAN, HE'D'A GONE OFF LIKE GODDAMN THIRTY MEGATONS.
HE'D'A SHIT ON THEIR ASHES.

"HE WAS A FREE MAN.

"SO.
"I GOT OLDER.
"I SPENT MORE TIME OUTSIDE.
"I GOT STRONGER. I GOT FASTER.
"I LEARNED HOW TO KEEP A COOL HEAD WHEN SOMEBODY WAS TRYING TO KILL ME.
"I'D WATCH ***THEM*** FIGHT. I FIGURED OUT HOW TO PICK THE ONE WHO'D WIN MOST OF THE TIME.
"IT CLICKED INTO FOCUS FOR THE FIRST TIME. IT'S AMAZING HOW MUCH YOU CAN TELL BY HOW THEY CARRY THEMSELVES.
"LIFE GOT SIMPLE.
"IT'S DUMB, BUT TRUE: YOU JUST HAD TO BE FASTER OR SMARTER THAN EVERYONE ELSE.

"'JUST GOT TO BE SMARTER OR FASTER THAN ANYBODY ELSE.'

!
"SOUNDS SIMPLE. DON'T IT?

"WELL.
"IT IS.

"THAT I WAS RAPIDLY GROWING BIGGER THAN ANYBODY ELSE WAS OF INESTIMABLE HELP IN IMPLEMENTING THIS SIMPLE PHILOSOPHY."

--AND IF YOU GOT A PROBLEM WITH ME, YA FUCK, YOU CALL ME OUT PROPER! YOU DON'T DO THAT GIRL SHIT LIKE PULLING MY HAIR, GET IT??

HEY!

OH-- YOU CAN PULL MY HAIR ANY OL' TIME.
C'MON.
G'AHEAD. PULL MY HAIR.
GRAB A BIG HANDFUL. SEE WHAT HAPPENS.

"IT'S NOT THAT I HAD NO FRIENDS. IT'S JUST THAT I COULDN'T BE WITH ANY-BODY WHO ASKED ME THE QUESTIONS I COULDN'T ASK MY FATHER.
"THAT GOT ME INTO A SHITLOAD OF FIGHTS.
"IT WASN'T UNTIL I REALIZED I COULD JUST LIE--
(MAKE UP A NAME MAKE UP A STORY)
"-THAT I GOT SO I COULD PUT UP WITH THEIR GRINS AND HUNGRY EYES.
(FILL IN THE EMPTY SPACES WITH DETAILS THAT DON'T MATTER MAKE THE MOST IMPORTANT THINGS INCONSEQUENTIAL)
"AND YOU KNOW-- IT DOESN'T EVEN MATTER IF YOU TELL EACH ONE A DIFFERENT STORY. THEY LOVE IT.
"AND MY MOTTO WAS...
"DON'T FIGHT WITH THE OLD MAN. DON'T DREAM OF BREAKING HIS BONES -
(IF THE BLURS CAN'T BEAT WHAT THEY WANT OUT OF HIM, NEITHER CAN YOU)
"KEEP GOING OUT. KEEP GOING OUT. KEEP GOING OUT.

"SCHOOL FINISHED.
"SOME OF THE KIDS WERE SENT ON TO HIGH SCHOOL, OR TECH SCHOOL. MOST WEREN'T.
"I WASN'T.
"THE COMPANY KIDS WERE BEING MARRIED OFF--AT THIRTEEN, FOURTEEN, EVEN TWELVE.
"THE ONES WHO DIDN'T GO ON TO MORE SCHOOL WERE ROUTED INTO JOBS. OF COURSE, THERE WAS NO JOB FOR ME, NO WIFE. MY LIFE WOULD END WITH MY CHILDHOOD.
"NO SCHOOL. NO JOB.
"NO *BLURS?*
"NO REASON TO STAY IN TOWN.

"SO I GUESS IT'S NO SURPRISE THAT IT WASN'T LONG BEFORE I GOT INTO MY FIRST *REAL* FIGHT.

"A FIGHT WITH A *MAN*, NOT A KID.

"*THAT* WAS ONE I DIDN'T SEE COMING AT *ALL*.

"I WAS IN THE MARKET, THINKIN' ABOUT HOW YOUR OPINION OF WHAT YOU DO CHANGES WHEN YOU THINK SOMEBODY MIGHT BE WATCHING YOU.

THIS GUY SAID SOMETHING AND *I* SAID SOMETHING AND *HE* MADE SOME BAD NOISE ABOUT WHAT HE'D DO 'IF YOU WERE MY SON **MY SON MY SON**'

AND *BOOM*.

BAP
BAP
BAP
BAP
BAP

"PROBLEM IS, FIGHTS DECIDE WHERE PEOPLE GO IN THE ORDER OF THINGS. AND IN THIS TOWN I HAD NO PLACE.

"NOTHING PROVED THIS TO ME MORE UNDENIABLY THAN WHEN THE LAW LEVELERS TOOK THE *OTHER* GUY AWAY AND IGNORED ME ENTIRELY."

NUH
WAIT.. PLEASE, WAIT-- MY WIFE-- WE'LL LOSE EVERYTHING--
TSK
LIKE A WILD ANIMAL!
SAFEST THING TO DO IS JUST STAY AWAY
SHOULDN'T BE IN TOWN
"THE COMPANY'S NOT INTERESTED IN JUSTICE. THEY WANT LEVERAGE.

"SO I GO HOME, NOT KNOWING IF I WON OR LOST, TRYING TO FIGURE OUT WHO THE DRIVERS WOULD TAKE IT OUT ON IF I REALLY DID SOME BAD SHIT...

"I FOUND OUT WHO SOON ENOUGH.

"MARTHA.
"SHE WAS ONE OF THEIRS."
IT'S NOTHING, HENRY. THEY GRABBED ME OUT OF THE MARKET AND GAVE ME A FEW STRIPES.
SO WHAT?

JUST-- ONE OF THEIR STUPID MADE-UP REASONS-- SAID I ASSOCIATED WITH WILD ANIMALS OR SOMETHING--
SNIFF THEY PROBABLY MEAN THE BARN CAT--
YOU KNOW THEY'LL DO ANYTHING TO GET AT YOU, HENRY; IT'S JUST THE PRICE I PAY--

I'LL PAY IT ...
UNH
I'M GONNA GO LIE DOWN NOW...

"OH HOW HE ITCHED TO HIT ME.

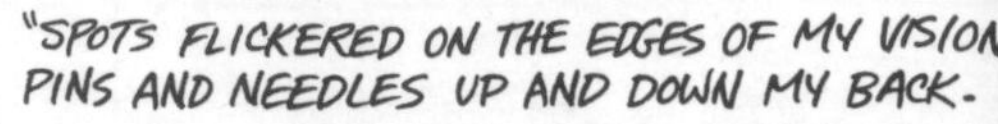

"THEN

"IT STOPPED.

SHE'S LYIN' DOWN, BABY.
OH.

LIE LOW FOR A WHILE.
I'LL KEEP 'EM IN. WON'T NOTHING ELSE HAPPEN.

--YOU SHOULDN'T SAY "WON'T NOTHING," YOU KNOW.
IT'S A DOUBLE NEGATIVE.

"I LAID LOW FOR A WHILE, ALL RIGHT.

"I WENT DOWN IN THE BOGS AND CAUGHT SOME GODDAMN DISEASE. SICK FOR... WEEKS... THOUGHT I'D GOT DEAD FOR SURE.
"A BLEEDING SAVED ME. I LAID UP FOR A WHILE TILL I FELT BETTER. BUT BY THE TIME I GOT HOME IT WAS MY FATHER WHO WAS DEAD.
"MARTHA LEFT ME A LETTER.
"SHE SAID HE PASSED OUT DRUNK ONE NIGHT AND LAY IN THE ROAD A WHILE.
"IT WAS COLD....
"HE CAME HOME, WENT TO BED, AND JUST NEVER GOT UP AGAIN.
"HE SANK.
"MARTHA TOOK THE KIDS AND RAN.
SHE WAS SORRY SHE COULDN'T WAIT FOR ME.
SHE WAS SORRY SHE COULDN'T TELL ME WHERE SHE WAS GOING.
"THE HOUSE WAS COLD AND STANK OF DEATH AND STRANGERS.
"THEY SAID THE HOUSE WAS MINE. HE LEFT IT TO ME.
"BUT I WOULD HAVE TO PAY THE PROPERTY TAXES IF I WANTED TO KEEP IT.
"IF MY FATHER HAD ANY MORE MONEY, MARTHA MUST HAVE TAKEN IT WITH HER.
"DID I KNOW WHERE SHE HAD GONE?
"THEY OFFERED ME SUCH A DEAL.

"I COULD KEEP MY FATHER'S HOUSE. I COULD HAVE A JOB WITH THE COMPANY. I WAS *MAYBE* THIRTEEN, FOURTEEN, BUT THEY'D PAY ME ENOUGH TO COVER THE TAXES. NO *MORE*, SINCE THEY WOULDN'T WANT TO INTERFERE WITH MY SELF-SUFFICIENCY, RIGHT?
"RIGHT?

"SIGN **HERE**, AND JOIN THEIR HAPPY LITTLE FAMILY.
OTHERWISE....
"THEY WENT ON ABOUT 'OTHERWISE' FOR QUITE SOME TIME."

GET OUT OF MY HOUSE.
I HOPE YOU DIE FORGOTTEN.
...EARTH SWALLOW UP YOUR BLOOD... VULTURES FIGHT OVER YOUR FLESH.
MAY YOU **NEVER** BE FOUND.

"THEY LEFT THEIR CONTRACT FOR ME TO SIGN IF I CHANGED MY MIND.

"I BURNED IT.

"I DIDN'T WANT TO SPEND THE REST OF MY LIFE ON THE PORCH WITH A SHOTGUN.

"AND ALL MY GHOSTS WENT UP WITH IT.
CRAK!
POP!
"**WELL**, OKAY, NO. I TOOK THOSE *WITH* ME.
"BUT THE HOUSE'S TERRIBLE TIDAL PULL WAS GONE.

"THAT SEASON, WHEN THE ASCIAN DRUM FIEF CAME THROUGH, I FOLLOWED THEM.
"I WAS A HALF-BREED, SO NOBODY WANTED ME. BUT I COULD KEEP UP, SO THEY *LET* ME.

"*LOT* OF FIGHTING THERE. ASCIAN KIDS FIGHT *DIRTY*. THEY DON'T NOTICE BROKEN NOSES OR BUSTED FINGERS. WHAT FEW OF 'EM *DID* BITCH TO THEIR FATHERS, THE DADS SAID, 'SO WHAT? IF YOU CAN'T BEAT 'IM, WHY COME CRYIN' TO **ME**?'
"IT WAS **VERY** ENCOURAGING.

"ALL THE ASS I KICKED, AND I **STILL** DIDN'T KICK THE ONE THAT *NEEDED* IT. LODR SHAKMAH, THE WEASELLY LITTLE SHIT. THAT'S *ANOTHER* STORY...
"I TOOK A BEATING BECAUSE OF HIM. JUST LIKE SCHOOL.

"ON *TOP*, IT WAS A GOOD TIME. IN MY GUT I'M ALWAYS AN ASCIAN. HOW COULD I NOT BE? THEY TAUGHT ME EVERYTHING MY FATHER DIDN'T.
"BUT UNDERNEATH, IT WAS A LOT LIKE TOWN.
"A FEW YEARS, AND I MOVED ON.

"SO I'M ALWAYS THE NEW GUY. PEOPLE GOTTA KNOW HOW IT IS WITH ME. SO THEY PICK FIGHTS. ...FRANKLY, I DIDN'T THINK ABOUT IT MUCH. I COULD **TAKE** IT, AND THAT SOLVES MOST FIGHTS BEFORE THEY START. I TOOK THAT FOR GRANTED, AS MOST GUYS WHO CAN TAKE A PUNCH DO.

"BUT DAMN I WAS GETTING TIRED OF IT! WASN'T I JUST MINDING MY OWN BUSINESS?
CLUNK
"ANOTHER DAY, ANOTHER BAR, ANOTHER ASSHOLE.

"I DIDN'T HIT THAT GUY TOO HARD.
"I KNOW HOW TO HIT A GUY SO AS TO KILL 'IM. AND I DIDN'T HIT THE SON OF A BITCH THAT HARD.

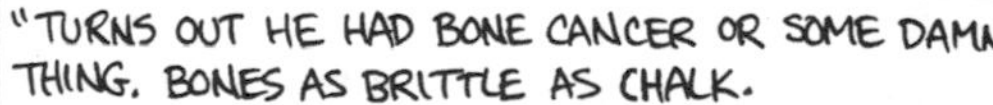

"TURNS OUT HE HAD BONE CANCER OR SOME DAMN THING. BONES AS BRITTLE AS CHALK.

"IT WAS HIS **OWN** DAMN FAULT FOR STARTING A FIGHT IF HE WAS SICK, BUT HE WAS STILL DEAD.

"AND I WAS STILL IN PRISON.

"I SWEAR, FIGHTING WAS THE ONLY THING THAT KEPT ME ALIVE IN PRISON. I CAN'T UNDERSTAND WHY THE OTHER INMATES DIDN'T GANG UP AND KILL ME.

"I JUST COULDN'T STAND IT... AS SOON AS THEY TURNED ME LOOSE I STARTED SHAKING. MY NERVE WAS **SHOT**. I COULDN'T THINK. MY ARMS AND LEGS JERKED OUT OF CONTROL... IF I TRIED TO HOLD STILL.

"SOMEBODY'D BUMP INTO ME AND I'D SINK MY TEETH INTO HIS SHOULDER. THEY'D PUT ME DOWN IN SOLITARY TO CALM DOWN AND I'D BOUNCE OFF THE WALLS LIKE THERE WAS NO GRAVITY.

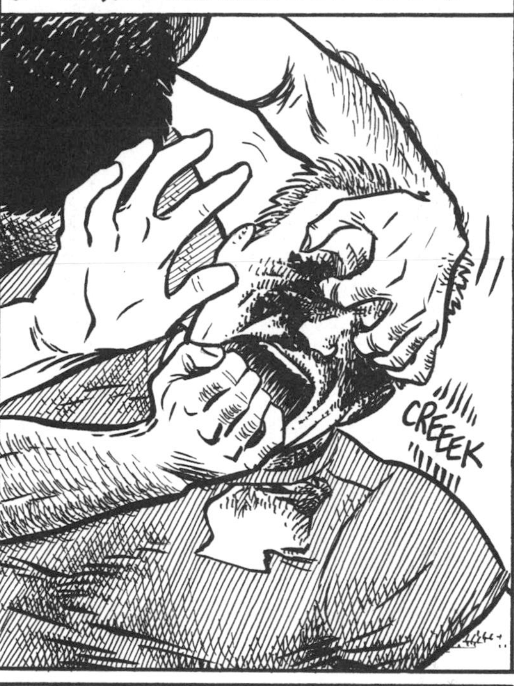

"THE GUARDS HAD THIS THING WHERE THEY'D STAGE FIGHTS TO BET ON. THEY WANTED GOOD FIGHTERS. OF COURSE, WHAT ***I*** WAS WASN'T SO MUCH A *FIGHTER* AS IT WAS A *RABID HOG*...

"THOSE POOR SLOBS DIDN'T DESERVE WHAT I DID TO THEM. BUT FIGHTING -- REALLY CUTTING LOOSE -- IT WAS ALL I COULD DO. I DON'T THINK I SLEPT TWO HOURS AT A STRETCH ALL THE TIME I WAS IN.

"I THINK I WAS AFRAID I'D **SINK**, LIKE MY FATHER. JUST LAY DOWN AND NEVER GET UP.

"IN THE ARMY IT WAS DIFFERENT--
"OH, YEAH--OUT OF PRISON, INTO THE MEDAWAR COLONIAL ARMY.
"MEDAWAR CLAN RUNS THAT PRISON. WHEN THEY WANT CANNON FODDER, THAT'S ONE PLACE THEY GET IT.

"SO. BOOT CAMP. THE GUYS IN BOOT CAMP DIDN'T HATE ME, EXACTLY--"
NONE-OF-US-HAS-HAD-ENOUGH-SLEEP. IF-WE-DON'T-PASS-INSPECTION-WE-GO-ON-A-FORTY. MILE. RUN!

LESSEE. I C'N GEDDUP AN' SPEND FOUR HOURS DOIN' MY KIT 'N' CLEANIN' UP THIS PLACE.
BRASS POLISH.
BOOT POLISH.
FRANTIC SOCK REFOLDING.
OR I C'N GET SOME SLEEP, AN' IN TH' MORNIN' GO ON A NICE FORTY-MILE RUN AWAY FROM ALL THE POLISH FUMES AND YOU 'CAUSE YOUR ASS WILL BE EATIN' MY DUST...
...HMMM...

FLUMP!
Z

WHAK
WHAK
WHUMP
THUMP
NH!
"ARMY PEOPLE UNDERSTAND PAYBACK.

"BESIDES-- BEFORE I GOT A CHANCE TO MAKE ANY REAL ENEMIES, THINGS STARTED GETTING OUT OF CONTROL WITH THE DRILL INSTRUCTOR.
HUFF

"BRIGHAM GROSVENOR.
"THINGS GET OUT OF WHACK WITH HIM REAL EASY SOMEHOW.

"THE MORE HE STEAMED, THE MORE SLACK THEY CUT ME. I DUNNO IF IT WAS PITY OR IF THEY WERE JUST GLAD HE WASN'T BUSTIN' THEIR 'NADS."
HHH HUFF HHH HUFF

WELL, SHIT, IF YOU DIDN'T STRIDE IN LIKE YOU OWN THE GODDAMN PLACE, THE LOCALS WOULDN'T GET BENT OUTTA SHAPE SO EASY.

YOU'RE JUST A DICK, MAN. I'M SORRY, BUT--
"AT TIMES I'M SORRY MY ARMY TIME WASN'T LONGER.

"NOT EVERY DRILL SERGEANT WAS LIKE BRIG. IN TIME I SAW THAT.

HUFF GASP UH HAFF HAH ERNT UH UFF HECH EH AAHH HUH EH

"GUYS WHO FALL IN LINE NATURALLY, WELL, NO PROBLEM. GUYS WHO TRIP ON THEIR WAY IN, THE DRILLS JUST HAMMER 'EM A BIT HARDER AND THEN WAIT. THEY KNOW THEY CAN WEAR 'EM OUT.

"DRILLS LIKE BRIG... THEY CAN'T **WAIT.** THEY CAN'T JUST **LET** A GUY FALL INTO STEP AND THEN PRETEND HE WAS ALWAYS THAT WAY.
"NO, THEY HAVE TO HAVE A, A **MOMENT.** WHERE THEY KNOW **THEY** PICKED YOU UP AND **PUT** YOU WHERE YOU GO.

"AND HE JUST COULD NOT WEAR ME OUT."

WHATSAMATTER WITH YOU? TOO CHEAP TO BUY SHAVING CREAM OR TOO LAZY TO LATHER UP A LITTLE SOAP?
SIR, NO SIR! NEVER USE THE STUFF, SIR!

NO?
SIR, NO SIR!
YOU MEAN TO TELL ME YOU DON'T USE SHAVING CREAM.
SIR, NO SIR!

OR SOAP?
SIR, NO SIR!

SO IF I WAS TO ASK MURPHY THERE IF HE'S EVER SEEN YOU USE SHAVING CREAM HE WOULD SAY NO?
SIR, YOU'D HAVE TO ASK HIM, SIR!

AND IF I WAS TO ASK TANETTA THERE OR ADELFI OR EVEN GODDAMN EVANS THEY WOULD SAY WHAT WOULD YOU SAY, DAVIES? DOES AYERS HERE EVER USE SHAVING CREAM?
SIR NOT THAT I'VE EVER SEEN SIR!

SIMBLETT! DOES AYERS EVER USE ANYTHING ON HIS FACE IN THE MORNING?
SIR, YES SIR!

YES! OKAY! WHAT DOES HE USE?
S-S- SOMETIMES HE SLAPS A LITTLE WATER ON THERE, SIR! SIR!

WHAT ARE YOU GRINNIN' AT?

SIR.
THAT OFFICER SAID SERGEANTS AREN'T ALLOWED TO HIT US.
SIR.

02:28
"SO THERE I WAS, NOT SNEAKING OUT OF OUR HUT TO RUN THE CAMP PERIMETER, MAKE SURE I KNOW WHAT ALL'S GOING ON, AND LET ME TELL YOU ONE THING FOR SURE: THAT IS NOT IN MY NATURE.
"IT MADE ME SWEAT FIRE. I GROUND MY TEETH TO PULP.
"AND FOR THE LIFE OF ME I COULDN'T TELL YOU NOW IF I WAS STAYING PUT TO BE GOOD OR BECAUSE NOT GIVING BRIG A CHANCE EVERY NIGHT TO CATCH ME DROVE HIM EVEN MORE BUGFUCK CRAZY.
"AND SMILING. I COULD NOT STOP SMILING. THAT AT LEAST BEGAN AS FUCKING WITH HIM. AND NOW IT WAS FUCKING WITH ME. MY LIPS FELT LIKE BOOTLACES. MY CHEEKS FELT LIKE SPRAINED ANKLES.
WHY, YES, SAR'NT MAJOR
"I WANTED TO FEEL MY TEETH CLICK ON BONE THROUGH FLESH."

"THE DAY CAME WHEN ALL THE OTHER GUYS IN TRAINING WEREN'T EVEN TIPTOEING AROUND TO SEE WHAT WOULD HAPPEN NEXT.
"THE DAY CAME WHEN EVEN THE OTHER TRAINERS WEREN'T TRYING TO TALK SENSE TO BRIG ANYMORE.
"THE DAY CAME WHEN ALL I COULD DO WAS MAKE MY CREAKING TENDONS WALK AND BREATHE AND PICK THE MOMENT TO SAY I'D BE OUT BACK OF THE COOK SHACK AT NINETEEN HUNDRED.
"THE DAY CAME."

YEAH, YOU **BE** THERE.

I'LL BE YOUR GODDAMN DADDY AND I'LL FUCK YOU JUST LIKE YOUR **DADDY** DID.

YEAH, THAT'S WHAT I THOUGHT.

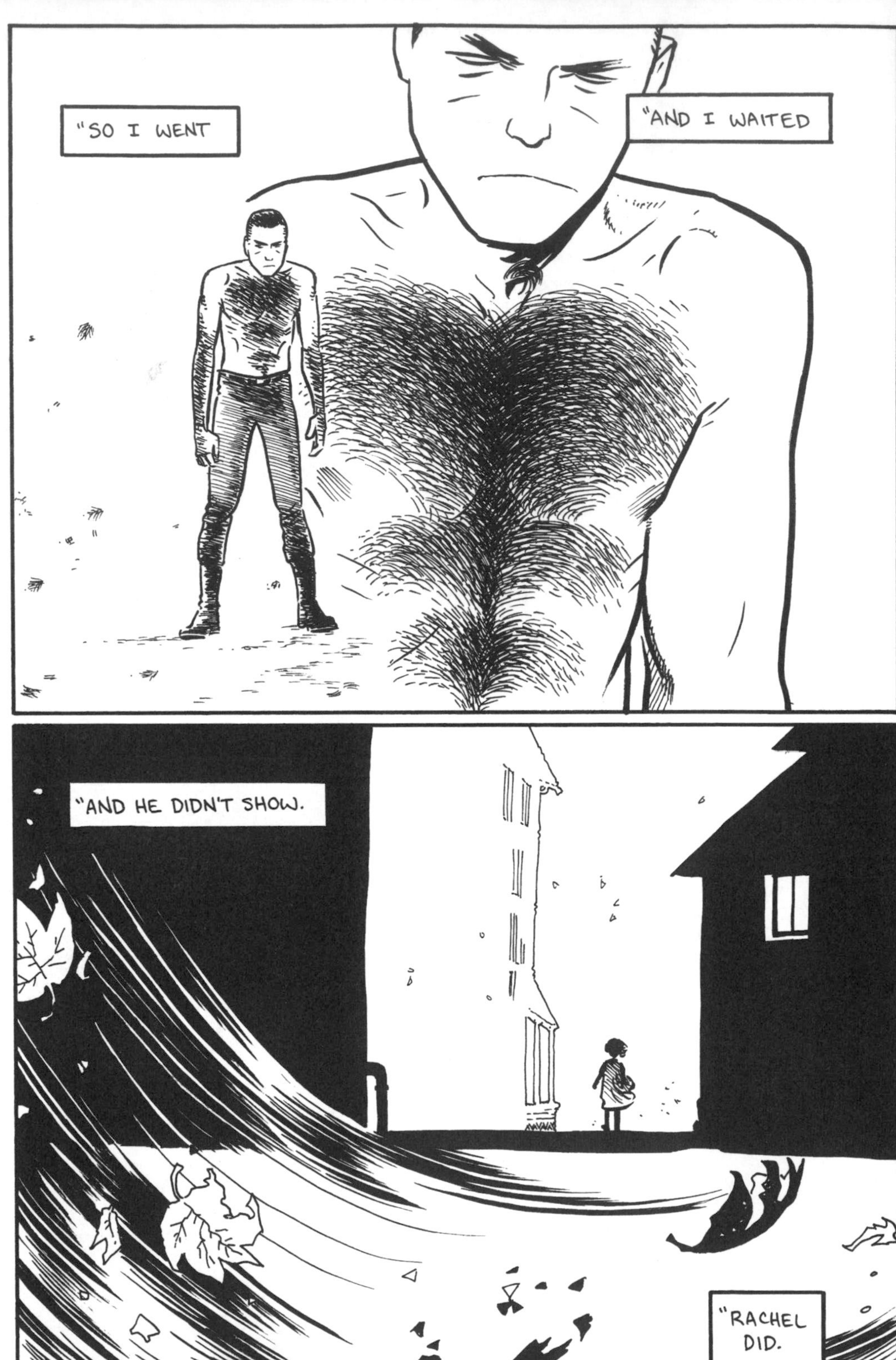
"SO I WENT
"AND I WAITED
"AND HE DIDN'T SHOW.
"RACHEL DID.

"SHE WAS ABOUT FOUR, AND CUTE, AND OBLIVIOUS, AND SHE HAULED ME OFF BY THE HAND.
"TO DINNER.
"BRIG TOOK ME IN. HE MADE ME WELCOME, HE HAD AN ABSOLUTELY GODDAMN GORGEOUS WIFE.
"I HAD THE SHAKES. SHE THOUGHT I WAS SICK. SHE PUT ME TO BED.
"FROM THAT MOMENT ON, THEY WERE MY FAMILY. I WOULD KILL FOR HIM. I WOULD HAVE DIED FOR HIM.
"I WAS HIS DOG AND I DIDN'T CARE.
"AND I FELL INTO LINE."
AN'T BE ERIOUS--
EMMA, IF HE'D RATHER SLEEP OUT AT THE FRONT DOOR, WHAT'S IT TO YOU?
YOU DON'T KNOW THESE PEOPLE LIKE I DO--

HAS IT EVER OCCURRED TO YOU THAT MAYBE BRIGHAM DIDN'T SHOW UP FOR THE FIGHT BECAUSE HE WAS AFRAID?
THAT YOU MIGHT WELL HAVE KILLED HIM? IF HE COULDN'T WEAR YOU OUT AGAINST YOURSELF, HOW COULD HE BREAK YOU BY HITTING YOU?
WHAT?
NO!

NO, I THOUGHT FOR A LONG TIME THAT HE NEVER MEANT TO COME. THAT HIS VICTORY OVER ME WAS WHEN THAT GRIN FELL OFF MY FACE. THAT THAT WAS WHAT HE WANTED, HE-- ADOPTED ME BECAUSE HE'D WON ALREADY.

NOW I THINK BRIGHAM NEVER THINKS THAT MUCH.

ABOUT ANYTHING.

"MY WHOLE LIFE HAS BEEN ONE 'MISSING TOP STEP' AFTER ANOTHER.
"I GET WOUND UP FOR FIGHTS THAT NEVER HAPPEN. MY DAD, THE BLURS, LODR, BRIGHAM-- THEY SHOULD HAVE HAPPENED.

"ALL THE STUPID SHIT I DID GET INTO... IF I HAD ANY IDEA WHAT I WAS DOING, I COULD HAVE AVOIDED MOST OF IT.

"DON'T GIVE ME THAT 'JOURNEY' SHIT. I'M AN ASSHOLE. I WAS AN ASSHOLE. ASSHOLES ARE ONLY POLITE TO *OTHER* ASSHOLES WHO CAN BEAT THEM UP. IT'S *SIMPLE*...

"POINTLESS, PUNK-ASS EXISTENCE, CAROMING AROUND WITH MY FISTS UP AND TRIPPIN' OVER MY DICK. ONE FIGHT LEADING TO ANOTHER, UNDERSTANDING NOTHING."

HEY!

"TRUSTING ONLY MY STRENGTH...
"KNOWING IT CAN'T LAST.

"EVERY PLACE IS AN INTRICATE CONSTELLATION OF DIFFERENT GUYS--
--THE GUYS WHO CAN'T FIGHT (MIGHT BE JERKS, OR MIGHT BE NICE GUYS, BUT THEY CAN'T FIGHT--)

"--THE GUYS WHO ARE SO EVENLY MATCHED THAT IT'S THE ONE WHO GETS IN THE FIRST PUNCH WHO WILL WIN--
"THEY MIGHT BE RIVALS, MIGHT BE FRIENDS, BUT THEY KNOW THAT BETWEEN THEM, FIRST PUNCH WINS--

"THERE ARE GUYS WHO CAN FIGHT BUT CAN BE MISTAKEN FOR GUYS WHO CAN'T BECAUSE YOU DON'T SEE THEM FIGHT VERY MUCH.
"THESE ARE THE ONES WHO DON'T GLANCE AT ANYBODY ELSE WHEN THEY'RE MAKING UP THEIR MINDS...

"...AAAND PUNKS."
WHAT ARE YOU, HALF A FAG 'R SOMETHIN'?
WHY, 'R YOU HALF CRUISIN' ME OR SOMETHIN'?
"FIGHT PICKERS.
"CHEST POKERS.
"ASSHOLES.
"THEY SERVE THEIR PURPOSE, I GUESS. EVERYBODY WATCHES THE FIGHTS THEY PICK AND JUDGES THE NEW GUY BY HOW HE REACTS.

"SO THIS GUY'S STUPID DRUNK AND GIVING ME SHIT, BUT HE AIN'T DOING ANYTHING. YET.
"HIS FRIEND IS LAUGHIN' BUT IT'S APPARENTLY NOT CONTAGIOUS.

"IF HE AIN'T GONNA BACK OFF, HE HAS TO ESCALATE--
"-- AND I LIKE THIS JACKET--

!
FAPBAPBAP!

"--NOW THIS OTHER GUY WANTS TO HELP BREAK IT UP---
"--BUT EVIDENTLY HE'S JUST A YIP-YIP TOO, 'CAUSE THE FIRST PUNK TURNS ON HIM--

"--ALL THE YIP-YIP'S FRIENDS COME TO HIS RESCUE--
"--AND HERE IT COMES; THE AIR IS CRACKLY WITH THE DAY'S RESENTMENTS--

"ALL THE FIRST-PUNCH WINS ARE DECIDING IF THEY'RE PISSED OFF ENOUGH TO SEIZE THE OPPORTUNITY, SETTLE SOME OLD SCORES--
"AND

"BOOM.
HEY!
FUCK!

"IT'S BEAUTIFUL, IN A FUCKED-UP KIND OF WAY.
"LIKE AN ECLIPSE.
I TOLD YOU I DIDN'T KNOW WAS ONLY
"I DIDN'T START THIS. I JUST SET IT OFF.

CRINKK =KTSSH

"PEACE AND QUIET.
"MINDING MY OWN BUSINESS.
"THE FIGHTS THAT COUNT ARE THE ONES THAT DON'T HAPPEN.

"THAT'S ALL."

SIN-EATER

PART TWO

CHAPTER SEVEN

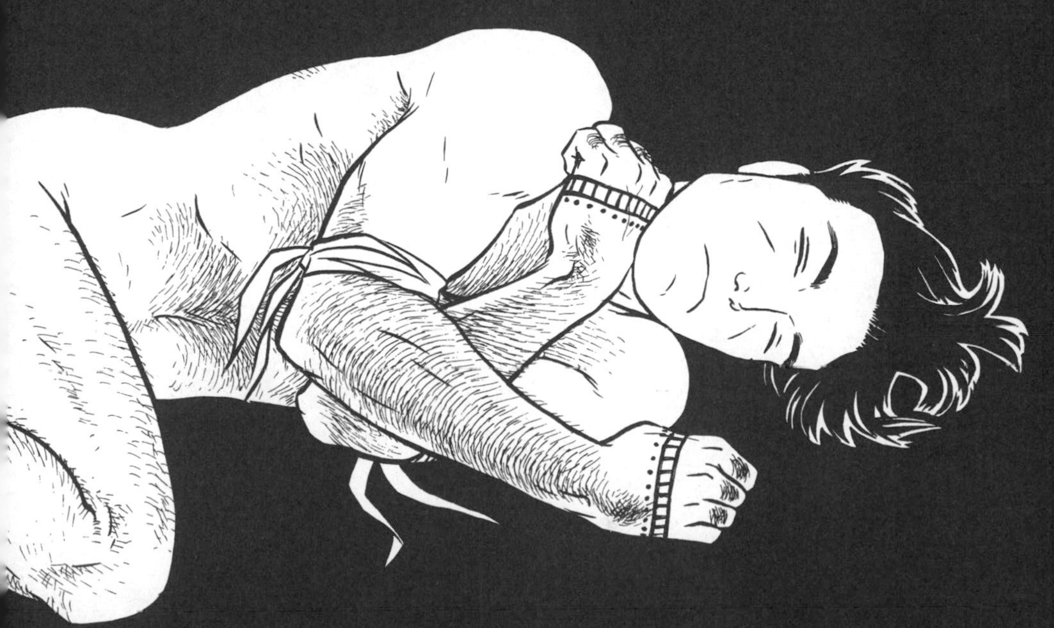

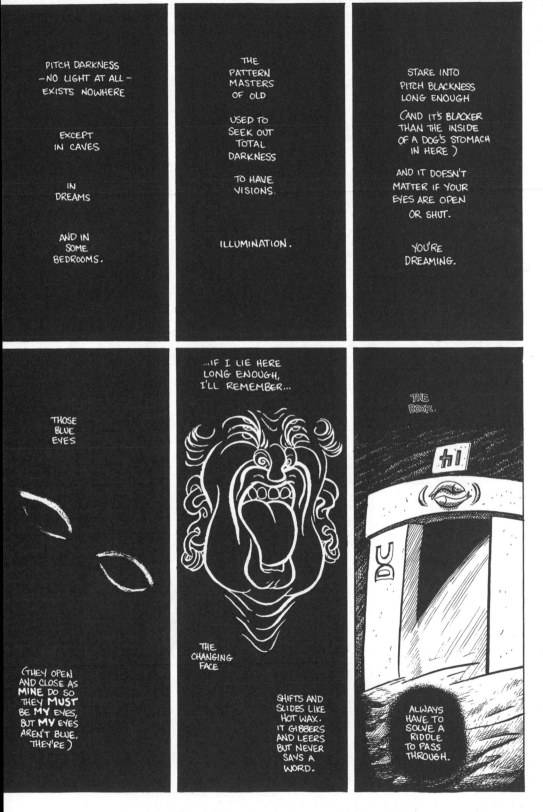

PITCH DARKNESS
-NO LIGHT AT ALL-
EXISTS NOWHERE

EXCEPT
IN CAVES

IN
DREAMS

AND IN
SOME
BEDROOMS.

THE
PATTERN
MASTERS
OF OLD

USED TO
SEEK OUT
TOTAL
DARKNESS

TO HAVE
VISIONS.

ILLUMINATION.

STARE INTO
PITCH BLACKNESS
LONG ENOUGH

(AND IT'S BLACKER
THAN THE INSIDE
OF A DOG'S STOMACH
IN HERE)

AND IT DOESN'T
MATTER IF YOUR
EYES ARE OPEN
OR SHUT.

YOU'RE
DREAMING.

THOSE
BLUE
EYES

(THEY OPEN
AND CLOSE AS
MINE DO SO
THEY **MUST**
BE **MY** EYES,
BUT **MY** EYES
AREN'T BLUE.
THEY'RE)

...IF I LIE HERE
LONG ENOUGH,
I'LL REMEMBER...

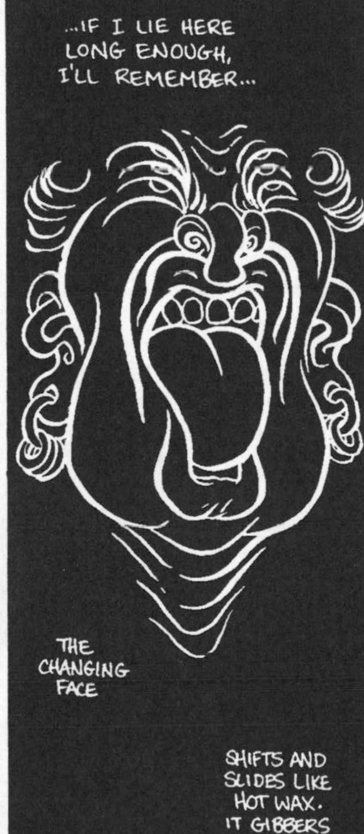

THE
CHANGING
FACE

SHIFTS AND
SLIDES LIKE
HOT WAX.
IT GIBBERS
AND LEERS
BUT NEVER
SAYS A
WORD.

THE
DOOR.

ALWAYS
HAVE TO
SOLVE A
RIDDLE
TO PASS
THROUGH.

AH, JE SUIS DÉSOLÉ --
MAIS JE N'AI PAS LE CHOIX...
JE SUIS DÉSOLÉ, MAIS LA VIE ME DEMANDE ÇA...
HAVEN'T THOUGHT OF THAT TUNE SINCE I WAS A KID.
WONDER WHY I ALWAYS DREAM OF EMPTY PLACES?
WONDER WHAT IT MEANS TO WONDER ABOUT YOURSELF IN DREAMS....
SON, THERE JUST NEVER WAS A GOOD TIME TO TALK TO YOU ABOUT ALL OF IT. THAT'S RIGHT, I DIDN'T DIE. BUT I HAD TO LEAVE, OR ELSE YOU--
DAD?
BUT IT'S GOING TO BE ALL RIGHT, SON; DON'T LOSE SLEEP OVER THE PAST. I THINK ABOUT YOU ALL THE TIME. WHEN I FIND YOUR MOTHER --
DAD?
SHIT!
SHADE'S DOWN--
YOU KNOW NEITHER OF US WOULD HAVE LEFT YOU IF IT HADN'T BEEN A MATTER OF LIFE AND DEATH. JUST THE SAME, I'M SORRY YOU COULDN'T GROW UP WITH FAMILY AROUND YOU--
DAD, DAD! IT'S ME! WAIT, WAIT, I CAN'T HEAR YOU!
BAM BAM BAM
I KNOW YOU CAN LOOK O FOR YOURSELF, BUT IT GRIE ME TO SEE YOU AS SUCH A STRAY CAT. FOR YOU NEVE TO KNOW YOUR OWN PEO YOUR BLOODLINES, YO HOME...

WELL, GOTTA GO, BOY; I'M SO GLAD I FINALLY GOT A CHANCE TO TELL YOU

NO!

DAAAD!

WHERE ARE YOU?

"ONE SWORD, AT LEAST, THY RIGHTS SHALL GUARD, ONE FAITHFUL HARP SHALL PRAISE THEE."
tikka tikka tikka DINNG!

THE MINSTREL FELL! BUT THE FOEMAN'S CHAIN COULDNA BRING THAT PROUD SOUL UNDER ~

WHAT THE HELL IS THIS?
SSSSH!
DON'T YOU SHUSH ME YOU TOY BIMBO!

sSHOOOOOOM

QUIET! YOU MUS' BE QUIET! YOU KNOW EET EES DANGEREUSE TO WAK' 'ER WHEN SHE EES EEN ZEES STATE!
EEF YOU WAN' 'ER TO WAK' UP ZEES WEEK, YOU WEEL LET 'ER WAK' UP NATURALLY. YES?

ALL RIGHT.
ALL RIGHT, FINE.
BUT WHEN SHE DOES, I'M TELLING HER ABOUT ALL THIS, SO YOU'D BEST BE GETTIN' YOUR STORY STRAIGHT.

eeuuww. WHAT A JEALOUSE LEETLE SNEAK EET EES.
WHAT'S THE MATTEUR, BUTCH? DON' YOU RELISH A LEETLE COMPETITION

THERE ARE SO **MANY** THINGS THAT COULD GO WRONG.
(THANK GOD.)
010110
WATCH OUR STEP

COUPLA NAILS STICKING UP OUT OF THE HARDWOOD FLOOR. THAT COULD BE ROUGH ON LITTLE BARE FEET.
011010
PUNCTURE WOUNDS. **VERY** PAINFUL.
BANDAGES. TETANUS SHOTS. MY LITTLE GIRLS LIMPING OFF TO SCHOOL.

BUT! I'M HERE, **I** CAN FIX THESE LITTLE THINGS. AVERT THESE CHILDHOOD TRAGEDIES WITH A LITTLE ATTENTIVENESS.
THEIR LIVES WILL PROGRESS SERENELY ON, AND THEY'LL NEVER EVEN KNOW I WAS HERE.

SEE, MY FAMILY LIVES HERE. WIFE, THREE KIDS, NO DOG. SHIT DIDN'T WORK OUT, AND THEY **LEFT** ME. NOW I'M JUST TRYING TO BE USE-FUL TO 'EM WITHOUT SCARING 'EM.
SO I'M MAKING IT MY JOB TO COME IN HERE WHEN THEY'RE GONE —
(AND I'VE BEEN LUCKY AS HELL SO FAR; THE PLACE IS ALWAYS EMPTY. I GUESS **THEY'RE** DROWNING THEIR SORROWS IN WORK **TOO**)
VERY NICE, EMMA. YOU MANAGED TO TURN THAT LITTLE HELL-RAISER INTO A LADY FOR A **MINUTE,** ANYWAY.
sktch
—AND I'M GONNA FIX **EVERYTHING.**

GOOD GOD, EMMA. YOU KNOW YOU'LL CUT YOURSELF WORSE WITH A DULL KNIFE THAN WITH A SHARP ONE.
LAZY.
SSSHK
FUCK!
THIS ONE'S NOT EVEN GROUNDED! WOMAN, WHERE IS YOUR BRAIN??
AND LOOK AT THE SHIT YOU'RE FEEDING THEM....
PLT

"MOST ACCIDENTS OCCUR IN THE HOME."

OH, THAT'S **BRILLIANT, THAT** IS.

HOME'S WHERE YOU **ARE,** MOST OF THE TIME. SO IF ANYTHING'S **GONNA** HAPPEN, IT'LL MOST LIKELY HAPPEN AT **HOME.**

SPLINTERS FROM THE FLOOR. KNIVES IN THE KITCHEN TO CUT THE SPLINTERS **OUT.**

WATER IN THE SINKS TO WASH THE CUTS OUT; BUT NO FILTERS TO KEEP THE WATER CLEAN.

WRONG KIND OF SOCKETS OVER THE SINKS. FIRES, ELECTROCUTION....

THIS FRIDGE AIN'T EVEN **HALF** COLD ENOUGH, EITHER.

GO BY THE DATES ON THE FOOD, AND YOU'D THINK IT WAS FRESH, BUT IT'S NOT.

KIDS DON'T KNOW ANY BETTER. MIGHT EAT THE STUFF ANYWAY, AND GET FOOD POISONING. MAYBE ONE O' THOSE GOD-AWFUL FOREIGN KINDS THAT THEY CAN'T KNOCK OUT EVEN WITH ANTIBIOTICS.

MY POOR BABIES....

THROW IT OUT OR **DON'T** THROW IT OUT...

NAH, THEY'D **KNOW** SOMEBODY'D BEEN **IN** HERE.

CAN'T JUST STAND BY AND LET MY KIDS MAYBE GET **SICK,** CAN I?

WORSE TO **SCARE** 'EM. THEY'RE SO PARANOID **ALREADY.** LIKE HOW YOU NEVER REALLY GET OVER FROSTBITE. HEAT'S AS PAINFUL TO A FROSTBIT MAN AS COLD IS.

AHA! *THING TO* ***DO*** *IS* ***REPLACE*** *EVERYTHING THAT'S GONE* ***BAD!***

—JUST GOTTA FIGURE OUT HOW TO CHANGE THE DATES ON THE **NEW** STUFF; THEY MIGHT NOTICE THAT...

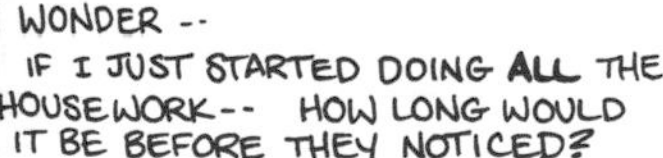
I WONDER --
IF I JUST STARTED DOING ALL THE HOUSEWORK-- HOW LONG WOULD IT BE BEFORE THEY NOTICED?
HUH! PROBABLY NEVER!
MMA ALWAYS DID SAY HOUSEWORK WAS THE GREAT INVISIBLE NECESSITY.
LIKE A LEAK IN THE ROOF.
YOU DON'T WANNA GO OUT IN THE RAIN TO FIX IT, AND IF IT'S NOT RAININ' YOU DON'T THINK ABOUT IT.
NOBODY NOTICES HOUSEWORK UNLESS IT DOESN'T GET DONE.
OT TILL THE TOILET STARTS STINKIN' AND HE DISHES ARE ALL DIRTY AND THE ORNERS ARE ALL FULLA HAIR...

SHWF
SHWFF

T HEY! THAT'S ME - NINJA EANING SERVICE!
UNDER THEIR VERY NOSES, I KEEP EVERYTHI~

NEVER MISS A~
WHAT THE HELL?

LOOKS LIKE HAIR...
STRAIGHT... BLACK... LONG...
NO DOG FOOD...
NO CAT BOX...
A BIG ANIMAL....

SHIT! WHAT KINDA THING'S BEEN CREEPIN' UP IN MY WIFE'S HOUSE WHEN AIN'T NOBODY HOME??

NGH!
≡SHIT!≡
BESIDES ME....

OH, IT'S JUST CRUMBLING TO BITS, JAEGER...
I'M NOT SO MUCH CUTTING IT AS WATCHING IT FALL APART!
ALL YOUR BEAUTIFUL HAIR...
AAH, RAE. IT'S ONLY HAIR.
IT WAS GETTIN' TOO LONG ANYWAY.
THOUGH I'LL ADMIT IT'S BEEN A WHILE SINCE IT WAS THIS SHORT.
MILITARY DAYS, HUH?
MMNO, I WAS THINKIN' OF A BIG GRASS FIRE IN RAMALAH TERRITORY ABOUT TWO YEARS AGO ACTUALLY...
I TOOK IT FOR GRANTED WHEN I WAS A KID.
ALL THOSE MANY WEEKS AGO...
PWOOOF!
I MEAN, YOUR HAVING BEEN IN THE MILITARY. I CAN'T EVEN PICTURE YOU IN THE ARMY NOW. YOU MUST HAVE BEEN MISERABLE.
NOT REALLY.
SCRITCH SCRITCH SCRITCHA
mmm... DON' DO THAT....
TURNS ME ON...
REEALLY.
SCRITCH SCRITCH SCRITCH SCRITCH
WHAT MADE THE ARMY OKAY?
IT BEAT PRISON.

ONE.
YOUR EYES SURE LOOK STRANGE WITH YOUR HAIR GONE
HOW MANY LICKS DOES IT TAKE TO GET TO THE
SHEESH, JUST ONE QUESTION... THAT'S WORSE THAN THREE WISHES!
WHY WERE YOU IN PRISON? WHAT DID YOU DO?
DID YOU DO WHAT YOU WERE CONVICTED OF?
HOW MANY THINGS HAVE YOU DONE THAT YOU WEREN'T CAUGHT FOR?
DID YOU KILL SOMEBODY?
HAVE YOU EVER KILLED ANYBODY?
GOD IF I DON'T MAKE THIS A GOOD QUESTION HE'LL ..HE'LL ..I DUNNO
DO I LOOK FAT IN THIS SKIRT?
ARE YOU IN LOVE WITH MY MOTHER?
WHAT DO I HAVE TO DO TO MAKE YOU LOVE ME?
DING! TIME'S UP! RUMPELSTILTSKIN!
up! HOW DO YOU GO FROM PRISON TO THE ARMY
IT'S AN OPTION OFFERED TO SOME CONVICTS, IF THE JAIL'S CROWDED OR IF THERE'S A BIG WAR ON.
MEDAWAR CLAN RUNS DAMN NEAR EVERYTHING IN UNIFORM IN THIS PART OF THE WORLD, RIGHT?
WELL, THERE'S A KIND OF RIVALRY BETWEEN THE MEDOS THAT RUN THE COPS AND THE ONES THAT RUN THE ARMY.
SIMPLY PUT, SOMETIMES THE COPS SLOUGH OFF PRISONERS THEY DON'T WANT, OR THE ARMY BRASS TAP CONS THEY THINK WILL MAKE GOOD CANNON FODDER.
BUT THE ODDS ON MY GETTING MY HEAD BLOWN OFF WERE GREAT COMPARED TO MY CHANCES OF SURVIVING PRISON.
BUT WHY~.
AND DO YOU KNOW WHO TAPPED ME? GOT ME UP OUTTA JAIL? SAVED MY LIFE?
DON'T TELL ME.
YOUR DAD.

IS THAT WHY YOU ...
NOPE. NOPE. NE PER CUSTOMER. ALREADY SAID THAT.
SCRRIPPT

BUT I DON'T ....
um.

WHAT THE HELL ARE YOU DOING?
WHAT'S WRONG WITH SHOELACES?
WHAT HAPPENED TO YOUR BOOTS?
SCRRPTTCH

HERE'S A FREEBIE. YOU DON'T UNDERSTAND BECAUSE YOU DIDN'T ASK THE RIGHT QUESTION.

DON'T ASK
DON'T ASK ...
DON'T ASK ...

WHEN THERE'S A BIG THING YOU WANT TO KNOW, YOU GOT TO FIGURE OUT WHAT'S THE RIGHT QUESTION TO ASK. SOMETIMES THE RIGHT QUESTION GETS THE WHOLE THING TO COME OUT ALL NICELY STRUNG TOGETHER.

BBUT-- HOW CAN YOU POSSIBLY KNOW WHICH ONE THAT IS?

IF YOU CAN'T, YOU JUST ASK THE ONE THAT BOTHERS YOU THE MOST.
I'VE GOT ONE.
GO, LYNNE.
WHY ARE YOU SO SURE YOU'D HAVE DIED IN PRISON?
RACHEL'S SECOND QUESTION WAS BETTER.
BREAK MY HEART.
JUST KEEP IN MIND; IF YOU ALWAYS ASK THE QUESTION THAT'S BURNING A HOLE IN YOU, YOU GIVE AWAY A LOT.
YOU'LL NEVER MAKE AN INFO TRADER THAT WAY.
EWW, MR. CRYPTIC. YOU'RE STILL STALLING.
I'M HALF SKIN.
AND ALL BULLSHIT. KEEP IT GOING.
NO, "SKINS" ARE WHAT MY MOTHER'S PEOPLE CALL THEMSELVES WHEN SPEAKING TO PEOPLE LIKE YOURSELF. THEIR SKIN IS BROWN.
MY FATHER WAS PINK SKINNED LIKE YOU CITY MONKEYS. BUT I GREW UP ON THE OUTSIDE.
OH... I THOUGHT YOU WERE FROM HERE.
ANVARD.
ANT FARM, YOU MEAN.

IT'S SUCH A WEIRD PLACE.. I DON'T KNOW HOW TO.... IT'S LIKE THE WAY GASOLINE SMELLS TO ME... MAKES ME HUNGRY AND SICK AT THE SAME TIME. SO I DUNNO....
ANY- HOW.
YOU LOCK UP SKINS; THEY DIE.
SO YOU HAD TO FOLLOW SUIT TO PROVE YOU'RE ONE OF THEM, IS THAT IT?
NOW YOU'RE GETTIN' NASTY.
NO, YOU DIDN'T ANSWER MY QUESTION. WHY DO THEY DIE?
HAVE YOU EVER BEEN LOCKED UP?
YOU KNOW WE HAVE. BY OUR OWN BELOVED BREADWINNER BRIGHAM.
LY-YNNE!
THEN YOU SHOULD NOT HAVE TO ASK THAT QUESTION.
THINK HOW IT WAS.
THEN TELL ME IT WOULDN'T HAVE KILLED YOU.

PRISON.....
WHAT MOST PEOPLE DON'T, OR CAN'T, REALIZE, IS HOW IMPORTANT JUST A LITTLE BIT OF PRIVACY CAN BE.

JUST ONE OF THOSE THINGS YOU DON'T MISS TILL YOU DON'T HAVE IT ANYMORE.

LIKEWISE YOU CAN'T EXPLAIN IT TO ANYONE WHO'S NEVER EXPERIENCED IT. LIKE TRYING TO DESCRIBE SEX TO SOMEBODY'S NEVER HAD IT, OR NEVER HAD IT **GOOD**.

EVEN MOST CONS WOULD NEVER UNDERSTAND WHY I ACTUALLY PREFERRED SOLITARY.

TEN BY EIGHT BY FIVE ROOM, PITCH BLACK, AND IT'S A PUNISHMENT.

WORK YOURSELF INTO ENOUGH OF A FRENZY TO GET THROWN **IN**, AND IT'S EASY TO LET THAT FRENZY JUST KEEP ON ROLLING.

TIME PASSES LIKE NOTHING, DAY AFTER DAY, RICOCHETING OFF WALLS, FLOOR, CEILING, FREE OF GRAVITY, IN TOTAL DARKNESS.

CAN'T TELL DARK FROM LIGHT OR NOISE FROM SILENCE AFTER A WHILE OF THAT.

IT'S BETTER.

GET HUNGRY ENOUGH TO REALIZE THERE'S A WEEK'S WORTH OF FOOD ON THE FLOOR, AND COME DOWN TO GET IT, AND HEAR A STRANGE NOISE; THINK, SOMEBODY'S SCREAMING;

AND THEN,
OH;

THAT'S
ME.

Rules, rules, rules... we were only allowed to move around by night.

Our father told us how **bad** it was on the outside; how people were so desperate they'd kill for anything.

Always talking about how the homeless might come over the neighborhood wall any time, and set the house on fire.

He, himself, was gone all the time. Hunting. Patrolling. Leading "clean-up" missions.

He never told us any details. Said it wouldn't do us any good to be afraid.

But.

He'd take me out on little walks. To get air. He'd get very tense. He'd Talk and talk.

About how he'd seen other people's kids torn apart like fresh bread. How he'd found a living woman with all the skin neatly torn off of her legs down from the knee, her arms down from the elbow, and her face. Said she looked like a red Siamese cat.

He'd talk and talk.

Then he'd pull himself up short, like he was coming out of a trance, and apologize, and he'd hug me close.

Sure, it sounds lame. But I was a kid. I fell for it. Oh, **how** I fell for it.

Then it was back to the house for another day of sitting, reading, in total silence.

Years after, I finally told the others what he'd told me. That's when we all realized he'd pulled the same shit with each of us. Of course.

Except Mom. What he told **her**, she'd never say.

STRIDE
STRIDE
STRIDE
STRIDE
STRIDE
OH, HELL ...

THERE'S NO TALKING TO HIM WHEN HE'S LIKE THIS....
AAAH, LYNNE. WHAT ARE YOU DOING, YOU LITTLE TROLL?

GO ON, MARS. IT'S OKAY.
BUT SIR ...

ONE QUESTION PER CUSTOMER, RIGHT?

HAHAHA
OKAY, OKAY, SURE
HAHAHAH
I CAN PLAY GENIE-INNA-BOTTLE. C'MERE, SWEETS.

NOW, WHAT'S YOUR BURNING QUESTION?
uh... what kind of ... uh...

IS THAT REALLY WHAT YOU WANT TO ASK?
no...
WHAT'S ON YOUR MIND, BABY?

WHERE'S MY DUST BUNNY? HAVE YOU SEEN HIM?
AAWHGH!

IN-FUCKIN'-CREDIBLE. MY MARCIE STILL HAS THIS.

I REMEMBER WHEN I GOT IT FOR HER.
KEPT THE TOYS BUT SOLD THE GOOD SILVER... EMMA, YOU'RE NUTS.

SHE MEANS HER STUFFED TOY. MAMA USED TO JOKE ABOUT KNITTING DUST BUNNIES AND THE NAME SORT OF **STUCK.**
YEAH; IT'S PROBABLY IN A BOX SOMEWHERE, BABY.

OH MARCIE... **WHY** CAN'T YOU JUST SLEEP WITH SOME **OTHER** TOY?
WILL YOU FIND HIM FOR ME?

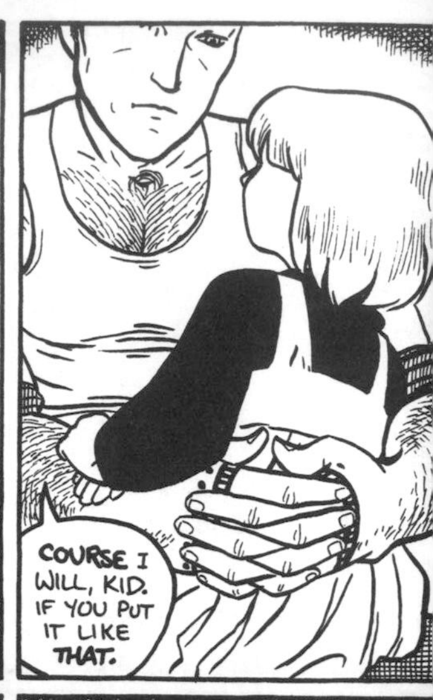
COURSE I WILL, KID. IF YOU PUT IT LIKE **THAT.**

=SIGH=
AND MARCIE'S MEDICAL BILLS. WHAT DID THE INSTALLMENTS TURN OUT TO BE?
ANUZZER SEEX SEEXTY-FIVE PER MONTH, MADAME.
FOR HOW LONG?
FIVE YEARS, MADAME.

=SIGH=

SO, BLYTHE, MY GIRL... NOW THAT I'M FINALLY **IN** MY DREAM HOUSE, NOW THAT ALL THESE UNEXPECTED EXPENSES HAVE POPPED UP.... **HOW** LONG WILL I BE ABLE TO **STAY** HERE?
A-ABOUT SEVEN WEEKS, MADAME.

I.. I'M **SORRY,** SIR...
WELL, **STOP** IT.
IT'S NOT **YOU.**
IT'S **HIM.**
THEY'RE **ALL** LIKE THAT.
THEY ACT LIKE SOMEDAY YOU'LL JUST MAGICALLY KNOW **EVERY-**THING....

EEF ZE STEPFORDS CAN BE PUT OFF ANUZZER WEEK, ZE MONEY OF ZEE BANKHEADS WEEL ~-

WE ARE LEAVING... LEAVING

LEAVING ON THE TIDE, COME AND STAND BESIDE ME, LOVE, THE WATER IS SO WIDE... YOU CAN HEAR THE SAILORS CALLIN' AT THE DAWNING OF THE DAY... YESTERDAY IS FALLING, LOVE, AND JE SUIS DÉSOLÉ...

OH, I **HATE** IT WHEN I GET A TUNE RUNNING THROUGH MY HEAD... MAYBE IF I COULD JUST REMEMBER **ALL** OF IT....

MADAME... EEF YOU PLEASE...

OH ~ I'M **SORRY,** BLYTHE...

OH NO **NO,** MADAME; EET'S JUST ..

'AVE YOU EVER BEEN TOLD ZE STORY OF ZEE CAT IN BOOTS?

PUSS IN BOOTS.

A-CHEM.

ZEES PUSS, SHE EES ZE ONLEE INHERITANCE OF ZE MILLER'S YOUNGES' SON, YES? AN' ZEES YOUNG MAN, 'E S'INKS ZAT 'E WEEL SURELY BE REDUCE' TO BEGGAR'S ESTATE.

YEAH... **AND?**

BOT ZEES CHAT, SHE ASK ONLEE FOR ZEE PAIR OF BOOTS, AN' FOR 'IM SHE ACQUIRE ALL ZAT 'E COULD EVER WEESH FOR.

YES?

SIR?
DON'T CALL ME "SIR."
YES SIR... JAEGER REALLY SAID HE'S PART "SKIN"?
HE MEANS "ASCIAN."
ASS-SEE-AN, OKAY; AND THEY HAVE REAL DARK BROWN SKIN, RIGHT?
BUT HIS SKIN ISN'T DARK, NOT EVEN A LITTLE.

IN FACT, HE'S LIGHTER THAN WE ARE.
HE GETS REALLY DARK IN THE SUMMER. HE USUALLY LIVES OUT IN THE BARRENS THEN, AND OUT THERE, THERE'S NO DOME TO PROTECT YOU.
WEEEIRD... HE ACTUALLY CHANGES COLOR IF HE STAYS IN HERE?
POP

YEAH, WELL.
LOTS OF WEASELS TURN WHITE IN WINTER.
RUB RUB

EMMA..?
sShhh...

HELL, IS SHE IN LA-LA LAND AGAIN?
MMHMM... SHE'S EARLY TODAY.

USUALLY SHE DOESN'T DISAPPEAR TILL EARLY AFTERNOON.

WELL, WHEN YOU GOT NO ROOM TO BREATHE, YOU GO AWAY ANY WAY YOU CAN.

I'D JUST LIKE IT IF SHE'D GO BACK TO NOT DOING IT ON THE WEEK-ENDS. IT'S NOT THAT I REALLY MIND FIXING LUNCH FOR EVERYBODY, BUT I'D REALLY...
SHE ALWAYS LOOKS LIKE SHE'S TRYING TO REMEMBER SOMETHING, DOESN'T SHE?

CHAPTER EIGHT

SKIIIIIIIIIEEEEE

"WELCOME TO THE ANCIENT DOMED CITY OF ANVARD!

"OUR CIVIC WALKING TOUR BEGINS HERE, IN RABBIT TUBE STATION, ENTRY POINT FOR ALL VISITORS!

"THE 'RABBIT WARREN' IS ONLY ONE OF TWELVE, ENCIRCLING THE OUTSKIRTS OF OUR GREAT KRATOPOLIS!"

SO, HEAD **UP** THE GRAND ESCALATOR, TURN RIGHT, FORWARD TEN PACES, CHECK FOR WILD TRAFFIC, DART FORWARD RAPIDLY, STOP IN THE CENTER ISLAND, AND AWAIT FURTHER INSTRUCTIONS...

DOWNING STREET LIMITED BOARDING NOW, WEST PLATFORM.... ALL ABOARD NOW FOR THE DOWNING STREET LIMITED....
BLINK BLINK
SCRITCH

SIGH
FLUMP!

TUG!

BAMBAMBAM
BAM

DOWNING STREET LIMITED NOW DEPARTING... NEXT STOP, MADURO HUB... FORTY MINUTES....
STAND CLEAR

WHOOOPS.

WELL, KID.... I GUESS YOU'RE ALONG FOR THE RIDE, HUH?

<AWWW, BABY... DON'T WORRY!>
<SO, WE'RE IN A STRANGE CITY WHERE WE DON'T SPEAK THE LANGUAGE, THOUSANDS OF MILES FROM HOME, AND WE JUST LOST OUR FOUR-YEAR-OLD SON. SO WHAT? WE'LL GET HIM BACK. YOU KNOW THAT BOY LEADS A CHARMED LIFE.>

THAT'S RIGHT, GOUA. REMEMBER THE TIME HE FELL OUT THAT THIRD-FLOOR WINDOW?>
<YEAH, LANDED RIGHT IN ALL THAT SHAVING CREAM?>
<AND HOW ABOUT THAT TIME WITH THE TARASCAN KING MANTIS AT THE ZOO?>
<BESIDES WHICH, THIS IS ANVARD. IT'S SAID THAT GETTING LOST IS AN INTEGRAL PART OF THE TOTAL PHILOSOPHICAL EXPERIENCE.>
:KHOFF:

SOMETHING IS GONNA HAPPEN.
TODAY.
I KNOW IT BUT I DON'T KNOW WHAT.
I NEVER BACKED OFF FROM ANYTHING IN MY LIFE, BUT I'M TIRED.

DAILY L
WASTE OF PAPE
MORE DEAD PEOPLE
IF ONLY ONE BAD THING WOULD PASS ME BY FOR A CHANGE...

THIS IS THE BACK WAY TO MY FAMILY'S HOUSE.

I'VE BEEN COMING HERE FOR **THREE** DAYS, SNEAKING IN NOT ABLE TO STAY AWAY.

I **STARTED** TO SETTLE INTO A GOOD ROUTINE. STARTED TO FEEL LIKE A PART OF THEM AGAIN, EVEN IF IT'S IN SUCH A SKULKING AND PATHETIC WAY.

STARTED TO FEEL **OKAY** AGAIN, LIKE EVERYTHING **COULD** BE OKAY AGAIN.

LIKE SOMEDAY I COULD JUST WALK IN THAT DOOR AND BE **HOME,** JUST LIKE ORDINARY MEN DO, AND EVERYTHING WOULD BE FINE. LIKE NOTHING EVER WENT WRONG AT ALL.

UP TILL NOW I'VE STAYED HIDDEN FROM THEM. THEY'RE AFRAID OF ME, AND I GUESS THEY'VE GOT THEIR REASONS.

BUT I'M BASICALLY LIVING HERE. EATING, SLEEPING, HIDING. ALERT, WATCHFUL, MAKING SURE THAT THE ONLY CLUES I LEFT TO MY PRESENCE WERE **GOOD** THINGS, LITTLE CHORES.

THOUGHT I'D JUST BEEN REAL SKILLED AND REAL LUCKY. THEY'D NEVER HAD ANY SIGN OF ME.

BUT NOW I REALIZE THAT ***I*** HAVEN'T SEEN ANY SIGN OF ***THEM*** EITHER.

NOT IN **THREE DAYS.**

THREE DAYS AND THEY HAVEN'T COME HOME.

(SOMETHING'S HAPPENED.)

I'M GONNA GO **IN** AND STAY TILL THEY **DO.**

(SOMETHING'S HAPPENED TO MY WIFE AND KIDS AND HERE ***I*** WAS, PLAYING ***HOUSE***)

THREE DAYS I'VE BEEN WALKIN' ON EGGS, SO PROUD OF MYSELF FOR BEIN' SO **SLICK.**

(SOMETHING'S **GONNA** HAPPEN AND I'M PRETTY **SURE** IT'S GONNA BE **ME**)

THIS IS IT.
HIS IS LIKE HEN YOU LIDE THAT TICK UNDER HAT DEAD AT AND LIFT, ND THE CAT ISES UP LIKE CARDBOARD UTOUT, AND OU'VE NEVER BEEN TOLD BOUT RIGOR MORTIS.
IT'S UNPLEASANT, INCOMPREHENSIBLE, AND NOT TOTALLY UNEXPECTED.
COME ON, BRIGHAM!
MONEY BE DAMNED! COME ON, LET'S GO, AND I MEAN NOW! LET'S GO DRIVIN', LET'S GO FISHIN', LET'S GET OUTTA THIS ANTHILL WHERE YOU KNOW YOU CAN'T THINK! WE'LL GET DRUNK TILL WE DON'T KNOW WHAT YEAR IT IS ANY-MORE, JUST COME ON AND WE'LL GO RIGHT NOW!
I CAN'T...
I CAN'T LIVE LIKE YOU, DAY TO DAY, PICKIN' STUFF UP, NEVER SLEEPIN' IN THE SAME PLACE TWICE... I WANT MY KIDS... GOTTA HAVE A HOME...
RIGOR MORTIS.
YOU DON'T KNOW YOU'RE GONNA FIND SOMETHING LIKE THAT WHEN YOU START TURNING OVER DEAD THINGS, BUT YOU GOTTA KNOW IT'S GONNA BE SOMETHING BAD.
K-CLK

OH MIGHTY GOD!
DAA-- DY....
AH AH
AAAAAA...
BAM!

THE HOUSE ITSELF WAS BOTH OLD AND NEW. OLD, IN THAT IT HAD OCCUPIED ITS PLACE ON THE CORNER OF CINCINNATUS AND SEPTIEN STREETS LONG BEFORE EITHER WAS NAMED OR PAVED. NEW, IN THAT EACH YEAR IT BLOSSOMED AND PUT FORTH NEW LEAVES, AND GREW NEW ROOMS. UNTOUCHED BY TRUE SUNLIGHT, RAIN, OR SEASONS, IT NONETHELESS GREW SLOWLY, PLACIDLY, AND INDOMITABLY, TENDING ITS FRENETIC HUMAN RESIDENTS.
IT WAS CALLED, UNACCOUNTABLY, THE GRASS HOUSE.
SOMETHING OLD, SOMETHING NEW, SOMETHING STOLEN, SOMETHING TRUE...
SOMETHIN' FORGOTTEN BY THE MOVING CREW
SOMETHING THAT FELL DOWN THE CHIMNEY FLUE
HOP
MARR-CIE... YOU'RE NOT DOING MAGIC AGAIN, ARE YOU?
OH NO... THIS IS...UM...PLAGIC.
AND THESE AREN'T MAMA'S GOOD PEARLS, EITHER...
<THIS IS BY THEM AN ARCHITECTURAL MASTERPIECE! IT'S GROTESQUE.>
<OH, I DON'T KNOW...>
<=PTCH= CONTRARY MAN.>
nn.. N!
GOOD, 'CAUSE YOU KNOW MOM TOLD YOU NOT TO. REMEMBER WHAT HAPPENED TO THE FRONT DOOR LAST TIME.

VZZZZZZZZZZZ

PATHWAYS, KID...

PEOPLE PAVE STREETS SO THEY CAN'T SEE THE RUTS THEY TRAMP AROUND IN.

COURSE, IT'S **REALLY** MORE LIKE THE RUTS ARE SO DEEP THEY CAN'T SEE **OUT** OF 'EM ANYMORE.

NOW, MAYBE FREEDOM'S **EVERY**BODY'S TREASURED ILLUSION, MINE INCLUDED BUT **I** THINK **MY** BEATEN PATH IS A **LOT** MORE ***FUN.***

OO- WEEE...
WOULDN'T IT BE SO EASY TO PICK ME OFF RIGHT NOW?
SEE, KID? YOUR MOMS IS RIGHT DOWN THERE. WE'LL NEVER BE TOO FAR FROM THEM.
BLAH BLAH BLAH
IF HER MOM'S DOWN THERE, WHAT'S SHE DOING UP HERE?
HEY, SWANN.
HE. HE AND HIS MOM ARE BOTH DOIN' THE SCENIC WALKING TOUR... HE'S JUST DOING THE REALLY SCENIC TOUR.
AH.
WELL, I GUESS IT BEATS SUMMER CAMP. C'MON DOWN, TEA'S ALMOST READY.

HELLO AND WELCOME TO CHECKPOINT SEVEN, LOCATED IN THE COURTYARD OF THE NOBLE HOUSE OF LLAVERAC!
<LLAVERAC..NOW THERE'S AN UN-PRONOUNCEABLE NAME.>
THE COURTYARD AFFORDS A GLORIOUS VIEW OF THE ... CALLED "LAKE OF THE ... IN WHICH MANY OF ... CLANS MAINTAIN THE...
<OH YES; ISN'T THAT THAT CLAN OF ALL WOMEN?>
<ABSURD. HOW CAN THEY BE A CLAN OF ONLY WOMEN~ NO BREEDING STOCK?>
LLAVERAC
MAYBE THEY GIVE AWAY OR DENY MOST OF THE BOY BABIES, LIKE THE LION-WOMEN?
SSSHH-<DON'T TALK ABOUT THEM IN THEIR OWN LANGUAGE. AND ANYWAY THAT'S NOT WHAT THE NYIMA DO.>
ANVARD IS THE ANCESTRAL HOME OF THIS AND TEN OTHER GREAT CLANS. SIXTY-THREE OTHER CLANS MAINTAIN EMBASSIES HERE AND INNUMERABLE CRAFTS AND GUILDS BASE THEMSELVES UNDER ANVARD'S PROTECTIVE DOME.
<WELL, THEY CERTAINLY HAVE GOOD CONFORMATION. THEY LOOK VERY MUCH ALIKE.>
<YOU MEAN "CONFORMITY.">
<PAAH... SURELY THE WHOLE CLAN DOES NOT HAVE SUCH A REMARKABLE UNIFORMITY. THEY SET THEIR BEST EXAMPLES AT THEIR GATES.>
<PUREBRED DOGS DON'T LOOK SO MUCH ALIKE.>
HMF. <TOUR GUIDE DOESN'T TELL YOU THESE LOOK-ALIKE CLANS CONTROL EVERYTHING. THEY ARE THE RULING CLASSES.>
THIS MULTITUDE OF CLANS IS IN PART WHAT GIVES ANVARD ITS COSMOPOLITAN AIR. NOT DOMINATED BY ANY ONE CLAN ANVARD HAS A LOVELY, FULL PALETTE OF FACES AND FORMS.
<EVERY GROUP OF PEOPLE HAS ITS DISTINGUISHING MARKS. THEY'RE JUST, I GUESS, A LITTLE MORE.... STRINGENT!>
<THEY ALL LOOK ALIKE ... YET THEY PRIDE THEMSELVES ON BEING A CITY OF MANY FACES.>
TOURS OF HOUSE LLAVERAC ITSELF MAY BE PURCHASED AT THE GATE HOUSE. FROM HERE WE PROCEED...
LLAVERAC
MEDAWAR
MILO
SYLVAN

WELL, THEN, JAEGER MONSTER... I DON'T SUPPOSE YOU'LL BE NEEDING ANY MORE APARTMENTS CLEANED OUT, EH? TWO IN ONE MONTH...

NAAH, NAW. I'D STAY CLEAR OF THE SECOND ONE- THE RISING ROAD PLACE?- FOR A WHILE.

THE GUY IT WAS SET UP FOR IS IN SORT OF A DELICATE STATE OF MIND.

AT LEAST, HE WILL BE BY NOW...

I
AM NOT
A SIN-EATER.
SIGH
NO MONEY, DAMMIT... NO CHEERING CROWDS, NO "OH MY HERO" AND TEETH-TEETH FOR THE CAMERAS...
RUB RUB
NO NICE OLD LADIES WHO'D KEEP ME IN THEIR BACK BEDROOM AND FEED ME WITH A SPOON IF I WERE TO BREAK MY BACK...
YOU'D THINK SWANN WOULD KNOW THESE THINGS... HIS CLAN'S BOUND BY ALL SORTS OF BLOOD LAWS, RULES... RITUALS... HELL, I CAN'T EVEN TELL 'IM "NO THANKS" WITHOUT LOOKIN' LIKE AN ASSHOLE! YOU JUST DON'T PAY FOR...FOR...
"NO GIFTS!"
-YES SIR-!-
"WRONG, WRONG, WRONG!"
-YES SIR!-
"SO IF SOME POOR WELL-INTENTIONED SAP GIVES YOU OH, SAY, A BEAUTIFUL KHALAKAN WAR CLUB IN PRIME CONDITION WITH NO LESS THAN SIXTEEN POWER POINTS..."
DUCKY SOAP
BOOM!
TWIRL
YOU CAN'T KEEP IT... YOU HAVE TO BURN IT.
SNAP THE SPEAR AND BREAK THE BOW ASUNDER...
CAN'T TAKE PAY, THAT MAKES YOU AN EXECUTIONER... OR WORSE.
IF YOU DO WITHOUT WEAPONS YOU'LL NOT HAVE TO DESTROY THINGS YOU FIND BEAUTIFUL.

GOOD GOD! WHAT IS HE DOING IN THERE?
AAH-- HE'S ALL RIGHT.
ALL RIGHT? SOUNDS LIKE HE'S HAVING A SERIOUS SHIT ATTACK!
LIKELY HE IS. HE DOES, FROM TIME TO TIME. BUT HE ALWAYS MAKES UP FOR WHAT HE BREAKS, AND HE'S GOOD TO HAVE AROUND.

UNMENTIONABL NECESSITY
YAAH! CHECK OUT THE CAVEMAN!!

UNGH! OOOLA COME WITH!
HEE! TOUGH DAY ON THE JOB, BABY?

YYEP-- IT'S S'POSED TO BE A THANKLESS JOB, YOU KNOW.
YOU OUGHTTA STAY HERE, WORK FOR MR. TEMPLE. BE A PROFESSIONAL BEAUTY.

INSTEAD OF JUST SCENERY.
NAAH.
WHY NOT? YOU'RE INVENTIVE ENOUGH.

D' I EVER TELL YOU GUYS I WORKED AS A BOUNCER FOR A HOUSE IN MERECINAË ONCE?
NOO! KID IN A CANDY STORE, HUH?

OH, AT FIRST, SURE. AFTER ABOUT FOUR MONTHS, THOUGH, I SUDDENLY REALIZED I WAS STANDING IN A BALLROOMFUL OF PRITTY YOUNG THINGS, ALL LAUGHING AND HAPPY, MOST OF WHOM WOULD BE GLAD TO BUNDLE UP WITH ME, JUST TO MAKE ME SMILE, SHOW THEIR APPRECIATION... AND ALL I WAS WONDERING WAS IF I'D GET OFF WORK IN TIME TO GO TO MY FAVORITE POTATO JOINT FOR DINNER BEFORE IT CLOSED.

SOO, I CONCLUDED WORKIN' REGULAR DIDN'T AGREE WITH ME, AND SO I QUIT. BEEN SWORN OFF PAYCHECKS EVER SINCE.

WHY DID THAT ONE JOB RUIN YOU FOR ANY JOB?

I GUESS I COULDN'T THINK OF ANYTHING I LIKED WELL ENOUGH TO DO FOR A LIVING THAT I WOULDN'T MIND BEING SICK OF INSIDE O' FOUR MONTHS.
GLOOG
AH. WELL, WORKING AS A BOUNCER ISN'T QUITE THE SAME AS BEING A WORKING ARTIST.
I/I JUST DON'T THINK SO....

NOT ENOUGH AMBITION? IT IS A DEMANDING PROFESSION.
BUT IT'S ONE THAT ONLY TESTS YOU AGAINST YOURSELF. LIKE ANY ART. AND YOU HELP PEOPLE. AND IT'S FUN~ IN THE RIGHT HOUSE.
FLOOM!
Chocolate Addiction

THERE'S GOOD HOUSES AND BAD, O' COURSE ... I HEARD GAIMAN COMPARED IT TO A MUSICAL. SEE, A BAD MUSICAL HAS NO PLOT AND LOUSY SONGS. A MUSICAL CAN SKATE BY ON GOOD SONGS AND NO PLOT, BUT IT CAN'T EVER BE TRULY GREAT UNLESS IT DOES BOTH THINGS WELL, AND THAT'S TOUGH.
IT'S THE SAME THING WITH SEX HOUSES. WITHOUT THE SEX, IT'D JUST BE A HANGOUT, NICE OR NOT; AND WITHOUT OUR ... PAYING ATTENTION, IT WOULD BE .... WELL. A BAD HOUSE.
PEOPLE PAY US MONEY; WE PAY ATTENTION.
CRACKLE
FIZZZZ

YEAH... BUT YOU STILL GET PAID.
OOOH... THAAT'S NICE...
GIMMEE THAT BACK! YOU GONNA SMELL ALL THE FLAVOR OUT OF IT!
FIZZZZ
PECK
FZZZZ~

HE'S A FAKE.
FIZZZZ

HUNH??
I THOUGHT HE WAS, YOU KNOW ~-TRIBAL.
A REAL CAVEMAN. LIVES IN THE WOODS, SHITS ON THE GROUND. PRIMITIVE.

NOW, I'VE
EARD ALL SORTS OF
LK ABOUT HOW WE
OULDN'T GET PAID
FOR OUR ART...
ANDERING AND
ALL THAT...
AND YOU THINK THAT AMOUNTS TO "PRIMITIVE," DO YOU?
COME ON... A CAVE MAN THAT SAYS "WHOM."
...BUT HE MAKES IT SOUND LIKE IT'S MORALLY WRONG TO GET PAID FOR ANYTHING. I MEAN HOW DOES HE FEED HIMSELF??

"WHY IS A FAVOR OKAY, BUT MONEY ISN'T? HE'S NOT, LIKE, A THIEF, IS HE?"
PLAYROOM
HE'S A SWEET ONE, JAEGER. I ALWAYS KNEW YOU HAD TO HAVE ONE STASHED AWAY SOME-WHERE!

YOU TREAT HIS MAMA NICE, OKAY?
PLAYROOM
OH YEAH... WOMEN LOVE TO SEE A GUY WITH A KID. "OOOH. HEEE'D MAKE A GOOD DADDY, SQUEEEL!"

HEY, MILES. WORKIN' FRONT DOOR STILL?
HEY, BROTHER.

YOU TAKING THAT ANKLE BITER ON THE WARPATH WITH YOU?

NNWELL...

NOW, Y'KNOW, MILES... WAY BACK EAST, THERE'S A CLAN CALLED EXEDOR.
AND THEIR BIRTHRATE IS SO HIGH, AND HAS BEEN FOR SO LONG, THAT THEY'VE INNOVATED A MARTIAL ART THAT ACTUALLY WORKS BEST WHEN YOU'VE GOT A KID ON YOUR BACK.
THEY STRAP TEN-POUND BAGS OF FLOUR ON EIGHT-YEAR-OLDS TO TRAIN 'EM.

THIS IS SORTA LIKE HOW YOU KICK SOMETHING TOO HARD TO GET YOUR MIND OFF A BROKEN FINGER, SEE? HE'S SAFE WITH ME.

IF I'D BEEN PAYING **ATTENTION,** HE WOULD NEVER HAVE BEEN SEPARATED FROM HIS **MOTHER** IN THE ***FIRST*** PLACE.

GETTIN' LAZY, GETTIN' DULL; TOO USED TO JUST SAYIN' OKAY AND DOIN' LIKE PEOPLE EXPECT ME TO.

PEOPLE EXPECT A MAN WITH NO JOB, NO FAMILY, NO MONEY TO BE A BUM OR A CRIMINAL, SO THAT'S THE WAY I DRIFT WHEN I'M AROUND PEOPLE.

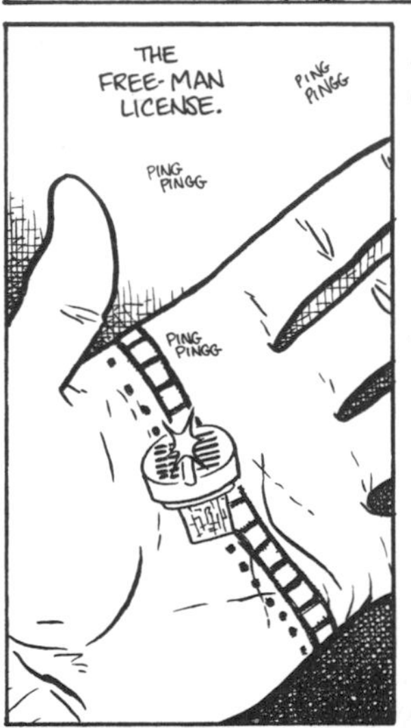

GOT A KID TO LOOK OUT FOR, THOUGH, THAT SHARPENS UP FEAR THE ***FAST*** WAY.
LLAVERAC QUAR

THE FREE-MAN LICENSE.

IT MAKES LIFE **SO** EASY FOR SOME EX-CONS; THEY GET OUTTA JAIL EARLY IF THEY'LL USE ONE OF THESE THINGS. FITS INTO THIS GOD-AWFUL **JACK** IN THE BASE OF THEIR **SKULLS... ≥BRRRR≤!**

IT SCREWS WITH THEIR BRAINS -- ENDORPHINS FOR THE DEPRESSED, SEDATIVES FOR THE SLEEPLESS - **AND** IT TRIGGERS CHEAP, EVER-AVAILABLE HIGHS FOR THE USER THEY'RE KEYED TO. I'M TOLD THEY'LL **REALLY** SCREW UP ANYBODY **ELSE** WHO TRIES TO USE THEM, AND THAT'S A CRIMINAL OFFENSE IN ITSELF.

THEY ALSO HOME **IN** ON THEIR USERS, IF THE USER'S IN RANGE. I THINK THE COPS USE SOMETHING SIMILAR TO CATCH 'EM IF THEY SKIP OUT ON MEETING THEIR PAROLE OFFICERS.

THEY'RE BASICALLY **LEASHES.** SOFT, **COMFORTABLE** LEASHES.

NG PINGG
PING PINGG
PING PINGG
PING PINGG
PING PINGG
PING PINGG PING PINGG
I'M SURE IT GAVE BRIGHAM QUITE A TURN TO FIND HIS GONE.
LEAD ME PRECISELY...

...WHERE I NEED TO BE.
PING PINGG PING PINGG PING PINGG
I'M SORRY, I'M SO SORRY... **SHE** TOOK 'EM AWAY, NOT **YOU... SHE** PUT MY GIRLS IN DANGER, **I** NEVER... IF SHE'D A STAYED PUT **NONE** A THIS **EVER** WOULDA HAPPENED... I'M SO, **SOOO** SORRY... I FORGOT WHERE I WAS... YOU ALL LOOK **ALIKE...**

JAEGER...
OH **GOD**- **DO** SOMETHING --I--

WAY AHEAD OF YA, BUDDY.

nnnh...

<I CAN'T SEE!>

OAHH

SHE'S GOT ONE OF THOSE POLICE-CODE THINGS- NO TELLIN' HOW FAST THEY'RE COMING....

NEET NEET
NO SOUNDS OF TRAFFIC SMASHING UP AS THE COPS MUSCLE THEIR WAY THROUGH --

NEEP NEEP
BUT PROBABLY LITTLE TIME TO DO MORE THAN MAKE A PRAYER FOR HER, BEFORE I GET MY FRIEND OUT OF HARM'S WAY.

IT'S A DELICATE MATTER WHEN ONE OF YOUR OWN GOES SO BAD, SO FAST...

FINALLY. GIRL, IF I WERE YOU, I'D WANT MY MONEY BACK.

AND THAT'S THE DIGITALLY RECORDED SOUND OF LONG TOM, THE FEVER CANNON, WHICH WAS FIRED EVERY DAY AT THIS TIME! IT WAS BELIEVED TO DISSIPATE THE "BAD AIR" WHICH CAUSED SICKNESS...
CHECKPOINT 37
<OMIGOD! LOOK!>

<SEE? I TOLD YOU NOTHING WOULD HAPPEN TO SUNFLOWER.>
<HE'S PROBABLY SEEN MORE OF THIS CITY TODAY THAN WE'D SEE IN A MONTH.>
SNIFF
<AN' DEN~ AN' DEN DE BAD SNICK HURT DE BLUE LADY AN' DERE WAS BLOOD AAALL OVER! AN' DEN DE OWL MAN BEAT UP DE BAD SNICK~>
<THAT'S HIS OLD PAPA'S BLOOD IN HIM. YOU KNOW MY GRANDAD WAS A FINDER.>
<AHH, DAD...>

<IT'S TRUE. ALL THE WORLD IS HIS HOME. HOW CAN SUCH A BOY EVER BE LOST?>
<AN' IT SOUNDED JUST LIKE BREAKIN' CARROTS FOR THE STEW POT!

BLAUE ENGEL WOMEN'S HOSPITAL

QUITE A COLLECTION, MISS MARIANE. IS THAT ONE REAL LEATHER? IT MUST'VE COST YOU A FORTUNE.

MATACORDA MEDAWAR CHARITY HOSPITAL
ADMISSION
FIVE MORE FOR THE JOHN DOE WING.
SIGHH

SIGH
FLOP

AHH, BRIG... WHAT AM I GONNA
WITH YOU? YOU POP, JUST LIKE
PCORN, UNDER THE SLIGHTEST
PRESSURE...

YOU BREAK ALONG THE SAME CRACKS EVERY TIME, NO MATTER HOW YOU'RE GLUED BACK TOGETHER.

CRAZED KILLER SHOOTS WIFE, KIDS, SELF...
YOU BELONG TO ME... IF I CAN'T HAVE YOU NOBODY CAN...
IF YOU REALLY LOVED ME...
POSSESS... ...SHUN...

DAUGHTON... ELEVEN-DOLLAR MURDERER.... KILLED EIGHTEEN WOMEN... ALL RESEMBLED PORTRAIT OF PRIME MINISTER DAUGHTON... ...OF BALDERMERE... PORTRAIT OFF THEIR 11-DOLLAR BILL...

OHGOD NOT ME NOT ME, JAEGER
I CAN'T HELP-- HELP ME GET
FF THIS TRACK 'CAUSE I KNOW
HERE I'M HEADED-- I CAN'T--
NOT MY FAULT--

THAT'S THE BONE MARROW TALKING.
HUH?
WISH I WAS A DRUNK.... AT LEAST THAT WOULD BE.... EXPLAIN THIS... DO SOMETHING ABOUT..

BITS OF BONE MARROW. THEY GET INTO THE BLOODSTREAM. IT HAS THE STRANGEST EFFECTS ON SOME PEOPLE.
CAN'T-- CAN'T TRUST MY INSTINCTS ANYMORE... MONSTER, UNSPEAKABLE....
MAKES 'EM GO DOWNRIGHT CRAZY SOMETIMES. PAY IT NO MIND.

CHAPTER NINE

METAPOLIS
·EMMA·

IT BEGAN AS A GAME... TO EVADE BOREDOM.

WHEN I WAS VERY SMALL I HATED BUSYWORK. I DIDN'T MUCH CARE FOR WORK IN ANY FORM REALLY... BUT I UNDERSTOOD THAT I HAD TO WORK IF I WANTED THINGS TO HAPPEN.

CREATION...
SNORT
EVERYBODY SINGS HOSANNAS TO THE CREATIVE LIFE.

THE ACT OF CREATION IS EALLY THAT SPLIT SECOND NSIDE YOUR OWN MIND, HEN AN IDEA COMES TO OU. IT'S UTTERLY PRIVATE, ERSONAL AND CRYPTIC.

EVERYTHING ELSE IS JUST TRYING TO GET OTHER PEOPLE TO SEE THE TINIEST FRACTION OF WHAT YOU SAW. IT'S ALL SO HAPHAZARD.

SIGH
ANY-WAY...

I'D BE SITTING OVER SOME TASK... BORED BEYOND DEATH WITH THE THOUGHT OF ALL THE WORK I HAD TO DO... WISHING IT WAS JUST DONE SO I COULD TAKE PLEASURE IN BEING FINISHED.
ND SOME-TIMES...
IT WAS ONLY OCCASIONALLY AT FIRST....
I'D JUST BLINK, AND IT WOULD BE DONE.

AND DONE WELL.
AS IF SOMEONE TWICE AS BRIGHT, TWICE AS SKILLED AND CAREFUL HAD DONE IT. SOMEONE WHO NEVER STINTED, SOMEONE WHO ALWAYS WENT BACK AND FIXED THINGS.

SOMEONE WHO HAD CONCENTRATION LIKE A DIAMOND DRILL. WHO COULD HOLD EVERY DETAIL IN HER MIND. CLEAN AND PRECISE AS GOD IN THE FIRST SEVEN DAYS.

'D LOOK AT THE CLOCK AND EE THAT IT HADN'T HAPPENED N AN INSTANT. MY TEACHERS OULD SMILE AND TELL ME HOW NTENSE CONCENTRATION CAN OCK OUT ALL ELSE, EVEN THE SENSE OF TIME.

I SKIPPED EVERY OTHER GRADE IN SCHOOL AND STILL NEEDED PRIVATE TUTORS. I HAD MY MASTER'S DEGREE AT SIXTEEN. MY FATHER HATED ME BECAUSE I OUT-OVERACHIEVED HIM.

AND I HAD NO MEMORIES OF HOW I'D DONE ANY OF IT. I COULDN'T TEACH ANYONE THE SIMPLEST PART OF IT. EVERYONE SAID I WAS TOO INTUITIVE, THAT NOT EVERYBODY HAS THE ABILITY TO EXPLAIN.

HUH
THOSE WHO CAN DO, CAN'T TEACH?

THE GREATEST WORK OF MY LIFE HAS BEEN THE TINY BIT OF GROUND I'VE RE-CAPTURED, OF BEING PRESEN AWARE, ALIVE, WHETHER I'M CREATING ONE OF MY SECRE GARDENS, OR JUST PLODDIN TO THE GROCERY.

BUT RA-CHEL...
KID, IF YOU NEVER REMEMBER YOUR DREAMS, YOU LOSE OUT ON HALF YOUR LIFE.
MORE LIKE A THIRD, ISN'T IT? RDA FOR SLEEP IS FOUR OUT OF EVERY TWELVE HOURS.
I'M NOT TALKING ABOUT TIME. IF YOU'RE A SLEEP AMNESIAC, YOU'RE JUST LIKE A COMA VICTIM WHO NEVER WAKES UP IN THIS WORLD.
MY LIFE IS WEIRD AND CONFUSING ENOUGH WHEN I'M AWAKE, THANK YOU. I DON'T NEED TO REMEMBER CRAZY JUNK LIKE BEING CHASED BY BLAZING HOOP SNAKES. AND I SURE DON'T CARE WHAT THEY MEAN.
HM.
IT ONLY BOTHERS ME WHEN I'M TOO PREOCCUPIED TO TELL WHETHER I'M AWAKE OR ASLEEP. I DON'T EVER SLEEP MORE'N A FEW HOURS AT A TIME, SORTA SPREAD OUT OVER THE COURSE OF THE DAY.
BOTH SIDES HAVE DEFINITE RULES AND AGENDAS, AND CROSSING BACK AND FORTH KINDA MESSES ME UP IF I'M NOT AWARE I'M DOING IT.
AND WHAT'S GOT YOU SO PREOCCUPIED RIGHT NOW?
DINNER.
THAT ALL?
THAT'S PLENTY. WHERE I GREW UP, NO WOMAN'D BOTHER WITH A MAN WHO COULDN'T COOK AT LEAST ONE THING REALLY WELL.
IT'S A COURTSHIP THING.
RRILLY.
YOU CAN HAVE SOME TOO. AFTER YOUR MOM AND I GET DONE.
IF YOU WANT.
GOT DEM JAIL BAIT BLUES.... DA NA NA NA NAH...

THE STREETS OF ANVARD...
THE DOME OVERHEAD...
YOU'VE GOT A LONG WAY TO GO, BABY.
TEATRO del HY-BRASIL
NEWS SPORTS STYLE OP-ED
CAFE BANADINO
CHECKPOINT 338... CHE

STAND BY
TEATRO del HY-BRASIL
NEWS SPORTS STYLE OP-ED
CKPOINT 338... CHECKPOI

CARNIVAL!
338... CHECKPOINT 338
KCHINGG!

AH YES, FOLKS, THAT WAS THE FIRST BLINK!
THAT MEANS CARNIVAL SEASON'S OFFICIALLY BEGUN!
AWW, SWEET-HEART! IT WASN'T EVEN AS DARK AS YOUR BEDROOM WHEN WE TURN OUT THE LIGHTS, AND LOOK! IT'S LIGHT AGAIN!
HUP
COME ON, HONEY, THIS IS SUPPOSED TO BE A HAPPY TIME!
TRUE, IT WASN'T SUPPOSED TO HAPPEN FOR WEEKS NOW...
BUT SCIENCE AIN'T EXACTLY AN EXACT SCIENCE WHEN YOU'RE DEALING WITH LOST TECHNOLOGY!

SEE, MARCIE? IT'S ONLY SNOW.
GATHER ROUND, KIDDIES, VISITORS, AND ALL THOSE SORELY LACKING IN LONG-TERM MEMORY!
AIR HANDLERS MUST BE OFF AGAIN. USUALLY THERE'S TOO MUCH OF A BREEZE GOING OUT FOR ANYTHING MUCH TO GET IN.
FIRST, LET'S TAKE A MOMENT TO CONTEMPLATE THE GODDESS IVITYE, PERSONIFICATIO OF THE SHELTERING SKY
MAÎTRESSE IVITYE
NOW - OUR DOME, WHICH PROTECTS US FROM HARD RADIATION AND THE WHIMS OF THE WEATHER, IS NOT ACTUALLY TRANSPARENT!
IT ABSORBS RADIANT ENERGY FROM THE SUN, TRANSMITTING TO THE INTERIOR ONLY THOSE WAVELENGTHS USEFUL TO THE INHABITANTS!
~ IN THEORY ~
OOOPS!
CRASH!
WELL, ANYWAY, VISIBLE LIGHT, A LITTLE ULTRAVIOLET, AND A FEW ODD BALL THINGS WE AIN'T GOT A CLUE ABOUT!
THAT'S HOW IT SHINES EVENLY AND PERPETUALLY OVER THE CITY, REGARDLESS OF THE SUN'S POSITION IN THE SKY!
BUT, WHEN IT'S WINTER OUTSIDE, THE SUN'S RAYS ARE TOO STEEPLY ANGLED FOR THE DOME TO CAPTURE ENOUGH ENERGY TO KEEP THE LIGHT ON! IT'S AS IF OUR DOME GOES TO SLEEP!
(COURSE, OTHER DOMES DON'T SEEM TO DO THIS -- BUT ANYWAY -)
Z
THE FIRST BLACKOUT IS CALLED THE FIRST BLINK!
MAÎTRESSE IVITYE
THE BLACKOUTS WILL GET LONGER AND CLOSER TOGETHER UNTIL WE HAVE TOTAL DARKNESS FOR SEVERAL WEEKS! THEN THE LIGHTS WILL BLINK BACK ON, AND THE PROCESS WILL REVERSE ITSELF UNTIL WE'RE BACK TO TWENTY-FOUR-HOUR LIGHT AGAIN

BUT TILL THEN, WE'RE GONNA PARTY HARD AND KEEP WARM, RIGHT?
COME to ANVARD
SEASONAL IMMIGRATION
TIME TO THROW ON YOUR BEST DUDS, EAT TOO MUCH, AND DANCE TILL OUR ANKLES CRACK! CAR-NI-VAL!
CAR- NI- VAL!
CAR-

MAA-MA! WE'RE HO-OME!
SHE MUSTA GONE OUT, KID, NOBODY HERE BUT LYNNE.

NOW, JAEGER, HOW DO YOU KNOW? YOU JUST GOT HERE TOO!
-- GOOD NUTRITION HAS GIVEN THE CURRENT GENERATION SEVERAL INCHES IN HEIGHT OVER THEIR PARENTS -

LOCK. NO OVER-RIDE.
FREEP!
HE EFFECTS N THEIR HILDREN AVE SO AR SHOWN HEM-ELVES --

-- GREATER BIRTH WEIGHT AND ACCELERATED SEXUAL MATURITY. GIRLS ARE ENTERING PUBERTY AT A MEAN AGE OF TEN YEARS OLD, A FULL THREE YEARS EARLIER THAN THEIR MOTHERS --

AYS ANNA NEWTON OF OCK CREEK PARKWAY, "WHY, HAD TO PUT A BRA ON MY HIRD GRADER, AND NOT TRAINING BRA, EITHER!" OYS NATURALLY TRAIL EHIND GIRLS BY A EW YEARS, BUT THEY TOO ~
CLAK!

FUCKING TRAITORS.
THEY HAD NO BUSINESS GETTING MARRIED.

HMPH.
POKE
PROD
GRIND
GOOD NUTRITION'S THE PROBLEM, IS IT?
PERMISSION TO LIVE ON BIRCH BEER AND DING DONGS IF I EVER HEARD IT.
THEY SAY THAT WHEN EVERYTHING IN YOUR LIFE IS TOO COMPLICATED, IT'S BECAUSE YOU WON'T FACE UP TO ONE BIG THING THAT'S VERY SIMPLE.
OR IS IT THAT ANY TOO-SIMPLE ANSWER SOUNDS LIKE GREAT WISDOM? NOTHING'S EASY.
WHINY RACHEL. ANYTHING'S EASY IF YOU LET IT.
HAH! EASY TO SAY, THAT'S ALL.
WHAT HAVE I GOT? A SWEET MOTHER - WHE SHE'S NOT ON MARS OR WHEREVER THE HELL SHE GOES. A FATHER IN PRISON AND I HOPE HE STAYS THERE. AN EQUALLY PSYCHO LITTLE BROTHER WHO'S BEEN RAISED AS A GIRL. A VERY POPULAR GIRLFRIEND I'M NOT IN THE LEAST ATTRACTED TO ~~
OH, YEAH? WHY AREN'T YOU ATTRACTED TO HER?
EH. TOO GIRLY, I GUESS.
AHA. YOU'RE LOOKING FOR SOMEONE A BIT MORE MASCULINE, THEN.

LAVERACS AREN'T ALL WOMEN. THEY'D JUST PREFER YOU TO THINK SO. THEY ALL HAVE WOMEN'S NAMES, CALL EACH OTHER "SHE" AND "GIRL".... BUT THE GUYS ARE STILL GUYS, EVEN IF THEY DO HAVE TITS. HECK, MY GIRLFRIEND IS A GUY, AND SHE'S STILL TOO GIRLY FOR MY TASTE. HAW!

Y'WANNA KNOW HOW TO REALLY BURN UP A LLAVERAC? CALL 'ER BY GUY'S NAMES. ASK 'ER "HOW'S IT HANGIN'?"

HO BOY, AND JUMP BACK!

HUH.

WELL, YOU KNOW I'M A GRAVES, OUR FAMILY'S PART OF LABRES CLAN. WITH US, THERE ISN'T MUCH MIXING BETWEEN GENDERS. GUYS MARRY GUYS, WOMEN MARRY WOMEN. I THOUGHT YOU WERE LIKE US.

THERE AREN'T VERY MANY OF US HERE.

AND YOU'RE CUTE.

HELL, HAVING TO KILL FOR A PIECE OF LAND SOUNDED PRETTY DAMN EASY COMPARED TO WHAT I HAD TO DO TO GET HOLD OF IT HERE...

ROYAL MEDAWAR 203RD PEACE KEEPERS
FOOD, WATER, SEED, MEDICINE ...
DRUGS, DISEASE, SERFDOM, "CLEANSING"..
T'SARSKO
TOWNSHIP
5 MILES
ALL ENTER
SUBJECT
SEARCH
HURRAH.
GRUNT
OH GOD... MORE OF THEM.
YOU SURE?
YEP.
SK!!!...
"ONLY THREE RANOS. THREE OFFICERS AND THEIR WIVES. AND ONLY ONE TRANSPORT TRUCK..."
AND ONLY ABOUT TWENTY MUTT SOLDIERS.
'TAIN'T A REGULAR THING, THEN. ONE A THOSE OFFICERS IS IN DISGRACE. BAD MARRIAGE, LIKELY.
HEY! WE'RE THERE NOW, RIGHT?
RACHEL, MY LOVE... IF YOU ASK ME THAT ONE MORE TIME, YOU'RE STEW MEAT, OKAY?

I BARELY REMEMBER TRAVELING THERE. IT'S AS IF PUBERTY BRINGS ON AMNESIA.
IF I'D KNOWN HOW LITTLE OF IT I WAS TO BE ALLOWED TO SEE, I'D'VE PAID CLOSER ATTENTION.
I REMEMBER MILES OF DUSTY ROADS. BARBED WIRE UNDER BLUEBELLS.
GREEN FIELDS.
ARMED GUARDS.
(JAEGER WAS ONE. HE CAME AND WENT AS HE PLEASED... NATURALLY.)
TREES, HILLS, MOUNTAINS... BIRDS IN THE SKY. ALL GROWING WILD.
DIDN'T SEEM REAL.
NOTHING OVERHEAD. I FELT LIKE A BUG ON A PLATE. IT BURNED ME TO THINK HOW GLAD I'D BEEN TO BE UNDER A ROOF AFTER ALL THAT SKY.
BIG, DARK HOUSE... THAT I REMEMBER EVERY INCH OF.
THAT I STILL GO BACK TO. IN DREAMS.
REALLY BAD DREAMS.

I NEVER KNEW THAT ONCE WE WENT IN, WE WOULDN'T EVER BE COMING OUT. NOT WITHOUT PERMISSION, ANYWAY.
"BUT BAY-BEE, THERE'S NO DOME OUT THERE. THINK OF ALL THE DISEASes THAT THAT UNFILTERED SUN CAN GIVE YOU"...
SNORT

BRIGHAM, FOR PITY'S SAKE, I HAVE NOTHING AGAINST-- AGAINST MEN! I MARRIED ONE, DIDN'T I? AND I HAVE EVERY REASON TO BELIEVE MY FATHER IS ONE! IT'S JUST NOT A FIT SUBJECT TO DISCUSS IN FRONT OF CHILDREN!
YOU RAISE THE GIRL, EMMA, FINE! BUT YOU DON'T HAVE A CLUE HOW TO RAISE A BOY! NOT THE FIRST GODDAMN CLUE!
WHAT DIFFERENCE CAN THAT POSSIBLY MAKE AT THEIR AGE?
TALK SENSE, MAN!

WAIT FOR IT...
NONE OF THE OTHER KIDS WOULD HAVE MUCH TO DO WITH LYNNE OR ME SINCE OUR MOTHER WAS NOT A MEDAWAR.
OUR FAVORITE GAME WAS MAKING UP BETTER WAYS TO MAKE 'EM ALL DIE SCREAMING.

DID I SAY WE NEVER GOT OUT OF THE HOUSE?
WAKE UP, RAE. SSSHHH.
nnuh...

I THINK JAEGER WASN'T WELL LIKED EITHER. HE WAS SORT OF A PET OF OUR DAD'S.
MAMA SAID IT WAS EITHER ADOPT HIM OR SHOOT HIM....

LOOK, KID.
RRRRMMMBBBRLLLL
IT'S A THUNDER-SNOW.
SEEMED LIKE EVERY-BODY HATED JAEGER FOR A DIFFERENT REASON. I GUESS THAT'S WHY WE LOVED HIM SO MUCH.

RARE THING, Y'KNOW.
MEDAWAR EYES ARE DARK BROWN; TOO DARK TO SEE THE IRISES OPEN AND CLOSE. EVERYBODY I KNEW HAD VERY DARK EYES.
HIS EYES WERE STRANGE. SHINY.
CCCC
SSHAC

IT WAS HARD TO BELIEVE HE SAW THE SAME THINGS I SAW WITH THOSE SPOOKY METAL-SHINY EYES.

HEY, KIDS!
BYELO CLUTCH HATCHING RIGHT NOW! WHO WANTS TO WATCH? FIRST TEN OUT THE DOOR, HUP HUP!
YAIP!

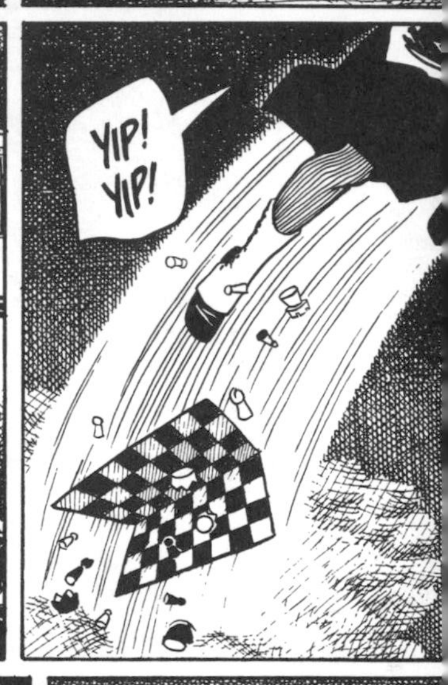
YIP! YIP!

EIGHT-- NINE--
THUMPATHUMPATHU

--TEN! OKAY, YOU BUMS, LET'S MOVE IT--
BUT CAPTAIN NELSON--

NO GIRLS!

…E BASTARD. AND …E'D ALWAYS …EEN SO NICE …O ME UP TILL THEN.
OR SO I THOUGHT.

HE'D ALWAYS SAID SOMETHING LIKE, "OH, HONEY, THERE'S ONLY SO MUCH ROOM" OR "OH, SORRY, WE LEFT SO EARLY, I MUSTA FORGOT TO WAKE YOU UP"…
…EXCUSES.

…AT TIME, THE TIME HE DIDN'T …THER, WAS A REVELATION. I …ELT THE WALLS OF A PINK TAFFETA …SON SNEAKING UP BEHIND ME.

OH. HEY.
YOU DIDN'T HAVE TO STAY BEHIND.

BUT YOU KNOW I'M KINDA GLAD YOU DID…

CLOCK!

OHH--
NOT AGAIN.
FIGHT
FIGHT!
FIGHT
BRIGHAM! COME PULL YOUR BRATS APART AGAIN!
FIGHT
WAAAAAA

I'M GETTING TO IT, I'M GETTING TO IT... THE WORST PART...
I— THIS IS WHERE IT-- STARTS TO GET HAZY. BUT...
SEE, EVERY TIME SOMETHING LIKE THAT WOULD HAPPEN, WE'D GET THE SAME LECTURE.

IF SOMEONE DOESN'T **ACCEPT** YOU, FOR **WHATEVER** REASON **FUCK** 'EM! DON'T **TRAIL AFTER** 'EM LIKE A **CHICKEN!** IT DOESN'T **GET** YOU ANYTHING!
YOU GUYS **CAN'T** JUST BE **AS** GOOD AS EVERYBODY ELSE, YOU GOTT GO **TWICE** AS FA BUT YOU **GOT** TO HAVE YOUR PRI

I WON'T **HAVE** THEM SNEERING AT **MY** KIDS. SINCE YOU HAVEN'T GOT ANY MORE SELF-CONTROL THAN TO FIGHT LIKE CATS AND DOGS, YOU CAN JUST STAY OUT OF THE GREAT HALL FROM HERE ON IN.

EVERY TIME, HE'D USE IT AS AN EXCUSE TO CUT US OFF A LITTLE MORE. BY SPRING OF THAT YEAR, WE WERE FORBIDDEN TO SEE **ANY**BODY. JAEGER MADE SNEAKING AROUND INTO A SORT OF GAME.

WE! CARRY! DEATH! OUT! OF THE VILLAGE!
WE! CARRY! DEATH! OUT! OF THE VILLAGE!
WE! CARRY! DEATH! OUT! OF THE VILLAGE!
JUST DON'T **UNDERSTAND** ...
I COULD EXPLAIN IT YOU, RAE, BU YOU WOULD LIKE ME IF I DID.

THAT WINTER JAEGER WAS **"DISCHARGED,"** SENT HOME. OR SO DAD **SAID.**

FOR FOOT SOLDIERS, THAT WAS USUALLY A EUPHEMISM FOR **"DEAD."**

AND DAD MOVED US OUT OF THE GREAT HOUSE ENTIRELY, THIS **TINY** LITTLE PLACE, ALL SEPARATE AND EXPOSED. DIDN'T EVEN LIVE IN **IT**, JUST ITS BASEMENT. **HE** SAID WAS BECAUSE HE COULDN'T TRUST THE OTHER MEDAWA ANYMORE. I WAS CHOKING ON MY OWN SHAME.
...HE WAS **SO PROUD** OF HIS LITTLE DECOY HOUSE

E ROOM. A
OMPOSTING
OILET. A
NK OF WATER.
WE COULD HEAR THE FIGHTING THERE, THROUGH THE FLIMSY WALLS. GUNS, SCREAMS. WHEN YOU'RE A KID YOU DON'T REALLY **ASK** WHAT'S GOING ON. YOU **KNOW** IT ISN'T GOING TO MAKE SENSE, NO MATTER WHAT THEY SAY.
NCE WE HEARD SOME-
ODY BREAKING ALL THE
NDOWS UPSTAIRS,
WLING AND DANCING.
RHYTHMIC POUNDING ON THE UPSTAIRS WALLS AT NIGHT. LOCKED DOORKNOB CLICKING... SHADOWS.

MOM HAD MARCIE. "MARCELLA" MEANS "CHILD OF WAR." MEDAWAR NAME.
MOM TALKED LIKE A TV KIDS'-SHOW HOST NOW--HIGH AND FAKE SOUNDING. SHE FED MARCIE A LOT OF PAREGORIC SO SHE WOULDN'T MAKE ANY NOISE. THEY BOTH SLEPT MOST OF THE TIME.
OH IVITYE... GUARDIAN OF LIGHT AND DARKNESS... SHIELD MAIDEN OF DREAMING AND WAKING...

AVING NO ROOM TO MOVE
ROUND MAKES YOU A LITTLE
RAZY... THEN A **LOT** CRAZY.
DAD STARTED WRAPPING US UP IN WET SHEETS DURING THE DAY. **ALL** DAY. ME AND LYNNE. TO KEEP US **STILL.**
I LEARNED TO SCREAM SILENTLY.
WE WERE **HIDING**. THERE WAS **DANGER** OUTSIDE.

ONE DAY I WATCHED MOM TRY TO SCRUB A SPOT OF SUNLIGHT OFF THE FLOOR. DIDN'T SEEM STRANGE TO ME AT THE TIME.

E-- DAD WAS GONE MOST OF
HE TIME. ONE NIGHT IN
UMMER SOMEBODY SET
HE HOUSE UPSTAIRS ON FIRE.
I-- I **THINK** IT WAS **MOM**-- UNTIED US AND TOOK US UPSTAIRS WHEN THE FIRE WENT OUT.

EVERYTHING WAS **GONE**.
THE GREAT HOUSE, THE FIELDS, THE STABLES -- ALL BURNED. THE PLACE WAS A GHOST TOWN.
I REMEMBER MAMA SAYING "THEY'VE BEEN GONE FOR A **LONG** TIME. **HE** DID IT **ALL**."
DIDN'T SEEM STRANGE.

≡SNIFFF≡
I-I'M GONNA GO...
I DON'T WANNA TALK ABOUT THIS STUFF ANY-MORE... I'LL JUST HAVE TO WAIT TILL JAEGER FEELS LIKE TELLING ME HIS REAL WHOLE NAME.
HEY! LISTEN UP! I DON'T WANT YOUR ANSWER ANY-MORE... LET ME OUT!
YOUR QUESTION IS ASKED, THE DEAL HALF-STRUCK. THERE IS NO OUT.
BUT — BUT I CAN'T REMEMBER ANY MORE! YOU WANT THE WORST THING THAT EVER HAPPENE TO ME, WELL, YOU'VE GOT AS MUCH OF IT AS I HAVE! BUT I TELLYA I DON'T HAVE A "GREATEST FEAR" TO TELL YOU ABOUT! I — I MEAN I DON'T WANT TO DIE OR GET RAPED OR GET PARALYZED FROM THE NECK DOWN AND I'M NOT WILD ABOUT THE IDE OF GETTING OLD, BUT WHO IS? I DON'T HAVE ONE BIG OVERWHELMING FEAR! I CAN'T PAY YOU! LEMME OUT!
AH... BUT KNOWLEDGE GROWS IN GOOD SOIL. PAY NOT MY PRICE AND YOU WILL... INTROSPECT.
HERE IN THE DARKNESS.
INSIGHT WILL COME.
IN TIME.

CHAPTER TEN

•RESUME REC.•
IT'S A FUNNY THING, PERCEPTION...
I KNOW PERFECTLY WELL THAT ANYBODY CAN BE LOOKING RIGHT AT WHAT THEY'RE LOOKING FOR--
•MARGIN NOTE•
-MAKE THAT "SEARCHING FOR"?-
-"OBJECT OF THEIR SEARCH"?-
•RESUME•
--AND NOT SEE IT-- BUT I NEVER GOT SO MANY TANTALIZING HALF GLIMPSES AT THE OBJECT OF MY--
-QUEST-?
TOO MELO-DRAMATIC.
15 MINUTES
WHILE I CAN'T HONESTLY SAY ALL THESE POLYGLOT OUT-CLANNERS LOOK ALIKE, THEY EACH LOOK SO DIFFERENT THAT THE EYE REDUCES THEM TO VISUAL NOISE.
I HAVE THIS OBSCURE CONVICTION THAT I'LL KNOW HIM IF I CAN SEE HIS EYES. WHY, I DON'T KNOW, AS I HAVE NO CLEAR IMAGE OF HIS EYES ON EXISTING FOOTAGE.
YOU'RE NOT HALF-BAD, YOU KNOW.
IF YOU DIDN'T STOP TO TALK TO YOURSELF SO MUCH, YOU'D LIKELY FIND YOU HAVE QUITE A KNACK FOR TRACKING.
KNACK FOR TRACKING. KNACK FOR TRACKING. YEAH, THAT ROLLS OFF THE TONGUE.

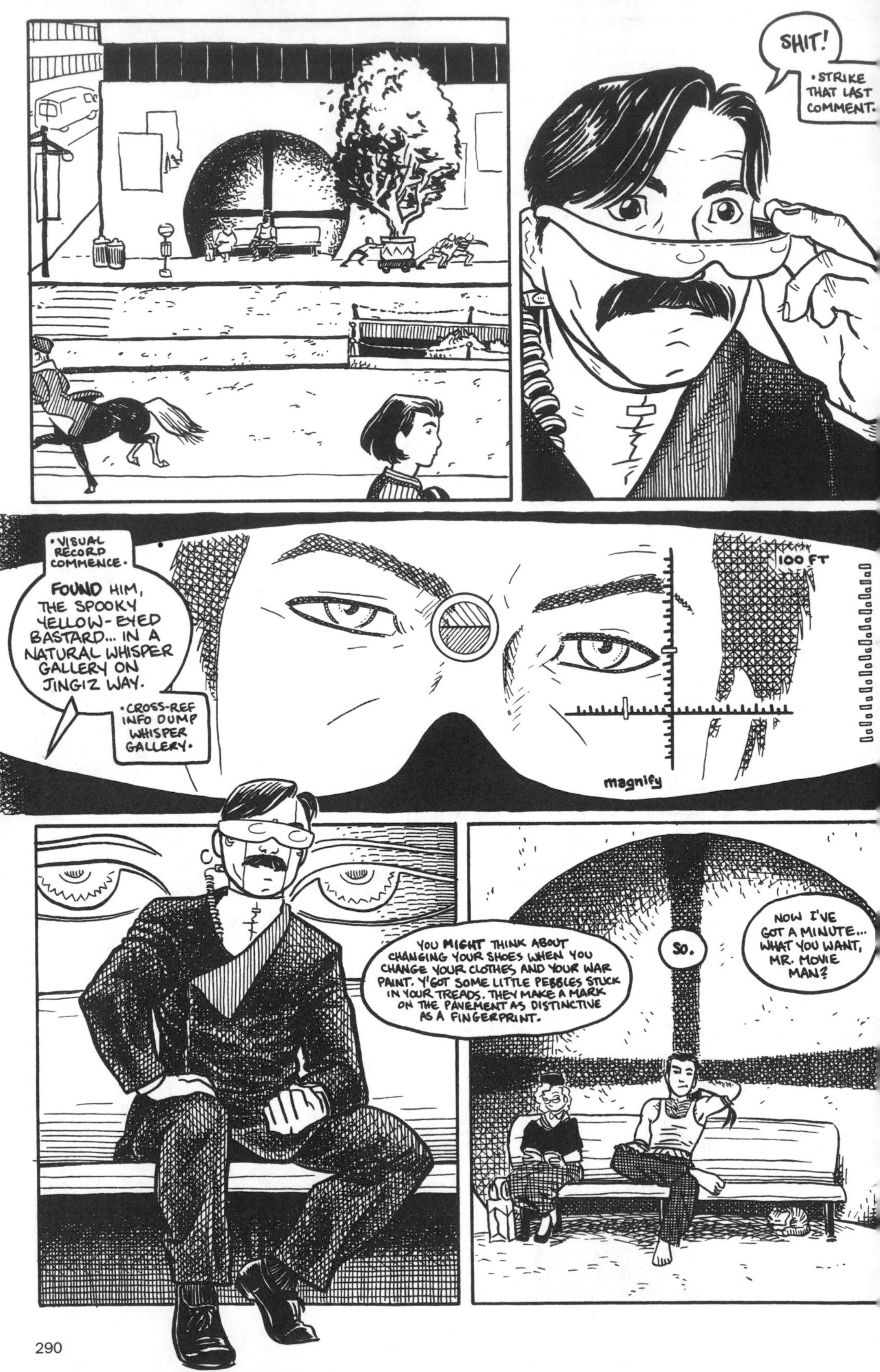
SHIT!
•STRIKE THAT LAST COMMENT.
•VISUAL RECORD COMMENCE•
FOUND HIM, THE SPOOKY YELLOW-EYED BASTARD... IN A NATURAL WHISPER GALLERY ON JINGIZ WAY.
•CROSS-REF INFO DUMP WHISPER GALLERY•
100 FT
magnify
YOU MIGHT THINK ABOUT CHANGING YOUR SHOES WHEN YOU CHANGE YOUR CLOTHES AND YOUR WAR PAINT. Y'GOT SOME LITTLE PEBBLES STUCK IN YOUR TREADS. THEY MAKE A MARK ON THE PAVEMENT AS DISTINCTIVE AS A FINGERPRINT.
SO.
NOW I'VE GOT A MINUTE... WHAT YOU WANT, MR. MOVIE MAN?

LIF
YOU
YOUR NE
REAL LIF
MOVIES
I REPRESENT SOMEONE YOU CAN HELP, MR. FINDER.

ISN'T THAT WHAT YOU DO? YOU SERVE YOUR PEOPLE. WHY AREN'T YOU WITH YOUR PEOPLE? WHO DO YOU SERVE OUT HERE?

I DON'T KNOW WHERE EVERYBODY GETS THESE HALF-BRIGHT IDEAS ABOUT WHAT A FINDER IS AND DOES. A FINDER IS A SCOUT. WE BREAK TRAIL. WE EXPLORE AND OBSERVE. AND THAT'S ALL.
AND AS FOR WHAT I'M DOIN' HERE, --SINCE YOU ASK ME SO NICE-- MY WIFE--

YOU JUST PICK SOMEBODY, IS THAT IT? SOMEBODY NEEDS HELP AND YOU SAIL RIGHT IN. MAN OF CHIVALRY, NINJA DO-GOODER. ISN'T THAT HOW IT IS?
•ETYM: JAEGER, SOFT J, ACCENT FIRST SYLLABLE. CHASER, HUNTER.•

WELL, I'M HERE TO SAY THERE'S SOMETHING YOU CAN DO. THERE'S A TIME WHEN IT TAKES A GUY LIKE YOU TO FIX A PROBLEM.

AND WHAT KIND OF GUY AM I, ACCORDING TO HOYLE?
AN OUTSIDER.
•CROSS-REF HOYLE: GAME RULE BOOK.•

A THROWAWAY, YOU MEAN. LISTEN, PAL, YOU AIN'T EXACTLY RACKIN' UP BROWNIE POINTS HERE--
WELL, MY HEART'S NOT REALLY IN IT, Y'SEE. I BELIEVE BUDDING MURDERERS OUGHT TO BE LEFT ALONE TO MATURE HOWSO EVER THEY WILL.
• SLOW ZOOM ENHANCE.
WHO EXACTLY ARE YOU THINKING THIS PIECE OF TRASH WILL KILL FOR YOU?

DOESN'T HAVE TO BE "KILL." AS LONG AS IT'S "NEUTRALIZE"... "RENDER HARMLESS"... WE LEAVE THAT TO YOUR DISCRETION.

YOU'RE STILL SITTIN' THERE WITH YOUR BARE FACE HANGIN' OUT ASKIN' ME TO--

•MONTAGE: ANIMALS WITH YELLOW EYES. CATS. GOATS. OWLS. EPHANTS. DINETRIA.•

GRACKLES.

•AND GRACKLES.•

YOU KNOW PERFECTLY WELL WHO IT IS, OR YOU'RE NOT THE MAN I'M LOOKING FOR.

IT'S BRIGHAM GROSVENOR.

HIS OWN FAMILY.

WELL, THAT'S FINE...

THAT'S A CHEAP TRICK.

WELL, YOU KNOW NO ADULT KILLER HAS EVER BEEN SUCCESSFULLY REFORMED. THERE WAS THAT PROMISING NEW THERAPY, WHERE FEEDBACK THROUGH CRANIAL JACKS WAS USED TO INSTILL IN THE SUBJECT A TRUE UNDER-STANDING OF THE HEINOUS-NESS OF THEIR ACTS....
THE HORROR OF IT ALL, YOU KNOW?
GRAULS

BUT, FUNNY, ALL THE TEST SUBJECTS KILLED THEMSELVES.
SO THERE'S NO CURE, REALLY. DON'T YOU GUYS HAVE A TERM FOR THIS KIND OF THING? TOUCHED BY THE WENDIGO OR SOME SUCH THING?

I KNOW THIS ISN'T SUPPOSED TO BE YOUR DECISION. THE POWERS THAT BE DECIDE, AND THEN GUYS LIKE YOU TAKE CARE OF IT, RIGHT? EXECUTE THEIR ORDERS?

WELL, I'M A REPRESENTATIVE OF THE POWERS THAT BE IN MEDA-WAR CLAN. THIS GUY HAS GONE BAD. IF A DOG GOES RABID YOU WANNA SHOOT IT BEFORE IT STARTS TO RUN. WE NEED A SHARPSHOOTER.
WE WOULDN'T BE UNGRATEFUL.

WHAT YOU NEED'S A SIN-EATER. I DON'T DO THAT CRAP ANYMORE.
·CROSS-REF SCAPEGOAT·

NO, NO, FAR FROM IT. I WOULDN'T DREAM OF OFFERING YOU MONEY. BUT I CAN FIX IT SO ALL'S FORGIVEN. ALL OBLIGATIONS VOID.
I DON'T OWE YOU JACK CRAP--
NO? YOU DO OWE THE FAMILY OF LES SOFFIT.

...AND HE IS...?

THE MAN YOU HURLED OUT OF A SIXTH-STORY WINDOW A WHILE BACK. AND HIS TWO OUTCLAN FRIENDS, SINCE WE'RE COUNTING. THE LATE MARKET WARDEN'S WIFE WANTS RESTITUTION.

IT WAS A FAIR FIGHT.
IF I STOPPED TO FIND OUT WHY ANY PARTICULAR FOOL BROKE A BOTTLE OVER MY HEAD, I'D A BEEN DEAD IN GRADE SCHOOL. IF THERE'S ONE, THERE'S A HUNDRED AND ONE. AS FOR HIS WIDOW--
OH, MORE THAN THAT. MEDAWARS NUMBER IN THE HUNDREDS OF THOUSANDS.

YOUNG, EAGER TO CURRY FAVOR... IF YOU DON'T DEAL WITH THIS NOW, SOMEDAY SOME PRETTY THING WITH LONG BRAIDS IS GONNA PUT A TENT PEG THROUGH YOUR HEAD--

HAHAHAHAHAHAA MAYBE I WANT THAT! MAYBE THAT'S WHAT I NEED TO ADD POIGNANCY TO MY HUMDRUM LIFE, HUH? YA THINK?

DON'T YOU SAVAGE MY FAITH. JUST DON'T YOU DO IT. THE MODERN WORLD NEEDED A NEW CONCEPT OF BLOOD SACRIFICE. WE AT THE CHURCH OF HUITZILOPOCHTLI UNDERSTAND THAT.
nngh
MOVIES, MY ABORIGINAL FRIEND, HAVE ALWAYS BEEN RECOGNIZED AS THE COLLECTIVE DREAMS OF SOCIETY. FILMMAKERS REFLECT WHAT'S IN THE MASS MIND- IF IT'S TAWDRY AND SHAMEFUL, THEN THAT'S THE SAD TRUTH, BUT PEOPLE NEED THAT RELEASE--
BLOOD AND GUTS ON THE SCREEN DON'T CREATE VIOLENCE, THEY ALLEVIATE IT! WITHOUT THEIR INFLUENCE, GIVEN THE OVERCROWDING OUR ECONOMIC SITUATION PREDICATES, WE'D BE AWASH IN BLOOD! FOR MOST FOLKS JUST VIEWING CARNAGE IS ALL IT TAKES TO SOOTHE THE NEED TO COMMIT IT AWAY... AND THOSE FEW FOR WHOM IT ISN'T END UP ON THE TUBE. IT'S THE ONLY WAY. WITHOUT IT THE HUMAN RACE WOULD PERISH IN A SEA OF ROAD RAGE!
SEE- WHAT THE CHURCH DOES IS A MIXTURE OF REPORTAGE AND FICTION. WE TRY TO ALLOW THE HEART OF DARKNESS TO SHOW ITSELF IN MUNDANE LIFE-- LIKE A STATUE REVEALING ITSELF TO THE SCULPTOR IN THE GRAIN OF A BLOCK OF MARBLE
•VOICE-OVER•• FOR ONLY IN OUR DREAMS CAN WE LIVE FULLY, FREED OF CONVENTION AND MORALITY. THESE THOUGHTS DON'T STOP JUST BECAUSE THEY ARE BAD FOR SOCIETY...•
•CROSS-REF-- ONLY IN DREAMS ARE WE TRULY FREE. 'TWAS EVER THUS, AND EVER THUS SHALL BE.•
YEAHH.

AH, BRIG, **BRIG**... THE VULTURES ARE ALREADY CIRCLING. SHOULD I JUST LET 'EM **HAVE** YOU? 'F I HADN'T PUT YA IN THAT HOSPITAL BED, THEY'D ALREADY BE SELLIN' BLACK-AND-RED BOOKS ABOUT YOU IN THE TRUE-CRIME STORES ALL OVER TOWN....

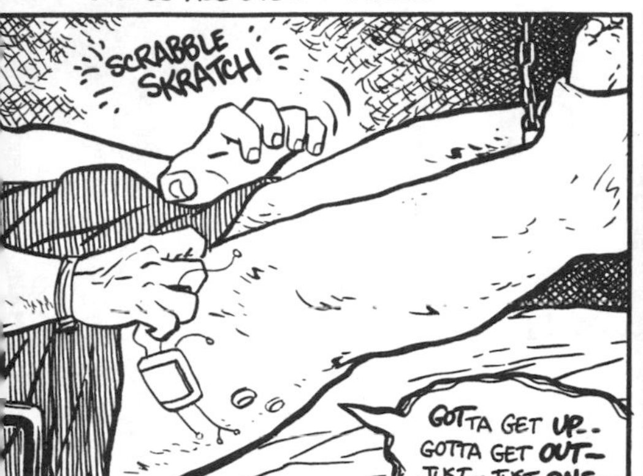

I CAME TO DICKER WITH THE ORACLE FOR SUCH A **SIMPLE** PIECE OF INFORMATION... I JUST WANTED TO KNOW A FEW THINGS ABOUT MY MOM'S MYSTERIOUS BOYFRIEND...

I ADMIT, IT WAS BECAUSE I'M - I **WAS** KINDA CRUSHED OUT ON HIM.

STUPID, TAIL-WAGGING **IDIOT** THING TO DO... LIKE WANTING TO READ ABOUT AN ARTIST'S MORE SORDID HABITS IN A MAGAZINE.

OH!

OH, NO, NOoo...
HOLD UP, I DON' WANNA BE HERE...
I KNOW WHAT COMES NEXT...

JAEGER!
THE HALL, IT'S SHRINK--

AH~!

HELP!

KRTESSSH

MHH

SCRRPTTCH

MMNGH

THIS IS A DREAM THAT PLAGUES YOU.
Y-yeah ... HFF
ITS ROOTS ARE MASSIVE. IT IS OF AN ANCIENT TREE.
SNKK SOB I don't
SNK DON' KNOW WHAT YOU MEAN
NAME IT.
wuh-- ? I
NAME YOUR FEAR.
OH, I--
I- IT'S-- IT'S LIKE IT'S WORSE TO TRY-- TO-- I DON'T KNOW- TO TRY TO GET AWAY THAN TO STAY-- BETTER TO STAY PUT THAN RUN BECAUSE--
BECAUSE YOU GET HURT WORSE IF YOU TRY TO--
LIKE- BETTER THE DEVIL THAT YOU KNOW?
AH YES. WELL PUT.
BUT YOU DON'T BELIEVE IT.
YOUR COIN IS ACCEPTED.
YOU ASKED WHO YOUR LOVER IS.
HE IS ROYLE SUDAMER AYERS.
BUT-- THAT'S STUPID- -EVEN I KNOW HOW STUPID THAT IS--
BUT--BUT I ALREADY KNEW THAT, YOU CRETINOUS FREAK!

SANCTUM
TESTIMONIAL CONFESSION
AUDITORIUM
NO WAY, YOU MOTH-EATEN GOBLIN! YOU CAN'T PUT ME THROUGH HELL AND THEN CHEAT-
TESTIMONIAL
AUDITO
~YAWK!
HURTLE!
SKID!
HEH-HEHH... BURNED AGAIN, HUH, KID?
OH LORD, WHAT NOW?
NO ORACLE EVER GAVE ANYBODY A STRAIGHT ANSWER, RACHEL.
ASK YOURSELF, HONEY; WHY DO YOU NEED TO KNOW ABOUT THE MAN'S PAST? ANYBODY CAN MAKE UP A STORY AND SAY IT IS THE PAST.
HOW IS HE TO BE WITH? WHAT DOES YOUR GUT TELL YOU? DO YOU TRUST HIM, AND IF SO HOW FAR? IF YOU DON'T, IS HE STILL GOOD FOR ANYTHING?
THESE ARE THE QUESTION THAT COUNT, AND NO ORACLE CAN CHEAT YOU OF ANSWERS.
John

ALL I WANT IS FOR SOMEBODY-- ANYBODY!--IN MY LIFE TO BE HONEST AND OPEN WITH ME FOR A CHANGE! WHY DOES EVERYTHING HAVE TO BE SUCH A BIG GODDAMN SECRET? HOW MANY TESTS DO I HAVE TO PASS? THIS IS MY FAMILY, FER CHRISSAKES, EVEN THE BABY'S GOIN' AROUND WITH THIS SLY "I-KNOW-SOMETHING-I-WON'T TELL" LOOK ON HER FACE!
VAGUE, MADDENING SENSE OF DISQUIET
SOMETHING MISSED, OR UNSAID, OR DID I MAKE AN IDIOT OF MYSELF? ... AGAIN?
AND I STILL SAY I WAS CHEATED!
LAME
OKAY, SO I'M NOT BETTE DAVI —...
SORRY, MISSIE!
DJOO SAY SOMETHIN'?
DON'T TAKE NO 'FFENCE, I'D'N MEAN T'BE RUDE, 'S JUSS WHEN I GOT THIS THI ON, Y'KNOW IN A WORLD O' MY OWN YUH WORK H LONG ENOU Y'GET SO YO 'PRECIATE A THING N AN' MORE
I WONDER IF THERE'S A WORD FOR WHEN YOU WISH YOU WERE SURPRISED ...
MISSIE?
Y'ALL RIGHT?
DON'T MIND MY YABBERIN' ON, I'LL SHUT UP ANY MINUT

I-I'M SORRY, MA'AM, IT'S JUST REAL HARD, BEIN' SO STUCK IN BED LIKE THIS.... GUESS IT'S GETTIN' ON MY NERVES SOME--I'M A PACER BY NATURE ~HIGH STRUNG, Y'KNOW....
SOO.. SO HOW LONG TILL I CAN EVEN TRY TO GET ON UP OUTTA HERE?
OH, WE DON'T WANT TO WORRY ABOUT THAT JUST NOW. YOUR TIME WILL PASS BEFORE YOU KNOW IT.
YOU 'PRENTICES GET YOUNGER ALL THE TIME... OR MAYBE IT'S JUST ME--
YOU MAY FEEL A SLIGHT STING-
AH! IT'S BURNING!
BUT IT'S REAL, MAMA, I'VE SEEN IT! I SAW YOU!
REAL LIFE TV
OH, MARCIE.... YOU MUST HAVE BEEN DREAMING, HONEY. GAN GARIDAN IS JUST A MADE-UP PLACE IN MY HEAD. THERE ARE NO GODDESSES REALLY...
REAL LIFE TV
GET A LIFE!
NEWS OF THE ODD
AND THAT'S ANOTHER FASCINATING NON SEQUITUR FROM "STRANGER-THAN-FICTION"! HAVE YOU HAD YOUR FIFTEEN MINUTES? SEND IN YOUR RANDOM FOOTAGE OF YOUR NEIGHBORS' ANTICS AND SOONER OR LATER IT'LL BE YOU --

YOU'RE DEAD, EMMA.
nnn...
YOU'RE DEAD, EMMA, YOUR HUSBAND KILLED YOU YEARS AGO.
SHUT UP! I'VE GOT WORK TO DO--
HE DID. YOU PUSHED HIM TOO FAR, AND HE BEAT YOU TO DEATH WITH A CHUNK OF STOVE WOOD. YOU NEVER SAW WHAT HE DID TO THE CHILDR AFTER--
NO!
BULLSHIT!
I DIDN'T DIE! LOOK AROUND! DO YOU THINK THEY HAVE RAT TURDS IN HEAVEN OR ROSES IN HELL?
I DON'T KNOW ANYTHING ABOUT THAT. I JUST KNOW YOU DIED. YOU NEVER GOT OUT OF THAT HOLE IN THE GROUND HE DUG FOR YOU. HE BEAT YOUR BRAINS OUT AND YOUR LITTLE SON PUT OUT HIS HAND TO TOUCH THEM, AND THAT'S WHY HE WON'T EAT SPAGHETTI
AAAH SHUT UUUUP!! I DIDN'T DIE! I MIGHT HAVE, BUT I GOT MYSELF UP AND OUT OF THERE BEFORE HE COULD DO IT! I AM NOT A WEAK WOMAN, SO CAN IT!
CHUP CHUP
YOU WEREN'T AFRAID HE'D KILL YOU. YOU WERE MORE AFRAID HE WOULDN'T. THAT IT WOULD JUST GO ON AND ON FOREVER. YOU WERE GLAD TO DIE - YOU BROUGHT IT ON Y

huhh ...
huhh ...

I DIDN'T DIE. HOW CAN I KEEP... REMEMBERING IT AS IF I HAD? EVERY DETAIL, AS IF IT HAD HAPPENED...
IS THIS A FALSE MEMORY? SOMETHING I IMAGINED TOO MANY TIMES?
HE'LL COME FOR YOU, YOU KNOW.
HE'S NOT QUITE RABID ENOUG TO RUN JUST YET, BU WHEN HE IS READY, HE'LL COME FOR YOU. HE'LL SNIFF YOU OUT, AND YOU'LL KNOW WHAT THE FATE WORSE THAN DEATH IS--

LET HIM COME.
LET'S FACE IT, I DON'T KNOW IF I'M INSANE BECAUSE OF HIM, OR IF I WAS CLEAREST WHEN HE WAS AT HIS WORST.

LANDSCAPER'S TALKING TO HERSELF, MUM.
ARTISTIC TEMPERAMENT, POOKIE. DON'T INTERFERE, SHE'S VERY PRESTIGIOUS.

PATH GUIDES ME... MY FEET ARE EVER SET ON THE PATH OF MY OWN MAKING... I FOLLOW THE PATH UNTIL I FIND THE FEET SET IN THE MARKS ON THE EARTH, TILL I COME TO THE PLACE WHERE THE PATH ENDS IN THE CLEARING.

≡SIGH≡
JUST CAN'T FUCK THIS UP.
IF BRIG WERE AN EARTHQUAKE I HAD FORESEEN, OR A TIGER WITH A TASTE FOR HUMAN BLOOD, WHAT TO DO WOULD BE SO SIMPLE.

BUT HE'S A MAN, AND EVEN IF HE DOES STINK OF CRAZINESS- I STILL OWE HIM SO MUCH. JUST GOTTA... RIDE THE RIDGES.
dingg
SHHMP

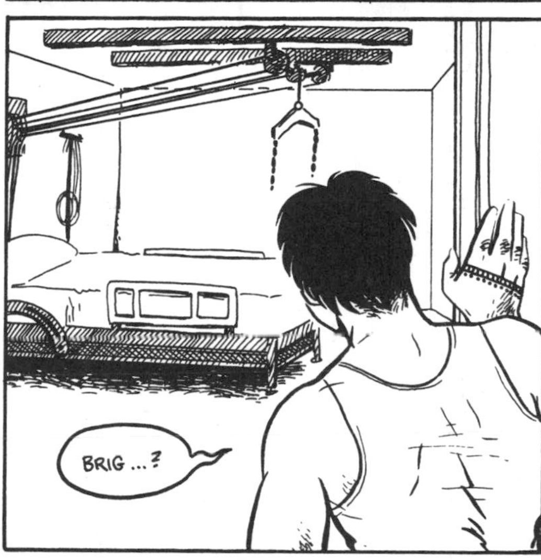
BRIG...?

EXCUSE ME. I'M GOING TO ASK YOU TO LEAVE NOW.
HUNH~? I JUST CAME TO LOOK IN ON MY FRIEND-- I'VE BEEN IN AND OUT ALL WEEK--

YOUR FRIEND HAS BEEN MOVED. I'VE ASKED YOU TO MOVE. ONCE MORE AND YOU AND YOUR UNDERSHIRT ARE GOING TO ANSWER SOME QUESTIONS.
SGM DURGA

THAT'S A VALID THREAT. I ACKNOWLEDGE THAT. BUT PLEASE, MA'AM -- IS HE WORSE? WHAT'S HAPPENED?
MISTER NO-PARTICULAR-CLAN, CERTAINLY-NOT-MY-CLAN, I HAVE BEEN ADMINISTRATING THIS HOSPITAL FOR TWELVE YEARS, AND IN ALL THAT TIME I HAVE NEVER HAD ONE OF MY PATIENTS INJECTED WITH BATTERY ACID UNDER MY VERY NOSE. YOUR FRIEND HAS BEEN MOVED TO A MORE SECURE LOCATION. AND NOW YOU ARE MOVING OUT OF HERE, BEFORE I HAVE YOU DETAINED AS A SUSPECT.
YOU WOULD BE GOING DOWN IF A MEMBER OF MY STAFF HADN'T VOUCHED FOR YOU.
I'LL GO, AND I WON'T KICK, IF YOU'LL PLEASE JUST TELL ME-- IS HE STILL LIVING?
YES.
DISAPPOINTED?

A2 L GROVE

VACANT
PAK!

THAT'S FOR DOING IT HALF-ASSED.

CHAPTER ELEVEN

THIS IS GOING TO HURT THE KID, ISN'T IT.
IF THERE'S ANY HOPE AT ALL FOR HIM, YES.

ALL RIGHT, SMARTY. JUST WAIT TILL IT HAPPENS TO YOU. I'LL WILL YOU THESE HILARIOUS TRAINING BRAS.
FINE! FROM THIS DAY FORWARD I HAVE NO SON.
THIS IS A GIRL.
SOMEDAY, BRIG OL' BOY, THIS KID'S GONNA KICK YOUR MUSHY BUTT FOR THE WAY YOU TREAT HIM.
LYNNE, DON'T YOU THINK THAT'S... OVERKILL, DARLING?

LYNNE ANTHONEY GROSVENOR.
WHY DID YOU TRY TO KILL YOUR OWN FATHER?
LET ME COUNT THE WAYS.
FIRST OFF, I HATE PINK.
THEY LOOK FINE, EMMA. TURNED OUT REAL FINE.
THEN WHAT'S THAT FACE FOR?
WELL, THAT ONE ON THE LEFT IS SUPPOSED TO BE A BOY, ISN'T IT?
WHAT'S THAT SUPPOSED TO MEAN? AND DON'T CALL YOUR OWN CHILD "IT"!
NOTHIN', NOTHIN'- JUST, IF THAT WAS A BOY, YOU'D KINDA WANNA LET IT BE A BOY, THAT'S ALL.
THAT'S ALL THE FABRIC I HAD--

THAT'S ALL?
THAT'S ENOUGH!
SO WHAT'S WRONG WITH BEING A GIRL?
NOT A THING, IF YOU ARE ONE.
BUT MOM SAYS--
JAEGER, TELL ME, DID YOU EVER SEE SUCH A STUPID KID? LOOK AT HIS EYES. DAMN, WHAT A STUPID KID! AND HIS MAMA WONDERS WHY I DON'T PAY MUCH ATTENTION.
SHEEEssh.
SOMEDAY, BRIG OL' BOY, THIS KID'S GONNA KICK YOUR MUSHY BUTT FOR THE WAY YOU TREAT HIM.
HAW! ANYTIME SHE'S READY!
AND I'LL HELP!
ANYTIME, PAL, ANY-TIME! HAW!
BULL-SHITTER!

HOW DO YOU KNOW HE WOULD HARM YOU OR YOUR FAMILY?
HE SNORED LIKE A CHAINSAW.
WE LEARNED HOW TO SLEEP THROUGH THAT.
IT WAS HARDER TO LEARN TO WAKE UP IF HE GOT QUIET.
GZZZZZT
TWITCH
mph ....
unh ... BRIG?
mmm?
BRIG AM
hmm? mwha?

THUNK!
unh!

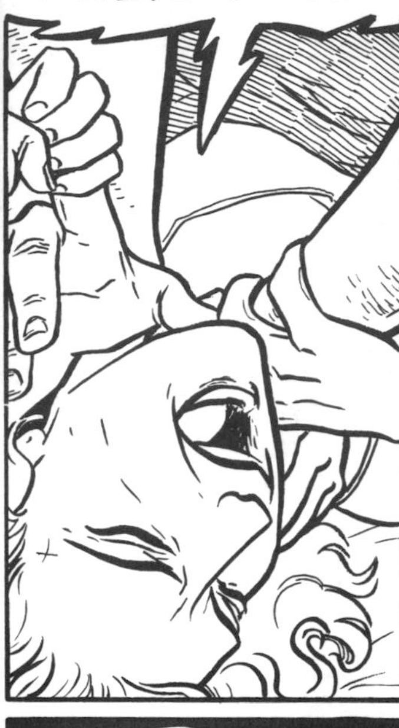
BRIGHAM, BRIGHAM WAKE UP! IT'S A DREAM! IT'S A DREAM! WAKE-

Gzuhh?
uh...
mmph.
HAHH uh
HAHH uh
HAHH uh
HAHH

TIK TIK TIK TIK TIK TIK TIK TIK TIK TIK TIK TIK TIK TIK TIK TIK TIK TIK

SKzzzZzz HAWWH
SKZZzz HAWWH

SKzzzz HAWWH
LET'S GO BACK TO SLEEP NOW, GIRLS.
unh!
GRIP.

YOUR DAD NEEDS TO BE BY HIMSELF FOR A WHILE. WE NEED TO GIVE HIM TIME TO GET USED TO US AGAIN.
AT NIGHT HE'D BE ALL BOO-HOO AND FORGIVE-ME AND I'M-SCUM. —IF HE WOKE UP AT ALL, THAT IS. BUT IN THE MORNING HE'D DENY EVERYTHING IN OUTRAGED TONES. EVEN IF WE SHOWED HIM BRUISES —OR CUTS. ...YEAH, RIP VAN STRANGLER.
MOM USED TO SAY:
IT'S THE FIGHTING THAT'S DONE THIS TO HIM.
WE HAVE TO TRY TO REMEMBER HIM AS HE WAS BEFORE.
THIS HAPPENS TO A LOT OF SOLDIERS. HE'LL COME OUT OF IT.
HE WAS BORN TO BE A FIGHTER; HE'LL SETTLE DOWN.
SHE HAD A MILLION OF 'EM.
I SAY
HAT GODDAMN
IFFERENCE
OES IT MAKE
HAT CAUSED
IM TO ACT
SO CRAZY?
KNOWING DOESN'T CHANGE HIS WAYS.
AND
OW LONG
AVE KILLERS
EEN ABLE TO
DE AMONG
WARRIORS?
MOM-- WHY IS -- IS HE IN THE ARMY ANYWAY?
WHAT DO YOU MEAN?
WELL-- HIS FAMILY-- THE GROSVENORS ARE ALL COPS. DON'T ARMY FAMILIES AND POLICE FAMILIES USUALLY STICK TO THEIR OWN BRANCH?
WELL .... YES.
USUALLY.
I HATE MY FATHER.
OH, YOU DON'T MEAN THAT.
THEN WHY'D I SAY IT?

"WAS THERE NO HIGHER AUTHORITY TO HELP YOU?"

LOOK... THINGS HAPPEN. BEIN' A FIGHTIN' MAN, IN HOSTILE TERRITORY, WELL, A LOT OF THINGS HAPPEN.

BEIN' A FIGHTIN' MAN MEANS LOOKIN' OUT FOR ONE ANOTHER, WATCHIN' EACH OTHER'S BACKS. WE ALL GET INTO SCRAPES, MAKE MISTAKES, DO THINGS WRONG... THIS AIN'T A BY-THE-BOOK KIND O' WORLD.

Y'WOULDN'T LIKE TO THINK YOUR OWN PARTNERS WOULDN'T COVER FOR YOU, IF YOU ... WELL, NEEDED A SECOND CHANCE?
SO YA GET A BAD EGG EVERY ONCE IN A WHILE. OR YA CATCH SOMEBODY OUT. EVERYBODY'S GOT REASONS FOR WHAT THEY DO. IT AIN'T FOR YOU TO JUDGE.
IT'S STILL BETTER TO PROTECT A FEW TARNISHED ANGELS THAN THROW DOWN THE INNOCENT.
MIX-UPS HAPPEN, MORE THAN ANYBODY LIKES TO THINK.

YOU GOT SOMETHIN' TO TELL THE HIGHER-UPS ABOUT LAST WEEK, YOU GO DO THAT. BUT YOU'D BEST BE THINKIN' OF WHO'S GONNA BE LEFT ON YOUR SIDE, IF YOU GO RUNNIN' YOUR MOUTH AGAINST ANOTHER OFFICER - ANOTHER MEDAWAR, YOUR OWN COUSIN!
AND OVER AN ENLISTED MAN?!

YOU WANNA HELP SOME CULL, FINE! TAKE 'IM INTO YOUR HOUSE, ADOPT HIM, LET EVERYBODY KNOW HE'S YOUR BOY- DO LIKE I'VE DONE WITH JAEGER AYERS.
AND KEEP YER FLAP MOUTH SHUT ABOUT WHATEVER YOU'VE SEEN.
KEEP IT IN THE FAMILY, COFFEY.

"HIGHER AUTHORITY." FEH.
COPS AND ARMY ARE ALL BROTHERS. ONE BIG HAPPY. THEY WOULDN'T DO ANYTHING TO HIM.

BUT YOU ARE PART OF THEIR BROTHERHOOD. YOU ARE OF THEIR BLOOD.
HUNH!
CAR-NI-VAL! CAR-NI-VAL!
WELL, I DON'T CARE IF YOU WON'T TALK TO ME, Y'KNOW I'M NOT THAT KIND OF GIRRRL--
FRY IN HELL FURYURE
OOM THUMPA BOOM
AND I DON'T CARE IF YOU WON'T WALK WITH ME, IT DON'T GIVE ME SUCH A THRILL--
AN' I DON'T CARE 'BOUT THE WAY YOU LOOK, YOU SHOULD KNOW I'M NOT IMPRESSED--

'CAUSE THERE'S JUST ONE THING THAT I'M LOOKIN' FOR, AN' HE DON'T WEAR A DRESS--
WHIT WHIT WHIT WHIT

I NEED A MAN! I NEED A MAN!
PLUCK!

BABY-BABY-BABY DON'TCHA SHAVE YOUR LEGS-- DON'TCHA DOUBLE COMB YOUR HAIR -- DON'T POWDER PUFF, JUS' LEAVE IT ROUGH, I LIKE YOUR FINGER BARE-- WHEN THE NIGHT COMES DOWN, I
TURN IT ROUND-- CAN TAKE YOU AN-Y-WHERE--

LOOK, GIRLS! THERE'S GRANDPA! ISN'T SHE GORGEOUS? WAVE TO YOUR GRANDPAPA!
I DON'T NEED LOVE-- FORGET THAT STUFF-- CUZ Y'KNOW THAT I DON'T CARE--
WOW! NICE CATCH!
≡TSK≡ REALLY, DADDY...

≡SHUDDER≡
CAR-
I NEED A MAN!
HEH! WELL IF YOU TAKE AFTER YOUR MOM'S SIDE ...
A.P.D.

"HYECH-HYECH-HYECH... Y'WON'T HAVE TO BUY PORNO TO SEE TITS! HYECH-HYECH-HYECH!"
I'M ONLY HALF MEDAWAR. A CULL.
AND THE OTHER HALF--
WELL, LET'S JUST SAY THE MEDAWARS WOULDN'T APPROVE.

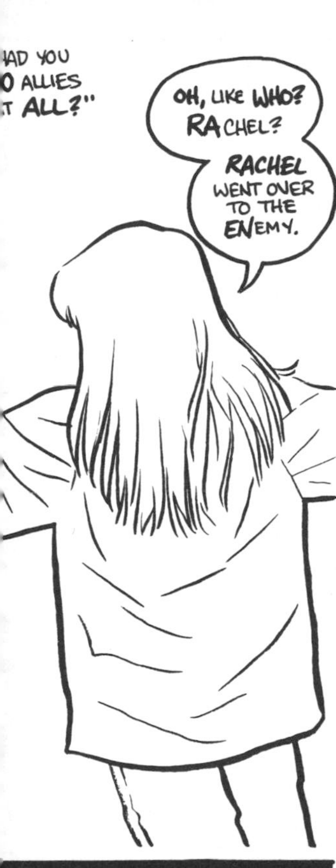

AD YOU
O ALLIES
T ALL?"
OH, LIKE WHO? RACHEL?
RACHEL WENT OVER TO THE ENEMY.

LOOK OUT THERE, LYNNE... CAN YOU SMELL THE RAIN?

DON'T TELL, OKAY? DON'T TELL, AND WE'LL COME UP HERE WHENEVER WE CAN.
WE'LL GET CAUGHT EVENTUALLY, BUT TILL THEN...
I'LL SHOW YOU THE STARS AND EVERY-THING.

OH, THAT I WERE A MAN, FOR HIS SAKE!
OR THAT I HAD ANY FRIEND WHO WOULD BE A MAN FOR MY SAKE!
SHE WAS MORE LIKE A BROTHER THEN.
MUCH ADO ABOUT NOTHING

BUT MANHOOD IS MELTED INTO COURTESIES, VALOR INTO COMPLIMENT, AND MEN ARE ONLY TURNED INTO TONGUE. HE IS NOW AS VALIANT AS HERCULES THAT ONLY TELLS A LIE AND SWEARS IT!

I CANNOT BE A MAN WITH WISHING.
THEREFORE I WILL DIE A WOMAN WITH GRIEVING.
RIVERSIDE SHAKESPEARE

NO HITTING! YELL ALL YOU WANT, BUT NO HITTING! HE'S LITTLER THAN YOU, SO WHAT CHANCE DOES HE HAVE? LET HIM PLAY!

LEN?
KILL 'ER!

DAD SAYS NO GIRL MY AGE SHOUL BE SEEN WITHOUT A DRESS. I MEA --HE MEANS NO GIRL SHOULD BE SEEN EXCEPT IN A DRESS.
BUT THEN HE SPINS RIGHT AROUND AND SAYS NO DECENT WOMAN WOULD GO WITHOUT TROUSERS! IT'S SO STUPID.
I BET MAMA'S CLAN ISN'T SO NUTTY.

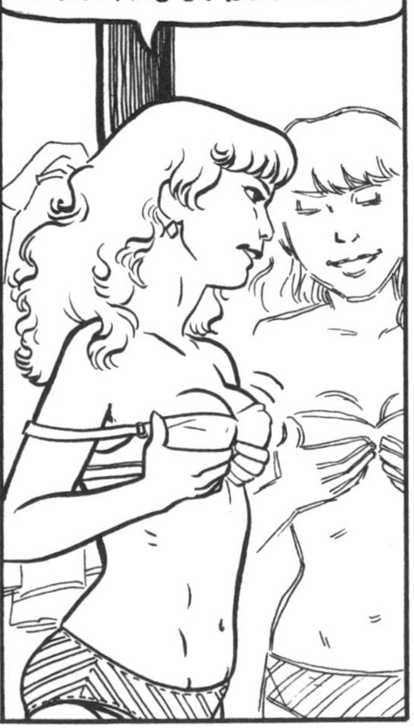

MAMA BEING LLAVERAC... IT'S HAPPENING TO ME EARLIER THAN THE MEDAWAR GIRLS. MAN, ARE THEY JEALOUS...
=SIGH= BUT IT'S KINDA SCARY. PUBERTY'S LIKE THIS MUTATION MACHINE, AND YOU DON'T KNOW WHAT YOU'LL BE LIKE WHEN YOU COME OUT THE OTHER SIDE. JUST THAT YOU'LL BE TOTALLY DIFFERENT.
WHICH I GUESS ISN'T BAD IN THEORY...

SOMETIMES I THINK IT'D BE SOO GREAT IF YOU COULD, Y'KNOW, SWAP THEM OUT. PUT ON SOME GREEAAT BIG ONES FOR GOING OUT IN THAT STRAPLESS GOWN; PUT ON SOME ITTY-BITTY ONES FOR JOGGING OR SLEEPING ON YOUR STOMACH?

HOW 'BOUT LEAVING 'EM OFF ENTIRELY?
=TSK= WHERE'S THE FUN IN THAT?

MARCIE'S THE ONE WHO NEEDS AN ALLY... POOR KID, THAT'S PROBABLY GOTTA BE ME.

I LIKE LITTLE BABIES. IT'S KIND OF MIND BOGGLING HOW UTTERLY HELPLESS THEY ARE.
REALLY-- HOW COULD ANYBODY HURT A PERSON WHO'S IN SUCH DIRE NEED OF THEIR HELP?

LYNNE ...
NO! MY BABY!

OH, LET HER. MARCIE SLEEPS SO QUIET WITH HER.

COME ON, BRAT-- SWAP YA A LITTLE DOLL FOR MY LITTLE DOLL, OKAY, GIRLY-BOY?
rrrh

BRIGHAM, LEAVE THE KID ALONE. HE'S GOT TO BE A FATHER SOMEDAY TOO.

NO, NO, NO, NO, NO!

UGF!

GET OVER IT, BRAT.

WHAT ARE YOU SPACED OUT OVER, SIR? WHEN I GET THAT FACE, IT'S BECAUSE I'M THINKING OF THINGS I CAN'T REMEMBER.
TAP TAP
YOU'RE WEIRD, MARCIE.
AND DON'T CALL ME "SIR."

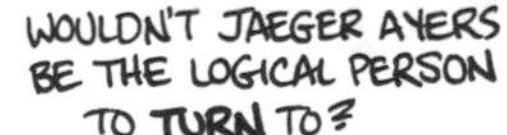
WOULDN'T JAEGER AYERS BE THE LOGICAL PERSON TO TURN TO?

JAEGER! HAH!

YING, CONNIVING, BACKSTABBING ONOFAWHORE... I OULDN'T ASK HIM TO PIT ON ME IF I WAS BURNING TO DEATH!

... SO, THE SCOUTMASTER SAYS, "A SMART ANIMAL WOULD BE SATISFIED TO KNOW THAT IF IT GOT CLOSE, IT GOT WARM-- AND IF IT GOT TOO CLOSE, IT GOT BURNT. BUT SOME ANIMALS," HE SAYS, AND THE BOYS ARE HANGIN' ON HIS EVERY WORD-- "SOME ANIMALS GET TO THINKIN' THEY'RE BIGGER THAN THE FIRE-

"...LIKE IT'S SOMETHING THEY'VE GOT TO CONQUER OR BE CONQUERED BY, AND NEXT THING THEY KNOW THEY'RE DANCIN' RIGHT IN THE MIDDLE OF IT, AND GET CONSUMED BY IT, AND ALL'S LEFT IS THE -- THE COLD EYES IN THE HOT FIRE, AND THAT'S WHY A CAMPFIRE IS SUCH A BIG-- --"
SSSH! LISTEN!

JUST DON'T UNDERSTAND MY HUSBAND'S ATTITUDE TO OUR CHILDREN
HE'S SO
mmm
SO...
WELL, RACHEL FOR EXAMPLE

RACHEL'S ALWAYS BEEN THE APPLE OF HIS LORDSHIP'S EYE
IT'S MAMA!
I KNOW. SSSH!
HE WAS SO
unh
SO HAPPY WHEN SHE WAS BORN ...
NOTHING
mmf.
NOTHING WAS TOO GOOD FOR HER.

...BUT BRIG WAS SENT OUT TO THAT BAD BORDER TROUBLE IN DAPTUM ... AND HE WAS NEVER THE SAME AFTERWARD ...
LYNNE WAS BORN WHILE HE WAS GONE, AND HE JUST NEVER HAD ANY USE FOR H
WHO'S SHE TALKING TO?
I DUNNO! SHUDDUP!

SO SHE TRAILS AFTER RACHEL, TRIES TO DO EVERYTHING LIKE HER... AND IT JUST MAKES BRIG MADDER
OH!

YOU'D THINK- AH!
--IF HE HAD SOME PECULIAR STANDARD FOR HIS SON, THAT HE'D TAKE AN INTEREST IN INSTILLING IT...

YOU'RE A-- A MAN, SURELY YOU KNOW HOW ALL THIS SORT OF THING IS SUPPOSED TO WORK; CAN YOU CLUE ME IN SOMEHOW? MAYBE I CAN SHOW HIM HOW TO ACT, IF I KNOW WHAT TO DO--
MUST BE JAEGER. BUT WHAT'S THAT WEIRD NOISE? IS HE CHEWING GUM?

WE OUGHT NOT TO EAVESDROP. C'MON, LYNNE, YOU DON'T REALLY WANNA HEAR --
EAVESDROPPING'S THE ONLY JOY LEFT IN MY LIFE. NOW SHUT IT!
I JUST WORRY
LYNNE- SHE'S
COLD-- WON'T
TOUCH
SHE
MARCIE
HEY, TRY AND CONCENTRATE, HUH? WHY D'YA WANNA TALK NOW?
AWW, POOOR BABY. BE MORE DISTRACTING.
DISTRACTION SHE WANTS--
THUMP
AH!
THUMP
=OOOH=
THUMP
AH!

oh!
=giggle=
oOOHH
THUMP
OH YESSs
THUMP
AH
THUMP
OHH
oOO

AT SICK SUCKING NOISE ND A SOUND SORT OF LIKE ARTING HAVE NEVER EALLY LEFT ME---
WELL, IF YOU WEREN'T SO ADDICTED TO LURKING AT KEYHOLES, YOU WOULDN'T'VE BEEN TRAUMATIZED.
HEY, WHAT IF I'M REALLY MARCIE'S FATHER? HANH? WHAT ABOUT THAT?
YEAHH, YOU TWO DO LOOK ALIKE. MAYBE YOU'RE BOTH HIS. WOULDN'T THAT BE A THIGH SLAPPER ON THE OLD MAN?
NO! SHE DOESN'T LOOK ANYTHING LIKE YOU!
SHE LOOKS LIKE ME!
YEAH, THAT'S JUST LIKE YOU, YOU'D DENY ME ON MY DEATHBED:
BECAUSE, YOU KNOW, IF JAEGER WAS OUR REAL DAD, YOU WOULDN'T'VE HAD TO DO ANY OF THIS.
DARLING, DO YOU REALLY THINK I'D CHOOSE A MAN LIKE THAT?
NO! KNOW HIM! EN IF HE WAS OUR THER, HE'D STILL BE LIAR AND AN EGG UCKER AND HE'S ONLY EN HOLDING DAD OFF L HE GETS GOOD AND RED WITH OUR MOTHER! EN HE'LL THROW US BACK THAT RAT BASTARD WHO EALLY IS OUR DAD AND BE NE WITHOUT A SECOND GLANCE!
OH, YOU SHUT THE FUCK UP! I AIN'T EVEN TALKING ABOUT YOUR PART IN THIS, MOM!

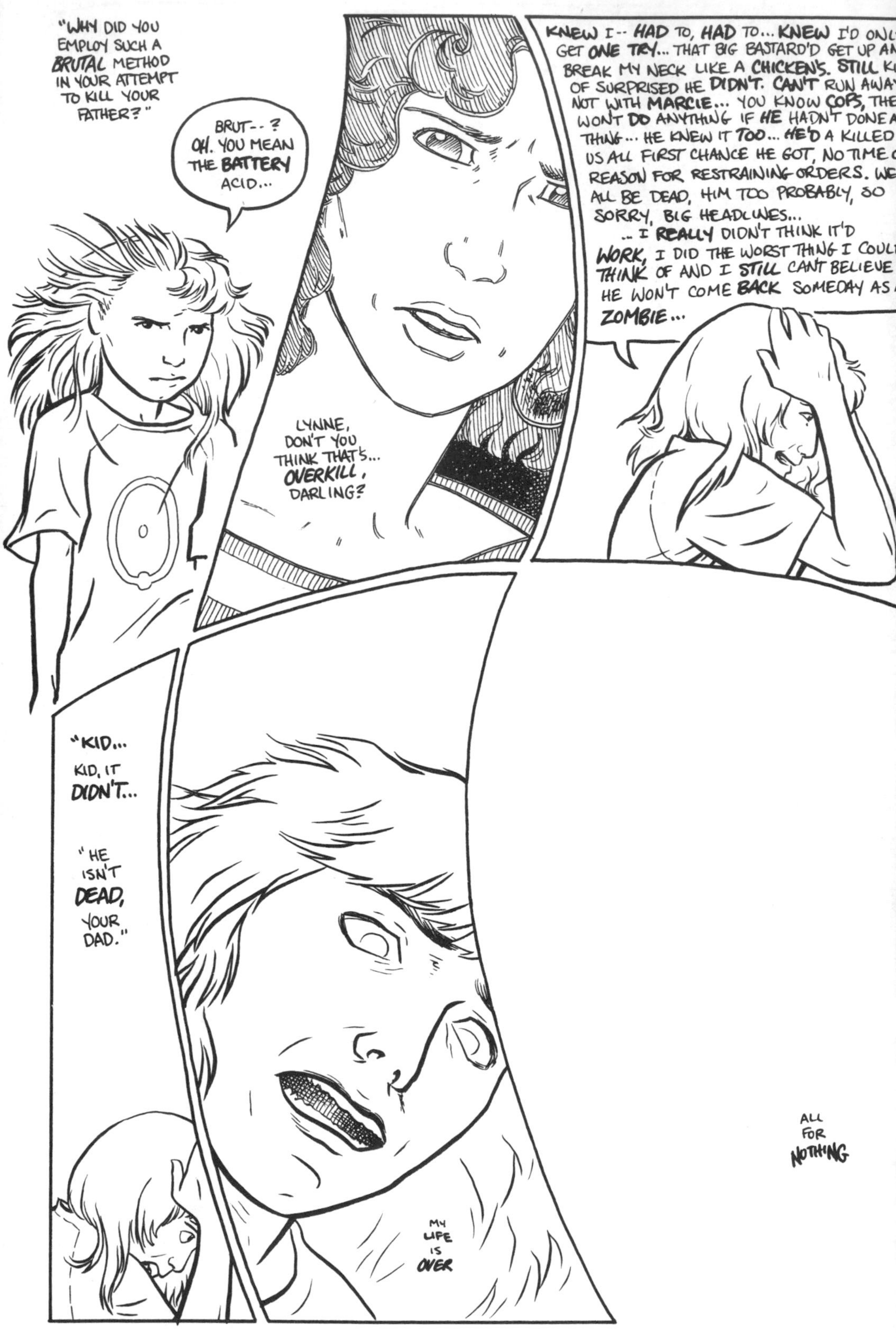
"WHY DID YOU EMPLOY SUCH A BRUTAL METHOD IN YOUR ATTEMPT TO KILL YOUR FATHER?"
BRUT--? OH. YOU MEAN THE BATTERY ACID...
LYNNE, DON'T YOU THINK THAT'S... OVERKILL, DARLING?
KNEW I-- HAD TO, HAD TO... KNEW I'D ONLY GET ONE TRY... THAT BIG BASTARD'D GET UP AND BREAK MY NECK LIKE A CHICKEN'S. STILL KI OF SURPRISED HE DIDN'T. CAN'T RUN AWAY NOT WITH MARCIE... YOU KNOW COPS, THE WON'T DO ANYTHING IF HE HADN'T DONE A THING... HE KNEW IT TOO... HE'D A KILLED US ALL FIRST CHANCE HE GOT, NO TIME OR REASON FOR RESTRAINING ORDERS. WE ALL BE DEAD, HIM TOO PROBABLY, SO SORRY, BIG HEADLINES...
... I REALLY DIDN'T THINK IT'D WORK, I DID THE WORST THING I COULD THINK OF AND I STILL CAN'T BELIEVE HE WON'T COME BACK SOMEDAY AS A ZOMBIE...
"KID...
KID, IT DIDN'T...
"HE ISN'T DEAD, YOUR DAD."
MY LIFE IS OVER
ALL FOR NOTHING

AAAAAA...
CALM DOWN, NOW.
CALM DOWN.
ALL RIGHT, THAT'S ENOUGH FOR NOW. LET'S BRING HIM OUT OF IT.
PUT YOUR HANDS ON HIM SO HE KNOWS WHERE YOU ARE.

SEE? HE'S A GOOD KID, REALLY-- MESSED UP, SURE, BUT MORE OUT TO HELP HIS BABY SISTER THAN ANYTHING ELSE.
rrnh..
PARRICIDE- EVEN UNSUCCESS PARRICIDE -- IS T MOST DIFFICULT CRIME ON EARTH TO FORGIVE. AND HERE, THERE IS NO TESTIMONY OF UNNATURAL ABUSE--
LIKE THERE IS SUCH A THING AS "NATURAL" ABUSE? BELIEVE ME. THIS KID HAS GOOD REASON TO BE AFRAID OF HIS FATHER. THE MAN'S NOT NORMAL.
THERE'S NOTHING TO FORGIVE.
...?
WE DON'T DISPENSE FORGIVENESS.
I WAS NOT SPEAKING OF THE FORGIVENESS OF THE COURTS, OR OF ANYONE MORE THAN THIS BOY, OF HIMSELF.
HE HAS A FEW CRACKS IN HIS ARMOR NOW. BUT MONSTEF BREED MONSTERS. YOU SEE HO VITAL IT IS NOW THAT THIS BOY' FATHER DOES NOT DIE? THAT HE HAS TO HAVE A CHANCE TO SEE HIS FATHER DIMINISHED, SMALL AS ANY MAN? NOT SOME... ANGEL OF DOOM?
mmp..
THANK YOU, SHRIVERS.
OUR DUTY, SIN-EATER.

WANTED

WHAT'S A "SIN-EATER"?
MEANS I TAKE THE BLAME FOR WHAT YOU DID.

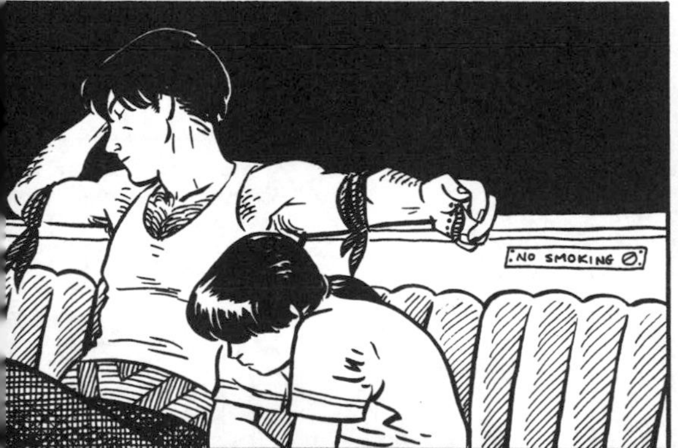
NO SMOKING

DID I TELL YOU THEY WON'T LET ME GO OUT FOR SOCCER ANYMORE?

NO, KID. YOU DIDN'T. HOW COME?
COACH FOUND OUT I'M NOT A GIRL.

....
..AH.

UNWANTED

IT ISN'T AS IF WE'RE NOT ACCUSTOMED TO MURDER ATTEMPTS IN THE JOHN DOE WARD. IT ISN'T AS IF WE DON'T HAVE MEASURES TO DEAL WITH THIS KIND OF THING...
BUT SIR, YOU'LL EXCUSE ME IF I'M NOT PREPARED FOR THIS KIND OF-- INTRIGUE!
SGM DURGA
ADMINISTRATOR
MATACORDA MEDAWAR CHARITY HOSPITAL
EXCUSE ME, SERGEANT MAJOR-- ...INTRIGUE?
A MEMBER OF MY OWN STAFF PROCLAIMED THIS MAN HER LONG-LOST FATHER, NO LESS! TRUE, SHE'S JUST A MED SCOUT, BUT--
A MED SCOUT?

LYNNE GROSVENOR. TEN YEARS OLD. TOO SMART TO LET RUN LOOSE. EAGER TO LEARN, CLEAR-HEADED, GUTSY-- MAKE A GOOD SURGEON SOMEDAY--
AND SHE IDENTIFIED A JOHN DOE? AS HER FATHER, AH... BRIGHAM GROSVENOR? JUST AFTER THERE WAS AN ATTEMPT ON HIS LIFE?
YES, SIR. HE WAS SENT HOME AT HER REQUEST.
UNDER GUARD?
NATURALLY. MY BEST.
IT WAS HER RIGHT TO REQUEST THIS, SIR. I'M SURE THAT YOU'LL SEE WE'VE PRUDENTLY OBEYED PROCEDURE IN ALL ASPECTS OF THIS CASE--
NOTHING TO WORRY ABOUT, MA'AM. THE CHURCH WON'T HAVE TROUBLE WITH YOUR ACTIONS AT ALL. YOU HAVE MY PERSONAL ASSURANCE. NO REASON TO WORRY ABOUT YOUR ENDOWMENT.

HAVE A SAFE AND BORING CARNIVA

Y'KNOW, KID... I NEVER SAW MY OLD MAN DEAD.
JUST A HEADSTONE ON A HILLSIDE.

SECURITY/INFO

FOR YEARS AFTERWARD I HAD THIS NAGGING FEELING THAT IT WAS ALL A BAD JOKE AND SOMEDAY I'D JUST WALK INTO MY KITCHEN AND... TA-DAA! THERE HE'D BE.
BAD ENOUGH TO GIVE ME NIGHT PANICS SOMETIMES...

JUST FOR A FEW YEARS? AS IN-- YOU DON'T HAVE THEM ANYMORE?

-4305

YOU BETTER RUN ON AHEAD, IF YOU WANT TO GET DAD OUT OF THE WAY BEFORE MOM OR MARCIE OR RACHEL GET HOME. IF THEY'RE NOT THERE ALREADY. I'D BE RUNNING MY BUTT OFF MYSELF, BUT I'M STILL A LITTLE WOBBLY--

KID--

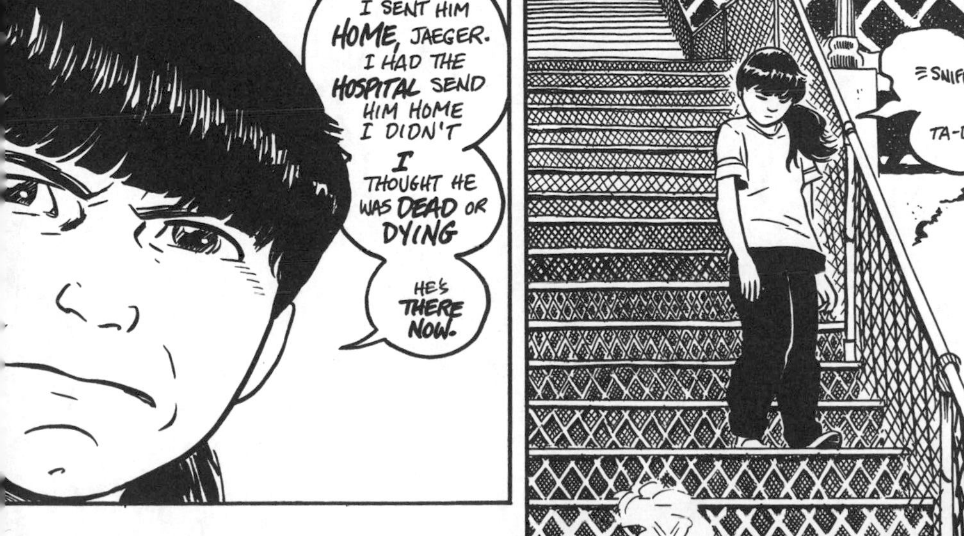

CHAPTER TWELVE

FREE WILL OR FATE?
IT'S AN OLD AND TRITE QUESTION.
IT'S A BASIC AND UNIVERSAL CONUNDRUM.

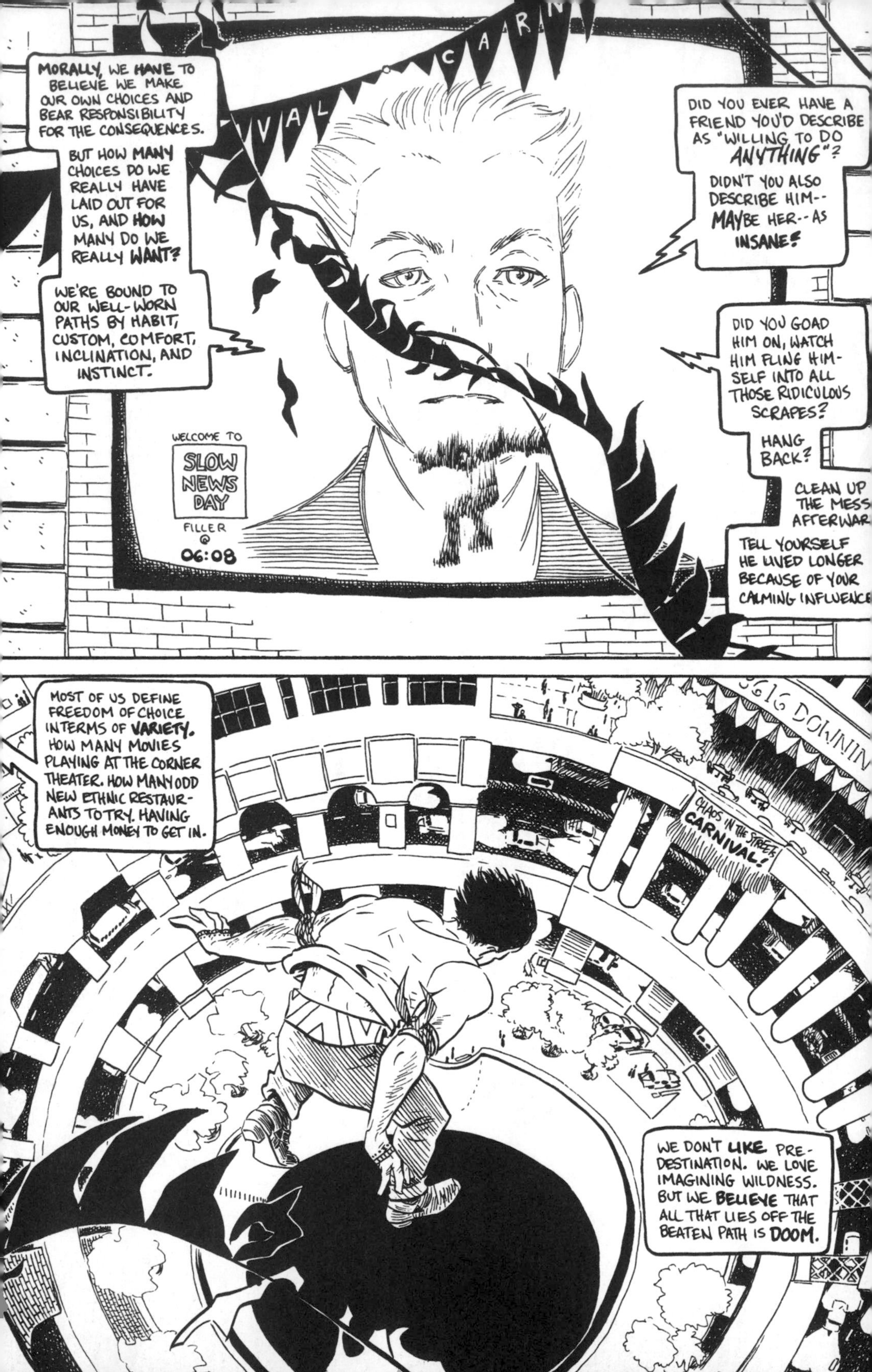

MORALLY, WE HAVE TO BELIEVE WE MAKE OUR OWN CHOICES AND BEAR RESPONSIBILITY FOR THE CONSEQUENCES.
BUT HOW MANY CHOICES DO WE REALLY HAVE LAID OUT FOR US, AND HOW MANY DO WE REALLY WANT?
WE'RE BOUND TO OUR WELL-WORN PATHS BY HABIT, CUSTOM, COMFORT, INCLINATION, AND INSTINCT.
DID YOU EVER HAVE A FRIEND YOU'D DESCRIBE AS "WILLING TO DO ANYTHING"?
DIDN'T YOU ALSO DESCRIBE HIM--MAYBE HER--AS INSANE?
DID YOU GOAD HIM ON, WATCH HIM FLING HIMSELF INTO ALL THOSE RIDICULOUS SCRAPES?
HANG BACK?
CLEAN UP THE MESS AFTERWAR
TELL YOURSELF HE LIVED LONGER BECAUSE OF YOUR CALMING INFLUENCE
WELCOME TO
SLOW NEWS DAY
FILLER @ 06:08
MOST OF US DEFINE FREEDOM OF CHOICE IN TERMS OF VARIETY. HOW MANY MOVIES PLAYING AT THE CORNER THEATER. HOW MANY ODD NEW ETHNIC RESTAURANTS TO TRY. HAVING ENOUGH MONEY TO GET IN.
CHAOS IN THE STREETS CARNIVAL!
WE DON'T LIKE PREDESTINATION. WE LOVE IMAGINING WILDNESS. BUT WE BELIEVE THAT ALL THAT LIES OFF THE BEATEN PATH IS DOOM.

PROBLEM IS, EVEN UNORTHODOX LIVES GET INTO PATTERNS.
EVERYTHING'S ORDINARY TO SOMEBODY.
CHANGING OUR WAYS:
IT TAKES A LEAP OF FAITH.

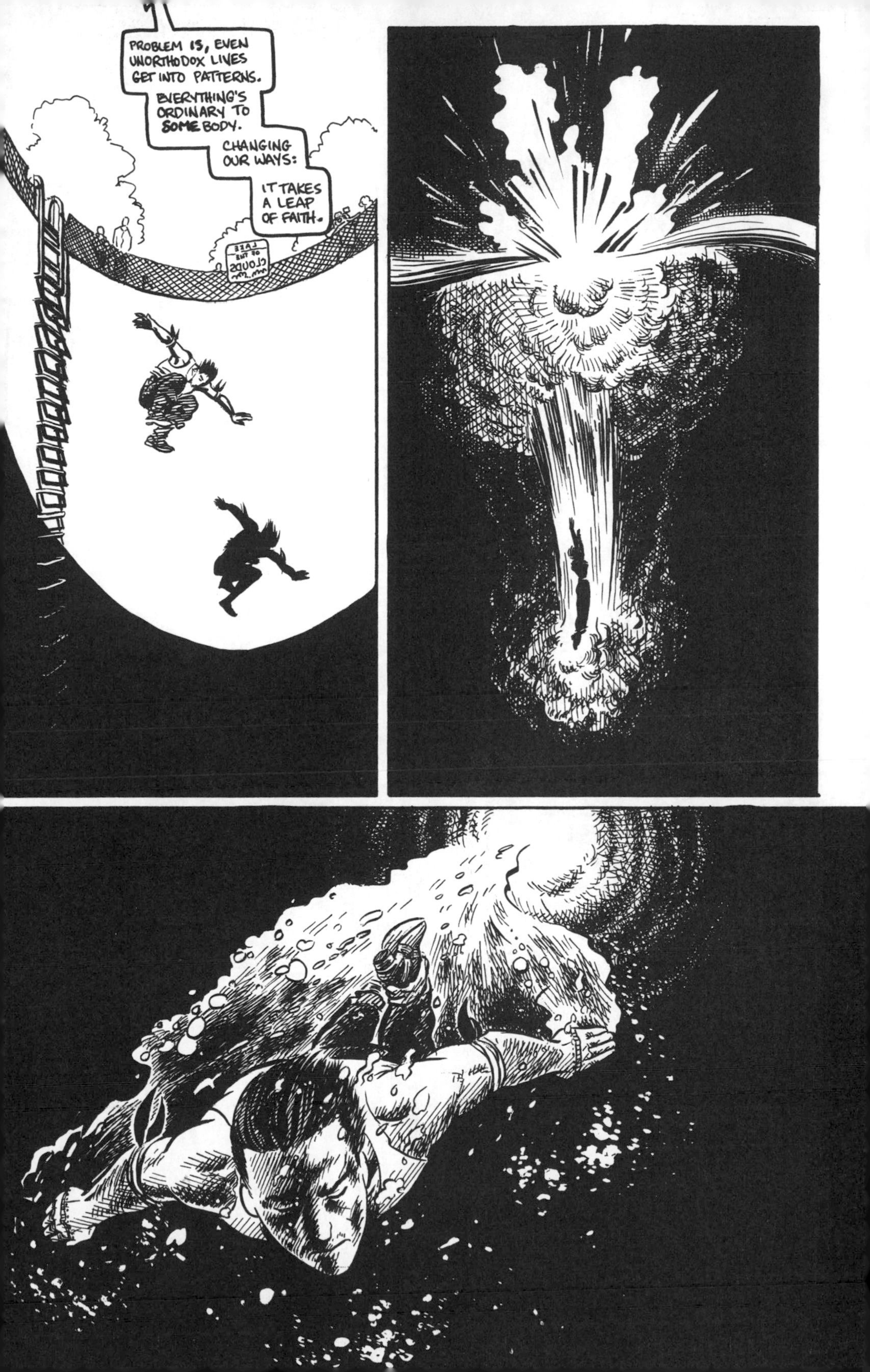

HFFFFF

HAAK!
THUMP!
PITTA
PITT
PTT
PATTA
PTT
PITT PTT
PATT PTT
PTT PATTA
PTT
PATTA
PTT
PTT-TT
KAFF
KHOFF
SOPP SOPP SOPP SOPP SOP
BINGG
HAAAHH
MAN!
ROOFTOP
GADDAM SHAME TO SEE A YOUNG FART LIKE YOU WITH SO LITTLE FAITH IN PUBLIC TRANSPORTATION.
SNIFFK
SORRY, BUZZ. I'D USE IT IF IT WENT WHERE I WANNA GO FAST ENOUGH.

I SHOULD BE HAPPY.
ONE WAY OR ANOTHER IT'LL ALL BE OVER SOON.
I'M GOING HOME.
BE WITH MY FAMILY AT LAST. KNEW I'D BE SCARED TO FACE THEM. PUT IT OFF. WANTED TO SHOW THEM RESPECT.
I JUST CAN'T GET OVER THE FEELING SOMEBODY'S BEEN TAKING ME FOR A RIDE.
GOT TO GO BACK INTO MY OLD LIFE AS IF IT WAS A STRANGE NEW WORLD.
DO EVERYTHING DIFFERENT.
IT'S THE HARDEST THING ANYBODY CAN DO, AND IF I SLIP UP, THEY'LL RUN AWAY FROM ME LIKE BEFORE.
SHROOMS.
KITCHEN GARDEN, I GUESS. NO MAGIC ONES... SNORT
"GRASS" HOUSE.
ALL ALIVE.
EW.
AND MY RUNNIN' DAYS ARE OVER.
ONE WAY OR ANOTHER.
PUB ALLEY DOWN BELOW
HE'S BEEN OUT OF IT FOR WEEKS NOW
SAFE HERE
IF MY KIDS DON'T KNOW ME I DON'T THINK I CAN TAKE IT.
JUST A QUICK ONE THEN.
I SHOULD BE HAPPY.
I SHOULD HAVE MORE THAN THIS COPPERY TASTE IN MY MOUTH.
CAN'T SHAKE THE FEELING I'VE BEEN SUCKER PUNCHED.
OOAHH..

CAN'T THINK. CAN'T THINK ABOUT IT AND GET MAD.
GOTTA BE CALM AND COOL FOR WHEN MY EMMA COMES HOME.
CLICK
FLOING!

CAN'T JUST SIT HERE AND STEW.
SKWI
EEKIK EEK IK EEK
GOTTA FIND SOMETHING TO DO TO KEEP MY MIND OFF.

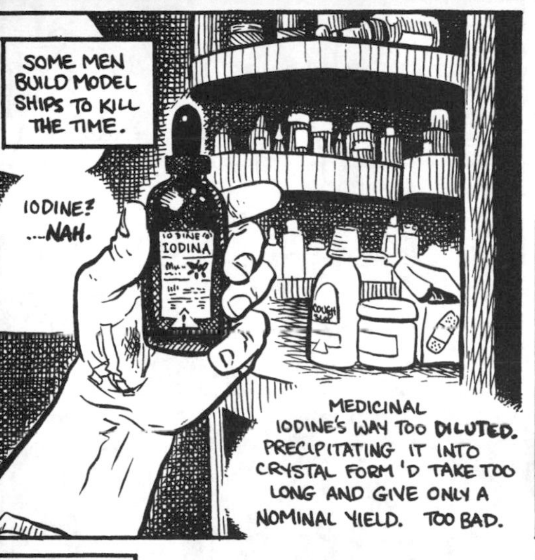
SOME MEN BUILD MODEL SHIPS TO KILL THE TIME.
IODINE? ...NAH.
IODINA
MEDICINAL IODINE'S WAY TOO DILUTED. PRECIPITATING IT INTO CRYSTAL FORM 'D TAKE TOO LONG AND GIVE ONLY A NOMINAL YIELD. TOO BAD.

NOT HAVING SUCHLIKE TO OCCUPY HIMSELF, THE RESOURCEFUL MAN DOES WITH WHAT HE CAN FIND.
CORN STARCH! YEAH BABY! --IF I GOT TIME TO DRY IT OUT IN THE OVEN. --IF EMMA'S UNPACKED HER COOKIE PANS.
DRAT!
CRINCHY
WELL, MAYBE NOT. I'D NEED A MORE ENCLOSED SPACE TO DEPLOY ANYWAY.
DAMMIT! WHY'S EVERYTHING UP SO HIGH?

I USED TO BE SO GOOD AT THIS. MAY GOOD OLD DAYS BE NOT FORGOT...
HEH! DRIED BEANS IN A JELLY JAR WITH TWO INNER LIDS. PUT YOU SOME WATER IN THAT BAD BOY, AND A SOLENOID SWITCH BETWEEN THE LIDS, AND YOU GOT A NICE LITTLE TIMING DEVICE. EASY-PEASY, YAP-A-NEEZY.
'CEPT I AIN'T GOT A SOLENOID.

CHLORINE BLEACH, CHLORINE BLEACH... DAMN! WOMAN'S GONE ALL NOBLE ON ME. NONE A THIS HAS CHLORINE IN IT.
PHOSPHATES? GOT PHOSPHATE LAUNDRY SOAP, BUT IT AIN'T ANY GOOD WITHOUT CHLORINE.
INHALANTS TAKE TOO LONG ANYWAY.
PRETTY SOON I'LL NEVER HAVE A NEED TO DO THIS AGAIN.
ONE WAY OR ANOTHER.

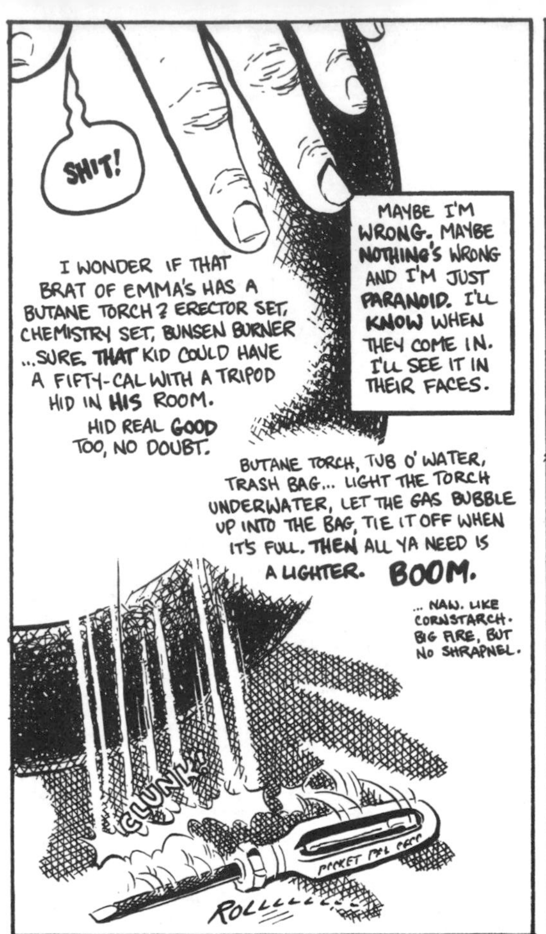
SHIT!
MAYBE I'M WRONG. MAYBE NOTHING'S WRONG AND I'M JUST PARANOID. I'LL KNOW WHEN THEY COME IN. I'LL SEE IT IN THEIR FACES.
I WONDER IF THAT BRAT OF EMMA'S HAS A BUTANE TORCH? ERECTOR SET, CHEMISTRY SET, BUNSEN BURNER ...SURE. THAT KID COULD HAVE A FIFTY-CAL WITH A TRIPOD HID IN HIS ROOM.
HID REAL GOOD TOO, NO DOUBT.
BUTANE TORCH, TUB O' WATER, TRASH BAG... LIGHT THE TORCH UNDERWATER, LET THE GAS BUBBLE UP INTO THE BAG, TIE IT OFF WHEN IT'S FULL. THEN ALL YA NEED IS A LIGHTER. BOOM.
...NAW. LIKE CORNSTARCH. BIG FIRE, BUT NO SHRAPNEL.
CLUNK
ROLLLLLL...

AHA! NITRATE FERTILIZER! YA-HEY, THANK YOU, GARDENER'S WEEKLY SUPPLY! NOW WHERE C'N I GET DIESEL FUEL...?
CAN I MAKE IT DOWN TO THAT ENCLOSED GARAGE AND BACK BEFORE THOSE DAMN IRRESPONSIBLE ORDERLIES COME DRAG ASSIN' BACK?
PROBABLY NOT.
METAL CANS, THUMBTACKS, LIGHTER FLUID, STAPLES...
IF MY KIDS DON'T KNOW ME I DON'T THINK I CAN TAKE IT.
DECOFFEINATED CAFFEE

CLUNK
RATTLE
CLICK
UNSCREW
TIGHTEN
SLIIIDE

SQUII'
CLICK
SHIFT
"DON'T WORRY, MARS.

"IF DEAR OLD DAD DOES COME BACK, YOU'LL BE READY."

...WE'LL BE PLAYING ANOTHER SELECTION OF SONG FRAGMENTS RECENTLY REMEMBERED BY OUR DEDICATED RESEARCHERS HERE AT THE PASTWATCH INSTITUTE! THE WORLD OF THE ANCIENTS OPENS UP TO THOSE FEW WHOSE DREAMS REVEAL THE JEWELS OF THE WEALTH OF HISTORY!
the HOPELESS DIAMOND
LAS FRIDAS
CORN CHIPS
EXTRA SPICY
nehi
WHEN DETAILS BECOME GARBLED, THE MIND STRIVES TO FIND THE LOST "SIGNAL"
THE HUMAN MIND MAKES PATTERNS TO COMBAT NONSENSE AND THEN BELIEVES THESE PATTERNS INHERENT...
WELCOME TO the Pastwatch Institute
CULTURAL MUSEUM NO. 166
"the past through tomorrow"
DOOMED TO REPEAT IT
ART, HISTORY, INDUSTRY
ONCE HEARD, NONSENSE-RESOLVING PATTERNS ARE HARD TO DISPEL.
SHE'S ALL RIGHT, SHE'S ALL RIGHT, SHE'S ALL RIIIGHT...
THUNK!
CO-CAINE!
sigh...
NO BONES
CLIK!
CHOOSE YOUR OWN INDENTURE
ALL THE WORLD'S A HOSPITAL, AND EITHER YOU'RE A PATIENT OR A NURSE
BLYTHE, I JUST DON'T KNOW ABOUT THIS PLACE. IT'S LIKE A COCOON.
A MORGUE.
A TAXI-DERMIST'S SHOP...
BBBBBZZZZSSSSS
AH KNOW, MADAME, BUT EVERY KIND OF REFUGE 'AS EETS PRICE.
WORK 'ERE AN' YOU CAN KEEP YOUR PRETTY GRASS HOUSE. AH BEELIEVE EET WAS MA MADAME 'OO SAID, EEF AH MAY QUOTE: "EEF AH HAF' TO TAK' MAH CHEELDREN AN' MOVE BACK EENTO MAH FATHAIR'S HOUSE, AH WEEL STAB MAH-SELF SEEX TAHMS"!
PAST DUE
COLLECTION
FINAL NOTICE
HOPCO
PLEASE PAY
DUE IN FU
sigh.
AH HATE ZE SMELL OF ARTERIAL BLOOD, MADAME. AH HATE IT.

IF I TOOK A JOB HERE, I'D BE GONE FROM HOME, HOOKED UP TO A DOZEN RECORDING DEVICES, FOR TWO MONTHS OUT OF EVERY THREE... REALLY, WHAT'S THE POINT IN DOING THIS FOR MY HOUSE IF I'LL HARDLY EVER BE LIVING IN IT?
EET WOULD STEEL BE YOUR 'OUSE, MADAME. YOUR PROPERTY. A CONTRACT EES NOT FOR FOREVER.
GUILT
Tell her about the state-of-the-art health care she'll get for FREE! PUSH her! She WANTS that HOUSE!
NonoNO! She KNOWS we only want her to take the job so she'll HAVE to give us a new UPGRADE for SHAME!
I SEE A RENOIR AND I WANT IT PAINTED BLACK... NO COLOR ANYMORE, I WANT IT TO TURN BLAACK
JUS' LIKE A ONE-WINGED DOVE, SINGS A SONG SOUNDS LIKE SHE'S SINGIN' OOH BABY OO
I WON'T SEE MUCH OF THE KIDS... WASN'T THAT THE WHOLE POINT OF.... STAYING OUT?
NOOOBODY DIES in HEAVen... MAKES ME FEEL SAD FOR THE REST... NOOOBODY DUZZm HALF AS GOOD AS YOU...
S'INK OF ZEE BETTER OPPORTUNITIES YOU CAN OFFER ZEM, MADAME. ZEY PAY SO WELL AN' ARE SO PRESTIGE', ZEES INSTITUTION.
SHE GOTT ELECTRIC BOOBS, A MOHAWK TOO, YA KNOW I READ IT INNA MAGGA ZAYEEEN, AH-HO.... BB-B-BENNY ANNA JETSSSSSSSsss
SOMEbody has to look after the KIDS and the HOUSE! WE'VE been doing the job of a MUCH bigger program for YEARS! It's PAYBACK time!
"INSTI-TUTION."
... JO-JO WAS A MAN WHO THOUGHT 'E WAS A WOMAN, BUT 'E WUZZA 'NUTHER MAN...
erk!
WHAT IF...
WHAT IF I'M ...NOT REALLY TAPPING INTO THE PAST? WHAT IF... THIS COMES FROM ... I DON'T KNOW...
SURE, but they'll still WANT her! LISTEN! We've been her BUFFER from the outside world for a long TIME now-- taken CARE of everything so she could get along! So she can be thought of only as a FLAKE, not a PSYCHO! We NEED more SMARTS to keep this UP!
Hmf!

<WAILING BRASS... DISTANT, FRENETIC BEAT>
SSSHHH...
<HARMONIZED HOWL>
PIF
PAF
M... MADAME?
I... I DEEDN'T SAY...
DEED I?
...THIS, OUR LATEST SONG FRAGMENT; ITS VIBRANT BRASS AND MANIC PACE MARK IT AS THE PRODUCT OF THE SWING ERA... HOWEVER IT
YOU WORRY TOO MUCH.. YOU MAKE YOURSELF SAD
SSHH... IT'S VERY FAINT...
MADAME, DON'T GO-
HUSH!
YOU CAN'T CHANGE FATE
SO DON'T FEEL SO BAD
ENJOY IT WHILE YOU CAN
CHK!
IT'S JUST LIKE THE WEATHER
SO QUIT COMPLAINING, BROTHER
NO ONE
LIVES FOREVER

CRIIIIIIKKK
SPLOTT
NO ONE, NO ONE, NO ONE, NO ONE, NO ONE, NO ONE LIVES FOREVER!
WHSPR
WHSPR WHSPR
SMAT!
YOU KNOW IT!

WAIT HERE, MISS! I'LL GET THE DIRECTOR!
OOOH
OH MY.
SHE HAS IT
SHE'S GOT THE GIFT
WOW.
YOU THINK YOU WANT WHAT'S IN MY HEAD...?
DECOF
CAF
TAP
TAP
TAP TAP
TAP
WHO CARES THERE'S NOWHERE SAFE TO HIDE NOWHERE TO RUN, NO TIME TA CRY?
SO CELEBRATE WHILE YOU STILL CAN, CUZ ANY SECOND IT MAY END
CUZ NO ONE, NO ONE, NO ONE, NO ONE

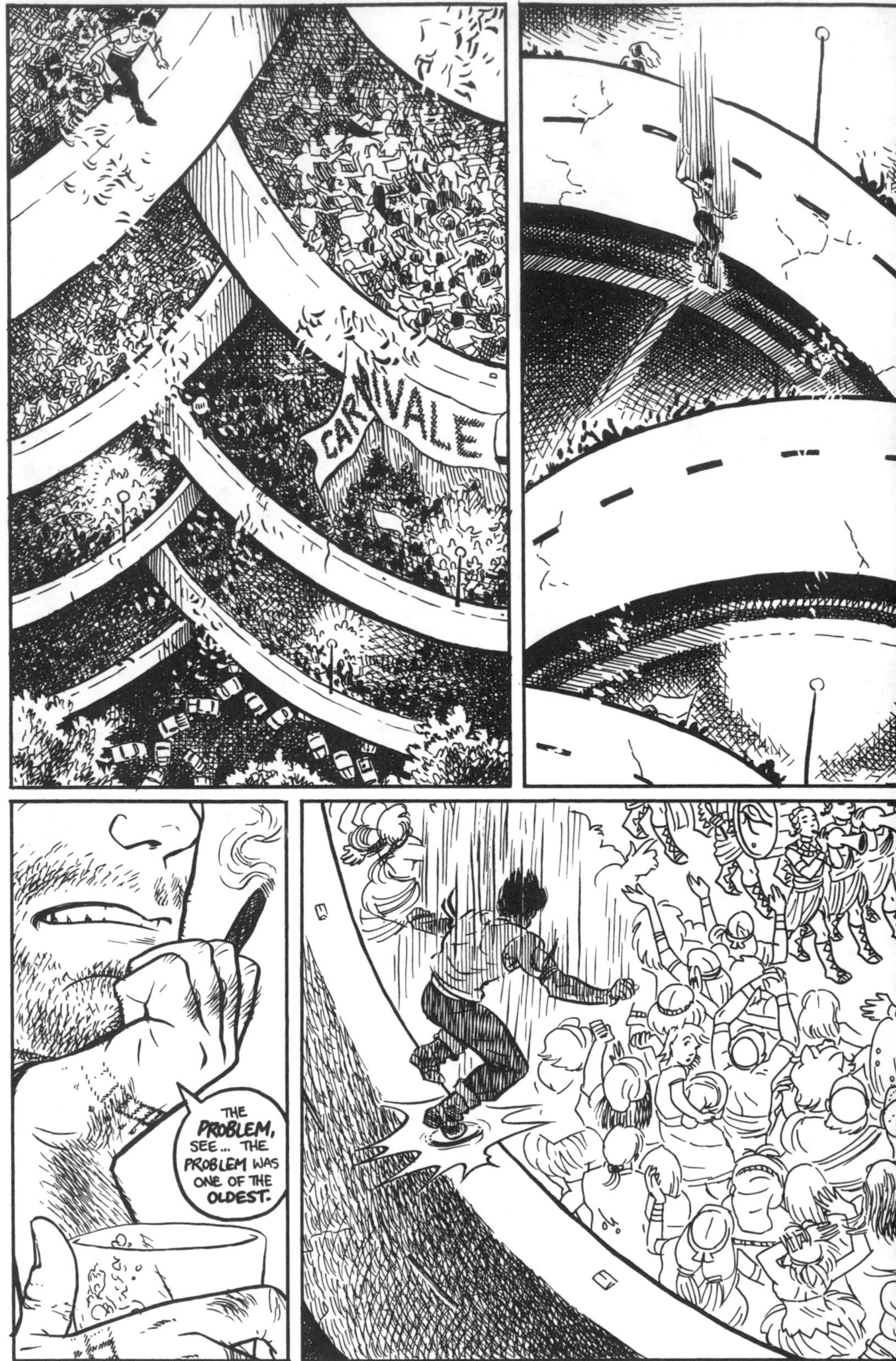
CARNIVALE
THE PROBLEM, SEE... THE PROBLEM WAS ONE OF THE OLDEST.

CAN'T ATTACK A MAN BEFORE HE'S DONE ANYTHING. A MAN-- EVEN A CRAZY MAN-- ISN'T A RABID DOG.
EVEN OUT IN WHAT PEOPLE SUPPOSE IS WILD AND UNLAWFUL COUNTRY, IT TAKES MORE THAN SUSPICIONS TO JUSTIFY A LYNCHING.
A MAN'S GOT TO BE GIVEN A CHANCE TO TURN HIMSELF AROUND.

MY PROBLEM WAS AN OLD ONE TOO.

PROBLEM IS...
HOW DO YOU GET A MAN TO LOOK AT HIMSELF?
ESPECIALLY A MAN WHO'S LIVED LIKE AN ISLAND, LIKE HE'S THE ONLY MAN ON EARTH, FOR SO LONG?
SURE, I SET BRIGHAM UP TO CRACK. I PUT THE SCREWS TO THAT MAN AND I DOGGED 'EM DOWN TIGHT. AN' POP WENT THE WEASEL.
I HAD THIS CRAZY IDEA THAT THAT WOULD SHOW HIM WHAT HE WAS IN DANGER OF BECOMING.
FINDERS.. MY KIND-- ARE TRAINED TO LOOK FOR PATTERNS. SOLVE PUZZLES. EVEN WHEN YOU DON'T KNOW WHAT THE PUZZLE IS, WHICH YA USUALLY DON'T.
HARDEST THING IN THE WORLD IS TO GET A WRONG IDEA OUT OF YOUR HEAD. A BAD PATTERN.
YOU MAY THINK YOU KNOW WHAT'S GOING ON, BUT YA DON'T.
GUYS LIKE BRIG, USUALLY THERE'S NOTHIN' YOU CAN DO WITH 'EM. EVEN THE SHRIVERS LOCK 'EM UNDER THE JAIL.
BUT I CAN'T DENY WHAT I DID TO HIM WAS PRETTY COLD BLOODED.
AND I'LL NEVER KNOW IF HE REALLY WOULDA BEEN OKAY IF I HADN'T TURNED UP THE HEAT UNDER HIM.
OR WHY I KEPT THE WHOLE THING SO CLOSE TO MY CHEST. DIDN'T CALL ANY COPS. NOT EVEN MY FRIENDS WHO WERE COPS.
THAT'S WHAT ATE AT ME, SAID IT WAS MY FAULT.

FORTUNATELY HIS POINT OF VIEW HARDLY **MATTERED** ANYMORE. YOU DON'T WASTE TALK ON RATTLESNAKES, EVEN IF IT **WAS** YOU THAT STIRRED 'EM UP.

THERE'S **MUCH** TO BE SAID FOR HAVING A ONE-TRACK MIND.

WOULDN'T IT BE **GREAT** IF IT WAS SOME BODY **ELSE** SITTING HERE IN MY FAMILY'S HOUSE WITH A HOMEMADE BOMB?

YEAH IT WOULD BE **PERFECT.**

WHAT IF THEY DON'T COME HOME **THIS** TIME **EITHER?**

LIKE THIS KID I HEARD ABOUT YEARS AGO.
HE'S ON HIS WAY TO SCHOOL AND SOME DUDE HANDS HIM A PACKAGE AND IT'S A **BOMB**. WHO **KNOWS** HOW HE GOT THE KID TO **TAKE** IT.
RELAX. YOU WERE IN THEIR **OTHER** HOUSE BEFORE. THEY **OBVIOUSLY JUST** MOVED **IN** HERE. THEY WEREN'T ... **HIDING** FROM YOU...
WHO COULDA TIPPED 'EM OFF ANYWAY? NOBODY.
NOT THE COPS. I MYSELF INTERCEPTED THE LETTER NOTIFYING THEM OF MY RELEASE FROM PRISON...
INSTEAD OF THROWIN' IT **AWAY**, THE KID SHIELDS THE CROWD WITH HIS OWN BODY.
BOOM. TEN-YEAR-OLD KID SPLATTERED ALL OVER THE TUBE STATION.
NOT JAEGER. HE'S UNRELIABLE BUT LOYAL. THAT DOESN'T MAKE SENSE BUT HE BELONGS TO NO CLAN SO I CAN'T EXPECT HIM TO.
HE'S LOYAL. HE **HELPED** ME.

THAT KID GOT HIS CHANCE TO BE A MAN AT **TEN** AND HE DIDN'T **BLOW** IT.
PRETTY WOMAN LIKE EMMA, NUBILE YOUNG THING LIKE RACHEL OH HE'S A FOX IN THE CHICKENYARD
DECOFFEE
CAFFEE
EXCUSE THE EXPRESSION.
NO. HE **HELPED** ME. IN THIS CHAIR I'M NO DANGER TO ANYBODY.

PERFECT SACRIFICE. HE SAVED ALL THOSE PEOPLE AND DIDN'T GAIN ANYTHING FROM IT BUT A HERO'S TOMB.
JAEGER PROTECTED ME. I LOST MY FREE-MAN LICENSE--
--SOMEBODY STOLE IT, YOU MEAN--
--I GO BACK TO JAIL IF I GET CAUGHT WITHOUT IT--

YOU KNOW HE WAS PROBABLY A BAD KID. CRAP GRADES. SASSED HIS PARENTS. DRUGS. MAYBE GOT DIRTY WITH KIDS WEAKER THAN HIM EVEN. BUT WHO CARES? WHEN HE GOT HIS CHANCE, HE REDEEMED HIMSELF.
--I NEEDED MEDICAL CARE--
-BECAUSE OF HIM!--

THAT'S ALL I EVER WANTED. A CHANCE TO MAKE GOOD. IF ONLY I COULD BE THAT KID.
I WOULDN'T CARE IF I HAD TO DIE, IF ONLY THEY'D LOVE ME AND THINK WELL OF ME.
--BECAUSE OF ME! I DESERVED EVERYTHING HE GAVE ME! I'D A DONE THE SAME!
--I GIVE UP--

I'VE MADE MY DECISION.
HE GOT ME HOSPITAL CARE--
--WITHOUT EXPOSING ME TO THE COPS THOSE BASTARDS WHO SHOULD BE MY BROTHERS
HE'S ON MY SIDE.

IF THEY DON'T COME HOME TONIGHT -- I WON'T GO ON WAITING.
AND IF THIS IS SOME KIND OF TRICK-- WELL, WHOEVER SET IT UP DESERVES THIS.

BOOM.
HEY--
WHY DO YOU DO THAT TO YOUR EYES?

I MEAN, MAKE 'EM GET ALL BIG LIKE THAT. I HEARD 'EM CRACKLE LIKE YOU CRACKED YOUR KNUCKLES. WHY DO YA DO 'EM LIKE THAT?

I
AH

SNIFF

IT--IT'S A TRICK--CKK: A TRICK I LEARNED--AT YOUR AGE--TO--REROUTE TEARS. I DON' NOTICE WHEN I DO IT.
THE NOISE... WAS--PROBABLY --MY NECK.
CKK

OH.
DEC

RACHEL!

hm!

I GUESS IT WORKED TOO MUCH.
sigh
WHAT DID?

WANNA KNOW SOME-THING?

MOM!
HOW DO, TWIN? HAPPY CARNIVAL!

SURE... huh honey.
OFFEINATED AFFEE

I DID MAGIC TO MAKE YOU COME BACK. I'M NOT S'PPOSED TO BUT I LIKE TO.
MAGIC. WELL --WELL THAT'S

SEE, I GOT MY FIRST LOOSE TOOTH. SEE? AND I DID A BIG SPELL AND WISHED ON ALL MY TEETH AND MY BONES TOO. I KNEW THERE WAS A BIG CHANGE HAPPENIN' AND I MADE SURE I'D BE IN ON IT.

AOW!!

nh!

OH JEsus!

DUD-- DON'T GIVE ME THAT LOOK! I DIDN'T MEAN TO --

TOOTH FAIRY!
AAA!

AW JEEZ KID YOU'LL NEVER FIND IT IN ALL THIS WHAT THE HELL IS IT, GRASS??

DON'T KNOW WHAT MAKES YOUR MAMA THINK DIRT BELONGS INSIDE A HOUSE BUT --
WHAT'S THIS?

LOOKS LIKE A JACK FOR A HEAD COMPUTER.
CAN YOU READ THIS FOR ME?

"FREE MAN."
IT SAYS "FREE MAN."
IT'S A LICENSE.
AND IT -- IT WAS--
HERE.

EMMA WILL SHIT SHE'LL ABSOLUTELY SHIT
SHE'LL DISAPPEAR INTO LA-LA LAND AND NEVE COME OUT
SHIT SHIT SHI SHIT

BOY!
I WONDER WHAT ELSE IS GONNA COME BACK!
THAT STUFF CAME WITH ME, HONEY.
SURE. IT DID. IT CAME BACK LIKE YOU DID. SEE, WE THREW OUT THIS VERY STUFF WEEKS AGO!
THREW IT OUT? MY LEATHER? THAT --THAT YOUR MOTHER-- --SAVED FOR ME-- ALL THESE YEARS?
OH, YEAH. RACHEL WAS SO HAPPY WHEN JAEGER TALKED MAMA INTO THROWING OUT ALL THIS OLD GARBAGE SO EVERYBODY COULD HAVE MORE ROOM IN THEIR CLOSETS.
BUT I GUESS IT'S ALL GONNA COME BACK NOW. DARN THAT TOOTH! ALL I WANTED WAS FOR JAEGER MONSTER TO STAY THIS TIME!
HOPE ALL THE GARBAGE DOESN'T COME BACK TOO! OOH... I HOPE THE TOILET STILL WORKS ... BOY! WOULDN'T IT BE GROSS IF THAT ALL CAME BACK!
SO-- SO THAT'S HOW IT IS, IS IT? I'M GARBAGE, I'M SHIT, YOUR OWN FATHER, JUST THROW HIM AWAY!
CRICKK
'MON, BRAT! ET'S HEAR YOU ALL ME "DADDY" IKE YOU NEVER ID EVEN WHEN YOU WERE TWO! NOT EVEN THEN!
C'MON! "DA DA"! LET'S HEAR IT! COME ON YOU LITTLE SHIT!
DECAFF CAFFE
WHOOOA!

OAHH...
WHAAAH
...
CLIK
FZZZZ

EMMA
...

UFF!

JAEGER!
SOB
HUFF
HUFF

NO-- NO--
EMMA--
WHINE
I-- I
DIDN'T
--
FZZzzz

AAH
FUCK
FZZZ
YOU!
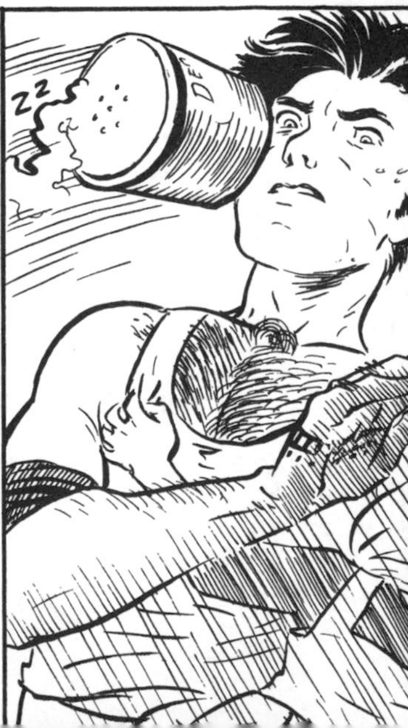
ZZ

DAMN THING YOU DAM
JAEGER LOOKOUT
AAAAAAAAAA
SPANG

KKOOOM!
bBBRRRRRMMBBLLLLLL

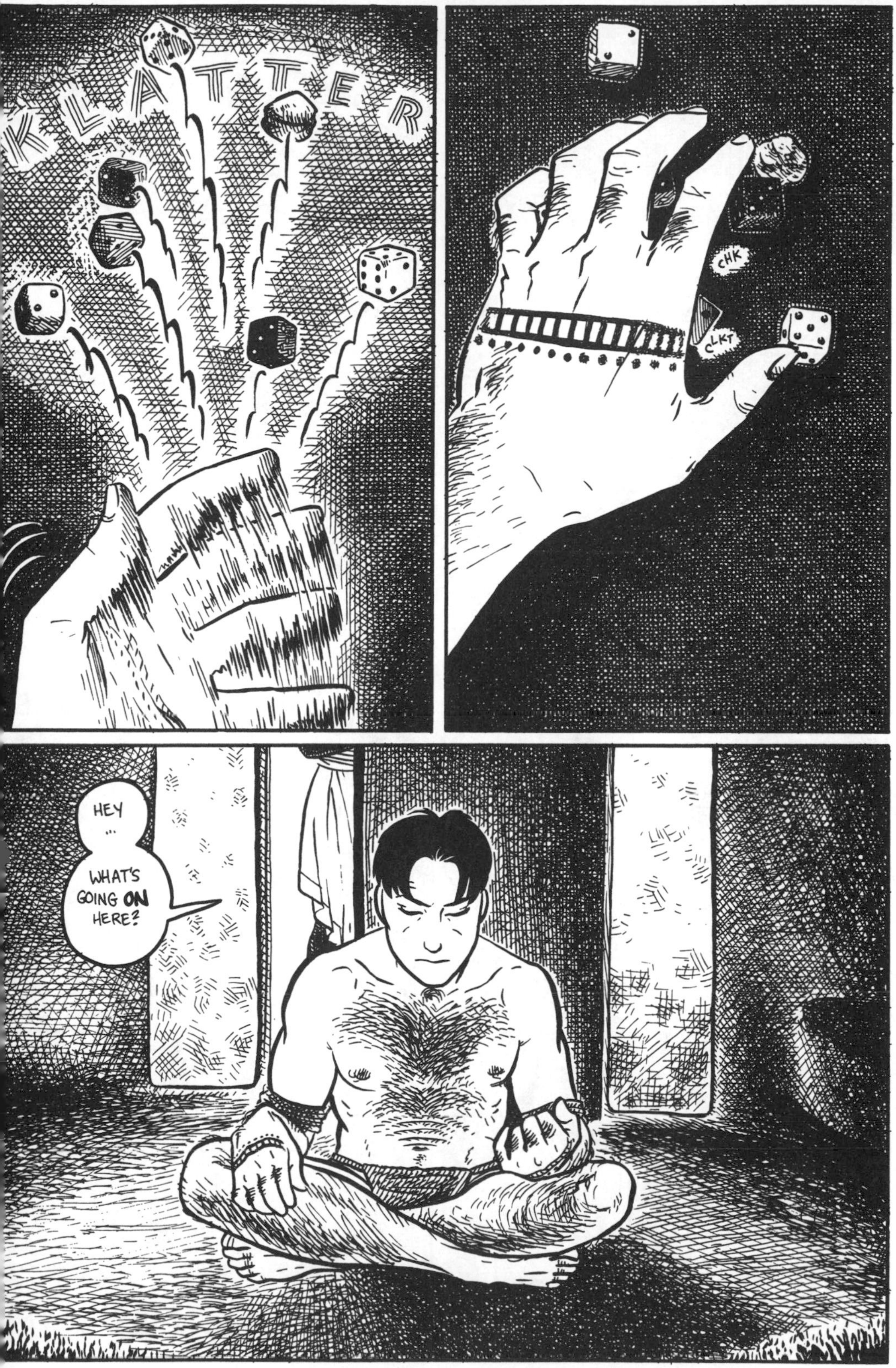

HEY ...
WHAT'S GOING **ON** HERE?

CHOOK
CHOOKA
CHOOKA
WHAT-
CHA
DOING?
KLATTER
THINKING.
CHOOKA
CHOOKA
CHOOK
WHAT
ABOUT
?
KLATTER
WHAT'S THE
USE...
EVEN A
BEATING'S
WASTED
ON YOU,
BOY...
WET FIRE-
CRACKERS.

AW!
POPP
POW!
OWEEOWEE
WELL, RUTH, I TOLD JA NOT TO LET "SWEATY" HENDERSON CARRY 'EM AROUND!
PIRATE STATION
POPP
PFFT
AW!
PERSONALLY? I WILL NOT BE DISAPPOINTED BY ANYTHING THAT FAILS TO EXPLODE FOR THE REST OF MY LIFE.
AOW SHIT!
BRIGHAM-- WHAT THE HELL DO YOU THINK YOU'RE DOING?
SO YOU UST LET THIS GUY ASTE YOU ACROSST HE HEAD WITH A OMEMADE BOMB.
IN A COFFEE CAN.
OUTTA PURE GOODNESS.
'CAUSE YOU'RE A BIG OL' HERO.
MORE LIKE A BIG OL' MASOCHIST.
'CAUSE THERE WEREN'T NO GOOD PLACE TO DEE-FLECT IT OFF TO.
TOOK IT RIGHT ONNA CHIN.
ULDN'T EE-VEN AT IT BACK AT E NUT WHO ADE THE BOMB?
HO ACTUALLY ESERVED A CE FULLA RAPNEL?
IF IT'A GONE OFF, WHICH IT DIDN'T.
WHICH PURTY-BOY FLOYD HERE HAD NO WAY A KNOWIN' IT WASN'T GONNA...
CAN'T COUNT ON THINGS LIKE THAT.
YOU GOTTA LIGHT 'EM TO FIND 'EM.

"I'D BEEN VISITING BRIG IN PRISON EVERY ONCE IN ...OH, A WHILE... WHAT I DIDN'T KNOW WAS THAT HIS WIFE WAS MESSED UP TOO..."
DON'T GOOOo
JAEGER...
SOB

YOU TELL 'EM... TELL EMMA... TELL 'ER I DIDN'T MEAN IT...
COURSE, BRIG. HERE CATCH... I GOT PICTURES FOR YA.

BRIGHAM-- MAJOR GROSVENOR-- HE WAS JUST BURNED OUT, I THOUGHT. SOLDIER'S DISEASE. COULDN'T SLEEP, COULDN'T EAT, COULDN'T THINK. HE'D CRACKED. IT HAPPENS. IT CAN MAKE A MAN DANGEROUS, OR HELPLESS. OR BOTH, SOMETIMES. EVERYBODY'S GOT FAULT LINES.
BUT HEY, I THOUGHT HE WAS RIGHT WHERE HE NEEDED TO BE. MEDAWARS PUT NUTS IN PRISON. MEDO WOMEN NEARLY INVENTED DOCTORIN', JUST TO PUT THEIR MEN BACK TOGETHER. WHEN HE GOT OUT... WELL, HE SEEMED OKAY. MEDAWAR WOMEN... THEY KNOW HOW TO HANDLE SHELL SHOCK.
THING WAS... BRIG'S WIFE, EMMA? SHE WASN'T A MEDAWAR WOMAN.
Z

EMMA?
HM?
CLANGG
CLINGITY
CLANG
CLANGG
ANGG
NGG
CLANGG
PLANTARS MARBLES

WHAT DOES, EH... "HORAGOROSI" MEAN, EXACTLY?

YOU TALK IN YOUR SLEEP, AND I WAS --HEY!
CLATTER

OH, JAEGER... I'M FINE. JUST ARRANGING SOME DEAD FLOWERS...

OU MUSTA HIT YOUR HEAD--
DRIED FLOWERS, I MEAN...

EMMA--! GIVE YOURSELF A BREAK, SIT STILL A MINUTE!
NATURALLY, YOU CAN'T PUT LIVE PLANTS IN A MENDED VASE; IT'LL ONLY LEAK.

NOW LOOK, YOU HORNY YOUNG THING, YOU HAVE GOT TO LET ME GET SOMETHING DONE TODAY!

"ALL THE REST OF THAT DAY, SHE WAS SO BRIGHT AND CHEERFUL I STARTED CHECKING CABINETS FOR DRUGS."
EM, IF YOU'RE PISSED ABOUT SOME-THING, I'D REALLY RATHER YOU JUST COME RIGHT OUT AND...

"CONCUSSIONS CAN MAKE PEOPLE ACT FUNNY... I'D HALF CONVINCED MYSELF THAT'S ALL IT WAS...
"THEN I RECALLED WHAT MADE HER FALL OUT IN THE FIRST PLACE."

IIORAGOROSI.

WHAT, EMMA...? WHAT?

SEEMS EMMA HAD A WHOLE MADE-UP WORLD IN HER HEAD, COMPLETE WITH A LANGUAGE.
ORACLE TOLD ME THE LANGUAGE GOES BACKWARD AND FORWARD. "HORAGOROSI" FORWARDS MEANS "THE END OF THE WORLD." BACKWARDS IT MEANS "HE IS COMING BACK SOMEDAY."

SO.
HERE'S BRIGHAM. FRESH OUT OF A PRISON THAT'S HALF NUTHOUSE, EAGER TO GET BACK TO PLAYING HOUSE.

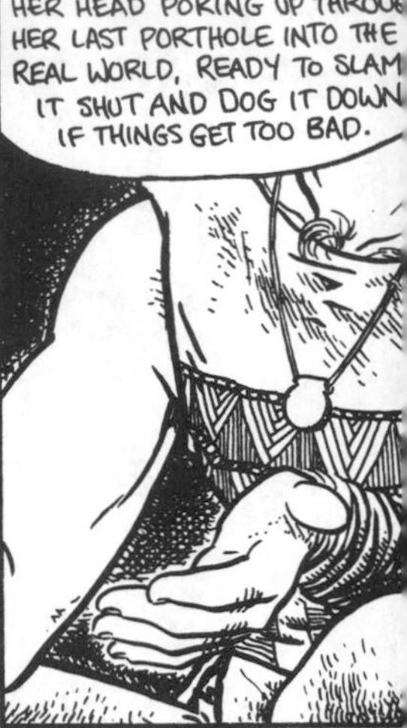
AND HERE'S EMMA, WITH HER HEAD POKING UP THROUG HER LAST PORTHOLE INTO THE REAL WORLD, READY TO SLAM IT SHUT AND DOG IT DOWN IF THINGS GET TOO BAD.

KIDS IN THE MIDDLE.
BOOM!

SECRET GARDENS
LANDSCAPING & GARDEN DESIGN
EMMA GROSVENOR
01010 RISING RD E ANWARD
8220-2706-8707 02 AI
"I KEPT 'EM APART..."
SOB I.. I DIDN'T MEAN IT-- I JUST --YOU ALL LOOK ALIKE--
"I TESTED THEIR FAULT LINES...

"THEY DIDN'T JUST CRACK. THEY WENT TO PIECES."

SIGH.
AND HERE'S THIS UNDERAGE BIT OF FLUFF WHO THINKS I'M SITTING ON ALL THE SECRETS OF THE UNIVERSE.

TAEGER, WHAT ARE YOU DOING?

--DON'T--
AH--

WHAT'S THIS?

OH! UH, I DUNNO... IT'S JUST FELT-TIP MARKER... I WAS ALL JUMPY SO I WENT TO SCHOOL TODAY JUST TO FEEL NORMAL, AND SURE ENOUGH I WAS BORED ABSOLUTELY STIFF, BUT I WAS STILL NERVY, AND I KINDA JUST DOODLED IT IN HISTORY CLASS AND IT'S STUPID, BUT I FELT A LOT BETTER
...

I DIDN'T THINK YOU'D BE MAD... ACTUALLY I DIDN'T THINK ABOUT IT AT ALL-- I JUST-- YOU'RE NOT MAD, ARE YOU?
I MEAN, IT'S JUST, UH

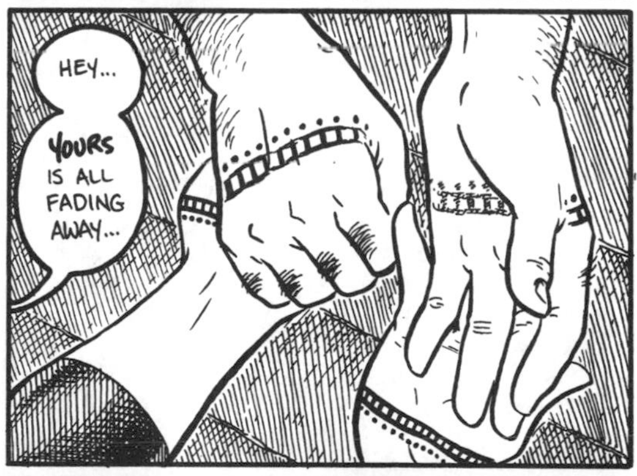
HEY...
YOURS IS ALL FADING AWAY...

SIT WITH ME, RACHEL.

KLATTER

HMPH.
FIGURES.

KLATTER

UHM.
THIS IS-- SOME SORT OF FORTUNETELLING THING, ISN'T IT?
SOME SORT, YEAH.

YOU DON'T-- ACTUALLY BELIEVE IN THIS STUFF, DO YOU? I MEAN -- YOU DON'T REALLY BELIEVE YOU CAN TELL THE FUTURE WITH A BUNCH OF PLASTIC DICE? I KNOW PEOPLE CALL YOU A--A CAVE MAN OR A TREE HANGER OR WHATEVER, BUT, UM-- YOU'RE THE MOST PRACTICAL, LOGICAL PERSON I KNOW, AND... WELL...

I... WELL, I ALWAYS WANTED TO BELIEVE IN ALL THIS MYSTIC STUFF, BUT WHEN I GET RIGHT DOWN TO IT, I JUST DON'T... IT SEEMS SILLY TO BASE ANYTHING IMPORTANT ON IT... SO... I MEAN, IS THIS SOMETHING YOU-- FOLKS FROM OUTSIDE -- DO TO SEEM MYSTERIOUS TO US, BECAUSE WE EXPECT IT, OR DO YOU REALLY... AND WHY DO YOU... ARGH. WHAT I WANT TO KNOW IS, WHY DOES THIS MEAN SOMETHING TO YOU?

I KNOW THIS--ISN'T VERY TACTFUL...
THIS ISN'T MAGIC. THIS IS JUST A WAY OF GETTING AT ALL ANGLES. SOME PEOPLE MAKE LISTS. SOME PEOPLE FLIP COINS.
I PROBABLY SHOULDA DONE IT AT THE BEGINNING.

FLIP A COIN?
THINK.

HEHH.. NOT FLIP A COIN, OH NO, HONEY, FOR IF I HAD, I CAN ALMOST ASSURE YOU I WOULDN'T STILL BE HERE.

UMBRAMANCY... THAT TAKES HOURS, MAYBE DAYS, IN PITCH DARKNESS. FEBRIMANCY... MEANS THOSE MOMENTS OF CLARITY THAT COME WHEN YOU HAVE A HIGH FEVER...
..THE FANCY WORDS DIGNIFY 'EM, BUT NO METHOD IS FOOLPROOF... BIBLIOMANCY... THAT'S A LINE IN A BOOK, CHOSEN AT RANDOM... DACNOMANCY... THAT'S WHAT THOSE LOONY BLOOD PRIESTS SAY PSYCHO KILLERS ARE DOING... HOCHIOMANCY... THE THINGS YOU SEE IN A HEAVY FOG... CATOPTRO-MANCY... THAT'S MIRRORS... ...ONEIROMANCY... ...APEIROMANCY...

THIS--THIS IS HOW YOU DECIDE WHEN, NOT IF, YOU'RE GONNA RUN OUT ON US?

U WON'T TALK ABOUT WHY OU DO THINGS. YOU DON'T ANT TO BE UNDER-STOOD.
BABY, INSIGHTS DON'T COME FROM POLLING THE NEIGHBORHOOD.
THEY DON'T COME FROM TEA LEAVES OR FANCY CARDS OR CRAP LIKE THIS EITHER.

NO, THEY DON'T. ALL ORACLES ARE ONLY MECHANISMS TO MAKE MIRRORS THAT TALK BACK.

OH, THAT'S GOOD-- YOU, YOU GONNA ROLL DICE TILL YOU GET THE ANSWER YOU WANT AND THINK THAT SINCE YOU HAD MORE OPTIONS THAN WITH A COIN TOSS, THAT MAKES IT BEYOND YOUR CONTROL?
YOU MADE YOUR DECISION THE SECOND DADDY CAME THROUGH THAT DOOR AND FUCKED EVERYTHING UP.
"CONFUCIUS SAY, TWO BULLS IN ONE PASTURE MAKE MUCH BULLSHIT"!
GONNA SAY, "IT'S OUT OF MY HANDS"? IT'S FATE, OR THE LUCK OF THE DRAW, OR SOMETHING?
WELL THERE IS NO FATE, BOY; NO WHEEL OF FORTUNE, NO SANTA CLAUS, NO TOOTH FAIRY!
NO PLAN, EXCEPT WHAT WE MAKE!
THINGS HAPPEN OR DON'T HAPPEN AND LUCK HAS NOTHING TO DO WITH IT!
RAE, YOU DON'T EVEN REALIZE THE CIRCLES YOU'RE TALKING IN.
THE WORD "HAPPEN," ITS OLDEST PART, IT MEANS "LUCK."
NO, DON'T... YOU DON'T GET TO BE NICE NOW...
YOU SAID THAT TO SHUT ME UP...
SIGH...
SUCKS WHEN PEOPLE GET TO KNOW YOU...
HOW COULD I TELL THE KID ALL THE SHIT THAT HAD BEEN GOIN' ON? THAT MOST OF IT WAS PROBABLY MY FAULT?
SNK
I---'M HAVING THESE BAD DREAMS LIKE I'M FALLIN'... THE BAD PART IS, IT'S NOT JUST THAT I'M FALLING BUT THAT --IT GOES ON AND ON, AND WHILE IT'S TERRIFYING IT'S AT THE SAME TIME BORING...
AND I KNOW, I KNOW, THAT I'M JUST GONNA GO ON FALLING AND FALLING FOREVER, AND NEVER HIT ANYTHING, BUT I CAN'T HELP BUT GO ON SCREAMING.
IF THERE'S A HELL AND I'M GOING, THAT'S WHAT IT'S GONNA BE LIKE.

THEN THERE'S THE WHOLE QUESTION OF BEING A SIN-EATER, THE HABITS AND ETHICS OF THE PROFESSION.
IT IS A PROFESSION, Y'UNDERSTAND: THE ONLY ONE OPEN TO A HALF-BREED LIKE MYSELF, WITH NO SPONSORS AMONG MY MOTHER'S PEOPLE.
WHAT I PRESUME ARE MY MOTHER'S PEOPLE.
ASCIANS.
SIN-EATER'S LOWEST OF THE LOW. UNTOUCHABLE. SCAPE-GOAT, WHO PURIFIES THE DYING SO THEY CAN GO ON TO A BETTER PLACE.
SIN-EATER'S LOW, BUT ALSO REVERED FOR HIS SACRIFICE. NOBODY MAKES THE SIN-EATER CLEAN WHEN HE DIES. NOBODY COULD EAT SO MUCH GUILT.
NO GIRL WOULD MARRY ONE.
BUT YOU'D BE SHOCKED AT THE NUMBERS WHO'D ROLL ONE...
ASCIAN LAW IS HEAVY ON THE HYSICAL STUFF. ENDURANCE PENALTIES, LOGGING, GAUNTLET, ALL THAT. BUT THEY 'NT PUNISH SOME PEOPLE THAT-A-WAY; EGNANT WOMEN, LITTLE KIDS, CRAZY OPLE. TABOOS. SO SOMETIMES A SIN-EATER IS CALLED UPON TO EAT THE SIN OF THE LIVING.
COUNCIL CAME ASKING IF ANYBODY WOULD STAND IN FOR A EMBER OF THE SHAKMAH FAMILY. I SN'T GONNA SAY ANYTHING, 'CAUSE OR SHAKMAH-- HE WAS MY AGE-- WOULDN'T PISS ON HIM IF HE WAS BURNING TO DEATH.
THEN THEY SAID IT WASN'T THE KID, BUT HIS DAFT D GRANDAD, CONVICTED OF MALICIOUS ROPERTY DAMAGE. MAN'S OLDER'N OD, WANDERING IN HIS WITS, AND LWAYS IN TROUBLE FOR SOME SHIT OR ANOTHER....
SOOO, I FELT BAD FOR THE OLD MAN, AND OBVIOUSLY SO DID HE COUNCIL, SO I SAID I'D DO IT. UNCIL ALL GOES, "YOU?" 'CAUSE I AS JUST A KID, AND THEY COULDN'T SHOW MERCY TO A SIN-EATER.
BUT THEY DIDN'T WANT TO BEAT THE OLD MAN, AND NO OTHER SIN-EATER COULD SPEAK UP ONCE I HAD. NOBODY EATS FOR THE SIN-EATER.
SO, THEY HUNG ME UP IN THE TOWN CIRCLE AND BEAT ME LIKE A GONG WITH A BIG, LONG LEATHER WHIP.

BEFORE THEY STARTED, I WAS COUNTING UP ALL THE BROKEN BONES I'D EVER HAD AND WONDERING HOW BAD THIS COULD REALLY BE.
THEN THAT FIRST ONE HIT ME AND I FOUND OUT. I WAS READY TO CONFESS TO EVERY SIN COMMITTED SINCE MANKIND CAME OUT OF THE TREES.
I SAW STARS. YOU REALLY DO SEE STARS IF THEY HIT YOU HARD ENOUGH. OPTIC NERVE FIRES OR SOMESUCH. I SAW COLORS I'D NEVER SEEN, BEFORE OR SINCE. I WAS... WELL, I WAS JUST GONE. NOBODY HOME. ON ABOUT THE SIXTH STROKE, COUNTING BACK FROM FORTY-FIVE, I GOT BACK INTO MY HEAD AND I FOUND OUT WHAT EVERY ANIMAL RUNNING FOR ITS LIFE KNOWS.
I HAVE THE WILL TO DIE.
LET THIS BE OVER, SAYS THIS LITTLE VOICE, SOUNDING REMARKABLY LIKE MY OWN; LET THIS BE OVER, OR LET ME DIE.
BOREDOM AND PAIN CAN KILL YOU. ENDURANCE IS WHITTLED AWAY AS MUCH BY HELPLESSNESS AS BY TERROR. THAT'S WHAT MAKES THE HARE STUMBLE, THE DEER DROP HIS CROWN, THE BEAR PINE AWAY FROM THE SPEAR POINT LODGED UNDER HIS RIB, LONG HEALED THOUGH IT MAY BE. THAT VOICE SPEAKS IN ALL OF US.
LET THIS BE ENDED, OR LET ME DIE.
THEN IT WAS OVER.
THEY CUT ME DOWN, AND I GOT BETTER.
THAT NIGHT, WHEN I COULD HEAR AGAIN, THE DOC WHO'D DECIDED TO LOOK AFTER ME STOOD UNHIDDEN AS A FINDER, A MEMBER OF A SECRET SOCIETY OF THE BEST HUNTERS, TRACKERS, AND SCOUTS IN THE NATION.
HE SAID I HAD A GIFT. HE WANTED TO SPONSOR ME TO HIS BROTHER FINDERS, TO TEACH ME TO BE ONE.
SECRECY. MASTERY. ACCEPTANCE.
BETTER TO BE ONE OF THEM THAN TO BE ROYALTY.
OF COURSE, I'D HAVE TO GO ON BEING A SIN-EATER; THAT, THE MEDICINE TALKER SAID, WAS A UNIQUE TWIST THAT THE BROTHERHOOD OF FINDERS WOULD RESPECT.
PAYBACK, THAT'S HOW IT FELT. KEPT ME FROM KILLING MYSELF, AS SIN-EATERS OFTEN DO.
IT'S ALSO WHY I DIDN'T KILL LODR SHAKMAH, EVEN WHEN I FOUND OUT IT HAD BEEN ALL HIS FAULT. THAT HE'D BEEN STIRRING UP SHIT AND BLAMING IT ON HIS OLD GRANDAD FOR YEARS.
I DID TELL ALL THE OTHER SIN-EATERS ABOUT HIM, THOUGH. WE KEEP OUR OWN COUNCILS, THOUGH FEW KNOW OR CARE. WHEN HE LIES DYING, HE'LL HAVE A HELL OF A TIME GETTING A SIN-EATER.
NOBODY COULD EAT THAT MUCH SIN.

DURGA
ADMINISTRATOR
MATACORDA
MEDAWAR
CHARITY
HOSPITAL
I'M A **HERO!** I'M A **HERO!** I SAVED MY FAMILY FROM THE **DAMN THING!**
CRASH
MODERN MEDIEVALISM
JULIA! HURRY UP WITH THAT HYPO!

MANY MEDICAL TECHNIQUES ONCE LABELED BARBARISMS ARE NOW SHOWING UNEXPECTED MERITS UNDER MODERN SCRUTINY.
PREFRONTAL LOBOTOMY, TREPHINING, AND BLOOD PACKING, SINCE THEY CAN NOW BE PERFORMED WITH GREAT PRECISION, HAVE PROVEN VERY EFFECTIVE IN CONTEMPORARY TREATMENT.
NO! YOU BITCHES GET YOUR **HANDS OFF** ME! NO MORE **DRUGS!**
THIS IS WHAT IS NOW DESCRIBED AS "MODERN MEDIEVALISM." DESPITE AIRS OF DRAMA AND SUPERSTITION, THE MEDICINE OF THE ANCIENTS HAS MUCH TO OFFER.
MMCH

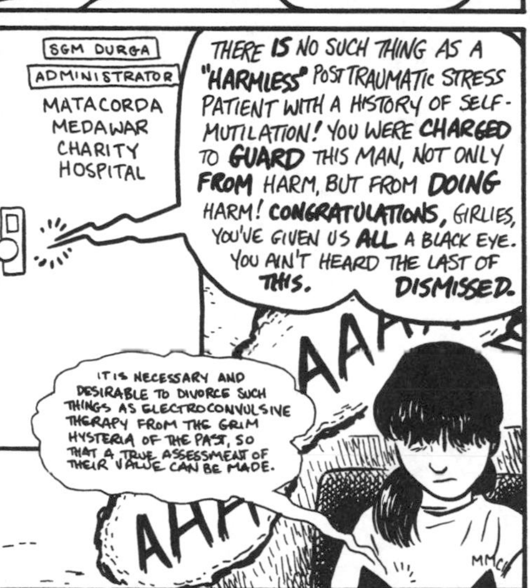

SGM DURGA
ADMINISTRATOR
MATACORDA
MEDAWAR
CHARITY
HOSPITAL
THERE **IS** NO SUCH THING AS A **"HARMLESS"** POST TRAUMATIC STRESS PATIENT WITH A HISTORY OF SELF-MUTILATION! YOU WERE **CHARGED** TO **GUARD** THIS MAN, NOT ONLY **FROM** HARM, BUT FROM **DOING** HARM! **CONGRATULATIONS,** GIRLIES, YOU'VE GIVEN US **ALL** A BLACK EYE. YOU AIN'T HEARD THE LAST OF **THIS. DISMISSED.**
AAAH
IT IS NECESSARY AND DESIRABLE TO DIVORCE SUCH THINGS AS ELECTROCONVULSIVE THERAPY FROM THE GRIM HYSTERIA OF THE PAST, SO THAT A TRUE ASSESSMENT OF THEIR VALUE CAN BE MADE.
AHH

SGM DURGA
ADMINISTRATOR
MATACORDA
MEDAWAR
CHARITY
AN INTENSIVE INVESTIGATION OF **EVERY** PRACTICE OF THE ANCIENTS IS CALLED FOR. NO MATTER HOW BIZARRE THEY MAY SEEM TO MODERN EYES. FROM PURGING AND BLEEDING TO COLD-WATER CURES, WE
OH GOD NO LET ME **GO** PLEASE, I JUST WANNA GO **HOME**

NNE, I WOULD LIKE TO MAKE A RMAL APOLOGY TO YOUR FAMILY R OUR NEGLIGENCE. THIS IS A ERRIBLE THING FOR THEM TO HAVE EEN EXPOSED TO, AND IT'S NTIRELY MY RESPONSIBILITY.
YOU CUNTS GET YOUR HANDS OFF--
MMCH
STAFF

CRASH!
SOB
WHINE WHINE WHINE
DON'T WORRY ABOUT YOUR FATHER.

WE'LL TRY SOME NEW THERAPIES ON HIM.

SKTCH SKTCH

DON'T **FIGHT,** YOU GUYS.

I'M SORRY, MARCIE... WE WOKE YOU UP.

IT'S OKAY... I CAN'T SLEEP... MY DREAMS ARE NO GOOD.

WOULD THEY BE BETTER IF YOU HAD YOUR DUST BUNNY BACK?

MY DUST...

...IT **MIGHT...**

BRIGHAM GRUSVENOR PERSONAL EFFECTS

DIDJA LOOK IN THAT **BAG?**

TSK! YES.

ALL THE WAY TO THE BOTTOM?

EWW!

EWWW!

EW!

I KNOW-- ON'T SAY IT--
"YOU MAY THINK YOU KNOW WHAT'S GOING ON--
"BUT YOU DON'T."
SIGH
WHUF!
BRRRSSSTTT
SO. MAJOR TIBBETS OF ZE ENOLA GAY 'AS RETURN TO ZE BLAST CRATER AT LAST, EH?
O BAD, YOUR PLANS R YOUR CAT'S PAW, EY COM' TO NUSSING. YOU ANNOT KEEP E SECRET ROM ME! U CANNOT K' ME PART!
AND DO I KNOW WHAT YOU'RE WHININ' ABOUT?
YOUR LEETLE SEESTER!
YOU EENTERFERE WEES ZE VER' COMPLEX DEVICES OF ZE DOCTEUR! YOU EENSERT SOME TER'BLE PROGRAM OF YOUR OWN EENTO 'ER MIND!
I WAS ZAT 'OUSE; I SEE EV-ER-Y-S'ING! ANY MACHINE ZAT ES PLUG EEN, ES PLUG EENTO ME.
ALL HOLES FILLED, HUH? HOW NICE FOR YOU.
DON'T WORRY, MARS.
IF DEAR OLD DAD DOES COME BACK, YOU'LL BE READY.
MMCH
OH, INDEED YES! SMALL GIRL CAN USE ZE GUN, ZE KNIFE!
YOU WOULD DO ZIS TO YOUR OWN BABY SISTER! SEND MARCELLA AWAY FOREVER TO 'OUSE OF INCORRIGIBLES!
WELL, I S'INK ET EES SOMEONE ELSE 'OO IS GO AWAY FOREVER ONCE MADAME KNOWS OF ZIS!

THAT PROGRAM DID EXACTLY WHAT I INTENDED IT TO DO.
WELL! BEST FOR ALL OF US, ZAT YOUR EGO EES SO MUCH MORE BIG ZAN YOUR BRAIN, AN' SO YOU WEEL TRIP OVAIR EET--
LOOK AT MARCIE.
USED TO BE, ALL YOU HAD TO DO WAS MENTION THE OLD MAN, AND SHE'D START TO WHEEZE. IF SHE GOT TO THINKING ABOUT HIM SHE'D GET SO SICK... WEEKS IN THE HOSPITAL WITH FLU IN HER LUNGS... WAY BEYOND SIMPLE PSYCHO SOMATIC ASTHMA.
SHE STOOD RIGHT IN FRONT OF THE BASTARD HIMSELF. SPOKE TO HIM. WAS TOUCHED BY HIM, AND WORSE.
AND LOOK AT HER.
SHE'S FINE.
um...
er...
AH STEEL SAY Y'ARE ONLY HALF BRIGHT, B'CAUSE AH CAN STEEL TRICK YOUR SECRETS OUT OF YOU. SO YOU 'AD BETTER BEHAVE--
I THINK YOUR BEHAVIOR WOULD BE AT ISSUE IF YOU TOLD MOM ABOUT THIS, CONSIDERING YOU DIDN'T TELL HER WHEN IT HAPPENED.
I THINK YOU ARE PARADING YOUR BRILLIANCE FOR MY EDIFICATION BECAUSE WE'RE IN AN ORGANIC HOUSE NOW, WHICH YOU CAN'T BE FULLY INTEGRATED INTO, AND SO YOU'RE A VERY REDUCED LITTLE HOLOTOY. WHAT'S MORE, YOU WON'T HAVE MOM'S EAR MUCH LONGER, SO YOU WON'T BE RUNNING THINGS ANYMORE.
YOU KNOW A LOT LESS THAN YOU LET ON. BE GRATEFUL FOR THE CRUMBS I SEE FIT TO THROW YOU.
hmph!
ALL TOO EASY.
PWOOF!

BRIGHAM HADN'T DONE ANYTHING WRONG.
BUT I WAS SURE HE WOULD. HE EVEN HAD THAT GOATY SMELL OF CRAZINESS SOMETIMES.
GIVEN EMMA'S MENTAL STATE... HE WOULDN'T A HAD TO DO MUCH.
WHATEVER HE'D DONE TO HER IN THE PAST... EVEN THE SLIGHTEST ...
AAAH..
MINUTE I BURST INTO THE HOUSE, I THOUGHT IT WAS ALL OVER... ALL FOR NOTHING... DAMAGE DONE.
WHEN I SHOVED HER OUT OF THE LINE OF FIRE, SHE WAS HEAVY AND STIFF. RACHEL WENT DOWN TWISTING LIKE A FISH; ALIVE AND KICKING. BUT EMMA...
LIKE SOMETHING ALREADY LONG DEAD.
KIDS SCREAMIN', BRIG SCREAMIN', THIS FIVE-POUND CAN OF NAILS AND LAUNDRY SOAP AND I SWEAR PEANUT BUTTER HITS ME SPANG IN THE HEAD, AND THE KIDS SHUT UP LIKE SOMEBODY'S UNPLUGGED 'EM, AND THERE'S JUST BRIG SNIVELIN', AND I'M LAYIN' THERE IN THE OPEN DOOR, USELESS AS A TURD ON THE HIGHWAY, TRYIN' MY DAMNEDEST TO UNCROSS MY EYES, WHEN EMMA SAYS, CLEAR AS A BELL:
SNAKE PIT.
BE HEALED OR BE KILLED.
MAYBE THE OLD WAYS ARE BEST.
AND I SWEAR TO GOD I THOUGHT SHE WAS DEAD.

I DON'T UNDERSTAND YOU...

YOU SHOW UP, YOU ALWAYS SHOW UP WITH GIFTS... BREAK INTO THE HOUSE AND LEAVE FIFTY BUCKS' WORTH OF OUR FAVORITE FOOD... AND LITTLE THINGS WE MIGHT'VE SAID "I WANT" OR "I WISH" ABOUT MONTHS OR EVEN YEARS AGO...

EVERY TIME ONE OF US SAYS THE "W" WORDS, I SEE YOU TAKING MENTAL NOTES...

YOU MAKE YOURSELF SO USE FUL, YOU CAN DO ANYTHING... YOU'RE SO HELPFUL AND ATTENTIVE... YOU KNOW JUST WHAT TO SAY AND HEAVEN KNOWS YOU'RE DECORATIVE...

BUT YOU DON'T STAY!

JUST WHEN WE'RE REALLY GETTING TO LIKE HAVING YOU AROUND... GOD FORBID, TO THINK OF YOU AS ONE OF US, EVEN IF YOU ONLY SLEEP HERE THREE NIGHTS OUT OF EVERY SEVEN AND WE NEVER KNOW WHERE YOU ARE OR WHAT YOU'RE DOING OR WHO WITH--

BUT JUST AS WE REALLY START TO GET COMFORTABLE WITH YOU, WHOOP! OUT YA GO! ZOOM!

DOOR AIN'T BEEN MADE THAT'S FAST ENOUGH TO SMACK YOU IN THE BUTT ON YOUR WAY OUT!

IT'S LIKE... YOU CAN'T JUST HANG AROUND!

YOU GOTTA BE DOING SOMETHING, BUILDING SOMETHING, BRINGING US SOMETHING, DIGGING UP THE GARDENS IN SOME NEW AND BRILLIANT WAY FOR MAMA! IT'S MORE THAN JUST NEEDING SOMETHING TO DO!

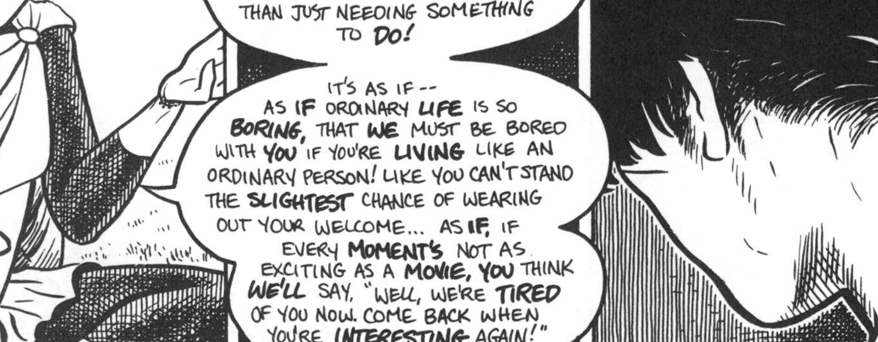

THAT WOULD BE IT, YES.
FOR HEAVEN'S SAKE, GIRLS... WHAT IS IT, CIVIC "LURKING IN DOORWAYS" DAY?
ODD WAY TO CELEBRATE CARNIVAL...

THERE YOU ARE.
HELLO, LOVELY. FEELIN' OKAY?

HOW'S THE EAR? TORN-OUT EARRINGS ARE THE WORST.
STILL HURTS, BUT--
WHAT TH-- WHAT'S THIS IN YOUR --

WHAT THE HHHNNGHH

NNNNGH!

I'M SORRY, THEY SAID I'D LEARN TO CONTROL THEM, BUT IT'S NATURAL FOR THEM TO BE ATTRACTED TO WHATEVER I'M FOCUSED ON...

FOR GOD'S SAKE, EMMA... WHY?
WHY WHAT? THEY'RE FOR A NEW JOB -- DON'T YELL AT ME -- THEY'RE JUST MULTISENSORY DATA LINES. SOPHISTICATED ONES, BUT--

NO JOB -- NO JOB IS --
YOU REALLY DON'T TRUST ELECTRONIC DO YOU? THESE -- THIS IS NOTHING. NOTHING TO BE AFRAID OF, I MEAN THEY'RE JUST SO THE INSTITUTE CA -- FULLY TAP INTO MY MIND, SO THE CAN GET EXACTLY WHAT I GET--

OH, COME ON, YOU LUDDITE! YOUR PRIESTS USE CRANIAL JACKS! I SAW IT ON TV--
NOT PRIESTS, SHRIVERS! AND NOT FOR MONEY, NEVER FOR MONEY!

YOU DON'T TRUST MONEY, EITHER. THIS IS JUST A SOCIETY OF WHORES TO YOU, ISN'T IT?
WELL, MAYBE WE ARE.
I'M ENGAGING IN THI KIND OF DEPENDENCE IN ORDER TO HAVE A MEASURE OF INDEPENDENCE. THAT'S HOW IT WORKS. DON' YOU SEE THAT?

YOU DON'T, DO YOU.
LISTEN, IT ISN'T JUST FOR MONEY. THEY'LL HELP ME. IT'S A HIGH-STATUS JOB. NOTHING'S TOO GOOD FOR--

EMMA, DON'T DO THIS! IT'S A TRA THEY'LL TELL YOU YOU CAN'T BAC OUT AND YOU CAN! DON'T LE THEM THREATEN YOU WITH WHAT YOU MIGHT LOSE- --ALL THIS --MISCELLANEOU SHIT! THIS HOUSE-- EVERYTHING! IT'S SHIT!

WHAT'S YOURS IS YOUR PRECIOUS MIND -- WHAT'S IN HERE, THE RECORD OF YOUR LIFE! DON'T SELL THAT!

MAYBE I'M NOT OVERFO OF WHAT'S I MY HEAD.

MY GODS WERE INFINITELY KIND TO ME ONCE
NOW THEY LIE.
THEY LIE.
LOOK-- CRAZY PEOPLE DON'T OFTEN GET OFFERED STATE-OF-THE-ART MENTAL-HEALTH CARE, OR CHILD CARE OR A NUMBER OF OTHER RESCUE ROPES, NOT ONLY FREE, BUT OFFERED UP ON A VELVET PILLOW.
BUT
I'D --FEEL A LOT BETTER-- ENTRUSTING THE KIDS TO A NANA, THAT IS--
--IF YOU WERE AROUND TO--
NNN--
H-H-HUHHH--
YOU'LL ...
AHEM
ALWAYS BE WELCOMED. WHEREVER... WHENEVER.
SO.
THAT.
AS THEY SAY.
WAS THAT.
ALK ABOUT UR WET ECRACKERS.
I THOUGHT BRIG WAS NUTS.
DID I KNOW?
I TESTED HIM BY PUTTING HIM UNDER ENORMOUS STRESS. OF COURSE HE CRACKED; I CRACKED HIM.
MAYBE ... HE COULD'VE HEALED. HE'S A LIAR BUT MAYBE HE WASN'T A SLOBBERING PSYCHO TILL I CAME ALONG.
AND EMMA.
I THOUGHT SHE'D CRACK, BE IRREPARABLY HURT JUST BY SPEAKING TO HER MAN, LET ALONE WHAT HE MIGHT DO TO HER. "IF I CAN'T HAVE YOU, BLAH BLAH BLAHH..."
DID I KNOW?
ORACLES DON'T LIE, BUT THEY SAY WHAT SUITS THEIR OWN MURKY PURPOSES.

IT'S QUITE POSSIBLE THAT I SAILED IN LIKE HELL AND DAMNATION AND FUCKED EVERYBODY'S SHIT UP ALL ON MY OWN. MY WIFE AND I -- WE SPLIT THE BLANKETS NOT SIX MONTHS BEFORE I WENT BACK TO ANVARD. MAYBE I HAD A HOLE IN MY LIFE THE SIZE OF A WIFE AND KIDS.
A HOLE TOO BIG TO SEE.
TCHC

FINDER BY NAME.
SIN-EATER BY NATURE.

WHEN I'VE GROWN ANOTHER ONE THIS LENGTH, I'LL GO BACK.
AND IF, WHEN I DO...
TOK
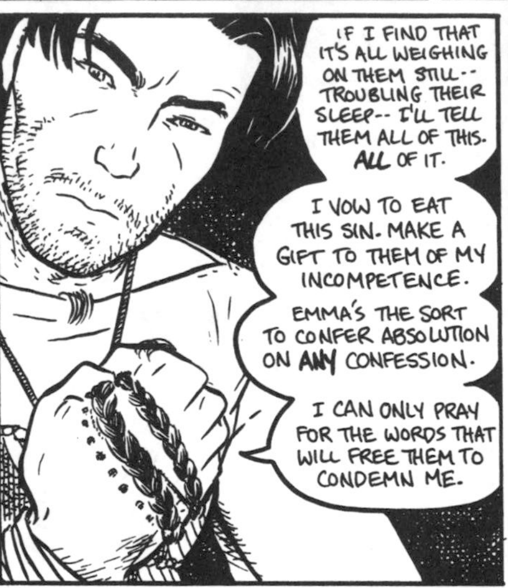
IF I FIND THAT IT'S ALL WEIGHING ON THEM STILL-- TROUBLING THEIR SLEEP-- I'LL TELL THEM ALL OF THIS. ALL OF IT.
I VOW TO EAT THIS SIN. MAKE A GIFT TO THEM OF MY INCOMPETENCE.
EMMA'S THE SORT TO CONFER ABSOLUTION ON ANY CONFESSION.
I CAN ONLY PRAY FOR THE WORDS THAT WILL FREE THEM TO CONDEMN ME.

WHAT'S YOUR OPINION, BAL?

WELL-- IN THE PAST, I'VE THOUGHT YOU A BORDERLINE PERSONALITY, AS HAVING DEFINITE PARANOIAC TENDENCIES. YOUR AVERSION TO BEING SEEN. YOUR IDEA THAT YOU CAN'T BE SEEN AGAINST YOUR WILL.
I BELIEVE YOU'VE CROSSED OVER ENTIRELY INTO DELUSIONS OF GRANDEUR; YOU'RE DEFINITELY A SEMIDETACHED BPS WITH SCHIZOID TENDENCIES.

AH, NOW THAT'S WHAT I LIKE ABOUT YOU, BAL.
Z
Z

YOU DON'T LISTEN.

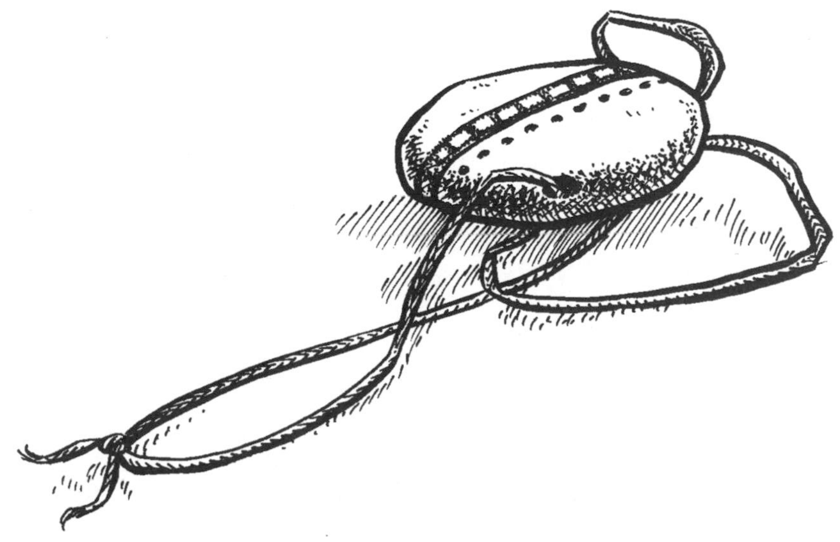

KING OF THE CATS

prologue

AHA.
HERE'S ANOTHER BAND... I MAKE OUT MAYBE EIGHT.
NICE BUNCH OF BACHELORS.
GROUPED VERY TIGHT. MOVING PRETTY FAST. WHAT ARE YOU HIDING, BOYS?

"LOOK AT THOSE TWO BAD OL' BOYS... THEY'D CONQUER MOUNTAINS GIVEN HALF A CHANCE."
"OH --"
"SHIT. THERE SHE IS."
GOT HER?
YAH.
RISHI'S LITTLE RUNAWAY, FOUR MONTHS TOO LATE.
WELL, WELL.
IS IT FUN, SISTER? BEING THE ONLY GIRL IN THE ROOM?
RUNNING SO WILD AND FREE?
BLAM!

THERE, BUT FOR OUR FATHERS' BLESSING, GO WE ALL.
BLAM
BLAM
BLAM
BLAM
BLAM

WRETCHED QUEAN.

CHAPTER ONE

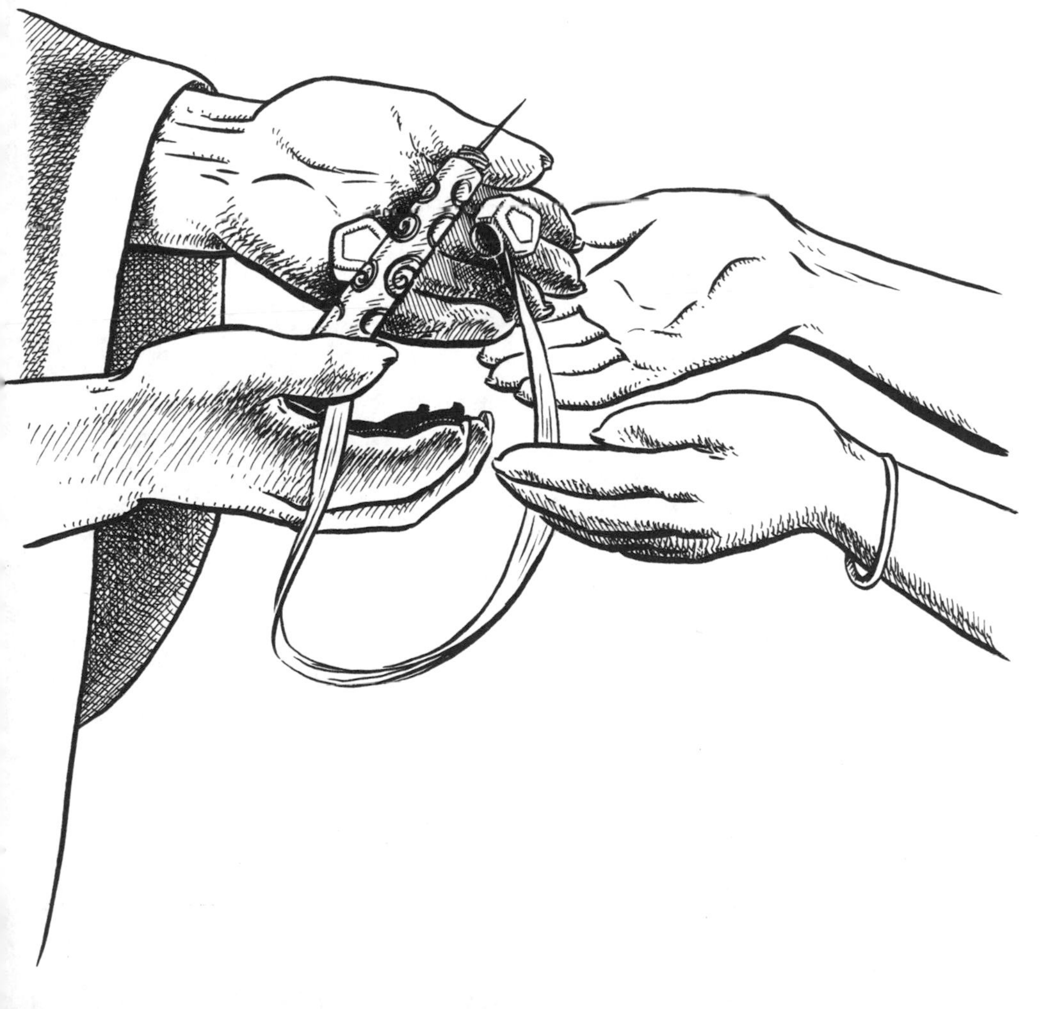

SHOOKA
SHOOKA
RATTLE RATTLE RATTLE
SHOOKA
RATTLE RATTLE RATTLE
SHOOKA
RATTLE RATTLE RATTLE

CHOOKA CHOOKA CHOOKA CHOOKA

PIFF!
FUMPETA

HO! HO-HO!

O-HO HO

GUH

SNAP!

HO-H

-HO!

THOOM!

HEY!

HO-LEE SMOKES!
THANKS, COUSIN!

OH, SURE! =HEH= LEAST I COULD DO.
HERE YOU'VE BEEN LOOKING AFTER US ALL THIS TIME.

SOME GUNNER YOU ARE! HOW COME NOBODY SHOWED UP TO GET SHOT AT? WHEN MY COUSIN SPENCE MADE THE TRIP, HE SAID--
AW, SIT BACK, KNOTHEAD DON'T BOTHER THE MAN.
SIT DOWN, ROY! THAT'S UGLY!

BEAUTIFUL OUT HERE... SO WELL KEPT! COURSE, IT WOULD BE... COULDN'T BE ANY TROUBLE ONCE WE PASSED THE OUTER MARKERS.
THEY LOOK OUT FOR YOU WHEN YOU'RE ON THE PILGRIMAGE TRAIL, KIDS.
HAK PTHEH

SORRY-- I'M JUST REMEMBERING MY TRIP OUT HERE AS A BOY... SUCH A WONDERFUL EXPERIENCE... SO GOOD TO BE BRINGING MY OWN CHILDREN HERE NOW. THAT'S WHAT IT'S ALL FOR ANYWAY; THE KIDS.
HONK SPLURTCH

I'M SO GLAD OUR NUMBER CAME UP NOW, WHEN MY YOUNGEST IS OLD ENOUGH TO APPRECIATE IT. THE KIDS MAY ONLY SEE THIS PLACE ONCE IN THEIR LIVES;
TOO BAD TO SPEND IT AS A BABY WHO WON'T REMEMBER.
NUMBER? LIKE A DRAFT?
VOWM

NO, MORE LIKE A LOTTERY.
DADDY WON!
THAT'S RIGHT, BABY. SO DID EVERYBODY ON THE BUS. WE'RE ALL CHOSEN, ALL SPECIAL.
SELECTED BY A LOTTERY? TELL ME THIS ISN'T ONE OF THOSE WEIRD RELIGIONS WHERE --

--THEY--

OH, KIDS! DID YOU SEE HIM, DID YOU SEE MUNKY? THAT MEANS WE'RE THERE! JUST AROUND THE NEXT CURVE IS THE VISTA!
RE GONN MISS IT!
OH, LOOK!
I SAW ON THE CHANN
"MUNKY"?

OKAY, BIG SMILES FOR MOMMY NOW, I'M FILMING.... ...GET READYYY.. THERE IT IS!!!

THERE IT IS, KIDS!
THERE'S ONLY ONE FIRST TIME TO SEE THE VISTA!

IT'S-- BEAUTIFUL!
SO IT IS.
SOMETHIN' MUST BE WRONG.
the Nyiman
CROWN JEWELS EXHIBIT

HA! YOU SOUND LIKE MOM WHEN WE BOUGHT OUR NEW HOUSE!
OH, A SKEPTIC.
WHY SHOULD THERE BE ANYTHING WRONG?

NO REASON. IF IT WAS WHAT I THOUGHT IT WAS.
FROM THE WAY YOU AND EVERYBODY ELSE TALKED ABOUT IT ALL THE WAY HERE, I THOUGHT--
I'VE SEEN SOME BEAUTIFUL HOLY CITIES IN MY DAY, BUT THIS--

MUNKY
WELCOMES
YOU!
ONLY 22 STONES
FROM THIS SPOT!

--I DON'T KNOW WHAT THIS IS.
THAT'S MUNKY!

'MUNKY' IS SHORT FOR 'HOMUNCULUS'--
--HIS BODY IS PROPORTIONED SO AS TO REPRESENT--
--A MAP OF MOTOR, SENSORY, AND NERVOUS-TISSUE DISTRIBUTION--
--IN THE HUMAN BODY.

THERE BEING MORE SENSORY NERVES LOCALIZED IN THE HANDS, FEET, AND FACE--
--AND CORRESPONDINGLY LARGE CENTERS IN THE CEREBRAL CORTEX--

--HE IS EFFECTIVELY A DIAGRAM OF THE INFORMATION GATHERED BY THE BODY AND ATTENTION PAID TO IT BY THE BRAIN.
HE'S SO EDUCATIONAL

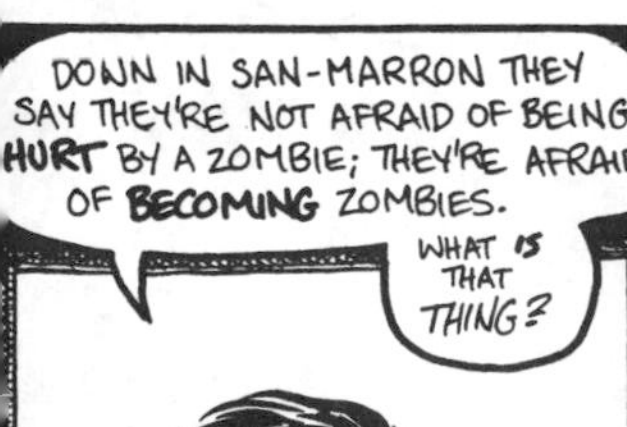
DOWN IN SAN-MARRON THEY SAY THEY'RE NOT AFRAID OF BEING **HURT** BY A ZOMBIE; THEY'RE AFRAID OF **BECOMING** ZOMBIES.
WHAT IS THAT THING?

IKON STEREOREALIST PHOTO INTERFACE. NEXT BEST THING TO BEING THERE.
BUT YOU'RE "THERE" NOW--
OH LOOK!

OVER HERE! CHANGE SIDES!
WOW
OH!
LOOK!
HEY!
OUCH
HUH?

OOH
AH
WOW

CHANGE SIDES!
OVER HERE!!
SCREEE

SEE, KIDS? YOU NEVER KNOW WHAT YOU MIGHT MISS!
MAKE 'EM DO IT AGAIN, DADDY!

YAYYY!!
TA-DAAAH!!
OKAY, KIDS, LET'S SING A HAPPY SONG!
SKURCHH---.
SKWRIIIIII....

SING SING SING SING I'M SO HAP-PY SING-ING
BAIL OUT, BAIL OUT...

HERE WE GO, KIDS!
ALL BE HAPPY NOW
YAYYY!

BOUNCE BOUNCE
BOUNCE BOUNCE
I'M SO HAP-PY BOUNCING
BRUMM BRUMM

HEY, CAP! WHY YOU LET THAT RUBBER MONKEY TAKE YOUR BUS?
AIN'T THERE NO TOWN OUT HERE?
THEY BOUGHT MY RIG YEARS AGO; I STILL MAKES THE RUN TO AND FRO, THOUGH. AIN'T NOTHIN' B'LONG TO NOBODY IF THESE FOLKS WANTS IT.

EN'T NAWT OUTSIDE, 'CEPTIN' SHANTYTOWN. NOW, MEBBEE YOU C'N STAY OUT HERE, GET HIRED ON T'THE NEK' BUS OUT, MEBBEE.
TODAY'S WINNING NUMBERS!
THEY COMES ALONG RIGHT QUICK LIKE SOMETIMES. MEBBEE THEY'LL BE ANOTHER BUS 'FORE YOU EVEN GETS HONGRY, MEBBEE

NOW MEBBEE YOU C'D GIT A JOB ONCE INSIDE, WAIT FO' A BUS WHAT IS HEADED YOUR WAY. YOU C'D GET HIRED, MEBBEE, IF THEY LIKE YOUR LOOKS.

JUS' CALL ME DREAD PIRATE JIM-BOB, EH!

"NUMBERS"? WHATIZZ'S, ANOTHER FRIGGIN' LOTTERY?
NO! NO!

I WANT THESE NUMBERS! I'VE BEEN PLAYING THESE NUMBERS SINCE I WAS A GIRL!
PLEASE TAKE A NUMBER!
GUESS SO...
SIGH

NO TIME LIKE THE ...
?

OH...
THANKS, GREAT-GRANDAD...

YOUR NUMBERS LOOK BETTER THAN MINE.
YEAH, AND MY BOOTS LOOK BIGGER THAN YOUR ASS, TOO, PAL.

TODAY'S WINNING NUMBERS
3501

"CONFUZIUS SAY, 'NO RULER BIG ENOUGH TO MEASURE THE WORLD.' "
CUTE.
NEXT--
XT--
--OKAY--
--OKAY--
--NEXT--
--OKAY--
--NEXT--
--OKAY--
HOLD IT.
NOT YOU. THAT HAIR'S TOO LONG.
YOU--C'MON, HONEY.
C'MON, JUNIOR-- YEAH, YOU--
OKAY. YOU AND YOU!
MOVE IT, URCHINS!
PENALTIES FOR COUNTERFEITING

WHAT?
FEE SCHEDULE
TIES FOR

IS THIS NOT A REASONABLE RESPONSE?
YOU STATED YOUR CONDITION; I MET IT.

SO, I SUPPOSE IF I SAID YOU HAD TOO MANY FINGERS, YOU'D GLADLY CUT OFF SOME OF THOSE **TOO**?
LOOK, COUSIN, THAT "IF-ALL-YOUR-FRIENDS-JUMPED-OFF-A-CLIFF" LOGIC DIDN'T WORK FOR MY **MOTHER**, EITHER.
WHY DON'T YOU **TELL** ME WHAT IS NEEDFUL TO MY GETTING HIRED ON, AND I'LL DECIDE IF IT'S **WORTH** IT.
FEE SCHEDULE
FOR COUNTERFEITING
MITS

YOU'LL DECIDE.
WELL, THAT'S **GOOD.**
PENALTIES FOR COUNTERFEIT

STATISTICAL PROF
HEIGHT/WEIGHT ALLOWAN
WELL, HERE YA GO, MISTER INDEPENDENCE. STATS FOR MALE EMPLOYEES. UPDATE 2-1-64.

"NO EARRINGS. NO FACIAL HAIR. NO NAIL POLISH. NO VISIBLE TATTOOS OR BODY MARKS."
OH, **YOU'RE** WHITE-COLLAR MATERIAL, YOU BET.

"HAIR OFF THE BACK OF THE NECK. NO MISSING OR DEAD TEETH. NO DECORATED TEETH."
WHAT'S GOING ON?
SSHH

"NO VISIBLE HAIR ON NECK, CHEST, OR EXTREMITIES"?
"NO—"

MOST OF THIS I CAN FIX WITH A RAZOR.
Y'WANNA TELL ME WHAT I'M SUPPOSED TO DO WITH THIS ONE? "NO VISIBLE BULGE OR PROTRUSION IN CROTCH OF PANTS"?
NALTIES FOR COUN

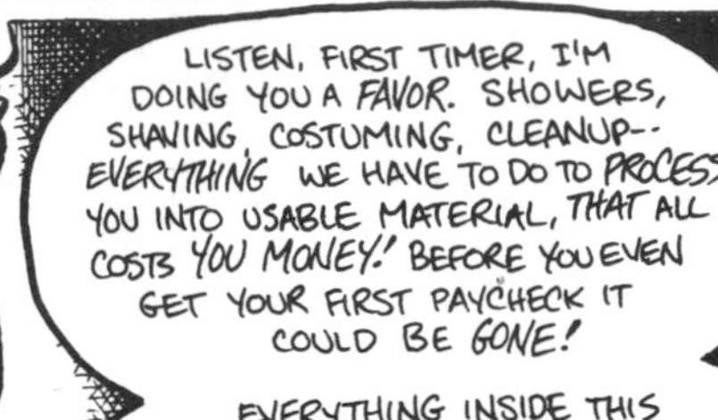
LISTEN, FIRST TIMER, I'M DOING YOU A FAVOR. SHOWERS, SHAVING, COSTUMING, CLEANUP-- EVERYTHING WE HAVE TO DO TO PROCESS YOU INTO USABLE MATERIAL, THAT ALL COSTS YOU MONEY! BEFORE YOU EVEN GET YOUR FIRST PAYCHECK IT COULD BE GONE!
EVERYTHING INSIDE THIS CITY IS CAREFULLY ORCHESTRATED, DESIGNED, AND ARRANGED--LIKE A MOVIE. EVERYTHING HAS TO FIT, SO THAT EACH GUEST'S EXPERIENCE IS JUST WHAT WE WANT IT TO BE.
YOU-- DON'T-- FIT.
WE HAVE NO ROLE FOR YOU TO PLAY. WE CAN'T USE YOU.

EVEN IN A MOVIE, NOT EVERYBODY--
I DIDN'T NOTICE THE EYES BEFORE. NO, THEY'RE TOO WEIRD.

YOU THINK YOU CAN EVER AFFORD THAT KIND OF REPLACEMENT SURGERY?

NEXT-- OKAY.
NEXT--
NEXT-- OKAY.

"THREE... FIVE... OH... ONE."
DAM, BWAH! THAT'S A GOOD NUMBER!

IF THIS WAS THE HOLY CITY OF HAURVATAT, I'D EXPECT THAT THE GUARDS WOULD CUT OUT THEIR OWN EYES TO ATONE FOR THE BREACHING OF THE WALL.
WORSE THAN THAT; TO CONSIDER THEMSELVES DAMNED FOR LETTING ANY-BODY SLIP BY THEM.
IF THIS WAS THE CARNY-DOME AT LES ANGES, I'D EXPECT THAT SECURITY WOULDN'T HAVE MANY REASONS TO KEEP PEOPLE OUT.
I DON'T KNOW WHAT THIS PLACE'S TRUE NATURE IS.
EITHER WAY.
I'M GETTING IN.

ALL CITIES WEAR SKIRTS OF SLUMS AND SUBURBS, RIBBONS OF CLEAN WATER AND FILTH. GREEN FIELDS AND BATTLE FIELDS, SCRAP HEAPS AND LAZARETTES FOR THE HOPELESSLY ILL.

...NO KIDS...

...NO MARKET...

...NO LIVESTOCK...

...WHAT IS UP WITH THIS PLACE?!...

WATER, FOOD, AIR, LIGHT, GEWGAWS-- EVERYTHING ANYBODY WANTS OR NEEDS HAS TO GO **IN** SOMEHOW. DOORS, WINDOWS, VENTS, PIPES, ACCESS TUNNELS.

AND **PEOPLE**. PEOPLE WHO **WANT** SOMETHING ARE DOORS.

SAY, BUD, WHERE COULD A GUY GET--

KEEP IT MOVIN', ROADIE. THIS ISN'T A HOTEL.

OR WHO'VE LOST SOMETHING.

M-HM.

SULLIVAN'S FIFTY-EIGHT-DAY SUSPENSION IS ALMOST UP... HE'LL BE BACK INSIDE IN NO TIME...

=SIGH=

SPLOSH

MAYBE HE'LL MOVE BACK IN WITH HIS FOLKS UNTIL HE GETS BACK ON HIS FEET, I DON'T KNOW.

=SNIFFF=

OH, I SHOULD BE GLAD AND I AM, REALLY; Y'KNOW, MEETING HIM-- SOME GOOD HAS TO COME OUT OF BEING SENT OUT HERE, BUT I JUST--

KAT, SSHH-- SH--SHH

Y'KNOW, HELL, AT LEAST I'VE LOST A LOT OF WEIGHT!

=WAHHHAHASHIT=

SNIFF

C'MON, KAT GET UP. LET'S GO TO MY PLACE.

OSTRAKON. JUNKYARD. PLACE OF BANISHMENT.

CALL IT WHAT YOU WANT.

IT'S STILL A PRISON.

SHANTYTOWN SITS IN A GULLY, HUDDLED UP AGAINST THAT GREASY CONCRETE WALL--
--AS IF THIS--
--WAS ALL DESERT.
I MAKE RIPPLES IN THE WOODS LIKE A PADDLE IN A CLEAR GREEN LAKE.
A HUNDRED SMALL SCUFFLES AND CRACKLES TELL OF THE PREY ANIMALS NOTING MY PRESENCE.
MOST OF 'EM DON'T CARE.
FAR TO THE WEST, SOME MINOR PREDATOR IS JUMPING AT GROUSE AND CURSING HIS LUCK.
BEYOND HIM, A SMALL HERD OF ANGU PICK UP THEIR AMBLING PACE A BIT, A WAVE BREAKING IN FRONT OF A BIG PREDATOR. A LAESKE, MAYBE, OR EIDECTUS.
CLOSER TO ME A FLOCK OF GROUND-RUNNING HAWKS VEERS NORTH-NORTHWEST, SENDING INNUMERABLE SMALLER CREATURES DIVING FOR COVER.
THEIR SQUAWKS AND COMPLAINTS TRAVEL OUT FROM THE POINT OF DISTURBANCE, TAKEN UP AND TELEGRAPHED BY MANY OTHERS.
THE SOUGHING WIND IN THE TREES CARRIES ALL THIS NEWS AND GOSSIP.
BUT THERE IS SOMETHING BIG OUT HERE BESIDES SHANTYTOWN; IF THE ANIMALS RIPPLE A BIT TO AVOID ME, WHATEVER'S AROUND THE PERIMETER TO THE NORTH--
--MUST BE QUITE A SANDBAR--

SOMETHING'S ON THEIR MINDS.
A NYIMA CAMP IS USUALLY A PLEASANT BUSTLE OF ACTIVITY; WOMEN COOKING, WEAVING, CLEANING ANIMAL HIDES; WOMEN SCOLDING KIDS, PRACTICING MUSIC, TALKING AND LAUGHING IN VELVETY VOICES WITH HANDS ALWAYS BUSY.

HERE, THERE'S ONLY THE SMELL OF INCENSE AND A SOMNOLENT HUM LIKE A BEEHIVE. EVERY LEAF'S ALIVE WITH IT.
FUNNY THAT A SOUND CAN FEEL SO LIKE SILENCE.

TROUBLE MAKES PEOPLE TWITCHY. I'D JU
AS SOON LET THEM BOOT ME OFF THE
LAND THAN START SIDLING AWAY AN
GET PUNCTURED FOR SHOWING THE
MY BACK.
SNIFF

I DECIDE TO BE MANNERLY AND LET THEM FIND ME.
<WHAT DO YE HERE, GYPT?>
NO HARM TO YOU OR YOUR KIN. JUST PAYING MY RESPECTS.

WHAT?

SIGH NO, FORGET IT, I MISSPOKE.
?

IT'S A BAD TIME TO BE ASKING PERMISSION TO HUNT WITH US. BETTER BE ON YOUR WAY NOW.

ACTUALLY, I WASN'T LOOKING TO GO HUNTING.
I WAS LOOKING AT THAT DOOR DOWN THERE.

IT'S ALL THE SAME TO YOU WHETHER I GO AWAY THROUGH THE WOODS OR THROUGH THAT DOOR, I'D LIKE A CHANCE AT THE DOOR.

AND YOU COULD GET THROUGH THAT DOOR?
CAN'T KNOW TILL I GET A GOOD LOOK AT IT.

I CAN GET THROUGH IT. WE ALL CAN.
"'EASILY IN BUT NOT EASILY OUT,' SAYS THE LOBSTER CAUGHT IN THE LOBSTER POT."

MY PROBLEM WILL BE SATISFYING MY CURIOSITY BEFORE THEY SAIL ME OFF THE BACK STEPS LIKE LAST NIGHT'S CHICKEN NECKS.
BELIEVE ME, SISTER, GETTING OUT IS JUST A MATTER OF TIMING.

TWITCH

COME AND TALK TO THE DOWAGERS.
HANH?
COME-AND-TALK-TO-THE-DOWAGERS.
URRLL??

HURRAYY!!
TINKA DING

YAYY!
TINKA-DWOYNK-- DINKY-DINKY
-BOINNG-

BINKA-BINK DINKA
YAYY

TINGG TING TINKA TINKA BIN
YAYY!
HOOULG
YAY

JING TINKA DING-DONG DINKA-DINKA DING-
GHASP
STAGGER

TWITCH

KLIK-KA SHEEEN

YAYY!
DOOT-DOOT-A-DOOOT!!
POP!

DING DINKA
DINGA
CLAP

WHOOAA...
SNIFF
DAMN BUT I WANT A CIGARETTE.

DON'T SEE **ONE** OTHER PERSON LIT P ANYWHERE SO IF I DON'T WANT TO STAND OUT, I CAN'T SMOKE.

HA-FLTCH!

ANYTIME I'M IN A CLOSED-UP PLACE FULL OF PEOPLE, MY NOSE PRETTY MUCH CATCHES **FIRE** AND ALL I WANT'S A DAMN CIGARETTE.
...ANNNHH...

PEOPLE LIKE THESE, THOUGH, THEY'RE BOUND TO LOOK AT A LIT CIG LIKE IT WAS A GOOSE TURD ON A WEDDING GOWN....

I KEEP WAITING FOR THAT HAND ON MY SHOULDER. BET THE COPS IN HERE JUST **LOVE** TO CRACK A GUY IN HIS HEAD JUST FOR--

HAAHH
PTSCHOO!
SHIT!
TSK!

I FEEL LIKE A KID PLAYING HIDE-AND-SEEK, THINKING THAT SINCE **I** CAN'T SEE ANYBODY THEN MUST BE NOBODY CAN SEE **ME**.
SNIFF
THINKIN' ALL I HAVE TO DO IS NOT **SMOKE** AND THAT MAKES ME **INVISIBLE**....
HEY!
POKE

HEY. YOU LOST?
SHNIRF
AREN'T YOU SUPPOSED TO BE PERFORMING WITH THE REST OF YOUR CROWD IN TWENTY MINUTES?

...THAT WAY AND BEAR LEFT PAST THE OFFICES OF FLARNE, FLARNE, FLARNE, FILTH, AND FLARNE (ASSOC.), AND YOU CAN'T MISS IT.

HEY!
WHAT HAPPENED TO YOUR **HAIR?**
-- DON'T RUN, DON'T RUN --

SO I COME ALL THIS WAY, THROUGH **ALL** THIS **STUFF** LIKE I AIN'T SEEN SINCE THE LAST TIME I SMOKED LAMBENT WEED ON TOP OF A QUART OF "OLD OVERCOAT" AND **WHERE** DO I END UP?

HOME.

IN SPITE OF THE FACT THAT THESE AREN'T THE PEOPLE I GREW UP WITH.

IN SPITE OF THE UGLY LITTLE THUNK IN MY CHEST.

I NEVER **MEANT** TO GO HOME.

WELL, **HEYY!**

WHAT TRIBE ARE YOU?

NOTHING SADDER THAN A SMOKE HOLE WITH NO SMOKE.
AIN'T THAT THE TRUTH.
ANYWAY-- SEVEN DRUM CHIEFS ARE GATHERED UP HERE. BEEN HERE TWO MONTHS NOW.
HUH! YEAH. WE CAME HERE TO PLASTIC TOWN 'CAUSE THIS WAS THE ONLY NEUTRAL TURF ANYBODY COULD AGREE ON.
WE'RE S'POSED TO SIT DOWN WITH KING KOKUTSOLADO-- HE'S ONE OF THE NYIMA KINGS--FOR A BIG PALAVER.
CHIEF COWARD SET IT UP.
YEAH AND THAT'S GOT TO BE SOME KINDA MIRACLE 'CAUSE THOSE CATS DON'T HAVE ANY SERIOUS DOIN'S WITH ANYBODY.
"YOU CAN HUNT WITH US IF YOU CAN KEEP UP WITH US." YEAH SURE.
COWARD'S THE BEST PEACE CHIEF WE EVER HAD. SO WE'RE GONNA SIT DOWN AND SEE WHAT HAPPENS.
PEACE IN OUR TIME, MAYBE. HARD TO PICTURE, THOUGH, HUH?
I GOT SOME BAD NEWS FOR YOU, THEN.
YOU CAN TELL CHIEF COWARD THERE ISN'T GONNA BE ANY PALAVER.
THE KING OF THE CATS IS DEAD.

CHAPTER TWO

THE HELL YOU SAY. OPPORTUNITY FOR WHAT?
TO GET SOME ANSWERS! OLD KING KOKUTSOLADO IS DEAD, RIGHT? WE'D JUST HAVE A NEW CHIEF, SNAP-SNAPPO, WHOEVER'S NEXT IN LINE.
WHO'S NEXT IN LINE, IF ALL THE NYIMA ARE WOMEN?
MAYBE THE KING'S A WOMAN TOO. YOU KNOW THAT TRIBE UP THE TSONG RIVER SOMEWHERE, THEY GOT A WOMAN CHIEF.
NAW, NAW. THEY GOT TO HAVE A REAL CHIEF. WHERE DO THEY GET KIDS FROM, OTHERWISE?
THE QUESTION IS, WHAT DO THEY DO WITH THE KIDS?
DO WHAT?
THE BOYS! THEY RAISE UP THE GIRL CHILDREN; THEY BECOME THOSE AMAZONS WE ALL KNOW SO WELL. WHAT ABOUT THEIR SONS? ONLY ONE KING-- WHAT HAPPENS TO ALL THE REST?
I DUNNO, BUT MY POINT IS, WHERE ARE THEY NOW? THINGS ARE BOUND TO BE ALL SHOOK UP WITH THE OLD BOY DEAD; ANYTHING COULD HAPPEN. LOADS OF OPPORTUNITY FOR THE LIKES OF US. THOSE WOMEN MUST KEEP A PRETTY TIGHT GRIP ON 'EM. THEY CAN'T LIKE LIVING THAT WAY.
YEAH! SO! WE GO FIND OUT IF THERE IS A YOUNG GUY! MAYBE WE STEAL 'IM OR SOMETHING; LIKE, GIVE 'IM A TASTE OF FREEDOM -- GET 'IM ON OUR SIDE! THAT WAS WHAT WE WANTED WITH THE OLD GUY, WASN'T IT?
ONE THING'S SURE. OLD KING KOKUTSOLADO WAS SOME HARDASS.
HIS WIVES ARE HARDASSES. MAYBE HE WAS A PUSHOVER AND THEY REALLY RAN EVERYTHING.
THEY TALK A LOT, BUT DON'T WORRY. THEY'RE REALLY VERY IMPRESSED.
YEAH, WHATEVER-- EXACTLY, SEE, THAT'S HOW WE GET HIM ON OUR SIDE! WE GO GET 'IM, GET HIM OUT FROM UNDER, HE'S BOUND TO BE SO--
RIGHT. HOW YOU GONNA GET BY THOSE ATTACK BEASTS OF THEIRS? THOSE THINGS GOT TEETH AND TEMPERS.

HE GOT PAST 'EM. JUST BREEZED RIGHT IN, NO PROBLEM.
HEY! HOW ABOUT IT, MAN? DID YOU SEE THE KING? REALLY SEE HIM?
YEP.
WELL COME ON, GIVE!
HUT! SAVE THAT TALK FOR THE COUNCIL.
WELL, KID, EVERYTHING'S GREAT.
THE DRUM CHIEFS ALL WANT TO HAVE A FORMAL MEETING WITH YOU IN THE MORNING. FORMAL, SO ALL SEVEN TRIBES WILL KNOW IT'S YOU WHO BROUGHT US THE NEWS.
EVEN THOUGH IT'S BAD NEWS.
YEAH, EVEN THOUGH. WHAT TO DO NEXT, THAT'S FOR CHIEFS TO WORRY ABOUT. YOU'RE A GOOD SCOUT--YOU DID A FINDER'S JOB. YOU FOUND OUT A CRUCIAL THING.
SO! WHERE YOU FROM? WHAT CLAN, WHAT TRIBE, WHO'S YOUR MAMA?
CHIEFS'LL WANNA KNOW--HELL, I WANNA KNOW!

HI-DUDHA-"TRAVEL WIFE"-HOSPITALITY TO A GUEST

IN THIS WOMAN'S FACE, I SEE A WHOLE LIFE LAID OUT BEFORE ME.
THIS IS ALL I'D EVER GET OUT OF HER. SHE'S MAD NOW, BUT SHE'LL SOON SOOTHE HER EMBARRASSMENT WITH COOL FORMALITY.
CITY PEOPLE LOOK ON TENT NOMADS AS WILD AND UNCIVILIZED, BUT THEY'RE REALLY AS BOUNDED ABOUT BY RULES AND ETIQUETTE AS CITY-BRED ROYALTY.
I CAN'T EVEN BLAME HER.
YOUNG GIRL LIKE THIS, NEWLY ESTABLISHED IN A HOUSEHOLD OF HER OWN; HER WHOLE FUTURE DEPENDS ON WHO SHE RECEIVES, HERE, WHO SHE ATTRACTS TO HER HEARTH.
I CAN LEAVE ANYTIME.
AND WHEN I COME BACK, THIS SAME LIFE WILL STILL BE WAITING FOR ME. OH, NOT THIS SAME GIRL; SHE'S NOT REALLY MY WIFE.
IF I EVER SEE HER AGAIN, SHE'LL BE A TOTALLY DIFFERENT PERSON.
I'LL STILL BE A SIN-EATER.
THESE ARE MY PEOPLE. OF THAT I HAVE NO DOUBT.
BUT WHEN I'M WITH THEM I FEEL MY LIFE GETTING SMALLER.
SHRINKING DOWN TO THE SIZE OF A SMOKE HOLE
THROUGH WHICH ONLY PRAYER CAN ESCAPE.

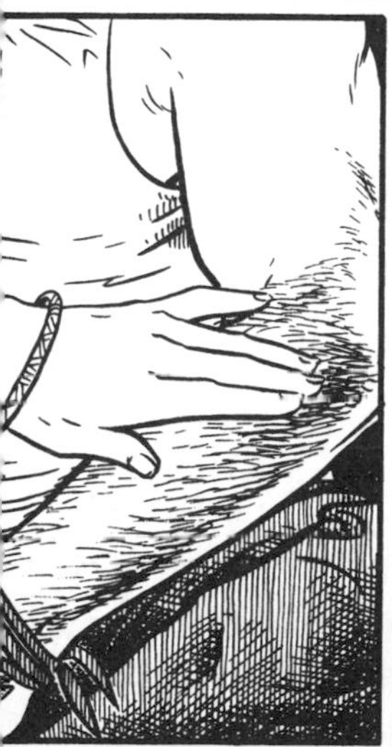

I'VE NEVER SEEN A MAN WITH SO MUCH HAIR ON HIS SKIN.

IT'S GOT TO COME OFF. I DON'T KNOW HOW I'M EXPECTED TO MAKE YOU PRESENTABLE BY MORNING.
DON'T HAVE A RAZOR... HATE TO DULL A GOOD SKINNING KNIFE...

WE'LL JUST HAVE TO TRY SEARING IT OFF. MAYBE THAT WAY IT WON'T GROW BACK.

HOOOH! I'LL BE HEARIN' IT FROM LELE EDGECOMB FOR MONTHS, BUT WHAT ELSE COULD I DO?

I DON'T BLAME HER. I WOULDN'T HAVE THAT HAIRY APE IN MY TENT.
HEY, MAYBE HE IS PART APE. ONE OF THOSE, UH, SIMI THINGS?
JOB TO DO. JOB TO DO. JOB TO DO.
DID YOU SEE HIS EYES? I'VE NEVER SEEN SUCH EYES.
IGNORE ALL THIS. YOU GOT A JOB TO DO.
SIT STILL AND BE QUIET, KIDS, AND I'LL TELL YOU ABOUT THE FADH-FELEN. THAT'S A NASTY EVIL SPIRIT THAT LIVES IN THE MARSHES. IT LOOKS LIKE A MAN, BUT IT HAS GOLDEN EYES LIKE A HAWK, AND IF YOU LOOK INTO ITS EYES, IT CAN GET INSIDE YOU AND MAKE YOU TERRIBLE SICK.
THE QUEENS OF DEAD KING KOKUTSOLADO GAVE YOU A JOB.
YOU'RE ON HER MAJESTIES' SECRET SERVICE.

So.
IF I WAS A BUNCH OF WEIRDHEAD GIRLS WITH FUR AND TAILS AND A DEAD ROYAL DADDY, WHERE WOULD I BE?
RUMBLRUMBLRUMBL
EYAAAAA
WHERE ELSE?
BIGGER THAN YOUR HEAD!
NOW SERVING

I AM NOT AT MY BEST IN CROWDS.
TODAY'S DRAMA IN REAL LIFE BEGINS NOW IN THE WESTERN FANTASY PAVILION!
SAUNTER ON DOWN AND BE AN EXTRA IN DRAMA IN REAL LIFE!
SOME SAY THEY LIKE THE ANONYMITY OF CROWDS.
PERSONALLY, I CAN'T SEE IT.
YOU NEVER KNOW WHOSE BODY YOU'RE BUMPING INTO OR WHO MIGHT BE TOUCHING YOU OR LOOKING AT YOU. I GUESS THAT'S ANONYMITY.
IF IT'S BAD, I START IMAGINING THEIR CASU GLANCES AS HOT SPO MOVING OVER ME LIK LASER SIGHTS.
MOST OF THESE PEOPLE ARE FROM FORMAL CLANS, WHICH BY DINT OF INBREEDING AND AESTHETICS ALL LOOK ALIKE.
I'M ALWAYS LEFT WITH THE FEELING THAT I'M SEEING THE SAME FIVE PEOPLE OVER AND OVER AGAIN.

NO POINT OF REFERENCE, IN CROWDS, THAT REMAINS CONSTANT.
WEIRD WEIRD WEST
...EVERYTHING KALEIDOSCOPES.
YOU ARE NOW LEAVING "CIRCUS CIRCUS"
MAP
HOLO HABILIMENT
SHIFT
BZZZZZZ
BZZZZT!
HOLO HABILIMENT
BZT
BZT
NGH.
DISORIENTATION ISN'T THE WORST PART OF IT.
ONE SMOKE. GOTTA HAVE ONE--JUST ONE--ELSE MY NOSE WILL ROT OFF MY HEAD.
SWEAT
MUSTARD
OLD COFFEE
TOOTHPASTE
COLOGNE
PATCHOULI
HOT DOGS
PERFUME #2
PLASTIC
AFTER-SHAVE
BUBBLEGUM

SECURITY MAY HASSLE ME BUT THEY'RE NOT GONNA KICK MY ASS OUT OVER ONE -- WHO'S GONNA CARE ABOUT ONE DAMN CIG?
FFFFP..
OH, I KNOW!
REALLY, THEY SHOULD ALL BE IN SERIOUS THERAPY.
THEY KNOW IT'S BAD FOR THEM AND EVERYBODY AROUND THEM BUT THEY TOTALLY DENY RESPONSIBILITY. THEY JUST SAY "I GOTTA HAVE IT"...
OHH, I KNOWW...
HAHHH
KFF
IF IT WASN'T... SMOKING... IT'D BE OVEREATING OR ALCOHOL OR DRUG ABUSE OR SEXUAL OVERINDULGENCE...
THEY'RE JUST-- ADDICTIVE BY NATURE. IT'S PATHETIC, REALLY.
OHH, I KNOWW...
FFFP!
YOU'RE SO MUCH MORE ATTRACTIVE WITHOUT THIS.
MY MY, WHAT NICE-LOOKING HOOKERS WE DO HAVE HERE IN THE MUNKY HOUSE!
PAHH

UNHH...
PYEEOWN
PINK!
GURK!
PANGG
SHREEK
PTEEEENG
COME ON OUT, DAGGETT! WHAT, Y'WANNA LIVE FOREVER?!?
POW!
CLAP CLAP CLAP
STAY DOWN, HONEY, EVERYTHING'S FINE..
IT'S SO GREAT FOR THE KIDS WHEN PEOPLE REALLY GET INTO IT LIKE THAT.
NH?!?
I BET THE KID GOT SOME GREAT FOOTAGE!
AHH, I DON'T LIKE THAT "EXPRESSIONIST" STUFF.
hee hee!
SMAK!
MAMA, MAMA! DID YOU SEE, WE WENT ALL WHOOSH AN' I WAS-.
TONIGHT'S DRAMA IN REAL LIFE, "BAD DAY AT DRY MULCH," CONTINUES OVER AT THE BAR-T RANCH, SO SLIDE ON OVER, SIDEWINDERS! YEEEE HAH!

HEY!

TAKE OUR PICTURE, WOULD YA, MISTER?
DISPOSABLE CAMERA
STEREO-REALIST
PEACH TREE

OHH.
I GET IT NOW...
PRESS HERE
DISPOSABLE CAMERA
IKON
STEREO REA
36 SHOTS

uh... umm...

TRUST ME, HONEY-- IT'S CLEANER THAN MY HANDS!
CLIK!

Y'GONNA HAVE TO WORK HARDER THAN THAT TO GET MY FINGERPRINTS.
BABE.

THE VELDT
PARDON OUR PROGRESS!
CLOSED TO VISITORS
PLEASE BE PATIENT!
TREASURES of the LION KING

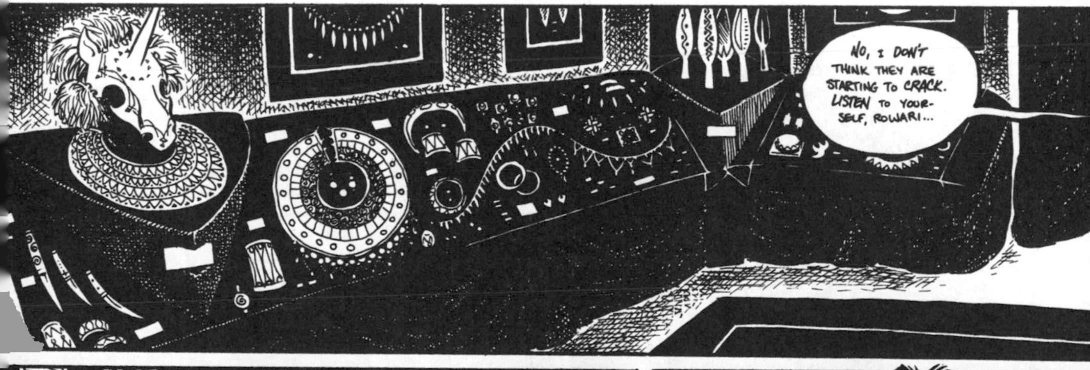
NO, I DON'T THINK THEY ARE STARTING TO CRACK. LISTEN TO YOURSELF, ROWARI...

HURRRrRrRrAAHHH...
HSSSSs
ALL WE NEED ARE A FEW HAMMERS.
I WOULDN'T SULLY MY HANDS.

I WOULD. IF THIS WERE HONEST STONE, AND NOT THAT BASTARD PLASTIC-CRETE, I'D RESCULPT THESE SLANDEROUS GROTESQUES MYSELF.

UH...
NONE OF US LIKES HAVING OUR HANDS TIED, SISTER.
RMRUH.
BUMP
BZZT... POP WELCOME TO "THE WATER HOLE" GIFT SHOP! YOU'LL FIND MANY AUTHENTIC REPLICAS OF... BZT POP
THIS IS A WAITING GAME, A MATTER OF DIPLOMACY.
"DIPLOMACY"!
THESE SKIN MONKEYS DON'T KNOW THE MEANING OF THE WORD.
THAT WAS OUR FIRST MISTAKE, AND WE'VE HAD TIME ENOUGH TO MEDITATE ON IT!
MORE FOOLS WE, TO THINK THEY OFFERED US HOSPITALITY AS VISITING DIGNITARIES!
TO THE MASTERS O THIS PLACE, W ARE NO MORE IMPORTANT THAN A-- A MALFUNCTION MUSIC BOX, WHICH NEED A GOOD SHAKING.
=GROAN= I CANNOT SEE WHY WE MUST GO ON GNAWING THESE DRY BONES. WE SHOULD JUST HAVE DONE WITH THIS PLACE.
YES! LET'S GO, NOW THAT WE CAN!
LET THERE BE ENMITY BETWEEN OUR TWO CITIES. LET THEM HUNT NO MORE ON OUR LANDS!
INDEED. WE CAN FIN SOME OTHER PLACE FO THE KING TO SIT DOW WITH THE ASCIANS
=HRRRH= AS WE FOUND THIS ONE

I SAY WE MUST NOT GO, UNTIL WE HAVE BEEN GIVEN SATISFACTION.
...AND ERASE THIS MONSTROUS INSULT!
THERE IS UCH WE CAN O, WHICH IS ITHIN OUR GNITY, TO BEND THEM TO OUR WILL...
TREASURY
DAUGHTERS BY BLOOD, DAUGHTERS BY BOND, OF KOKUTSOLADO.
KNOWING I HAVE NO RIGHT TO SPEAK HERE, I ASK YOUR LEAVE.
SPEAK, THEN.
I CAN BRING A MESSAGE OUT TO THE QUEENS. WHAT INSULT SHOULD I RELATE, THAT IS SO TERRIBLE, THAT YOU WILL NOT BE ATTENDING YOUR FATHER THE KING'S FUNERAL?
AH NO...

WHUP--
THEY WEPT NO OILY ANIMAL'S TEARS. THEY MOURNED IN A GREAT WICKERWORK OF HARD MUSCLE AND RAGGED BREATH. THE HOT SMELL OF THEIR COATS; THEIR BLACK LIPS PULLED BACK OVER IVORY TEETH, STIFF SPRAYS OF WHITE WHISKERS; THEIR HEAVY HAIR PLAITED WITH SILVER AND FAIENCE. THEIR THICK HIDES SHIVERED, AS CATTLE WILL SHIVER AWAY FLIES.
I SWEATED AND TRIED NOT TO CLEAR MY THROAT.
ALL RIGHT.
TIME TO GO.
I AM MARICCH, HEIR TO THE LATE KING KOKUTSO-LADO.
THESE, MY ADOPTED SISTERS, AND I THANK YOU.
I'M JAEGER.
I'M AN OUTLIER, OF ASCIAN DESCENT.
SKNURCH
SNFF
THE GUARDS OUTSIDE HAVE TO BE DISCREET, SO THE ZOMBIES DON'T GET UPSET. YOU **MIGHT** COULD JUST *BULL* YOUR WAY OUT.
HNH! NOT **US.**
THE CROWDS SETTLE ON US LIKE **GNATS.** WE WERE NEAR TRAMPLED BY THE MOBS ONCE.
NO, WE'LL USE THE TUNNELS

THIS PLACE IS AS RIDDLED WITH SECRET BYWAYS AS A TERMITE MOUND.
WE'LL USE THE TUNNELS, AND WHAT WE HAVE HIDDEN IN THE TUNNELS.
WHAT, THERE AIN'T ANY PEOPLE IN THESE TUNNELS?
NOT LIKE OUT IN THE OPEN. I EXPECT WE'LL HAVE TO KILL FEWER, THIS WAY.
SCRITCH
YOU DO UNDERSTAND.
HEY, THEY AIN'T NONE O' MINE, SIS....
TREASURY
HEY, WAIT! WHAT ABOUT THAT STUFF?
YOUR MA SAID TO MAKE SURE YOU BROUGHT OUT THE FAMILY TREASURE.
MMNH. SHE WOULD.
AS IF I WOULD DISPLAY MY BIRTHRIGHT LIKE A COMMON BAUBLE!
IT IS A PITY TO LEAVE THE DISPLAY. IT IS PRETTY STUFF.
BUT WE ALREADY HAVE THAT WHICH IS VITAL, AND TIME IS SHORT.
21

TILL WE MEET AGAIN, ASCIAN MAN. YOU WOULD MAKE A GOOD SISTER.
BROTHER.
TSK!
CLANG!
OVER THIS, THEY'RE READY TO GO TO WAR?

WHOOP-DE-DOO.
HOME CRAP HOME.

"FORMAL MEETIN'S ALL ARRANGED: SEVEN CHIEFS GONNA HONOR YOU, KID."
YEAH RIGHT.

IF I SKIPPED OUT, IT'D MAKE THEM HAPPY. "WELL, WHAT CAN YOU EXPECT," AND GO ON THEIR MERRY WAY.
BUT IT AIN'T GONNA BE THAT WAY. THEY WON'T BE ASSEMBLED, WAITING FOR ME, SHAKING THEIR HEADS OVER MY DISRESPECT.
GUESS I JUST WANNA BE THERE TO WITNESS THEIRS.

THERE YOU ARE YOU YOU WEASEL!! DAMN YOU DAMN YOU!

CRACK
SMAK
SMAKK
WHY YOU DISAPPEAR ON ME YOU MANGY MONSTER WHEN YOU KNOW IT'S UP TO ME TO MAKE YOU LOOK LIKE SOMEBODY GIVES A SHIT ABOUT YOU ONLY SEVEN CHIEFS WAITING IN MY TENT FOR A BUTTMONKEY LIKE YOU AND LOOK AT Y--

A-- AH~!

WHOP!

HOLY SHIT!
SHE DID THIS ALL IN ONE NIGHT?!

AW, FUCK ME.. WHY DID I CUT MY HAIR?

AS THE ASCIANS RECKON THINGS, A SIN-EATER HAS NO SOUL AT ALL.
JUST A HOLE FOR ALL THE WORLD'S SHIT TO POUR INTO. BOTTOMLESS.

A CHIEF HAS THREE SOULS.

HIS OWN; HIS SELF.

ANOTHER, WHICH MAY GO ON TO BECOME SOMETHING GREATER AFTER HIS DEATH. THE HERO SOUL.

AND THE SOUL OF HIS PEOPLE. AN AGGREGATE SPIRIT, WHICH STANDS FOR ALL THE ANCESTORS, FOR CUSTOM, WISDOM, HISTORY.

NO CHIEF STAYS CHIEF IF IT'S THOUGHT THAT SOUL HAS DESERTED HIM.

A MULTITUDE INDEED.
AND ME. THE EMPTY SPACE.

EMPTY.

EMPTY.

EMPTY.

AH, THERE'S OUR GOOD SIN-EATER. COME SIT WITH US, BOY.
THEY CALL ME COWARD.
THAT'S A GOOD NAME, SIR.
I'D LIKE TO HEAR THE STORY OF IT SOMETIME.
HA!
MANNERLY SAID, BUT A MANNERLY MAN KNOWS HE'S NOT APT TO HEAR ONE UNLESS HE SITS!
DON'T TAKE IT SO HARD. MY BROTHER CHIEFS, THEY'RE USED TO THINGS BEING ONLY ONE WAY.
THERE'S NOTHING IN THE BOOKS THAT SAYS SIN-EATERS MUST BE SHUNNED. IT'S JUST AN OLD CUSTOM.
CHIEFS AND CAMPS LIVE BY OLD CUSTOMS, SIR.
TRUE ENOUGH. BUT THERE IS AN EVEN OLDER CUSTOM WHICH HAS IT THAT SIN-EATERS ARE TO BE VENERATED.
PEOPLE HATE CONTRADICTIONS.
IN REAL LIFE, ANYWAY. CONTRADICTIONS MAKE THE BEST STORIES.
THE DAY TWENTY-ONE SPIRITS MET TO HONOR NO SPIRIT AT ALL.
THAT STORY MAY LIVE LONGER THAN ANY CHIEF CAN HOPE TO.
IF ANYBODY TELLS IT.

OH I'LL TELL IT. AND THEY CAN'T OBJECT.
THEY ARE NOT HERE WITH EYES AND EARS.
THEY SENT THEIR SOULS.

YOU COULD TAKE THEM, YOU KNOW.

STEAL THEIR TOTEMS. THEIR MAGIC BAGS, THEIR HISTORY BLANKETS. HELL, EVEN THEIR DRUMS.
TOOMB
DON'T TRY TO TELL ME YOU DIDN'T THINK OF IT.

WOULD SERVE 'EM RIGHT, WOULDN'T IT? THAT I'D BE THE ONLY ONE TO KEEP MY TOTEMS? I, WHO CAME?

...NAH.
WHAT WOULD I DO WITH THE STUFF, ONCE I HAD IT?
SELL IT?
DESTROY IT?
USE IT TO HUMILIATE THEM?
BESIDES, THEY'D ALL GO TO WAR TO GET IT BACK.

WAR IS ONE OF THOSE FAMOUS TIES THAT BIND, MY PEREGRINO.
BETTER TO BE HATED, THAN TO BE OF NO CONSEQUENCE AT ALL.

AND IT WOULD BALANCE OUT CERTAIN THEFTS OF THEIR OWN.
SIR...?

THOSE CATS BROUGHT SOME SORT OF TREASURE TROVE HERE. NOBODY'S SEEN IT, EXCEPT ON POSTERS... THE CATS HAVE KEPT THEIR CAMP CLOSED UP TIGHT.
BOYS AND MEN ALIKE, ALL HOT TO STEAL THE CAT KIN GOLD. I CAN'T PROMIS THEM ANY DRAMA IN THE WAY OF A PEACE TREATY, NOW.

NO ASCIAN CHIEF HAS EVER MADE PEACE WITH A NYIMAN KING.
YOU GOT SIX CHIEFS WHO CAN'T AGREE ON THE TIME OF DAY TO COME TO THIS CRAZY PLACE, TO DO JUST THAT... NOW HE'S DEAD, THEY'RE GONNA ROB HIS WIDOWS.
AND YOU WANT ME TO ROB THEM.

IT'S ONLY COUNTING COUP.
IF WE'RE NOT TO HAVE OUR TREATY, WHY SHOULDN'T WE GET OUR LICKS IN AGAINST AN ANCIENT ENEMY?

WHAT AMAZES ME IS THAT YOU WERE INTERESTED IN PEACE AT ALL.

THAT'S WHY THEY CALL ME COWARD.

DRUM-CHIEF, I BEG YOUR INDULGENCE TO LET ME GO. I HAVE JUST REMEMBERED A SMALL ERRAND OF NO IMPORTANCE THAT I MIGHT AT SOME POINT PERFORM.
HAH! GO, BOY, GO ON.

SIGH
COMES IN WITH HIS NASTY DIRTY BOOTS ON... AT LEAST I DIDN'T HAVE TO WASTE MY BEST CAKES ON HIM...
GO MAKE SOME TROUBLE..
SKTTCH SKRTTCH

I NEVER SPARED TOO MUCH THOUGHT FOR CITY PEOPLE.
THEY'RE NOT VERY SMART. THEY'RE NOT VERY STRONG. THEY DON'T CARE ABOUT ANY-THING I CARE ABOUT.
INSIDE THOSE BIG DOMED CITIES IT'S LIKE A DIFFERENT WORLD... AND IF THEY COME OUT OF THAT WORLD INTO THIS ONE, THEY GET SICK.
IN THIS GOOD LAND, WHERE I'VE LIVED ALL MY LIFE, THEY STARVE. THEY GET STRUCK BY THE SUN, DRY UP, FREEZE TO DEATH.
THEY DIE "OF EXPOSURE". GO FIGURE.

CHAPTER THREE
BUT SINCE I WAS A BOY I'VE CRAVED TO KNOW...
DID WE COME OUT OF THAT SAFE OVERCROWDED WARREN OF THE CITY?
OR DID THEY BUILD THE CITIES AND THEN FILL THEM UP?
ALL THE CITIES, THE CITIES ARE ANCIENT. THEY SAY THE WAYS OF MAKING THE GREAT DOMES WAS LOST.
MAYBE... THEY NEVER HAD IT?
THEY TAKE CREDIT FOR INVENTING ALL KINDS OF THINGS THEY MERELY ACQUIRED.
THEY DID BUILD THIS.

THEY'RE NOT SMARTER THAN WE ARE. THEY'RE NOT BRAVER. THEY'RE DAMN NEAR BLIND, AND DEAF TO THE SOUND OF THEIR OWN HEARTS BEATING.
DID THEY COME FROM US?
OR WE FROM THEM?
EITHER WAY, WHAT THE HELL ARE THEY DOING OUT HERE?

~WELCOME~ to the GRASSLANDS.
YAWN
SHADDAP.
....ANOTHER ONE-OF-A-KIND DAY IN MUNKYLAND! OUR FANTASIERS WANT ONLY THE BEST FOR OUR HONORED GUESTS, SO THIS EXPERIENCE IS NOT YET ONLINE--
ALL-I-WANT-TO-KNOW-IS-WHEN-IT-WILL-BE.
NYIMA PAVILION
CLOSED
--NO MAGICIAN EVER REVEALS HIS SECRETS--
ACTIVATE SILENT COMLINK.
YOU LIVE HERE! MY KIDS MAY NEVER SEE THIS PLACE AGAIN!
PARDON OUR PROGRESS!
CROWD VISCOSITY OUTSIDE NYIMA PAVILION (WEST GATE) INCREASING. EXPONENTIAL SLOWDOWN IMMINENT.
--WHERE WOULD THE FUN AND SPONTANEITY OF LIFE BE IF WE ALL KNEW HOW IT WAS DONE?
WHAT'S GOING ON?
WHY CAN'T THEY SEE THE GOLD EXHIBIT AT LEAST??
INITIATE DIVERSION IN GRIDS ONE-ONE-THREE AND EIGHT-ONE-THREE.
THERE ARE MANY FASCINATING EXPERIENCES YOU MAY MISS--
BOOM!
OOH
AAH
ENJOY THE VIEW, PLEASE!
~welcome~ to the GRASSLANDS.
DA-AAD! FOR GODS' SAKE COME ON! WE'LL BE THE LAST ONES THERE!
SIGH
I'M RUNNING OUT OF WAYS TO SAY "NO" WITHOUT SAYING NO, GIRLS...

WHAT'S WRONG WITH THESE STUCK-UP WEIRD-HEAD LION-GIRLS ANYWAY? WHY DON'T THEY WANT TO PERFORM FOR THE GUESTS?
SUPPOSEDLY THEY'RE ROYALTY. DIGNITY, Y'KNOW. IT ALWAYS SCREWS UP COMMERCE.
MAYBE SO, BUT I WISH THESE ASCIANS WOULD CALM DOWN!
BEEMP
SOMETHING'S UP-- THEY'RE ALL STRUNG TIGHTER THAN VIOLIN STRINGS AND WATCHING EACH OTHER LIKE HAWKS!
PUTTING ON A GOOD SHOW, THE GUESTS LIKE IT, BUT---
!
PUMFF!!
DON'T THINK NOBODY SEES YOU TRYIN'A SNEAK AROUND TO THE EDGES, WISE GUY.
WHERE D'YA THINK YOU'RE GOIN'?
OOH! FIGHT SCENE!
THEY USED TO SPEND ALL THEIR TIME WATCHING US....
I THINK WE BETTER NOT POST ANY ROOKIES IN THIS ZONE TODAY....

THE NYIMA CAMP S CLOSED OFF TO SITORS. NO TOURISTS. THAT'S GOOD.
WON'T BE ANY CROWDS TO HIDE IN. THAT'S BAD.
THERE'LL BE ONLY ONE OR TWO GUARDS, AND THOSE WILL BE AT THE GATES. THAT'S GOOD.
IF THERE BE NO GUARDS, THERE BE THOSE --EYES-- IN THE DARKNESS. THAT'S BAD.
THE LOOT IS MOSTLY ORNAMENT, SUCH AS WOMEN WOULD WEAR. IT SHOULD ALL FIT IN ONE BAG, EASIER TO HIDE. THAT'S GOOD.
THE WOMEN WE MEAN TO STEAL IT FROM ARE HEAVILY ARMED. THAT'S BAD.
NOT FORGETTING THOSE SNAGGLE-TOOTHED HORRORS THEY KEEP FOR WATCHDOGS. I'D CALL THOSE A WORLD OF BAD.
HNH!
COUNTING COUP ON THOSE ARROGANT LION HEADS.... THAT WOULD BE GOOD.
...GO IN THROUGH THE AIR VENTS...?
=TSK=
THAT IS SUCH A LAME IDEA.

SNAKE EYE
SECURITY

HELLO, KIDDIES! IT'S A GOOD DAY TO BE PARANOID! AS THE PROVISIONAL ASCIAN AMBASSADOR TO THE COURT OF MARICCH, HEIR TO KOKUTSOLADO, KING OF WESTMARCH, I DO HEREBY SEIZE THIS PAIN-IN-THE-ASS SECURITY DEVICE!

DAHHGUNNIT!
I WILL NEVER TRUST ANTHROPOLOGY PROGRAMS AGAIN. THEY SAID ON "WILD WORLD" THAT THESE PEOPLE ARE PRIMITIVE!
DISGUSTED SIGH
UNDY! CAN YOU GIVE ME INFRARED IN THE NYIMA PAVILION?
NO WAY. THAT'S THE FIRST THING THEY DISMANTLED.
DAMN.
CLICK
HENH!
GODDAMN KID!

CHING!
CHING!
CHING!
CHING!
THERE ARE THOSE WHO JUST DON'T UNDERSTAND WHAT IS MEANT BY COUNTING COUP.
COUNTING COUP IS A GAME. A REALLY SERIOUS GAME; THE KIND THAT CAN GET YOU KILLED. A GAME THAT CAN MAKE YOU SHARP. MAKE YOU SMART. PROVE YOUR WORTH.
THE BEST KIND OF GAME.
COUNTING COUP IS SOMETHING BETWEEN WAR AND PEACE. CLOSEST THING TO IT, I GUESS, IS PLAYING A PRACTICAL JOKE.
CHING!
CHING!
CHING!
CHING!
CITY PEOPLE HATE PRACTICAL JOKES. "NOBODY LIKES A SMART-ASS" OUGHT TO BE TATTOOED ON THEIR COLLECTIVE FOREHEAD.
NOMADS LIVE FOR 'EM. "GOTCHA" IS THE FAVORITE STORY TOLD AROUND THE CAMPFIRE.
SO I STOLE THE NYIMA GOLD. NOT LIKE THEY CARED ABOUT IT; THEY LEFT IT BEHIND WITHOUT A THOUGHT.
BUT I TELL YA-- IF THE ASCIAN BLUEBLOODS CATCH ME WITH WHAT THEY ARE ALL FULL OF PLANS TO STEAL--
HEY! WHATTA YA GONNA DO WITH TWO GIRLS??
THAT'S, EH... MY PROBLEM...
...I AM HERE NOW...
CHING! CHING!
--THE JOKE WILL BE ON ME.

AND WHAT GOOD IS IT TO ME THAT YOU'RE HERE NOW?

WHERE WERE YOU TWENTY YEARS AGO, TEN YEARS AGO? HOW DARE YOU, HOW DARE YOU COME TO ME NOW, WHEN I AM THIS?

I WISH YOU HAD NEVER COME. WHY DO YOU COME NOW?
EMMA ...?
SHE IS THE LAST. SHE IS THE LAST UNICORN IN THE WORLD.

SHE WOULD BE.

IT WOULD BE THE LAST UNICORN IN THE WORLD THAT CAME TO MOLLY GRUE.

IT'S ALL RIGHT.
I FORGIVE YOU.

IT WASN'T EMMA. EMMA WAS NEVER AN ACTRESS.
AAAAA!

IT WAS JUST ANOTHER... WOMAN FROM EMMA'S CLAN. A LOOK-ALIKE, THAT'S ALL.
AND SOUND-ALIKE, SMELL-ALIKE FOR ALL I KNOW...

I SAID I'D GO BACK TO HER WHEN ENOUGH TIME PASSED THAT I GREW MY BRAID AGAIN.

DAMMIT. WHY DID I CUT MY HAIR?
SOMETIMES I CAN FEEL TIME CRAWLING ON ME LIKE FLIES.
PLOOK!

WHY DIDN'T THE LION-GIRLS CARE ABOUT THEIR ROYAL TREASURE?
IT'S WEIRD, THOUGH; WHAT KIND OF ARTISAN INLAYS COPPER INTO PLATINUM?
IF THIS IS FAKE, THERE IS NO REAL.

...WONDER HOW THEY'RE DOING...
sshh...

WHERE THE HELL AM I GOING...
CHING
CHING

LINE FORMS 45 MIN
CHING

CHING

CHING

CROWDS ARE FUNNY THINGS.
≡BEEP≡ DO NOT ENTER! THIS IS SOMEBODY ELSE'S PROBLEM! ≡BEEP≡
WILDERNESS TRAILS (TM) ARE CARPETED WITH GENUINE LOBLOLLY PINE NEEDLES!
HI HO HI HO

SOMETIMES ANYTHING OUT OF THE ORDINARY DRAWS THEM LIKE SHARKS TO THE SMELL OF BLOOD.
OTHER TIMES, THEY'RE MORE LIKE THE WATER ITSELF.

THE OCEAN DOESN'T NOTICE IF A FISH JUMPS OUT AND WALKS AWAY.

KNOWING THE "WATER" IS ALL PART OF THE FINE ART OF GETTING LOST.

NO, MOM, IT'S NOT THAT I DIDN'T LIKE JOVE CANYON--THE REAL ONE, I MEAN -- IT'S JUST, LIKE, THERE'S NOTHING TO DO THERE...
42

VWHISSH
!
YIPE!
CLANG!

GABLOOOSH!
IT'S A BAG... INSIDE A BAG!

OW!
HEY! WAIT FOR BABY!
SON, THAT AIN'T THE HALF OF IT...

WHUP!
DEEP SPOT!
PLOSH
SAAAAVE ME, SAAAVE ME! BLUPPA BLUB

?
SAAAAVE ME, SAAAVE ME! BLUB

SAAAVE ME, SAAAVE ME!
CLICK
HEY, MISTER! IS THIS BAG YOURS?

SAAAAVE ME BLUB
WHOA!
BMP!

SHYEEE--
SAAAVE ME, SAAAVE ME!

I'LL SAVE YA, UNCLE JED, JUST HOLD STILL A MINUTE!
HA HA HAHAHA HA
SAAAVE ME!

HEY! YOU'RE IN THE WRONG RIDE!
ROARR

THIS IS THE BIG TIMBER ADVENTURE, NOT PIRATES OF THE CAROB-BEAN!
CLICK
COOL!

HURRY, HURRY! YOU CAN MAKE IT!
HEH RUN, BWAH!
TSK

CLICK
AW--

ROOOSHH

HEY, MISTER!
GHASPP
MWHA?

YOU'RE WET EVERYWHERE BUT YOUR BACK!
HUH! SHNORFF!
THAT'S STRANGE, ID'N IT?

GASPLARSH!
AH!

THERE, ZAT BETTER?
HEY, DON'T ROCK THE LOG!
HA HA HA HA HA HAA
YES, IT IS...
IT'S NOT FUNNY!

HERE IT COMES, KIDS!
BE SURE TO SMILE BIG FOR YOUR OLD PAL MUNKY ON THE WAY DOWN!
ROARR

NGEE.

!!!!
GADÜSSHH!

WATCH YOUR STEP...
WATCH YOUR STEP...
WATCH YOUR STEP...

STEP... WATCH YOUR
WATCH YOUR STEP.. WATCH YOUR
GREAT RIDE!

EP... WATCH YOUR STEP...
YEAH, GREAT RIDE!
CHNG CHING CHNG CHING
SQUIS SQUIS SQUIS SQUIS

HEY YOU!
IRK!
EXIT

YOU RUINED IT! NOW WE DON'T GET OUR PICTURE!
OOH, OOH, I SPOILED IT FOR THE WHOLE LOG...

THIS PLACE IS SO CAREFULLY CHOREOGRAPHED; SCENES ROM A DOZEN DIFFERENT STORIES HAPPENING ON VERY CORNER AND DOWN EVERY SIDE STREET.

THE SHERIFF OR THE RAINMAKER... I COULDN'T CHOOSE BUT NO ONE CAN SAY I WASN'T ASKED...

THESE PEOPLE ARE HERE FOR A VERY SHORT TIME, AND THIS PLACE IS FAR TOO BIG FOR THEM TO SEE ALL OF IT.
THEY'RE DESPERATE NOT TO MISS ANYTHING.
THEIR EYES SNAG ON ANYTHING UNUSUAL.

EOPLE TALK ABOUT BEING 'A FACE IN THE CROWD." HEY MEAN BEING NOBODY. OBODY WORTH NOTICING, THAT IS TO SAY.

SUSPECT IT'S ALSO SUPPOSED MEAN FELLOWSHIP. BEING NE AMONG MANY, PART OF A HOLE. CAN'T SAY FOR SURE.

ESE PEOPLE PROBABLY LWAYS FEEL THAT WAY. MOST F THEM HAVE THAT INBRED ULL-BLOOD CLAN DESCENT LOOK ABOUT THEM.

ANS ASPIRE TO UNIFORMITY.

THE *SAMENESS* OF THEM ALL IS WEIRDLY BEAUTIFUL SOMETIMES.
LIKE AN ASPEN WOOD. EVERY TREE ALIKE; EVERY LEAF ALIKE.
LIKE PRAIRIE; ONLY BRIGHT SKY, BLACK CLOUDS, AND WAVING GRASS OVER STRANGE ALIEN HILLS.

YOU GET SO HUNGRY
TO SEE A FACE THAT LOOKS LIKE YOUR OWN
AND THEN THAT CROWD OF SAMENESS BREAKS--
AND YOU SEE YOURSELF REFLECTED
LIKE A VISION
OF ANOTHER LIFE.

THE FORCE OF YOUR GAZE HAS A WEIGHT. EVEN SUNLIGH RESTING ON THE GROUND WEIGHS SOMETHING. YOUR ATTEN TION PRESSES AGAINST ITS OBJECT; YOUR EYE PROJECTS I LIKE A HEADLIGHT.

BZZZT!
POP
BZT
HOLO HABILIMENT "EVERY OCCASION"
HH

I DON'T KNOW THAT IT DOESN'T WORK ON SPY CAMERAS.
BUT NOT KNOWING GETS ME SO WOUND UP THAT IT DOESN'T MATTER. THE TRICK DOESN'T WORK IF I'M SO...

I'M TOO TALL
TOO DARK
TOO WET.
I'M TOO WEIRD TO BE A TOURIST AND NOT WEIRD ENOUGH TO BE AN EMPLOYEE.

WORST OF ALL-- I'M ALONE. NO WIFE, NO KIDS--
GODDAMN.
WHEN DID I--
NOBODY SMOKES IN HERE, STUPID!
AT LEAST IT AIN'T LIT...

THAT BLANK SCREEN BACK AT THE PLASTIC LOG THING SHOULD HAVE MADE ME HAPPY-- I HATE TO SEE MYSELF CAPTURED ON FILM--

UT IT DOESN'T. THERE'S SOMETHING ERY WRONG THERE, BUT I CAN'T PUT MY FINGER ON WHAT--

DAD?
DAD, LOOK! IS THAT THE GUY?
MAYBE, SON, BUT YOU'RE NOT SUPPOSED TO BOTHER--

GOT SOMETHING TO SAY?

MUMBLE MUMBLE MUMBLE

..SIDLE SIDLE SIDLE

..HHNGH...

SNAP!

SNAP!

ULGH!

POURATORIUM

NOT AN ASCIAN...
TOO TALL...
DOESN'T WALK RIGHT...
?
?
??!

HEH-HA... GOTCHA!

BZZZZST

LADIES AND GENTLEMEN! CHILDREN OF ALL AGES!

COOL!
TODAY'S DRAMA IN REAL LIFE BEGINS RIGHT HERE, RIGHT NOW!

A PRIMAL TALE OF THE CROWD AGAINST THE INDIVIDUAL!
HUNTER AND HUNTED!

THE RULE OF KING MOB!

SEEK OUT, AND BRING DOWN...
THE RUNNING MAN!

AAA
FREE TICKETS BACK HERE TO MUNKY'S PLAYGROUND FOR WHOEVER GETS HIM FIRST!
RUMBLE RUMBLE

SHINK SHINK
SHINK
SHINK
SHINK SHINK SHINKS

SHIT
GHASP
DAMN BAG'S HEAVY AS LEAD
GASP
--OR IS GOLD HEAVIER THAN LEAD--?
SHINK SHINK SHINK
SHINK SHINK SHINK

SHINK SHINK SHINK SHINK
THUNDER THUNDER THUNDER
WHOOF
HAGH
GASP
YI!
AAH...
WHEW!
OH, WELL
DAMN CARTILAGE
UNGH.
SORRY, BABY...
WAAA!

ZZZOOWWNTT!!
HOLO HABILIMENT EVERY OCCASION"
DIANA
HOLO HABILIMENT
HOLO HABILIMENT

DAMN, HARRY! YOU GOT TO STOP UNPLUGGING THINGS JUST TO FIND OUT WHAT THEY ARE! IT'S VERY UNPROFESSIONAL!
OH WAAH, WAAH.

RUMBLE RUMBLE RUMBLE
DIANA

YOU GUYS ALL WORK HERE!!
RUMBLE
WHAT DO YOU WANT WITH FREE TICKETS?
RUMBLE
RUMBLE
RUMBLE
RUMBLE
IT'S ALL FAKE! WHAT A GYP!
ERIK

OUR COMPLIMENTS, MISS.
POP
for you
A REBATE COUPON?
OH MY GOD!
WOW!
CLUMP
CHING!
THE RUNNING MAN
HHH YOU
YOU FUHH
OH, THIS MUST BE FOR THE SEQUEL. REMEMBER, THEY DID THE SAME THING LAST KINDLE-MAS.
TSK! WELL-- AT LEAST THEY GOT A BETTER-LOOKING STAR.
TODAY'S ... IN REAL LIFE..."THE RUNNI

GODDAMn..n.nH. SHIT! HALnFLIA SIGK! UPiSHIT! IDOMMNT. SHIT! IMHZ-IYZIIMPSHIT! SHIT!
THIS WAY!

I BARELY KNOW WHY I DID THIS--
..."TH

MY CLOTHES WERE SO WET AND HEAVY--

I THINK I JUST
ANTED SOMETHING TO THROW--
SPLOT!
OH IT WAS SO WORTH IT TO GET THAT FIRST ONE RIGHT IN THE HEAD WITH A WET LOINCLOTH!

IN REAL LIFE..
THEN I'M JUST STANDING THERE LIKE A STUPID DRUNK, YELLIN' ALL KINDS OF INCOMPREHENSIBLE BULLSHIT-- CAN'T REMEMBER A DAMN WORD OF IT..
OH JEEZ... IS THIS SUPPOSED TO HAPPEN?

ARDS FINALLY
AD BLOOD IN THEIR EYES--
SCREENS ALL FLIPPING TO CARTOONS--
OOK-OOK--
BIG SMILE FOR YER OL' PAL MUNKY!
SON OF A--
OH
--TOURISTS THROWING THEMSELVES OVER THEIR KIDS LIKE I'M A LIVE GRENADE!

I AIN'T SO TOUGH-- I MIND AN ASS BEATING AS MUCH AS THE NEXT GUY-- BUT IF I'VE GOT ONE COMING I'M FER DAMN SURE GONNA GET MY MONEY'S WORTH--

HUP HUP HUP
EEX...
IGNORE IT, IT'S JUST SOMEBODY ELSE'S NIGHTMARE...
GOLD OUT, GOLD OUT-- GOT TO GET THIS GOLD OUT--
CAN'T HIDE IT--
CAN'T COME BACK FOR IT--
MEDIEVAL
WARFARE

YES!

VWEEE

YES!

WONKK!!

CRINTSSH!

YES!

WELL, I'M RRY YOU GOT RNED AROUND, T I *NEVER* SAID E WAS ON THE CATAPULT TOWER!

IF YOU FLAMING IDIOTS WOULD *STUDY* THE NEW SECTIONS, YOU'D *KNOW* WHAT A BALLISTA IS AND I WOULDN'T HAVE TO *SAY* IT WAS ***LIKE*** A *CATAPULT!*

Y'KNOW, RALPH; I'LL TELL YA THE *BIG* REASON I HATE THIS FRICKIN' PLACE SO MUCH.
YEAH; WHYZAT, GEORGE.
IT'S THE WAY, Y'KNOW, IF YOU DON'T LIKE THE HAPPY PLACE, PEOPLE ACT LIKE YOU MUST BE SOME KIND OF *PERVERT*.

IF YOU GO SO FAR AS TO LIKE ANYTHING THAT ISN'T SQUEAKY CLEAN, YOU MUST BE SOME SORTA GOAT RAPER!
NO IN BETWEEN, NO SHADES OF GRAY-- EITHER YOU'RE GOOD CLEAN AND WHOLESOME, OR YOU'RE A VILE PUS SUCKING MONSTER!
HEH- HA!
GOOD ONE, GEORGE...
HEH... YEAH, EITHER YOU'RE RAGGIE ANNIE OR YOU'RE A BIG HOT STEAMING TURD ON TOAST--
BUT WAIT! THE WORST THING, THE MOST DIABOLICAL PART IS THIS!
MFF?
MOOSE
AFTER A WHILE, THERE STOPS BEING ANY DIFFERENCE BETWEEN THE TWO EXTREMES! CUTE BECOMES EVIL! RAGGIE ANNIE IS A BIG HOT STEAMING TURD! IT'S BIZARRE, IT'S LIKE A TRAP!
...
HEY, UH... SHIT, ARE WE STILL LIVE??

SUNDOWN SIDE OF MUNKYTOWN...

HRRGH--
OH MY GOD! HARRY! GET SOME TAP DANCERS OR SOMETHING DOWN HERE, PRONTO!
! mom--?
sniffle
OOF!
FWUMP!
WHOO!
GASP

HEY!
LEAP!
RIJI, NO!
WHMP!
NOT NOW!
RRALGH!
BAD BOY, BAAD!
HOLD THEM OFF.
NO ONE IS TO INDULGE UNTIL AFTER THE FUNERAL AND CORONATION.
THEY'RE GOING TO BE HARD ENOUGH TO MANAGE AS IT IS; DON'T MAKE IT ANY WORSE.
LET'S GO.

2: ON THE SUNUP SIDE...

21
CLIK
KERCHUNK
EEB

GUH!
WHUMFT!

HEH-EH-EH KOFF
FUNF!

'F I'D'A KNOWN THAT'S ALL YOU WERE GONNA DO, I WOULDN'A WORRIED!
HEE HEE

21
AWW!
WHAT SENTIMENTAL PEOPLE!
AND ONLY TWO SIZES TOO SMALL!

3: COWARD ALWAYS SMILES.
COMING THIS SUMMER

A NEW FILM ARRANGED BY
MESNIE HARLEQUIN

THE RUNNING MAN
IT'S ABOUT A YOUNG MAN IN A BIG HURRY.
SUMMER

SHSS!
THEY REALLY DO STEAL YOUR SOUL WHEN THEY TAKE YOUR PICTURE!
YEAH, STEAL IT AND SELL IT!
COOL!

well

RRR

NICE PARADE, CHIEF.
WE DO LOVE IT WHEN OUR PERFORMERS GIVE THE PEOPLE THAT CERTAIN SOMETHING MORE.
RRR

KTIK
KTOK
KTIK

BUT BEFORE WE GET MUCH FURTHER ON THIS LITTLE SUNDAY DRIVE...
MAY I POINT OUT THAT YOU, CHIEF COWARD, AND YOUR PEOPLE, ARE UNDER CONTRACT FOR FORTY-TWO MORE PERFORMANCES?
I'D BE GLAD TO RECORD THIS... SPECTACLE AS ONE SUCH, BUT THAT STILL LEAVES YOU WITH AN UNFULFILLED COMMITMENT TO FORTY-ONE MORE.

KTIK
KTOK

MAY I ALSO POINT OUT THAT IF YOU EFAULT ON THAT COMMITMENT, YOU-- ND YOUR PEOPLE-- WILL BE SUBJECT TO HEAVY FINANCIAL LOSSES?
IF YOU'RE NOT PERFORMERS, YOU'RE GUESTS. GUESTS ARE LIABLE FOR ALL THE COSTS OF THEIR ROOM AND BOARD. MEALS, WATER, ENTRY AND EXIT TARIFFS, IMPORT TAXES, DUTIES, SANITATION FEES... ALL THAT ENTIRELY ASIDE FROM CONTRACTUAL PENALTIES.
I ASSURE YOU, IT'LL ADD UP TO A PRETTY PENNY. NOW, IF YOU STAY, AND LIVE UP TO YOUR CONTRACT, YOU NEED HEAR NO MORE ABOUT IT.
IF YOU DON'T, WELL... I'M AFRAID WE'LL HAVE NO CHOICE.
RONK
!
SUBPARAGRAPH 2-2-8 OF SECTION 12-5 STATES PLAINLY THAT NO MERCHANDISING OF ANY ASCIAN LIKENESS, INDIVIDUAL, ART OR CRAFT SHALL BE UNDERTAKEN BY ANY NON-ASCIAN ENTITY.
FAILURE TO COMPLY WITH THIS PROVISION WILL RESULT IN PENALTIES AS SET FORTH IN PARAGRAPH 3-1 OF SECTION 21-5.
NOBODY HAS---
YOUR "RUNNING MAN" IS OUR SIN-EATER. HE IS MOST DEFINITELY ONE OF US.
BUT, BUT, BUT--
YOU'LL BE GETTING A BILL IN A FEW DAYS. I RECOMMEND YOU PAY IT.
BUT HE HAD SHORT HAIR!

4: SMOKE SIGNALS.
LGH!
RRR!
HRRG!

RRRGH!

WHAK!
YRL!
STOP IT.

URRWLL!
I KNOW YOU DON'T LIKE IT. JUST TRY TO STAY CALM.

!
FEH.
WITH LUCK... IT WON'T BE FOR LONG.

OH!
OH NO, NO...
E KNEW... HE KNEW HE
OULDN'T LIVE MUCH LONGER.
OHY THE HELL DIDN'T WE
JUST STAY HOME?
A KING HAS HIS REASONS.
"WE'D BETTER GO.
"THE KING IS DEAD.
"IT ISN'T SAFE."
AH, KOKUT...
IT'S TRUE, WE WON'T SEE HIS LIKE AGAIN--
?
TNK
SKSHH
WELL, FOR PITY'S SAKE... HOW DID THIS GET OUT HERE?

HENCEFORTH THE HUMAN WORD "QUEEN" SHALL BE STRICKEN FROM ALL USE, FORMAL OR INFORMAL, AS IT CARRIES UNSEEMLY CONNOTATIONS.

Z.

MORE SUITABLE TRANSLATIONS OF YMA FORM OF ADDRESS ARE BEING RESEARCHED. UNTIL FURTH NOTICE, SUBSTITUTE "CAPTAIN" OR "EXECUTIVE OFFICER." *NO* HUMAN FEUDAL RANKS ARE TO BE USED.

WHAT ABOUT "KING"?

NO. =SIGH=

NO, RETAIN "KING."

DECREED THIS DAY BY MARICCH, HEIR OF KOKUTSOLADO, BLAH BLAH BLAH, ETC. ETC. ETC.

MARICCH.

MY DARLING. YOU SHOULDN'T WAIT.

IT'S NOT SO BAD FOR YOU GIRLS. BUT WE WHO WERE WIVES TO THE LATE KING, WE'LL SUFFER IF THERE ISN'T A NEW KING SOON.

WE DON'T HAVE MUCH MORE TIME BEFORE IT SETS IN.

I AM IN NO WAY ATTEMPTING TO INFLUENCE YOUR CHOICE. *YOU* ARE THE THRONE.

JUST DON'T WAI FOR THE SAKE O WAITING. WE WON' BE OF ANY USE T YOU IF YOU DO

SIGH
YOU FOUND THIS WHERE?
IN THE WOODS.
WITH THE GOLD.
SCATTERED OVER A HILLSIDE.
EVIDENTLY IT WAS ALL ROLLED TOGETHER IN A BAG AND... EJECTED FROM THE DOME WITH GREAT FORCE.
IT'S A MIRACLE THE COAT WASN'T SHREDDED ALONG WITH THE BAG.
THIS KIND OF BEADWORK IS TREASURE TO THE ASCIANS.
THEIR WOMEN SPEND YEARS MAKING THESE, AS LOVE GIFTS FOR THEIR MALES... FOR, UH, FOR PROSPECTIVE HUSBANDS.
THIS DESIGN IS A COMMON MOTIF. I BELIEVE IT'S A TOTEMIC CLAN MARKING.
IT SMELLS OF HIM. HE MUST BE A HIGH-STATUS MALE, TO OWN SUCH A COAT.
ONESTLY, I CAN'T SAY WHAT HE EW. I JUST SPOTTED HIM, TWO DAYS , A HUMAN MALE, ASCIAN. HE SEEMED KNOW KOKUT WAS DEAD. HE SAID I CAME TO PAY MY RESPECTS.'
HOW COULD HE KNOW, TYI? HOW COULD ANYONE SNEAK INTO THIS CAMP-- AND BACK OUT?-- WITHOUT BEING SEEN?! IS THE STANDARD OF OUR GUARDS SO LOW?
I BROUGHT HIM TO THE DOWAGERS BECAUSE I THOUGHT HE'D BE USEFUL. AND HE WAS.
HNN.
I WOULDN'T PUT IT PAST CERTAIN ASCIANS.
THEY MAY BE PRIMITIVE PEOPLE, BUT DON'T UNDERESTIMATE THEM. THEY HAVE A SORT OF... PRIESTLY CLASS OF SCOUTS AND TRACKERS. THEY CALL THEM FINDERS. IF HE'S ONE OF THEM, THERE'S NO TELLING WHAT HE'S CAPABLE OF.
NOT A TAME MALE.

"ALSO... HIS HAIR WAS CUT SHORT."
"AND...?"

"ASCIANS DO THAT WHEN THEY ARE IN MOURNING."

IN MOURNING.
TYI... =SIGH=
DON'T MISUNDERSTAND. I AM GRATEFUL WE HAVE IN YOU SUCH AN EXPERT ON THE ASCIAN CULTURE AND TEMPERAMENT... BUT REALLY... DO YOU MEAN TO IMPLY THAT A SKIN MONKEY WOULD MOURN THE PASSING OF A NYIMAN PATRIARCH?

I DON'T KNOW THAT, AMARSINE.
BUT THE ASCIANS HAVE DON A LOT OF THINGS LATELY THAT WE NEVER EXPECTE
NH. WHO KNOWS. MAYB THEY ACTUALLY WANT THIS PEAC TREATY.

RRNGH! DAMN!
THE KING KNEW HE WAS DYING! HE KNEW HE'D NEVER SEE ANOTHER SPRING!
WHY NOW? WHY DIDN'T HE STAY HOME AND SAVE HIS STRENGTH?

...TROUBLE BREWING WIT KING KETZAWAHDI... AND WITH THE HULDRES TO T WEST... TROUBLE EVER WHERE. AND HE WAS SO TERRIBLY ILL...
HE... MUST HAVE... PUSHED THIS TREAT WITH THE ASCIANS FOR THE SAKE OF HIS SUCCESSOR.

HE SPENT THE LAST OF HIS LIFE TRYING TO NEUTRALIZE THE THREAT ON ONE FLANK: THE ASCIANS.
...TO GIVE US A CHANCE TO GET SETTLED WITH A NEW HUSBAND.
THAT'S THE ONLY THING THAT MAKES SENSE. ANY OTHER REASONS DIED WITH HIM.
AH, PAPA...

"HOW TAME WERE YOU?"

AMARSINE: A-MAHR-**SEE**-NEE -- KING'S CHOSEN/KING'S WEALTH

SORRY, FRIEND. I COULDN'T HELP IT.

TWIRL

SNAK!

COULDN'T HELP IT THAT TIME EITHER, HUH?
NO.

YOU REALLY CAN TALK. I THOUGHT MAYBE YOU WERE ONE OF THOSE ONES WHO JUST CROAK LIKE CROWS.
THOUGHT I WAS STUPID, HAH? ALL YOU SKINS THINK THE SAME. ANYTHING THAT CAN'T TALK MUST BE STUPID.

TRUTH IS, LOTS OF THINGS THAT CAN TALK ARE STUPID.
WHERE'S YOUR KEEPER, COUSIN?

HOO!
URUHAAHR RRHAGLA' A'AHHR!!

WHAT I CAN TRANSLATE OF THAT SOUNDS HIGHLY UNFEASIBLE, ANATOMICALLY SPEAKING.
SO YOU'RE ONE OF THE BUMS.
BETTER THAN BEING A SELL-OUT!

A WHAT?
A SELLOUT! THEY SELL OUT TO GET LAID!
--LOUNGING AROUND CAMP LIKE FAT STUPID DOGS--
SOMETHING BETWEEN MEAT DILDOS AND PETS!
THINK THEY'LL GET TO BE KING IF THEY STAY CLOSE--

DON'T THEY?
ONLY ONE KING. SAME BAD CHANCES FOR THEM AS FOR US.
WHY WORRY? IF THEY GET TO GET LAID--

THEY HAVE NO SAY IN WHAT GOES ON.
ONLY THE KING MAKES BABIES, NOT US FOUR LEGGERS.
BEING KING, SOMEBODY HAS TO CHOOSE YOU. NO CONTROL.
NOT BETTIN' ODDS.
BETTER TO LIVE OR DIE MY WAY. I'LL PROBABLY NEVER BE THEIR KING BUT AT LEAST I'M MINE.

"BETTER TO REIGN IN HELL," HUH?
BUT I STILL SEE YOU HERE WITHIN SNIFF DISTANCE OF A BUNCHA WOMEN WITH NO KING, DON'T I?

I CAN'T HELP IT!

MARICCH, IT'S TRADITIONAL!
TRADITIONS EXIST BECAUSE THEY WORK! THEY MAKE TRANSITIONS EASIER.
THE OLD KING'S LAST SON IS ALWAYS CHOSEN TO BE THE NEW KING!
YAWN

LOOK!
HE'S BRIGHT EYED, STRONG, AND HEALTHY!
MBL'H?
?

YOU ARE PUTTING OFF WHAT IS ESSENTIALLY NO DECISION AT ALL TO LORD IT OVER THE REST OF US!
Umwrr?
SNZZ.

WELL, GIRL, IT'S TIME YOU REALIZED THAT YOU ARE NOT STARRING IN "THE STORY OF YOU." WE ALL HAVE LIVES TO GET ON WITH AND YOUR AUTHORITY WAS GIVEN TO YOU ONLY TO BE GIVEN TO THE NEW KING.
SIGH.

SO DO IT!
SIGH
STOMP
STOMP
STOMP
STOMP

IT DOESN'T HAVE TO BE ONE OF THE CHILDREN.
CHOOSE ONE OF THE ADULTS IF YOU... IF YOU MUST, BUT... A BABY HUSBAND GROWS UP GENTLY, IN LOVE.
THERE'S NO SHAME IN CHOOSING A BLOOD RELATIVE.

INDEED.

NO SHAME IN BLIND INFANTS DROWNED IN EVERY WELL, LAME ONES LEFT TO CRY THEMSELVES TO DEATH ON EVERY HILLSIDE, FEEBLE ONES SHOT IN EVERY CLEARING FROM HERE TO ISKANFORD?
NO SHAME, INDEED.
Z.

STILL ... IT'S A NEW-CROWNED KING'S RIGHT TO KILL THE LAST CHILDREN OF THE FORMER MONARCH, IF IT PLEASES HIM TO DO SO.
SHALL I PLAY DICE WITH YOUR LIFE, LITTLE BROTHER?

SHOULD I SACRIFICE YOU?
OR SHOULD I CROWN YOU, TAKE YOU TO HUSBAND, AN SEE HALF OUR CHILDRE DROWNED IN THEIR MOTHERS' MILK?
SHOULD *MY* MOTHERS' FEAR FOR THEIR LIVING CHILDREN SIGN THE DEATH WARRANT FOR M OWN, AS YET UNGOTTEN?

≡SIGH≡
IT'S A HARD WORLD, LITTLE BROTHER.
HARDEST OF ALL WHEN THOSE YOU LOVE TRY TO MAKE YOU BELIEVE YOU HAVE NO CHOICE.

THUS IT IS.
I WAS RAISED UP TO BE A CAPTAIN, AND SERVE WELL MY KING.

I MAY PLAN A HUNDRED WARS WIN A THOUSAND BATTLES, BRING A MILLION ENEMIES TO RUIN.

BUT *NOT* WITHOUT A KING.
I HAVE *ONE* CHOICE TO MAKE. ONE CROWN TO GIVE AWAY. ONE CHANCE.

ONE *DOSE*.
TUG
MY MOTHERS COUNSEL ME T CHOOSE A KIN WE CAN *CONTROL*.
THEY CA CONTROL
THERE'S MERIT IN THAT IDEA.

OH, TAKE IT EASY! IN THE OLD DAYS YOU ALL WOULD HAVE BEEN KILLED AT A TIME LIKE THIS. THERE ARE CHILDREN ABOUT!
RRR... NOISY BRATS!
GNAW
GRITT
SNARL

!
FLOP!
FLOP!
FLOP!
FLOP
FLOP!

OH, IT'S YOU, AMARSINE.

OF COURSE, JINN HERE IS NOTABLE FOR THE CLARITY OF HIS SPEECH, BUT HE'S CROSS EYED.
BELAL, THERE, WAS CAPTURED ONLY LAST WINTER FOR HIS LOVELY BLACK MANE, SO LIKE OUR LATE KING'S.

...NOW, REIJAT HAS A VERY UNUSUAL STEEL-GRAY SHEEN TO HIS COAT. THAT DIDN'T COME OUT UNTIL HE'D BEEN BRUSHED AND FED UP A BIT...

BUT ABOVE ALL ARE MORO AND EBO HERE. TOO SMART FOR THEIR OWN GOOD, BUT MAYBE SMART ENOUGH FOR OUR GOOD, EH?
STRONG, FAST, CRAFTY, TOUGH-MINDED BRUTES.

AND LOTS OF SPIRIT!
TSK!
PHEROMONE ADDLED
PROD

RHUN... ARE YOU SORRY FIRST MOTHER EIDI CAUGHT YOU?
NO. NEVER BE KING, ME.

DO YOU REGRET THAT NONE OF THESE CUBS ARE YOURS?
ALL CUBS MINE.

URRWWRRR

MARICCH...?
SHE CAN'T BE SERIOUS- HEY, DON'T GO OUT THERE!
--NO, DON'T STOP HER--

KOKUT DID ALL HE COULD TO PREPAR US FOR WHAT IS COMING. I CAN DO NO LESS.
THEY'LL GO INTO A FRENZY. THEY'LL TEAR YOU APART.
SSHH! SHUT UP, WHAT'S WRONG WITH YOU??

OUR KING WILL COME TO YOU NONETHELESS.
WATCH YE FOR HIM.
..URRRRWNRRR..
RRHUUUHRRR
RRRWWRRRRRRR
Z.
UHRRRRHUHUHRR
...mm?
AAULWRRR
THERE YOU GO.
POOR FOOL.
ARE YOU WINNING OR LOSING?
ERRK
POP

HRRRURR...
MINE!
HMINE!
THUCH

HRRH!

LAST: TWO RIVERS.
WHAT NEXT?

I KNEW NOTHING OULD COME F IT. AND NOTHING SHOULD.
COWARD WASTES HIS SCHEMING ON PEACE TALKS. MAKES NO SENSE.
WHY SHOULD WE MAKE PEACE WITH OUR MOST ANCIENT ENEMY?
THEY ARE OUR GOOD FOE, THE NYIMA. THEY KEEP US STRONG, AS WOLVES DO DEER.
THEY RESPECT ONLY WAR. THAT'LL NEVER CHANGE.

KTF
KTF
KTFF
KTFF

HEIL, CHIEFS OF THE ASCIANS!
NOMAD KINGS, I AM ESVEYDY, HERALD OF KOKUT, ONCE KING OF WESTMARCH.
I AM SENT TO BRING YOU HIS REGRETS THAT HE CANNOT KEEP HIS APPOINTMENT TO DISCUSS OUR MUTUAL INTERESTS.

ISN'T HE DEAD? WHY DON'T SHE JUST SAY HE'S DEAD?
AND IF HE'S DEAD WHO SENT HER?
...HOWEVER, EVENTS OF LATE HAVE BEEN OF SUCH A REMARKABLE NATURE THAT THE THRONE WISHES TO KEEP KOKUT'S ARRANGEMENT TO PARLEY WITH THE COUNCIL OF SEVEN CHIEFTAINS.
KIDS! HUSH!

ASCENDANT KING HAKATSOLADO PROPOSES TO RECEIVE YOU, SHADOW-LESS ONES, WITH ALL GRACE AND HOSPITALITY, AT THE BRANCHING OF THE MAMAE AND MAETHI RIVERS, HALF A DAY'S RIDE FROM HERE.
HUH!
"SHADOW-LESS ONES"?
UM. IT'S A MIS-TRANSLATION OF "ASCIAN". I THINK.
GNRGH.

LAST... MY NEW-CROWNED LORD WISHES TO FEAST IN HONOR OF YOUR AMBASSADOR, FOR HIS MANY SERVICES TO THE THRONE.
GRRR!!!...

AMBASSADOR.
YOU'LL PARDON ME, SISTA, BUT SOME THINGS GET LOST IN TRANSLATION-- WHAT SINGLE MAN HAVE YOU DECIDED STANDS FOR ALL ASCIANS?

THE FINDER WITH THE YELLOW EYES.
HE WHO BROUGHT OUT HAKAT'S WEALTH.

YELLOW EYES?
A FINDER? ...THE VERY IDEA... DAMN CATS ALWAYS GET THE WRONG IDEA.... YELLOW...
YE GODS! DOES SHE MEAN THE SIN-EATER?

"LOOK, I'VE NOTHING AGAINST SIN-EATERS."
"BUT IF HE WAS WORTH ANYTHING TO ANYBODY, HE WOULDN'T BE A SIN-EATER."
"FINE. YOU TELL THE CAT KING TO THROW HIM OUT BEFORE WE START."
"HELL WITH IT. I'M JUST GONNA PUT IN MY TOTEM AND THEN GO FISHING."
"GO FOR IT. WE'LL LET COWARD ANSWER FOR YOU IN YOUR ABSENCE."
"YOU KNOW THIS IS ALL HIS DOING. TO SHAME US FOR BLOWING HIM OFF."
GROWL
SNARRL
GRIPE
GRIPE
GRIPE
=SIGH=
"SUCK IT UP, GUYS."
HMY GREETINGS, LORRDS OF THE WELLS AND WASTELANDS.
I AM HAKATSOLADO.
YOU'LL RRECOGNIZE YUR BROTHER CHIEFTAIN, COWARD.
...AND OUR NOBLE FRIEND, THE ASCIAN AMBASSADOR.
COWARD TELLS ME HE'S CALLED "SIN-EATER." SSUCH COLORFUL NAMES.

A SIN-EATER CAN'T LEAVE A TOTEM!

"A SIN-EATER IS JUST A BODY! HE HAS NO SOUL TO SYMBOLIZE!"

KKOOMB!!

ARMORED TOURS
ALLLL PART of the SHOW, folks!

AROUND CAMPFIRES, STORYTELLERS SPIN FANTASIES ABOUT PAX MA MAETHI, A RIVER GODDESS WHO JOINED THE NYIMA AND ASCIANS.
"A GREAT BEAST GAVE HIMSELF TO HER," THEY SAY. "A BEAST, AND A HOST OF SEVEN TRIPLE TOTEMS, AND ONE EMPTY SPACE. BECAUSE OF THE EMPTY SPACE, THEY MADE PEACE, AND THEIR ALLIANCE MADE THEM MIGHTY."
THE SYMBOLISM IS HARD TO EXPLAIN TO THE KIDS, BUT EASY FOR THEM TO REMEMBER.
ON TELEVISIONS, DOCUMENTARIES DEPICT BOTH NYIMA AND ASCIANS AS NOBLE WARRIORS, BUT A BIT PATHETIC IN THEIR PRIDE THAT THEIR LAND IS STILL THEIR OWN. EVERYONE KNOWS IT'S BECAUSE THERE IS NOTHING IN THEIR EMPTY LAND THAT ANYONE WANTS.
BZZT... HURRY BACK!
BZZT... HURRY BACK!

TALISMAN

MY BOOK
AND ART
SHALL
NEVER
PART

DEDICATION:

to the kid with the book; everywhere

INTRO:
MAMA'S
LITTLE
STRANGEL

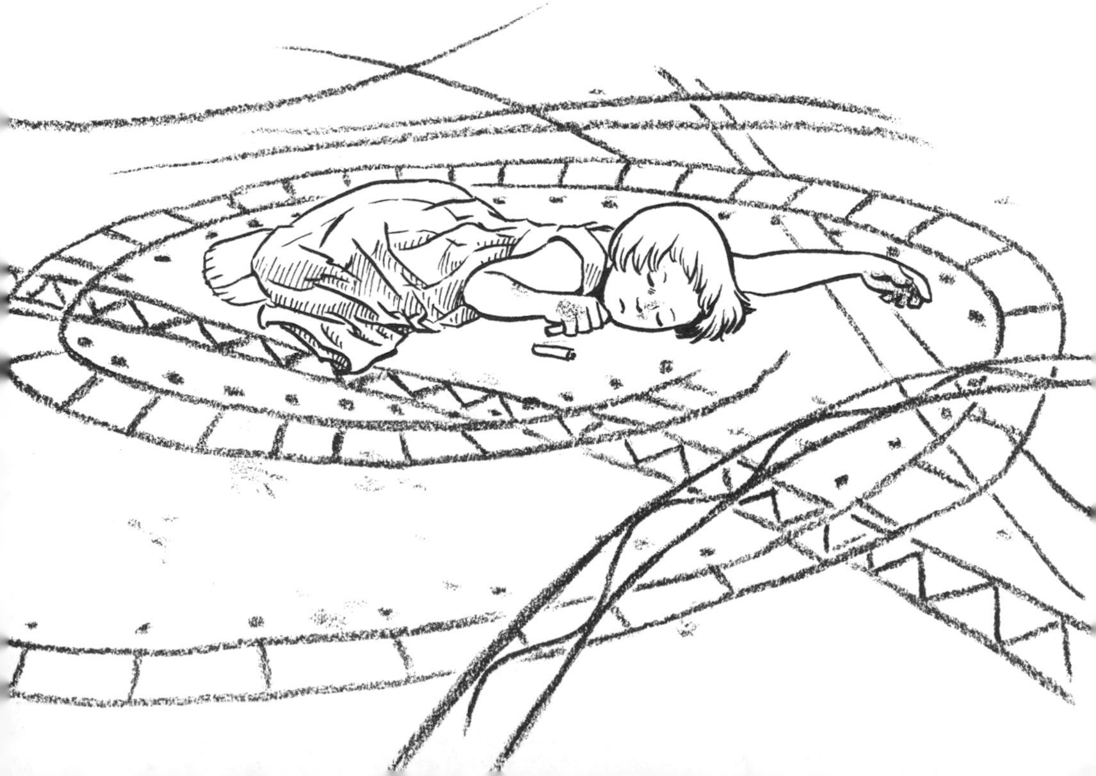

♪hm mmmmmmm

♪mmmmmmmmmm

mmmaaaaaaaaahhhhhhhhhhh

aaaaahhh mmmmm

mmm mmmmmmmmmmmmmmmm

mm
MARCIE!
NO MORE MAGIC!

BUT MOM ...
IT'S NOT OPEN FOR DISCUSSION!
BUT I WAS JUST-- THERE! A BAD
--IT BIT--
I JUST--
THERE'S A BAD FAIRY IN IT--
MARCIE...
LOOK. I KNOW HOW YOU LOVE THE WHOLE IDEA OF MAGIC. AND THERE ARE PEOPLE IN THIS WORLD WHO CAN DO AMAZING THINGS.
BUT YOU DID ALL THE TESTS, DIDN'T YOU? --YES, YOU DID. AND YOU JUST DON'T HAVE ANY MAGIC.
THEY CAN TEST YOU FOR THAT, AND I'D HAVE LOVED FOR YOU TO PASS THOSE TESTS.
BUT YOU DIDN'T, MY HONEY. THERE ARE NO FAIRIES. AND YOU'VE GOT TO STOP DOING THIS... PLAY MAGIC.
YOU'RE JUST BREAKING THING AND MAMA'S NOT MADE OF MONEY

BUT I WAS JUST GONNA FIX THAT CAB'NET DOOR THAT BITES YOUR HAND ...

SIGH
BABY, IT DOESN'T REALLY BITE ME. I JUST SAID THAT TO BE SILLY.

IT'S JUST A STICKY LATCH, AND THE KNOB GRABS MY-- *CATCHES* MY THUMB IF I GRAB IT JUST THE--

POP

CLUNK!

hsss! AOW! owowowow!

OW! daah-gunnit!
mm-hm♪.

CHAPTER ONE:

child of the pure unclouded brow

THE GREATEST GIFT I WAS EVER GIVEN WAS A BOOK.

IT WAS GIVEN TO ME BY A FRIEND OF THE FAMILY, WHO OFTEN TURNED UP UNEXPECTEDLY, LIKE A NEIGHBOR-HOOD CAT.

HIS VOICE WAS LOW AND GRAVELLY. THE ORDINARIEST THINGS IN THE WORLD SOUNDED DIFFERENT WHEN HE SAID THEM.
MY MOM SAID HIS VOICE WAS ROUGH BECAUSE HE WAS ALONE TOO MUCH, BUT THAT DIDN'T MAKE ANY SENSE.

I WAS SEVEN, BUT I HADN'T HAD MUCH SCHOOLING, AND I COULDN'T READ.

ALL I KNEW WAS, THOSE HEIROGLYPHS OPENED UP WHEN HE READ TO ME

CHAPTER ONE:
THE BRIDE.
AND I FELL IN.

"...WHEN SUDDENLY A WHITE RABBIT WITH PINK EYES RAN CLOSE BY HER...."
"...HENCEFORTH SHE KNEW SHE MUST GROW UP. YOU ALWAYS KNOW AFTER YOU ARE TWO. TWO IS THE BEGINNING OF THE END..."
"...'MY OWN GARDEN IS MY OWN GARDEN,' THE GIANT SAID. 'ANYONE CAN UNDERSTAND THAT, AND I WILL ALLOW NOBODY TO PLAY IN IT BUT MYSELF.' AND HE BUILT A HIGH WALL..."
"...IT WAS FOURTEEN YEARS OF HELL, ALL TOLD, BUT SHE HARDLY KNEW IT. FOR MOST OF THOSE YEARS SHE EXISTED IN A DAZE SO DEEP IT WAS LIKE DEATH...."
"...THE LAMB SAID, 'KI ME AND EAT ME. IF YOU DON'T CRACK AN OF MY BONES, THE FI LIGHT OF THE FOLLOWI DAY WILL RESTORE M TO LIFE ....'"
"...'I CAN'T ANSWER THAT,' REPLIED THE WEREWOLF. 'LIKE ALL GOOD DOGS, I'M A CYNIC, AND THEREFORE A LITTLE BLIND. I CAN ONLY SEE THINGS AS THEY ARE, NOT AS THEY OUGHT TO BE....'"
AFTER BLACKSHEAR!

"...UNTIL OTHER PEOPLE SAW WHAT I SAW IN MY MIRROR, I THOUGHT I WAS A MONSTER.."
"BYE, BOYS! HAVE FUN STORMIN' THE CASTLE!"
"...THE BOTTOM OF THE SMOOTH LAKE WAS JUMBLED NOT WITH SHARP STONES, BUT WITH KNIVES AND SPEARS AND SWORDS OF EVERY KIND EVER MADE..."
AWAKE, AWAKE...
WALKING TREES.
TALKING BEASTS.
DIVINE WATERS..."
ORDER TO RISE
ITS OWN ASHES
FIRST
..."
"...HE SAW HER FALL, AND, NOT KNOWING SHE HAD WINGS, LEAPED AFTER HER..."

MY FAMILY GRUMBLED ABOUT HOW UNRELIABLE HE WAS.

THE BOOK WAS FULL OF MISTS AND MONSTERS.
OHH, I'M SO GLAD YOU CAME BACK...
THE PEOPLE IN IT WERE SURROUNDED BY HUGE THINGS THEY DIDN'T QUITE UNDERSTAND.
JUST THE MAN I NEED.
SIGH CAN YOU KILL MY HUSBAND FOR ME?
...WHAT??
SIGH
YOUUUU... WHORE!
TELL 'EM T' GO AWAAAY.... PIG-FUCKA... I DON' WANNANY VISITORS.... OH SHIT IT BURNS!
EHHHHH...
SOB
HELP HELP AAAAAAA
BRIGHAM.
HE, UH...
FUCK! YOU FUCKIN' BITCH!
WHINE
...HASN'T BEEN ALL THAT COHERENT SINCE WE BROUGHT HIM HOME FROM THE HOSPITAL.
IT'S.. HARDER ON US THAN I THOUGHT IT WOULD BE.

LOTS OF FAMILIES HAVE WORSE THINGS TO DEAL WITH THAN...
EMMA, EMMA! WHERE
... I THOUGHT THE CHILDREN... WELL... NEEDED TO SEE THEIR FATHER AS HE IS...
NOT AS SOME DISEMBODIED BOGEYMAN...
TSK JUST IGNORE HIM! WE ALL DO.
DON'T YOUUU RUN FROMM MEEEEEE

I LOVED MY MOTHER. SHE WAS LIKE THE QUEEN OF THE FOREST IN THE STORY.

IN MY BOOK IT SAID THAT HER NAME, "EMMA", MEANT "GRANDMOTHER" OR "ANCESTRESS." I DIDN'T SEE HOW SUCH A SHORT NAME COULD MEAN TWO DIFFERENT THINGS, BUT I WAS EAGER TO FIND OUT.

YOU WANT TO LEARN TO **READ**, MY DARLIN'?
I THINK THAT'S A **FINE** AMBITION.

IT'S A RATHER ARCHAIC SKILL, LIKE PENMANSHIP, BUT I DO THINK THE OLD WAYS HAVE A LOT OF CHARM.
YOUR GRANDMOTHER WILL BE THRILLED...
CAN'T YOU READ, MAMA?

ME? OH, OF COURSE-- I WENT TO A TRADITIONAL SCHOOL. BUT I NEVER LIKED READING FOR PLEASURE; IT'S BAD FOR THE EYES.

LOTS OF PEOPLE WHO **CAN** READ **DON'T**; WHAT WITH SKULL COMPUTERS AND ACCESS-JACKS, EVEN PROFESSORS AT THE COLLEGE MISS IT LESS AND LESS.

MY SWEET OLD-FASHIONED GIRL.

GIVE ME A KISS, LOVE. I HAVE TO GO TO WORK NOW.

MY MOTHER MADE HER LIVING OFF OF GETTING LOST IN HER OWN WORLD.

I GUESS WE'RE VERY MUCH ALIKE.

USUALLY WHEN PEOPLE FIND OUT THEY'RE LIKE ONE ANOTHER, IT'S SUPPOSED TO BRING THEM CLOSER TOGETHER.

THAT'S HOW IT IS IN BOOKS.

HE DIDN'T SEEM TO **TRY** TO DO A DIFFERENT VOICE FOR EACH CHARACTER.
BUT I HEARD THEM ANYWAY.

THE **TERRIBLE** THING ABOUT THE REACHER MAN WAS HOW HIS VOICE OULD BE SO SWEET AND SOFT, WHEN HIS HEART WAS AS DRY AS A WASPS' NEST, AND JUST AS HOT WITH KILLIN'.

"CHILDREN?" HE CALLED.
"CHILLLL-DREN?
"I CAN FEEL MYSELF GETTIN' AW-FUL **MAD**...

"YOU COME ON OUT WHEN I COUNT THREE, NOW.
"ONE...
"TWO..."

AAA! AAA! AAA!!
DON'T PUT THOSE THINGS ON ME! AAA! AAA!

GASP GASP GASPP
OH **OH** FUCKERS, FUCKERS'RE CLOSING **IN**... **KEEP** THAT LITTLE SHIT **AWAY** FROM MEE **AAH**...
YOUUU.... YOU'VE BEEN A DISAPPOINTMENT TO ME SINCE THE DAY Y'R MUTHER **FARTED** YOU OUT OF 'ER WOMB...
uh!

OOH... SNIVEL WHINE WHINE
OHHH, MAN....
UH UH AAA!!

SHIT LICKER! BETTER RUN YOU YOU YOU

LINE UP, YOU LIMP-DICK MONKEY FUCKS!

I KNEW

THAT ALL STORIES LIKE THIS

YOU PIECE 'A SHIT! YOU LOUSY PIECE 'A SHIT!
ALWAYS COME DOWN TO SOMEBODY
HAVING TO OVERCOME SOME AWFUL FEAR.

THAT'S FINE FOR FICTION.

WHEN HE LEFT

(SUDDENLY, AS ALWAYS)

HE LEFT WITHOUT FINISHING IT.

I WAS DYING.
I'M DYING.
NOTHING TO DO BUT SETTLE FOR LESS.

I STARTED WITH MY BIG SISTER.
RACHEL?
HM?
WILL YOU READ MY BOOK TO ME?

YOUR BOOK? WHY?
...OH, I GET IT. THIS OLD THING HAS NO VOICE-CHIP AT ALL.
=SIGH=
SURE, HONEY.

OKAY THEN...
"CHAPTER NINETEEN: THE FOREST GLEN."

"THERE WAS NOTHING TO DO FOR IT UNTIL THEY WERE QUITE DRIED OFF. SO MARCIE AND HER FRIEND--"

HEY, ISN'T THAT COOL!
YOUR NAME'S IN THIS!

I ALWAYS LOVE TO SEE MY NAME IN A STORY, EVEN IF IT IS JUST A COINCIDENCE.

"SO MARCIE AND HER FRIEND WOLFE CLIMBED OVER THE SMOOTH ROCKS AND AWAY FROM THE RIVER. THE TREES WERE VERY TALL AND THICKLY LEAFY, AND BLOCKED OFF ALL THE SUNLIGHT.
IT WAS RATHER CHILLY.

"THEY WALKED ON, NOT WANTING TO GO FAR, BUT HAVING LITTLE CHOICE SINCE THERE SEEMED TO BE NO--"
WHAT?

I WAS JUST MAKING SUR YOU WERE IN THE RIGHT PLACE.
AM I?
WELL, I GUESS YOU MUST BE, BECAUSE I REMEMBER THI PICTURE.

UMM....
OKAY. --"SINCE THERE SEEMED TO BE NO REALLY GOOD PLACE TO STOP.
'GOODNESS,' SAID MARCIE. 'ISN'T THERE ANY PLACE TO SIT AND DRY OUT?'
'OH, I'M SURE THERE MUST BE.' SAID WOLFE.
'LET'S JUST GO ON A BIT FURTHER.'

"MARCIE WAS SUDDENLY TAKEN WITH A GREAT EXCITEMENT. 'LOOK!' SHE CRIED. 'LOOK OVER THERE!' FOR JUST AHEAD OF THEM, CLEARLY VISIBLE THROUGH THE STRAIGHT TRUNKS OF THE HEALTHY TREES, LAY ONE THAT HAD FALLEN.
SUNLIGHT STREAMED DOWN UPON IT, AND IT LOOKED WONDERFULLY DRY.

"'ISN'T THAT PERFECT!' CRIED MARCIE, AND WOLFE AGREED THAT IT WAS. THEY BOTH MADE THEIR WAY ACROSS THE EVEN FOREST FLOOR, AS SMOOTHLY COVERED WITH PINE NEEDLES AS A CARPETED ROOM.
'WE MAY AS WELL STAY HERE A WHILE,' SAID WOLFE. 'I MYSELF AM STILL QUITE WET, AND I WON'T BE MYSELF AGAIN UNTIL I GET MY TAIL DRY.'

"'SAME FOR ME,' SAID MARCIE. 'I CAN'T THINK OF ANYTHING ELSE BUT GETTING DRY WHEN I'M--"
HEY.
YOU SURE YOU WANT ME TO GO ON WITH THIS?
WELL-- WELL, YEAH! IT'S MY FAVORITE!

SO MARCIE AND HER FRIEND IADE THEMSELVES COMFORTABLE N A LOG IN A PATCH OF SUNLIGHT, AND WERE QUITE COMFORTABLE.
"PRESENTLY OLFE YAWNED ND STRETCHED AND OPENED HIS PACK--

"--FINALLY PRODUCING A PAPER BAG OF SMALL RASPBERRIES, A HALF-LOAF OF BREAD, AND A LARGE SOFT CHEESE, WRAPPED IN A CLOTH COVERED WITH BLUISH-GREEN OR GREENISH-BLUE SPOTS.

THIS WAS A GREAT RELIEF TO MARCIE, HO, UNTIL WOLFE HAD PULLED OUT THE OOD, HADN'T REALIZED HOW HUNGRY SHE WAS.
THEY ET AFTER THEIR UNCHEON ITH A WILL, ND SOON FINISHED IT OFF.

"AFTER THEY HAD FINISHED, THE SUN'S LIGHT WAS SLANTING DOWN RATHER MORE STEEPLY THAN BEFORE, AND MARCIE SUGGESTED THAT THEY HAD BEST BE MOVING ON.
'WOLFIE,' SAID SHE, 'THE DAY'S GETTING AWAY FROM US, AND WE STILL HAVE A LONG WAY TO GO. HADN'T WE BEST BE MOVING ON?'

"'YES, I SUPPOSE SO,' REPLIED THE OTHER, 'ELSE WE'LL LOSE THE IGHT ALTOGETHER, AND BE OBLIGED TO STAY HERE FOR THE NIGHT.'
'OH NO,' SAID MARCIE. WE MUSTN'T DO THAT ET'S BE ON OUR IMMEDIATE
THAT'S NOT IT!

WHAT--?
YOU'RE READING IT WRONG!

BUT-- BABY, I'M JUST READING IT. HOW CAN I BE READING IT WRONG?
MARCIE, I -- TSK! ARE YOU SURE THIS IS THE RIGHT BOOK?
OF COURSE I'M SURE! HOW MANY REAL BOOKS DO I HAVE?
I DON'T KNOW! YOU ARE! IT'S NOT LIKE THIS!
WELL, WHERE ON EARTH DID YOU GET THIS ONE --
GOOD-- LORD!
WHAT? WHAT??
I DON'T THINK YOU SHOULD BE READING THIS, MARCIE.
I CAN'T READ IT! I WANT SOMEBODY TO READ IT TO ME!
OH, NO. UH-UH. THIS GOES UP HERE.
NO!
NOW LOOK, LITTLE SISTER --
GUH! I SWORE I'D NEVER SAY THIS--!
THAT BOOK IS TOO OLD FOR YOU.
YOU'LL JUST HAVE TO WAIT UNTIL YOU'RE OLDER.
PROMISE ME YOU'LL LEAVE IT ALONE, NOW. PROMISE?
mumble.

SO.
D TRIED ONE SISTER.
OT MUCH POINT IN TRYING
THE OTHER ONE.
NOT THAT LYNNE
AS MY SISTER, EXACTLY.
SHE WAS REALLY A
OY WHO'D BEEN RAISED
S A GIRL AND WAS NOW
SORT OF BOTH.

NO, I DIDN'T GET IT EITHER. AT THAT AGE YOU GO ALONG WITH A LOT.
BUT BOY-OH-BOY COULD SHE BE A SON OF A BITCH.
SIGH

KID, YOU CAN STOP MOPING SO LOUD ANY TIME.

SIGH.
DON'T HASSLE ME WITH YOUR SIGHS, MARCIE.
BUT SIR...

AND DON'T CALL ME "SIR."
RACHEL TOOK MY BOOK AWAY.
SO?
IT'S MINE. IT WAS MY BIRTHDAY PRESENT.

SO?
IT'S NOT FAIR!

SO?
LOOK, MARS. THIS IS NOT SOCCER. THIS IS DEALING WITH PEOPLE WHO HAVE POWER OVER YOU; IN THIS CASE, OUR SISTER.
THERE ARE NO RULES AND THERE IS NO "FAIR."

BUT...
IF YOU WANT YOUR BOOK, GO GET IT.

I'LL GET A WHIPPIN'.
FROM RACHEL?
SNORT

SOUNDS LIKE YOU HAVE ONE OF THOSE DECISIONS TO MAKE.
IS THE PRICE YOU MIGHT PAY WORTH WHAT YOU MIGHT GET?

BUT I CAN'T EVEN READ IT.

WOULD YOU READ ME MY BOOK?
NO.

SIGH.

I GAVE IN AT LAST.
SCHOOL LOOKED LIKE MY ONLY HOPE.
SPONTANEITY is fun!
SCHOOL.
HMM
BEEP
AND BAAAck...
GOODNESS, CHILDREN-- GENTLE YOUR HANDS!
CLICK
SEAT OF KNOWLEDGE.
BZZZ
AAND SIP
KEY TO WISDOM.
AND DOWN.
DON'T SLURP!
=TSK= DO NOT TRY TO FORCE THE BOWL OF THE SOUP SPOON INTO YOUR MOUTH. SIP FROM THE SIDE, LADIES.
SACRED GROVES OF ACADEME.
MISS WENDY, WHEN DO WE LEARN TO READ?
OH, WE DON'T WANT TO GET AHEAD OF OURSELVES, MARCELLA. COME PICK OUT SOME COLORS!
DREET
HUMMM
CLICK
BEEP
HAND-EYE COORDINATION LOW NORMAL.
BALANCE SENSE ACCEPTABLE.
NEEP
BZZT
ANOMALOUS HAIR TEXTURE.
NO COLOR-VISION IMPAIRMENT.
CLICK
BZZTT
HIGHLY SELF-CONSCIOUS.
4 ON DEXTER MULTIPLE INTELLIGENCE SCALE.
CLICK-CLICK
THERAPY AND GROWTH REGIMEN COMPILING.

I DON'T CARE WHAT COLORS I LOOK BEST IN! I DON'T WANT A CUBBY-HOLE WITH MY NAME ON IT! I WANT TO LEARN TO READ!
MMM. WOW.
A SCHOOL OUR MOTHER PICKED OUT TURNS OUT TO BE FULL OF FLAKES.
A-MAY-ZING.

WELL, WHAT DID YOU THINK?
Y'THINK THEY WERE GONNA TEACH YOU TO READ ALL IN ONE DAY?
CLICK.

W...
W-WELL...
YEAH!

IF YOU REALLY WANNA LEARN TO READ FAST, I CAN FIX THAT.

EEEEE!!
NO HOOK UP!

ALL I HAD WAS THIS IMAGE OF THE STORY IN MY MIND. I TRIED TO RECONSTRUCT HOW IT WENT.
?
WROOOooo
THERE WAS A MONSTER IN IT.
ACTUALLY
WROOOoOOOo
THERE WERE A LOT OF MONSTERS.
ONE WAS A WEREWOLF. BUT HE DIDN'T CHANGE SUDDENLY UNDER THE FULL MOON.
INSTEAD, EVERY DAY HE WAS A LITTLE BIT MORE HUMAN, OR A LITTLE BIT MORE BEAST, WITHOUT EVER BECOMING EITHER ONE ENTIRELY.
WROO
KOF
ROOOOo
ONE WAS A THING THAT HAD EATEN A STAR. EVERYTHING WAS COLD AND DARK WITHOUT THE STAR IN THE SKY.
ONE WAS A KING ASLEEP UNDER A MOUNTAIN.
NOBODY KNEW IF HE WOULD EVER WAKE UP FROM HIS NIGHTMARE.
UH...
EVERYBODY THOUGHT THAT IF HE DID WAKE UP, THE WHOLE WORLD MIGHT GO OUT..
HMM...
POOF!
JUST LIKE A CANDLE.

MY NAME WAS ALL I COULD READ. BUT HEY! MY NAME WAS IN MY BOOK! I COULD READ MY NAME IN MY BOOK! ON EVERY PAGE!

H, HONEY. THOSE OLD-ASHIONED PAPER-PULP OOKS ARE PERISHABLE. WOULD ONLY HAVE GONE O ROT; IT WAS ALREADY URNING YELLOW.
OH, BABY, DON'T CRY...
MARCIE, THERE'S NOTHING TO CRY OVER... I SCANNED IT INTO THE HOUSE LIBRARY. IT ISN'T LOST AT ALL. ANY TIME YOU WANT TO, YOU CAN USE YOUR HOOKUP, AND IT'LL BE JUST LIKE HAVING THE REAL THING. YOU CAN TOUCH IT, HOLD IT, WHATEVER; IT ISN'T GONE AT ALL.
"I HAD NO IDEA IT WAS SO IMPORTANT TO HER. IT WAS A GIFT FROM JAEGER?
"OH DEAR. HE WILL TEASE ME..."
"MOM, EVEN IF SHE IS ONLY SEVEN, IT WAS HERS. YOU HAD NO RIGHT TO THROW IT OUT.
" I DO THINK SHE'S OVER-REACTING..."
"WELL, KID, WHAT DO YOU WANT ME TO SAY?
"IF YOU'D PUT IT SOMEPLACE SAFE, THEY COULDN'T'VE DONE THIS TO YOU..."
THE GREATEST GIFT I EVER HAD TAKEN AWAY FROM ME WAS A BOOK.

CHAPTER 2:

melancholy maiden

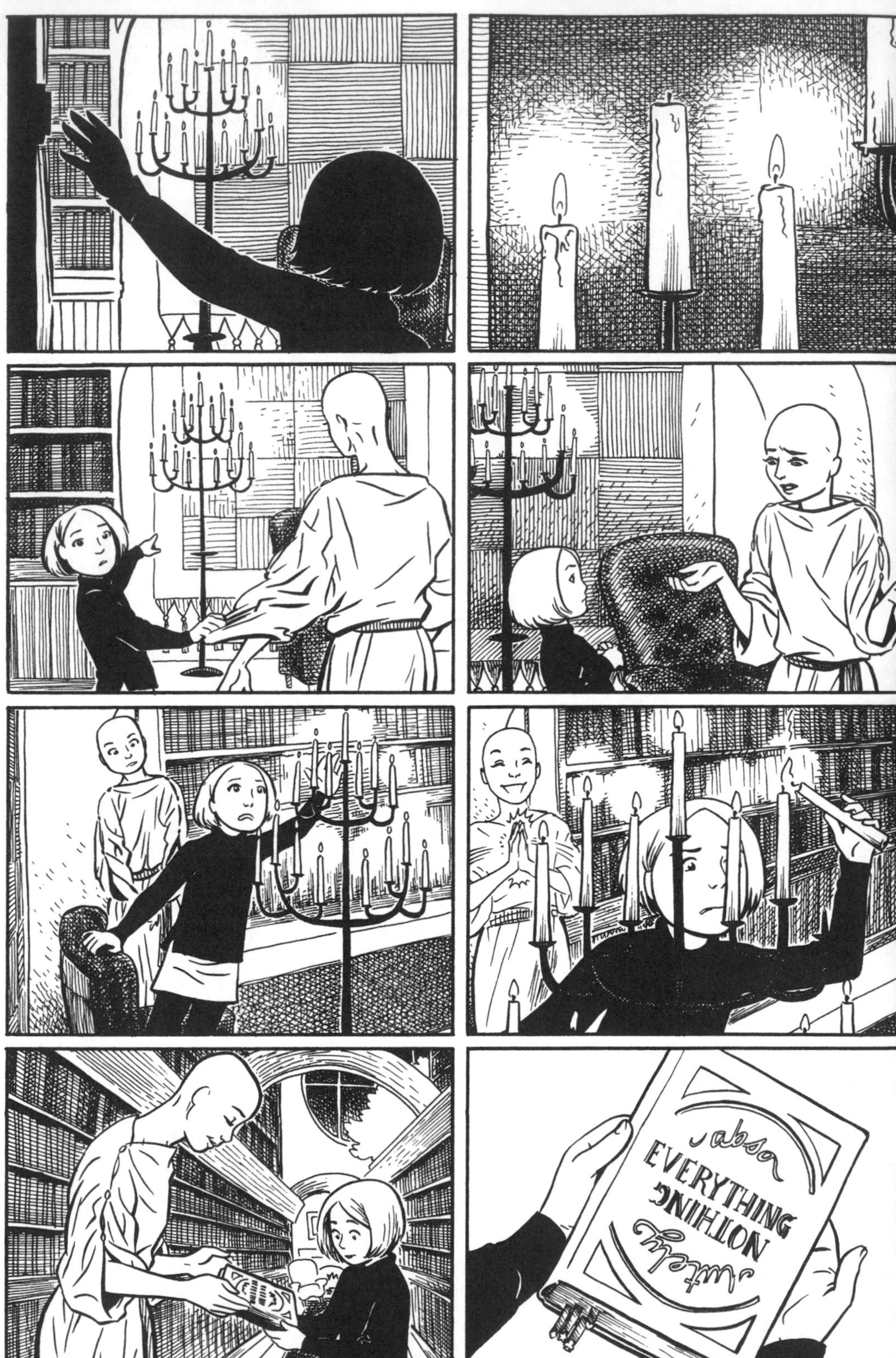
absa
EVERYTHING
NOTHING
lutely

UFF!

SIGH.

WHEN I WAS SEVEN, I LOST A BOOK.

WELL, ACTUALLY, MY MOTHER THREW IT OUT.
BUT I'VE LEARNED NOT TO THINK OF IT THAT WAY.
THE WRITER'S WAY

EVER SINCE THEN, I'VE HAD THIS RECURRING DREAM.
I'M TOLD IT'S A VERY **TRITE** DREAM. THAT EVERYBODY HAS THIS DREAM FROM TIME TO TIME.

SOMETIMES I CAN *FEEL* THAT BOOK'S BINDING IN MY HANDS BEFORE I LOSE IT.
IT'S A SAD THING WHEN EVEN YOUR *DREAMS* ARE CLICHÉS.

I DON'T KNOW WHEN MY BROTHER BECAME THE BEDROCK OF MY LIFE.

WE HAD A MOTHER AND AN OLDER SISTER, BUT HE MADE THE RULES.
MOM
RACHEL
ONE OF THE HARD, FAST RULES WAS I DIDN'T DARE CRY IN FRONT OF HIM.

IT'S NOT THAT HE WAS UNSYMPATHETIC. HE'D HUG ME, AND DOLE OUT MINTS, AND WAIT FOR ME TO CALM DOWN.

BUT THEN HE'D EXACT SOME INCREDIBLY BRUTAL REVENGE AGAINST WHOEVER OR WHATEVER HAD UPSET ME.
SOMEHOW MY TEARS INFURIATED HIM.

AND THERE WAS NO SLAP ON THE WRIST IN LYNNE'S BOOK OF RETRIBUTION. IT WAS THE JUGULAR OR NOTHING.
SO I DIDN'T DARE CRY OVER THE BOOK I LOST.

MARVELLO THE MYSTIC SEES A B-MINUS IN YOUR FUTURE.
C IF SHE TAKES OFF FOR BREVITY.
SO I HAD TO LEARN TO HOLD IN.

I HATE TO CRY, ANYWAY.

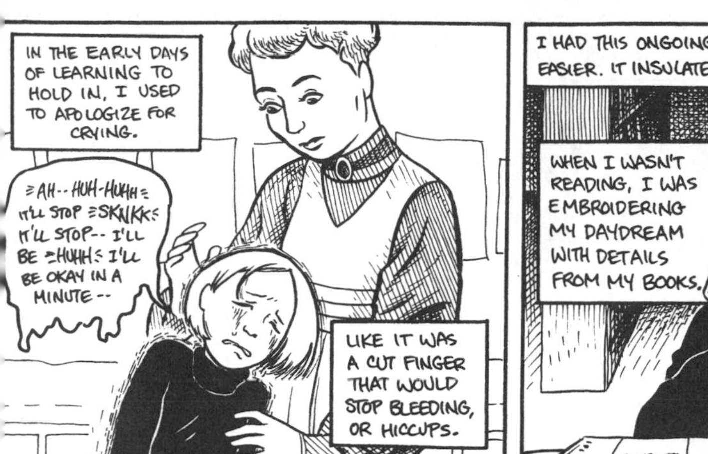

THE HILLS ARE NOT AS HIGH

"YOU ARE A LITTLE POT FULL OF SONGS, AND WHEN YOU CRY, THE POT BREAKS AND ALL THE SONGS SPILL OUT UGLY."

"...I ASK FOR SO LITTLE. JUST LET ME *RULE* YOU, AND YOU CAN HAVE EVERYTHING THAT YOU WANT. JUST *FEAR* ME; LOVE ME, DO AS I SAY. AND I WILL BE YOUR *SLAVE!*"

THE SEA SO DEEP

AS A DREAM

AFTER WILLIAMS

ALL MY LIFE
MY HEART HAS SOUGHT
A THING
I CANNOT NAME
"LOOK, EVERYONE," SAID THE STAR. "I'M BURNING SO BRIGHT!" AND THEN IT WENT NOVA. AND WHEN THE LIGHT FADED, THE STAR WAS NOWHERE TO BE SEEN. THE MORAL OF THIS STORY IS OBVIOUS."
"...HE STARED IN FASCINATION AT THE HOURGLASS, AT THE PHOSPHORESCENT CRYSTALS IN THE THICK GLOBE WHICH GAVE EACH INFANT HIS BIRTHRIGHT-- THE RADIOACTIVE TIMEFLOWER. HE STARED AT HIS OWN HAND, BLINKING RED-BLACK, RED-BLACK... "
"THERE WERE PLENTY OF RINGS IN THE AIR BUT ALL OF THEM WERE PALE IN COLOR, WHICH WARNED ME OFF. LIGHT YELLOWS USUALLY EXISTED IN PLACES SUCH AS EIGHTY KILOMETERS DUE SOUTH OF THE MOON, TEN METERS FROM THE BOTTOM OF MINDANAO DEEP, THE TOP OF ANNAPURNA, AND THE LIKE. BESIDES, I WASN'T READY TO GO BACK..."
"SOMEHOW, IT WAS HOTTER THEN: A BLACK DOG SUFFERED ON A SUMMER'S DAY; BONY MULES HITCHED TO HOOVER CARTS FLICKED FLIES IN THE SWELTERING SHADE OF THE LIVE OAKS IN THE SQUARE. MEN'S STIFF COLLARS WILTED BY NINE IN THE MORNING. LADIES BATHED BEFORE NOON, AFTER THEIR THREE-O'CLOCK NAPS, AND BY NIGHTFALL WERE LIKE SOFT TEA-CAKES WITH FROSTINGS OF SWEAT AND SWEET TALCUM... "

LYNNE DISAPPROVED OF CONSUMPTION WITHOUT PRODUCTION.
IF ALL YOU DO IS READ, WATCH, LISTEN, AND NEVER THINK, NEVER ACT, YOU ARE EATING WITHOUT BUILDING BONE OR MUSCLE.
FRANKLY, YOU ARE EATING WITHOUT EVEN SHITTING.

LYNNE ENCOURAGED ME TO WRITE IT ALL DOWN.
WORK EVERY DAY, KID, EVEN IF YOU DO THINK IT'S JUST SHIT.
MENTAL CONSTIPATION IS THE WORLD'S WORST SLOW POISON.
SO CHOP-CHOP! ON TO THE NEXT.

AT FIRST, I WAS WORRIED THAT MY DAYDREAMS WERE TOO PERSONAL, THAT IT WOULD BE INCREDIBLY EMBARRASSING TO LET ANYBODY READ THEM.
HA!

I LIKED THE KIDS IN MY HALF-TOON AT MY NEW SCHOOL. I WAS WILLING TO TAKE THE RISK OF MORTAL EMBARRASSMENT BY BARING MY SOUL TO THEM.
THEY'RE OKAY KIDS, THEY REALLY ARE... THEY TRIED TO BE COOL ABOUT IT WHEN THEY HAD TO TELL ME MY STORIES WERE BORING!

BORING?
HOW COULD SOMETHING I FOUND SO ABSORBING BE BORING? HOW COULD WHAT I FELT SO STRONGLY LEAVE THEM SO UNMOVED?
WHY DIDN'T THEY FEEL WHAT I FELT?

LYNNE SAID IT WAS A MATTER OF TECHNIQUE.
I WAS GRIMLY DETERMINED TO LEARN.

LYNNE ALWAYS HAD MONEY. IF I WANTED A BOOK, I GOT IT.
I KNEW MY HOME CITY AS A HUGE EMPTY SPACE WITH CONSTELLATIONS OF BOOKSTORES AND LIBRARIES. I BOUGHT, BORROWED, DEVOURED.
NOT FOR YEAR
DID I REALIZE
THAT I WAS
HOPING THAT TH
TALENT IN MY
FAVORITE BOOK
WOULD RUB OF
ON ME.
"...RIVETING!" "...ENGROSSING!" "...GOOD!"
MADIERAN
TITALIC
SELECT
IF NOT, WHY NOT
YOUR BOOK
NO REFUND OVER $1.00
I HOP TO LEAR WRITIN BY OSMOS I GUESS.

I *DID* REALIZE THAT HOW-TO BOOKS MADE ME FEEL STALE. THEY LOOK SO PROMISING ON THE SHELF; THEY MAKE WRITING LOOK SO *EASY*.

BUT WHEN YOU GET 'EM HOME, THEY'VE TURNED INTO JUST ANOTHER DRY LIST OF BORING RULES.
BAHGIN!
EVEN SO, I STILL COULDN'T STOP BUYING THEM.

ONE DAY I'D SCRIBBLE LIKE MAD, TYPE AWAY LIKE A PERKING COFFEE POT. WHO NEEDS THE MUSE? IT WAS ALL CRAP, BUT WHO CARED? NOT ME.

THE *NEXT* DAY I'D SWEAR I WOULDN'T PUT DOWN A *WORD* UNTIL IT WAS PERFECT IN MY MIND (WHICH MEANT, OF COURSE, THAT I NEVER PUT DOWN A WORD, *PERIOD*).

THEN I'D TRY TO GO BACK TO THE THINGS THAT EXCITE *ME*; THE FOUNDATIONS OF MY DAY-DREAM.

THAT USUALLY LEADS ME BACK TO MY LOST BOOK.

THERE WAS A COPY OF MY BOOK IN THE HOUSE'S COMPUTER. I COULD CALL IT UP ANY TIME I LIKED.

WITH MY STUDENT-LEVEL ACCESS JACK, I COULD SEE THE BOOK AS IF IT WAS REAL. I COULD HOLD IT IN MY HAND AND EVEN *OPEN* IT.

I JUST COULDN'T *READ* IT.
SOMEHOW, THE FILE HAD BEEN CORRUPTED.
EACH MONTH, THE HOUSE DUTIFULLY MADE A PERFECT COPY OF THE BAD FILE.

BUT I'M NOT UPSET ABOUT IT. I'VE LEARNED TO FACE THE WORLD WITH A COMFORTABLY AMBIVALENT INERTIA. I SHOULD CARE, BUT I CONSIDER MYSELF LUCKY THAT I DON'T.
LYNNE TELLS ME THAT THAT'S WHY MY WRITING IS SO DULL.

YOU KNOW, MARCE, MOVIE-MAKERS TALK ABOUT THIS ALL THE TIME. HOW IT'S THEIR JOB TO MAKE THE AUDIENCE FEEL WHAT THEY'RE SUPPOSED TO.
I HATE MOVIES.
TSK
WE **KNOW** YOU HATE MOVIES. BUT FACE IT-- NO BOOK CAN MAKE ANYBODY FEEL WHAT'S GOING ON AS INTENSELY AS IF IT'S REALLY *HAPPENING*.

OH. THAT'S NOT TRUE--
LOOK-- YOU KNOW *I* LIKE TO READ *TOO*, BUT IT'S JUST *NOT* THE SAME THING.
OH, *COME* WITH US. HOW CAN YOU GET TO BE A WRITER IF YOU DON'T EVER *DO* ANYTHING?

I *HARDLY* THINK THAT GOING TO THE *MOVIES* REALLY COUNTS AS A BIG, DRAMATIC, OUT-ON-A-LIMB, LIFE-ALTERING *ADVENTURE*....
FOR SOMEBODY WHO GOES AS RARELY AS *YOU* DO, IT DOES.
YOU'LL LIKE THIS ONE-- THAT FOOTAGE YOUR BROTHER SOLD TO STUDIOSIMA IS IN IT.

UNBELIEVABLE, HOW MANY PEOPLE LIVE FOR GOING TO THE MOVIES.
FOR PEOPLE WITHOUT THE JACK, A MOVIE IS JUST PICTURES AND SOUND.
JUST NOISE AND FLICKER, GUARANTEED TO GIVE ME AN INSTANT HEADACHE.
TONS OF PEOPLE WHO DON'T HAVE JACKS STILL LOVE THE MOVIES, WHICH I REALLY DON'T UNDERSTAND.
I MEAN, WITHOUT THE JACK ENGAGED, YOU CAN'T EVEN SEE THE SCREEN, OR EVEN HEAR OVER PEOPLE WHISPERING.
WITH THE JACK, IT'S LIKE THERE'S ONLY THE SCREEN AND YOU.
SO.
LOT OF FOLKS MAKE A LIVING SELLING RECORDINGS TO MOVIE STUDIOS. NOT JUST SCENES, STILLS, AND MUSIC --SOME PEOPLE SELL RECORDINGS OF NERVOUS IMPULSES. ANYTHING VIVID IS FAIR GAME.

STUDIOSIMA PRESENTS
A WEIRD FUCKER PRODUCTION
A STUDENT-ACCESS JACK CAN'T RECEIVE ALL THE RECORDED SENSATIONS---
AGAIN, I CONSIDER MYSELF LUCKY--
BUT THEY CAN MAKE YOU FEEL YOUR HEART RACE WHEN SOMEONE ON THE SCREEN IS SCARED--
UR GUTS CHURN IN SYMPATHY WITH SOME TWERP WHO'S SO FRUSTRATED THAT HE BREAKS A BOTTLE INTO JAGS AND STARTS SWINGING
YOUR THROAT BURNS WHEN THE STRONG, SILENT TYPES SWALLOW GRIEF, NO MATTER HOW MANY TIMES YOU'VE SEEN IT BEFORE--
THERE'S A BREEZY GIDDY FEELING THAT THEY SAY IS FALLING IN LOVE---
HEY PIECE TOGETHER ALL THESE INCONGRUOUS IMAGES, AND THEN LAYER EMOTIONS OVER THEM, SO NOBODY NOTICES IT MAKES NO SENSE AT ALL--
THEY LAYER A COLD SHOCK OF ADRENALINE OVER A SHOT OF ROSE PETALS FALLING, AND THIS IS SUPPOSED TO BE SO PROFOUND--
--PEOPLE WHO HAVE UNUSUAL EMOTIONS OR REACTIONS ARE PRIZED BY MOVIE STUDIOS---
HALF THESE THINGS I'VE NEVER EXPERIENCED IN MY OWN LIFE.

...UGH AT JOKES THAT AREN'T FUNNY
--SOMETIMES THEY RUN HUMOR AND FEAR RIGHT ON TOP OF EACH OTHER, PRESUMABLY TO SUGARCOAT THE FEAR, BUT I
AND FALL IN LOVE WITH WEIRD-LOOKING ACTORS...
--MOST MOVIES JUST HAVE A MOOD TRACK, LIKE A SOUNDTRACK. THAT'S WHAT MOST DIRECTORS PREFER, ACCORDING TO LYNNE
BUT FANCY THEATERS DON'T USE MOOD-TRACKS THEY HIRE CONDUCTORS
--NOBODY CAN TELL A JOKE THEY HEARD IN A MOVIE "YOU JUST HAVE TO SEE IT" AND THAT'S JUST HOW THE STUDIOS WANT IT--
IT'S A VERY INTENSE EXPERIENCE.

JUST DON'T UNDERSTAND
OW PEOPLE *ENJOY* GETTING
ANKED AROUND LIKE THAT.
TEAT
OPEN TEAR DUCTS, APPLY PLIERS...
I FEEL LIKE SOMEBODY PICKED ME UP BY MY HEAD AND SHOOK ME LIKE A MARACA.

I KNOW WHAT I *DO* WANT. I WANT THE BOOK I LOST. THE ONE MY MOM'S BOYFRIEND USED TO READ TO ME.

A REGULAR STORY, RIGHT ABOUT NOW,
D *FIND* THAT BOOK. LIKE *MAGIC*. I'D
UST TURN MY HEAD AND THERE IT
OULD BE.
AND I WOULDN'T BELIEVE IT, NO MATTER HOW MUCH I'D WANT TO.

IN **JAEGER'S** STORY, THE MAGIC ALWAYS HAD STRANGE RULES.

IN *THAT* STORY, I'D GET WHAT I WANT, BUT I'D STILL HAVE TO

--TO--

THERE COULDN'T BE ANOTHER ONE LIKE IT. IT WAS HAND-BOUND ESPECIALLY FOR ME. IT WAS UNIQUE.
ANDER

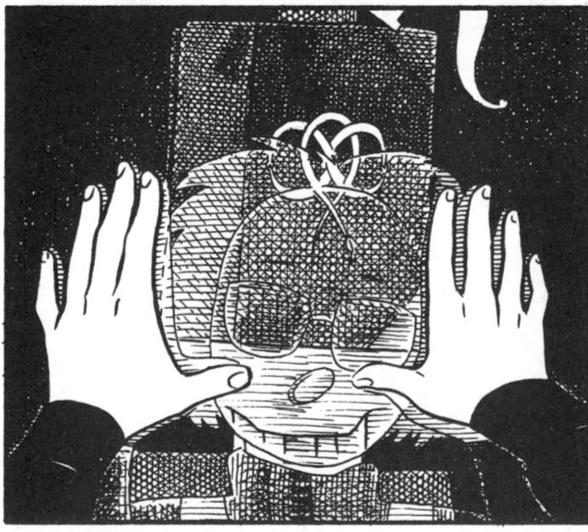

IT MUST HAVE BEEN SOLD AND SOLD AGAIN, CIRCLING AROUND THE CITY FOR YEARS UNTIL IT CAME BACK TO ME--
JUST LIKE JAEGER
WHO GAVE IT TO ME.

I'D BEEN IN THIS SHOP BEFORE, BUT NOT FOR A LONG TIME. THESE LITTLE PLACES DO APPEAR AND DISAPPEAR SUDDENLY.

THIS PLACE NEVER HAD MANY BOOKS OF INTEREST TO ME, BUT IT SMELLED OF THE PROPRIETOR'S SWEET PIPE SMOKE--

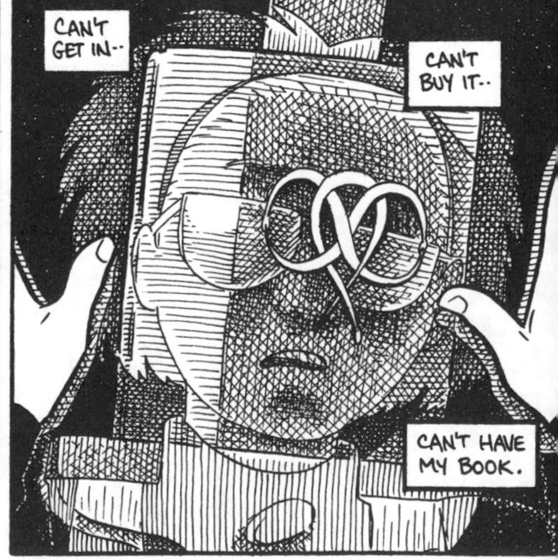

CAN'T GET IN--
CAN'T BUY IT--
CAN'T HAVE MY BOOK.

NO.
NO.
TIME TO BE A GROWN-UP.
I FOUND IT, BUT I CAN'T HAVE IT.

AND I AM NOT GOING TO SIT ON THE CURB AND HOPE SOMEBODY'LL BUY THIS PLACE AND OPEN IT UP AGAIN. THAT'S PATHETIC, AND, BESIDES, IT ISN'T GONNA HAPPEN.
SIGH.
IT ISN'T WORTH HOPING FOR.

EVEN IF THIS SHOP DOES REOPEN, YOU CAN BET THAT THIS PARTICULAR BOOK WON'T STILL BE ON THE SHELF.
FIRST THING A NEW OWNER DOES IS CLEAR OUT MOST OF THE OLD STOCK.
AND THAT'S WHAT IT IS, REALLY. OLD STOCK.

MAYBE THE RECYCLERS WILL GET IT THIS TIME.
OR A LIBRARY.
OR MAYBE IT'LL JUST GO INTO THE OLD PIPE-SMOKING GUY'S ATTIC, ALONG WITH ALL THE OTHER UNSOLD BOOKS. MAYBE... SOMEDAY... IT'LL COME BACK TO ME AGAIN.

I'LL GO MY WAY, AND THE BOOK WILL GO ITS WAY. THIS IS JUST A CHANCE MEETING BETWEEN OLD FRIENDS.
A CASUAL, BITTERSWEET HELLO--
--TO SOMEBODY WHO CAN'T STOP TO TALK--
--SOME STRAY WITH NO HOME--
--SOMEONE WHO CAN NEVER BE YOURS--

THERE ARE TIMES

WHEN YOU MAY THINK THAT PEOPLE ARE STARING AT YOU

THEY ARE.

THUMP!
CLICK-CLICK CLICKA
FUMBLE
BEEEP
THUNK

SLAM
HUHH!

OH
HUHHH HUHH
GASPP
HUHH HUHH HUHH

HUHH HUHH HUHH HUHH

I STOLE FROM THAT POOR OLD GUY I'M A BAD BAD PERSON
FUCK THAT IT WAS ABANDONED NOBODY WANTED IT

OH
HUHH HUHH
I DON'T CARE
HUHH HUHH
DON'T CARE IF NOTHING MAGIC EVER HAPPENS TO ME
WHEEZE
EVER AGAIN!
WHOOOH!
THIS IS ENOUGH!

SIGH

FLIP

FLIP
FLIP
FLIP

KFLUTTER
DUNK

NNNNNG!

WHAT'S THE MATTER, MARCIE?

NOTHING.

WHAT'S THE MATTER, MARCIE?
NOTHING, SIR.

?

PPP HAA HA HA HA HA HA HA HA HA HA HA!!

HO-HO-O, MAN!
THIS IS IT, ISN'T IT? THIS IS THE ONE HE GAVE YOU WHEN YOU WERE SEVEN.

YES, SIR.
I THOUGHT SO. YOU BAWLED OVER THIS THING FOR WEEKS.

SAD, SAD.
UP TO HIS OLD TRICKS I SEE.
WHAT DO YOU MEAN?

THIS IS ONE OF THOSE GIMMICK BOOKS. YOU'D FILL OUT YOUR KID'S NAME, AGE, FRIENDS' NAMES, FAVORITE FOODS, PETS' NAMES... THE COMPANY SENDS YOU A STORYBOOK WITH ALL THAT INFORMATION INSERTED.
IT WAS JUST A SCAM, A WAY TO START DOSSIERS ON FUTURE CONSUMERS AT A REALLY YOUNG AGE. ODD.
ALL THAT WAS OUTLAWED YEARS AGO. THIS THING'S A RELIC.

HE MUST'VE PICKED IT UP BECAUSE IT HAS YOUR NAME IN IT.
MARCELLA, Y'KNOW... IT'S A POPULAR NAME IN MEDAWAR CLAN.

TSK I.Q. 88 CHILDREN'S FICTION. ALL THE CHARACTERS DO IS TALK AND EAT.
WELL, THAT'S JAEGER ALL OVER. A BEAUTIFUL COVER ON A PIECE OF SHIT.

MAY I HAVE MY BOOK, PLEASE?

DON'T TAKE IT TOO HARD. HE DOES SERVE UP SPELLBINDING BULLSHIT.
HE USED TO DO IT TO US TOO, Y'KNOW.

WHAT DID HE DO?

HE'D MAKE THINGS UP, TELL STORIES, WHEN HE WAS SUPPOSED TO BE READING TO US.
HE'D JUST BULLSHIT, AND TURN THE PAGES WHENEVER HE FELT LIKE IT.

RACHEL ALWAYS LET HIM GET AWAY WITH IT.
RACHEL
JAEGER
I MADE HIM STICK TO THE STORY EVEN IF IT WAS A STINKBOMB.

WHY?
WELL...
I GUESS BECAUSE I WANTED TO READ. I LEARNED TO READ BY FOLLOWING THE WORDS WHILE SOMEONE ELSE READ TO ME.

UNH
I REALLY WANT THIS STORY... BUT IT DOESN'T EXIST!
IF I WANT TO READ IT, I HAVE TO WRITE IT, AND I CAN'T!
I'M NOT GOOD ENOUGH TO GET EVEN HALF OF IT RIGHT!

AHEM
KID...
...IF A THING IS WORTH DOING, IT'S WORTH DOING BADLY.

CHAPTER 3:

dreaming eyes of wonder

Isn't there any water here? Doesn't anything grow?
THERE IS THE IRON TARN.
THE TARN IS ALL WE WILL NEED.
THIS WEREWOLF DOESN'T CHANGE ALL AT ONCE UNDER THE FULL MOON INSTEAD, HE CHANGES A LITTLE BIT EVERY DAY. ONCE A MONTH HE'S NEARLY ALL WOLF AND ONCE A MONTH HE'S NEARLY ALL HUMAN.
GREEN EYES?
IT'S FUNNY HOW ADULTS DON'T USUALLY REALIZE THAT THE MAIN CHARACTER OF A KID'S BOOK DOESN'T HAVE TO BE A KID. DO THEY REALIZE THAT KIDS DON'T REALLY THINK OF THEMSELVES AS KIDS??
I HAVE NEVER IN MY LIFE FELT LIKE A KID.
ANY BOOK THAT HAS A KID FOR A MAIN CHARACTER GETS PUT IN THE KIDS' SECTION. ???
FFEE
TERS
IM262-PZ-883
MARTINENE144-BV-273
MEDIA HOMEWORK BLEH
HONEY, I'M SORRY, BUT I'VE LOOKED AND YOU'VE LOOKED AND THE BOOK YOU WANTED IS JUST NOT HERE ANYMORE.

BUT IT WAS HERE, IT WAS, AND IT WAS JUST FIFTEEN PENCE, AND TODAY I FINALLY HAVE FIFTEEN....
REMAINDERS
CHEAP! DEAD TREE SPECIAL
AS MARKED! ALL SALES FINAL!
EVERY DAY I'D STOP AND LOOK AT IT
SNIFF
'N I SAVED UP MY MONEY 'N I DIDN'T ASK FOR ANY---
the Dead Tre
BOOKSTORE
N-NOBODY HAD THE RIGHT TO JUST TAKE IT!
NOBODY TOOK IT. SOMEBODY BOUGHT IT. I'M SORRY, BABE... BUT THAT'S JUST THE WAY IT IS.
SNIFFFF
SOB
AW, BABY
NOW COME ON
WHAT'S GONE IS GONE
I'M PROUD OF YOU FOR SAVING YO MONEY
BWAAAH
HIC
SHNIFF
WHY DON'T YOU GET THIS ONE? IT'S ABOUT BIRDS TOO, AND IT'S ONLY ELEVEN PENCE.
--HONEY--
BUT I D-DON'T WANT THAT ONE!

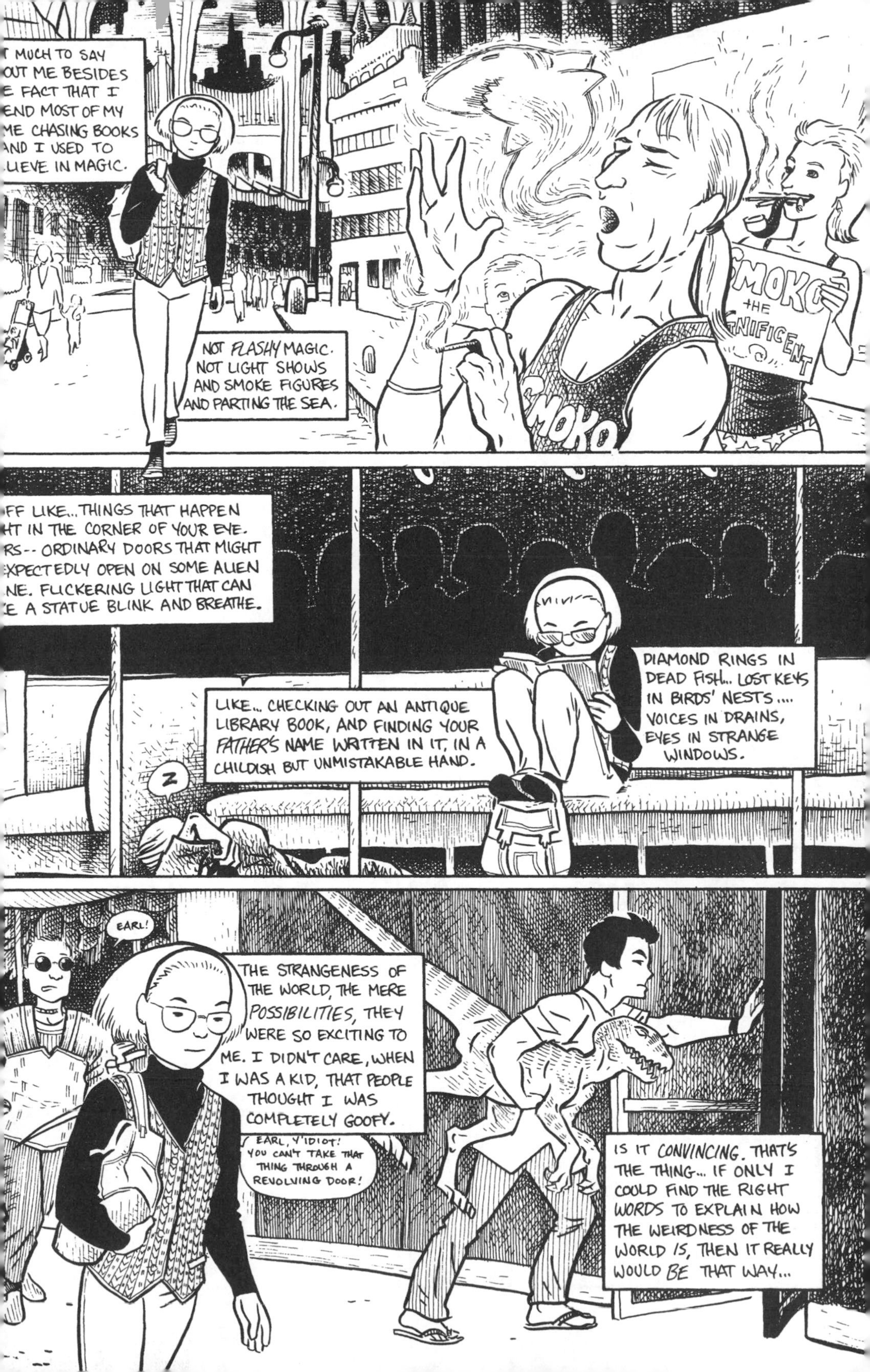
T MUCH TO SAY
OUT ME BESIDES
E FACT THAT I
END MOST OF MY
ME CHASING BOOKS
AND I USED TO
LIEVE IN MAGIC.
NOT FLASHY MAGIC. NOT LIGHT SHOWS AND SMOKE FIGURES AND PARTING THE SEA.
FF LIKE... THINGS THAT HAPPEN
HT IN THE CORNER OF YOUR EYE.
RS-- ORDINARY DOORS THAT MIGHT
EXPECTEDLY OPEN ON SOME ALIEN
NE. FLICKERING LIGHT THAT CAN
E A STATUE BLINK AND BREATHE.
LIKE... CHECKING OUT AN ANTIQUE LIBRARY BOOK, AND FINDING YOUR FATHER'S NAME WRITTEN IN IT, IN A CHILDISH BUT UNMISTAKABLE HAND.
Z
DIAMOND RINGS IN DEAD FISH... LOST KEYS IN BIRDS' NESTS.... VOICES IN DRAINS, EYES IN STRANGE WINDOWS.
EARL!
THE STRANGENESS OF THE WORLD, THE MERE POSSIBILITIES, THEY WERE SO EXCITING TO ME. I DIDN'T CARE, WHEN I WAS A KID, THAT PEOPLE THOUGHT I WAS COMPLETELY GOOFY.
EARL, Y'IDIOT! YOU CAN'T TAKE THAT THING THROUGH A REVOLVING DOOR!
IS IT CONVINCING. THAT'S THE THING... IF ONLY I COULD FIND THE RIGHT WORDS TO EXPLAIN HOW THE WEIRDNESS OF THE WORLD IS, THEN IT REALLY WOULD BE THAT WAY...

I LIKED THE IDEA OF FAIRIES AND GHOSTS AND MAGIC SWORDS AND CARDS TELLING THE FUTURE... BUT THOSE WERE FOR BOOKS. *WHY* WEREN'T THEY REAL? THEY SEEMED REAL ENOUGH WHILE I WAS READING.

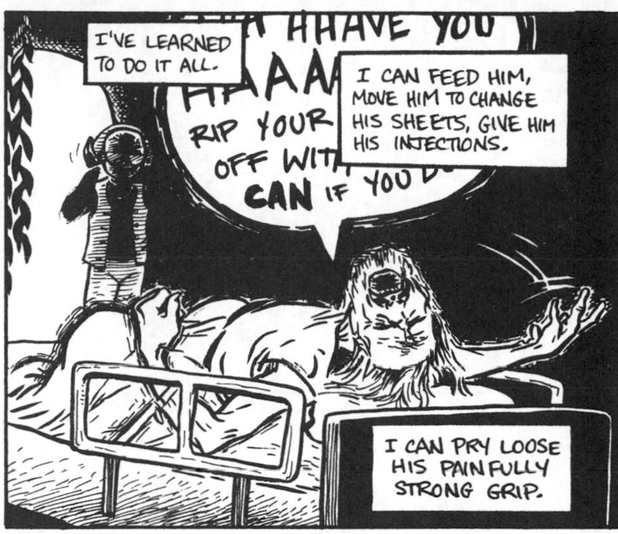

HE *USED* TO QUIET DOWN FOR ME. WHEN I WAS SIX, ALL I HAD TO DO WAS TOUCH HIM OR TALK TO HIM AND HE'D STOP BUSTING OUR EARDRUMS JUST LIKE *THAT.* WE COULD ALL RELAX AND GET SOME SLEEP.

THANK GOD I HAVE A JOB. A LEGITIMATE REASON TO GET OUT OF THE HOUSE.
ALL RIGHT, MARCELLA MY LOVE.
MOM'S ALWAYS WORKING OUR SISTER RACHEL'S OFF AT SCHOOL. NO SENSE OF OBLIGATION'S EVER BEEN SUFFICIENT TO MAKE LYNN STAY IN ONE PLACE FOR LON
MOM'S HIRED A NURSE TO LOOK AFTER HIM. SHE CAN AFFORD IT.
BUT IF I DIDN'T HAVE A JOB, I'D NEVER BE ABLE TO LEAVE HIM.
MY GRANDDAD RUNS A MOVIE STUDIO. HE SAYS ACTORS CAN TALK, THEY CAN JOKE, SOME CAN EVEN SORT OF SING.
THEY'VE GOT TIMING AND INFLECTION AND EXPRESSION DOWN PAT. THEIR VOICES ARE DISTINCTIVE AND MEMORABLE.
MAKE ME PROUD.
THEY CAN DO EVERYTHING A STORYTELLER REQUIRES OF THEM.
EXCEPT SCREAM.
MOST FACE ACTORS CAN'T SCREAM.
I SCREAM PART-TIME FOR MY GRANDDAD.

I'VE *HEARD* THE SOUNDS FACE ACTORS MAKE WHEN THEY TRY TO SCREAM. IT'S PATHETIC, REALLY. THEY *RASP.* THEY HONK LIKE *GEESE.* THEY MAKE THESE STRANGLY SQUEECHES. *AND* THEY TEAR UP THEIR VOICES DOING IT.
I HAVE A SCREAM THAT POURS OUT OF ME LIKE HOT METAL.

IT'S LOUD AND IT'S SATISFYING AND IT'S SKULL PIERCING. IT SETS THE BONES TO VIBRATING. IT'S FULL OF TRICKY LITTLE WAVE FORMS THAT BYPASS THE BRAIN AND GO DIRECTLY TO THE BASE OF THE SPINE.
SADLY... NOTHING LASTS FOREVER. PEOPLE *HAVE* GOTTEN USED TO MY SCREAM IN THE SIX MONTHS THAT I'VE BEEN RECORDING IT.

NOW, ALL THEY DO IS POP OUT IN COLD SWEAT, JERK SPASTICALLY, AND GRIN WEAKLY.
OH, MY LITTLE GRANDBABY... SHE'S GOT A GIFT!
UNH!

OH HOW I ***WISH*** I COULD DO THAT TO THEM WITH MY ***WRITING.***
...AND SHE'S SUCH A *PLACID* LITTLE THING USUALLY...

YOU CAN NEVER HOPE TO WIN UNLESS YOU BATHE IN THE TARN.
THAT IS THE GODDESS, DAUGHTER-OF-WAR. SHE WILL HELP YOU IF YOU ARE BRAVE.
EEEH...
HSSS
OH!
THE BOTTOM--
IT'S ALL-- ALL COVERED WITH--
OH, IT'S COLD...
ARE YOU HURT?
--NO--
THEN GO DEEPER IN.

...LIKE THIS?
DEEPER STILL.
HOW FAR--?
LIKE THIS--
BLUP
BLUPF
HNN...
BLUPP
BLUP
BLUPPA

HUAHH!
HEY--!
WHAT'S WRONG WITH HER?
SIGH
SHE ALWAYS WEEPS WHEN CHILDREN HAVE TO GROW UP TOO FAST.

SO, HOME I GO, SATCHEL FULL OF BOOKS, PACK FULL OF DATA PLUGS, HEAD FULL OF FANTASY LIKE A CAT FULL OF KITTENS.

BUT I FEEL SO *LIGHT*, AS IF, IF I TOOK A DEEP ENOUGH BREATH, HELD IT, MADE A WISH, LET OUT THE BREATH JUST RIGHT, I COULD RISE UP LIKE A HELIUM BALLOON.

AND I GET HOME AND I SIT DOWN AND I START WRITING AND THEN--

SIXTEEN OUTLINES, TWELVE GENEALOGIES, EIGHT CHARACTER SHEETS, ONE ALTERNATE TIME LINE, AND THREE MAPS LATER, IT'S ALL GONE.

I DON'T KNOW *WHAT* I EVER FOUND EXCITING ABOUT IT. I'VE GOT A DRY HEADACHE.

THE STORY THAT'S BEEN KEEPING ME ENTERTAINED FOR WEEKS... IT'S JUST NOT *THERE* ANYMORE.

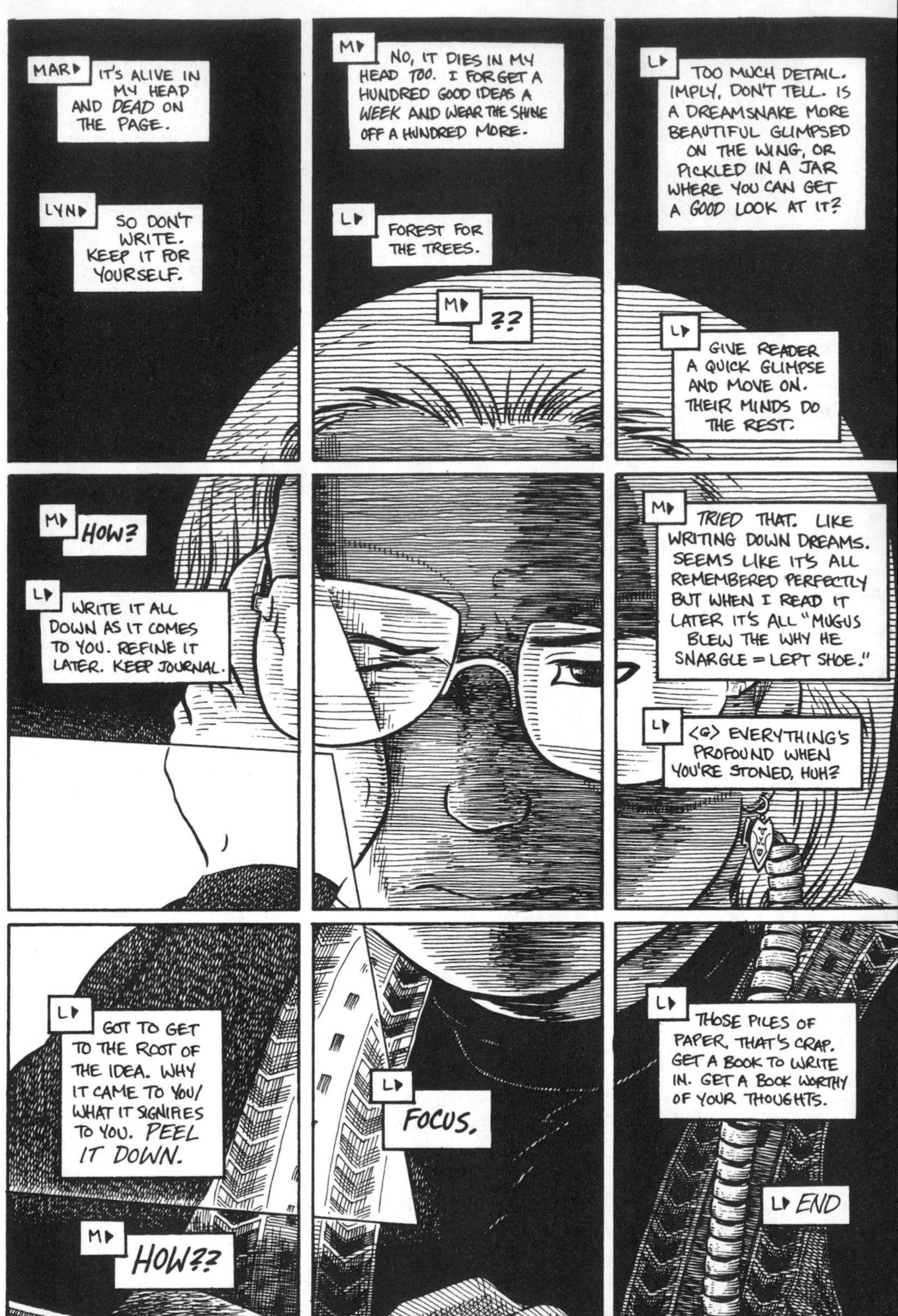

MAR▸ IT'S ALIVE IN MY HEAD AND DEAD ON THE PAGE.
LYN▸ SO DON'T WRITE. KEEP IT FOR YOURSELF.
M▸ NO, IT DIES IN MY HEAD TOO. I FORGET A HUNDRED GOOD IDEAS A WEEK AND WEAR THE SHINE OFF A HUNDRED MORE.
L▸ FOREST FOR THE TREES.
M▸ ??
L▸ TOO MUCH DETAIL. IMPLY, DON'T TELL. IS A DREAMSNAKE MORE BEAUTIFUL GLIMPSED ON THE WING, OR PICKLED IN A JAR WHERE YOU CAN GET A GOOD LOOK AT IT?
L▸ GIVE READER A QUICK GLIMPSE AND MOVE ON. THEIR MINDS DO THE REST.
M▸ HOW?
L▸ WRITE IT ALL DOWN AS IT COMES TO YOU. REFINE IT LATER. KEEP JOURNAL.
M▸ TRIED THAT. LIKE WRITING DOWN DREAMS. SEEMS LIKE IT'S ALL REMEMBERED PERFECTLY BUT WHEN I READ IT LATER IT'S ALL "MUGUS BLEW THE WHY HE SNARGLE = LEPT SHOE."
L▸ <G> EVERYTHING'S PROFOUND WHEN YOU'RE STONED, HUH?
L▸ GOT TO GET TO THE ROOT OF THE IDEA. WHY IT CAME TO YOU/ WHAT IT SIGNIFIES TO YOU. PEEL IT DOWN.
M▸ HOW??
L▸ FOCUS.
L▸ THOSE PILES OF PAPER, THAT'S CRAP. GET A BOOK TO WRITE IN. GET A BOOK WORTHY OF YOUR THOUGHTS.
L▸ END

I HAVE BLANK BOOKS.
THIRTEEN OF 'EM, TO BE EXACT.

EVERYBODY GIVES ME BLANK BOOKS FOR BIRTHDAYS AND HOLIDAYS.
THEY'RE ALL ANTIQUES AND GORGEOUS AND THEY'RE ALL STILL BLANK.

MOST OF 'EM, ANYWAY. THE ONES THAT AREN'T STILL BLANK--
EX LIBRIS
marcie
marcie
marcie
little fareys by and by light the candels of the sky
farey

--THEY MIGHT AS WELL BE.
PIF!

AH, SHIT!
HAOOH!
WEIRD--

THAT WAS NOT MY FATHER--
AH! GODDAMMIT!

GNRR!
SHIT SHIT
AH LET GO YOU YOU
HUFF!
HSS!
SNIVEL
NO, IT'S MY OWN DAMN FAULT, GIRL. I SAW HIS FACE, I KNEW HE WAS AWAKE--
MAGIC. I WANT MAGIC. I WANT MAGIC THAT WORKS.
THERE IS NO DOCTOR THAT CAN MAKE THE CREATURE BACK INTO MY DADDY. NO THERAPY THAT CAN MAKE HIM INTO WHAT HE SHOULD HAVE BEEN.
NO GOING BACK TO THE BEGINNING AND REWRITING. HE IS WHAT HE IS, AND IF I HAVE TO WRITE WHAT I KNOW, I'M DOOMED, BECAUSE I CAN NEVER WRIT ABOUT THIS, NEVER

I NEED MY FANTASY. I NEED MEMORY AND DREAM.
READING IS MY ANESTHETIC. IT ISN'T ENOUGH.
I POUR BOOKS INTO MYSELF AND THERE ARE NEVER ENOUGH.
THEY'RE GONE TOO FAST, LIKE PAPER ON A BONFIRE.
I NEED THE BOOK I LOST.
I NEED THE BOOK I ALWAYS LOSE. THE STORY THAT TELLS ITSELF.
THE BOOK THAT CAN NEVER BE FILLED UP OR FINISHED.
PALACE OF MEMORY
OH, THIS IS SUCH A DUMB IDEA.
I AM NOT GOING TO DO THIS.

NO WAY.
I AM NOT GOING OFF ON SOME FLAKY ADVENTURE TO FIND THE PERFECT BLANK BOOK.
IT'S STUPID AND WEIRD AND ANYWAY IT WON'T WORK. THERE IS NO PERFECT BOOK.
MY MOTHER'S FAMILY IS FULL OF KOOKS--
THEY MAKE A LIFE OUT OF BEING WEIRD-
--THEY DO ALL SORTS OF WEIRD STUPID THINGS TO SEEM ARTSY AND INTUITIVE BUT THEY DON'T EVER PRODUCE-- THAT'S NOT MAGIC, IT'S--
--THEY MAKE UP ALL THIS RITUALISTIC BEHAVIOR BECAUSE IT SOUNDS COOL, NOT BECAUSE IT REALLY HELPS THEM BRING ANYTHING NEW INTO BEING.
THEY CAWN'T WORK WITHOUT THEIR LUCKY PINK PENCIL, OR IF THE TEMPERATURE ISN'T JUST SO--
--OR IF THEY'RE NOT HOME IN THEIR FAVORITE CHAIR BETWEEN THE HOURS OF TEN AND TWO--
--OR THEY GOTTA HAVE THEIR WRITER'S HAT OR SIX DOZEN GREEN GUMDROPS OR A DAMN TEDDY BEAR OR SOME OTHER IDIOTIC LUCKY CHARM, SOME
TALISMAN
--AND IT'S JUST AN EXCUSE NOT TO WORK, SINCE THEY CAWN'T WORK IF EVERYTHING'S NOT PERFECT, WHICH IT NEVER IS.
IT'S SETTING YOURSELF UP TO FAIL, THAT KIND OF MAGICAL THINKING, AND I'M NOT GOING TO BOTHER WITH IT.
IF IT ISN'T ABSOLUTELY PERFECT, I'M NOT GOING TO BOTHER WITH IT. NO MAKE-DO OR SORTA.
ANTIQUE BINDERY
GREYHAWK BOOKS
AND IF I DON'T FIND IT TODAY, THAT IS THAT. I CAN BLOW ONE DAY ON THIS FOOL'S ERRAND.
HOURS:

MOST SHOPS CARRY TONS OF MOVIES AND DATA PLUGS. BUT COMPARATIVELY FEW REAL, BOUND BOOKS.
EMBOSSED LEATHER
GILT EDGING
DAMASK SILK
RIBBON BOOKMARKS
ANY COLOR YOU WANT
ENVIRONMENTALISTS HATE PAPER BOOKS. THEY SAY IT'D BE BETTER IF ALL BOOKS WERE DIGITAL FILES.
HUH..
BUT PEOPLE LIKE BOOKS...
MOSTLY FOR DECOR, MIND YOU... MY UNCLE MAG'S WHOLE LIBRARY IS BLANK. HE ORDERED FORTY YARDS OF BLUE BOOKS, AND THAT'S WHAT HE GOT.
IT WAS SAID--
(WHERE DID I READ THAT?)
--THAT ONLY ANOTHER SPHINX COULD BEAR TO MEET A SPHINX'S GAZE.
NICE 1/2 PRICE
$3.99
IT WAS SAID THAT IF TWO SPHINXES LOOKED INTO EACH OTHER'S EYES, ALL THE RIDDLES OF THE UNIVERSE WOULD COME POURING OUT.
MAYBE THAT'S WHY THE STONE GUARDIANS OF THE AMBERSON FAMILY'S PRIVATE LIBRARY (WHAT THEY CALL THE PALACE OF MEMORY)--
--MAYBE THAT'S WHY THEY FACE EACH OTHER.
30% DISCOUNT
VOICE CARD
SCAN-EX
DECORATIVE DUST JACKETS
1/2 PRICE
NICE PRICE!
THOSE SPHINXES ARE THE GUARDIANS OF THE GREATEST COLLECTION OF BOOKS IN THE WHOLE WORLD.
A PALACE OF BOOKS. A TEMPLE OF BOOKS.
THAT'S COOL.
I WANT A BOOK.
BUT I DON'T WANT A FANCY DIGITAL DAY PLANNER. NOR DO I WANT A CHEAP CARD-BOARD JACKET TO MAKE A PLAIN DIGITAL DAY PLANNER LOOK FANCY.

DJURI ANTIQUES
LAMPS-KEYS-BOOKS
OWL & PUSSYCAT
BOOKSTORE SALOON
JUNK SHOP
PALEO
RECLAIMED BOOKS
NOVELS·POETRY·LIBRETTI
OLD-FASHIONED BINDERY
GOD, THESE THINGS ARE GORGEOUS. HOW CAN I EVER WRITE IN ONE OF THESE?
MY HANDWRITING'S TOO UNEVEN. MY THOUGHTS AREN'T THIS ELEGANT. I'M NOT THIS COOL.
I CAN'T COMPROMISE ON THIS. IT JUST HAS TO BE THE ONE THAT JUMPS OFF THE SHELF YELLING "ME ME ME" OR IT ISN'T GONNA WORK.
....IF YOU WRITE IN THEM YOU RUIN THEM. A BLANK PAGE IS UNLIMITED. FLAUBERT WROTE IN THE SAME BLANKNESS AS STINE.
BUT A WRITER WHO HAS ONLY BLANK PAGES ISN'T MUCH OF A WRITER.
THERE IS NO PERFECT. THERE IS NO MAGIC. I'M NOT GOING TO FIND THE BOOK OF MY DREAMS.
nh.
I'LL HAVE TO MAKE IT.

THIS ONE--
THIS ONE--
SIMPLE BUT BEAUTIFULLY MADE. UNLINED, THICK CREAMY PAGES. HAND-STITCHED AND HAND-CUT. NO CHEESY CAR-TOONS, NO MESSY SMEARS OF GLUE.
BUT IT NEEDS AN ICON. A TOTEM. THE RIGHT SYMBOL. A SYMBOL OF ALL THE BOOKS IN THE WORLD, OF ALL MAGIC WHETHER FAKE OR REAL.
SPHINX. LIBRARY GUARDIAN. THAT GLOSSY CARDBOARD COVER, DUST JACKET FOR AN EXPENSIVE DAY PLANNER.
PERFECT.
IT WON'T MEAN A DAMN THING TO ANYONE BUT ME. BUT TO ME, IT'S THE ESSENCE. IT'S MYSTERY. THE ANCIENTS USED TO CALL THEIR RELIGIOUS RITES MYSTERIES.
IT WON'T STILL BE THERE.
COURSE IT WILL BE. IT'S ONLY BEEN A FEW HOURS.
IF IT IS, I'LL GET IT AND CUT IT OUT, GLUE IT DOWN TO THE COVER OF THIS ONE. I KNOW THE KIND OF GLUE TO USE.
I HATE WANTING THIS. IT WON'T BE THERE. I'LL GET THAT LEAD-WEIGHT FEELING. I'LL SMOTHER.
IT MAY BE GONE. IT MAY BE THERE. IT MAY BE GONE.
I MAY NEVER WRITE ANYTHING IN MY BOOK. I MAY NEVER WRITE ANY-THING WORTHY OF INSCRIPTION ON THESE PAGES. BUT EVERY WORD I WRITE WILL BE WRITTEN WTH THAT ASPIRATION. IT'LL BE ENOUGH.
HERE--
SS INC.
AND... IT'S NOT HERE.
IT'S GONE.
OF COURSE.
GONE
ALWAYS GONE

AAAAAAAAAH
HHHRRH...

A!
OIRRR!
OH--
AAAAAAAAP
SHUT UUUHP!
OHH...
SKLITTCCHH
OHH MY DAUGHTER--- I NEVER, I NEVER MEANT HARM TO YOU OR YOUR MOTHER-- I HAD NO CHOICE! I-- I ONLY LOVED YOU--- I--I --LOVED-- LOVED YOU---

AAAA!

AAAUWW

AA

HWAAAAA

I DON'T REALLY BELIEVE IN REINCARNATION.

CRITT
SCRITCHA
SKRIZZ
PARROT BEAK
TIN SHEARS
SCRITTCHASKTT SCRITTZ
a mere
MÜ
GLUE

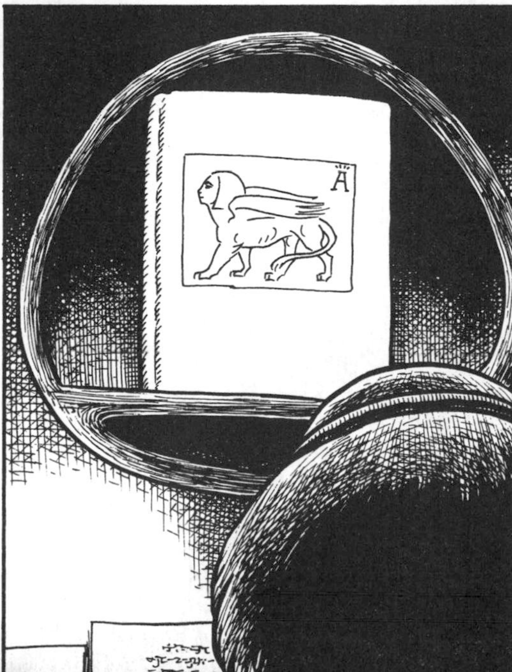

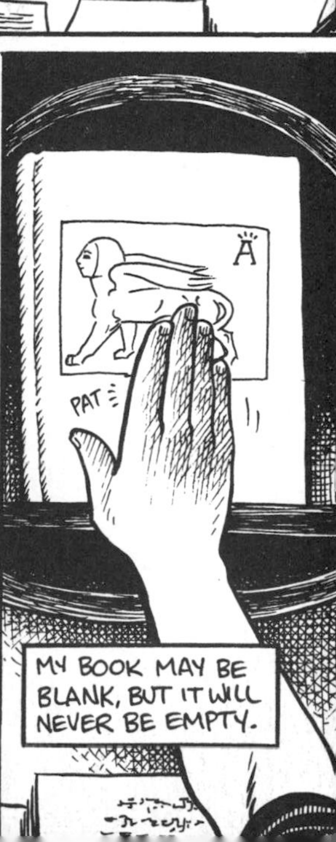

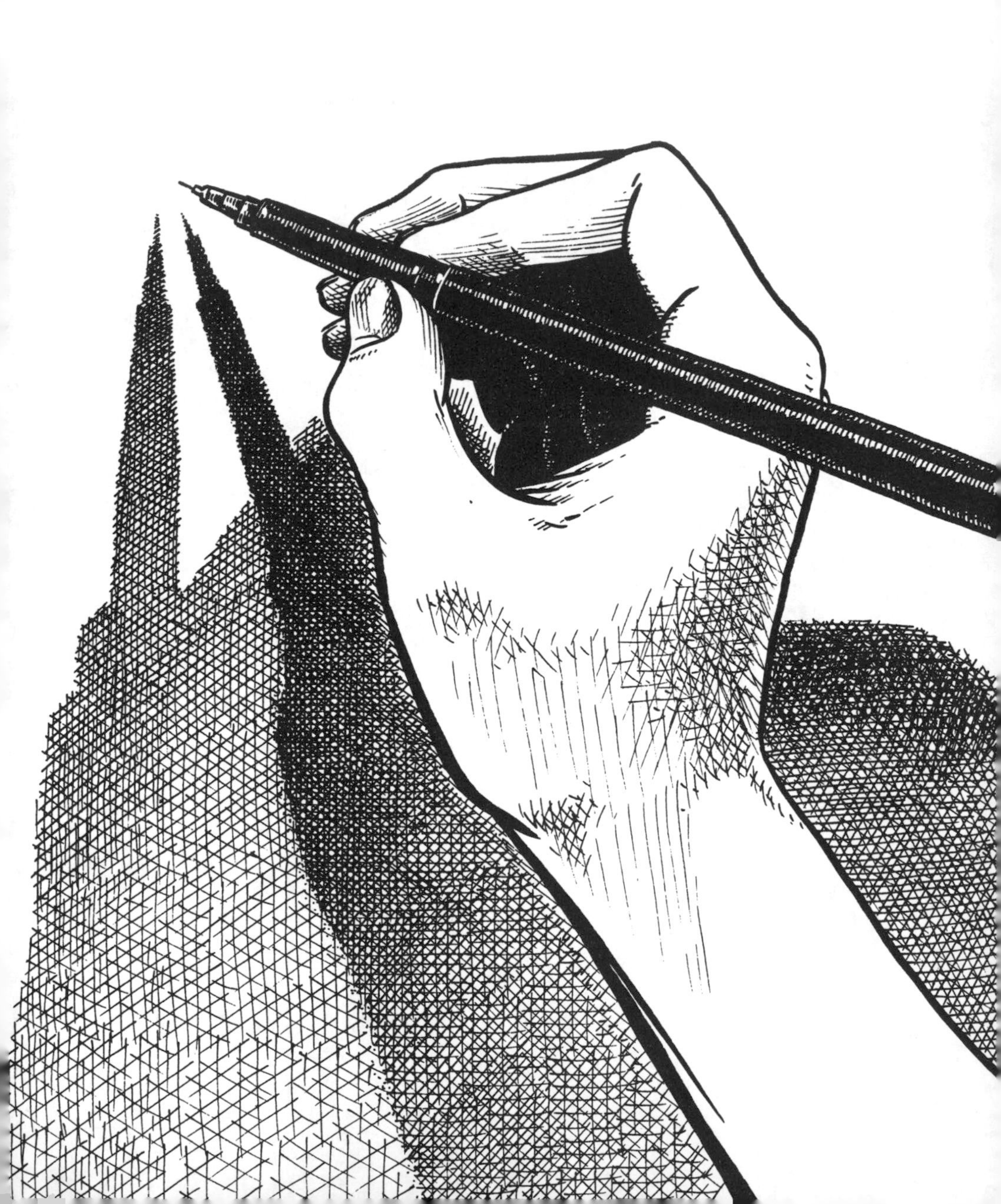

NOTES

SIN-EATER

PAGES 10–11
Inspired by the engravings and watercolors of David Roberts. This was drawn from Abu Simbel, when it was still full of sand. Animal on the left is a male Nyima named Kohut.

PAGE 17
Ganesha, Hindu deity. Hailed as the Remover of Obstacles, he is to be addressed at the beginning of any new venture. I couldn't get started on this story until I read about this custom first in Alan Moore's *From Hell*.

PAGE 18
Jaeger (pronounced Yae'gurr). He is the first of several Finders. He's much like an Indian scout or detective.

PAGE 19
First blood sacrifice. Ganesha is usually honored with fruit or candy, but this is all he's got.

PAGE 21
Trading post—these mark the outermost boundaries of the territory of the city of Anvard.

PAGES 22–23
City of Anvard, seen from the eastern road. The city fills up its dome rather than spread out on the tide plains. An almost unbreakable latticework inside and fixed to the dome serves as building foundation.

In the foreground is Mount Cino (Chee'noe), topped by a fortified lookout that is one of the oldest existing structures in Anvard. Cino is riddled with tunnels.

The name "Anvard" came from a kingdom in the books of C. S. Lewis.

PAGE 24
"Her Majesty"—the Beatles, *Abbey Road*. The LP was more fun.

Those mechasuits aren't suits; they're remotely operated robots. First reference to Hayao Miyazaki's Totoro. The suits appear only at the perimeter gates of the city or at severe trouble spots.

The free market—many of the city's inhabitants are resident and transient noncitizens. The free markets, mostly found on the lowest levels, are the only places they can buy, sell, and barter legally with full citizens. The full citizens have their own troubles with permits, ID, and accounting; most go to the markets to get away from paperwork.

Languages on the banner, left to right, are Arabic, English, Miremai (a trader's language, like Swahili), and Laeske (the big, feathery lizards).

Panel 5. Gilroy Garlic Doll. Gilroy, California—Garlic Capital of the USA. Won't do you no good to roll your windows up when driving through.

Jaeger's handmade leathers are ludicrously valuable in urban areas—very expensive and only barely legal.

PAGE 25
Panel 2. Ron Chitin's rookie card? Ron Chitin is a four-armed ex–hockey goalie from Evan Dorkin's *Pirate Corp$!* (renamed *Hectic Planet*).

Panel 3. Fat man with parrot is Sydney Greenstreet, as Signor Ferrari in *Casablanca*.

There are hundreds of TV channels in Anvard. It takes armies of busybodies with cameras and computers to fill 'em up. Careful what you sing in the shower; somebody will consider it an audition.

Free Traders are members of large, ill-defined tribes of nomadic and seminomadic people, recognized by law as being able to buy and sell within cities. They are exempted from carrying ID or permits, but they may not own any real estate, storefront, or permanent dwelling, nor may they receive what is considered a living wage for work. Some breeze in with goods to sell and then back out; others move tent towns in and out of alleyways, Dumpster diving as they go. They're the first to be hassled whenever trouble starts.

PAGES 26–27
Whiskey Jack is a victim of a peculiar sexually transmitted disease commonly called the Fey Plague. It randomly inserts animal genes into human bodies, and sometimes vice versa. It kills most, but is also believed to impart oracular abilities. The little girl with him is his rememberer, an attendant with a perfect memory trained to recall every addled word the poor man says.

PAGE 28
Tour guide. Members of her clan are very long lived, and are as such de facto historians. Her personal name is Medina.

PAGE 31
Panel 2. Inspired by the remarkable photography of Rene Jacques, in this case *Escalier, Montmartre*.

PAGE 32
The bookstore is named for the infamous Madame Marie Laveau, voodoo mambo.

PAGE 33
Hulger, male Nyima. Many folk in Anvard have animal characteristics in some way or another. Most common are "constructs" or living artifacts, genetically constructed servants or sex toys mostly. Least common are survivors of the Fey Plague, like Whiskey Jack. Somewhere in the middle are such as the Nyima, the centaurs or halfhorses, the Huldres, and so on. They are often treated with the same casual contempt as the constructs, and are very touchy about it.

"Nyima" is a phonetic play on "Nemea" as in "Nemean Lion."

PAGE 34
Bookshop counter slugs: Virgill, Gyles clan. Ann Handler, manager, Shingtown clan. Miss Lennie, owner, Llaverac clan. Almost all full citizens of Anvard are members of or employed by the clans. Here on the lower levels, the clans mix more comfortably, and nonclan people are better tolerated.

PAGE 35
Panel 4. Why do we see Miss Lennie in her youth? Lots of reasons, but that would be telling.

PAGE 36
Panel 3. The thing in the jar? He wasn't nice.

PAGE 38
Panel 2. No matter who looks into it, that mirror always reflects the face of the lady who first owned it.

PAGE 40
The sad fate of Bob Plant, who was my studio mate for years. Big areca palm. Lots of vitamin C, I guess.

PAGE 41
Panel 1. The river, once it gets within the confines of the city, becomes blood red.

Panel 3. Spalding Gray, from *Swimming to Cambodia*.

Panel 9. Camera brats from the market. The girl's name is Ruth. She's half Medawar clan and half Heinz 57. The halfhorse boy's name is Kalif (Ka-leef'); he mans the camera.

PAGE 43
Panel 6. Emma and her youngest daughter, Marcie. Emma is of Llaverac clan, but her kids are half Medawar clan. Most of the clans are not very tolerant of cross-clan marriage, these two in particular.

PAGE 47
Mount Cino, and Anvard, many thousands of years ago when it was a fortified town.

Absurdly large banner pinned to the side of the mountain depicts a Roman soldier's helmet. Jaeger always dreams of mazes and puzzles.

PAGE 49
Arrow with chevrons is an aviator's symbol indicating severe turbulence ahead. The banner, which changed from a soldier's helmet to the number 36, now shows a total eclipse. The marks above the doors are hobo code. The sands underfoot are composed of tiny, tiny bones.

PAGE 50
Meet Emma Grosvenor's kids. Rachel, fourteen; Lynne, ten; Marcie, six. Rachel's tall for her age, Marcie's small for hers, and Lynne is far too devious for anybody's good. Marcie is the only person in the world Lynne will admit to giving a shit about.

PAGE 55
Sawing for Teens—watch more Canadian cartoons. I recommend Richard Condie's stuff in particular.

PAGE 56
Tessa Jhara, Nyiman noblewoman. She's in town working on a medical degree. She would never be granted a license to practice within the city, but she won't need it back home. Ann Handler has it pretty bad for Tessa, who is the jock of her dreams.

Long-haired clerk: Lydia, who was out when Jaeger stopped by the previous day.

PAGE 58
Lynne knows Jaeger has a terrible blind spot for electronics. He doesn't understand them or like them. Only his essential rootlessness makes him hard to plant bugs on.

PAGE 59
"Don't look so good, don't feel so good" conversation courtesy of Mike McNeil when he wasn't feeling so good.

PAGE 60
The first movie is of course *The Night of the Hunter*, with Bob Mitchum, Shelley Winters, and Lillian Gish. Mitchum says he got that "love" and "hate" tattoo idea from prison.

The second movie, however, is *The Producers*, Zero Mostel and Gene Wilder. Springtime for, uh... you know who?

PAGE 61
Quoted passage is from *Journey*, by William Messner-Loebs.

PAGE 62
This quick-healing thing has many variables, and as many drawbacks as advantages.

PAGE 64
Emma keeps a lot of locks on her door, doesn't she?

PAGE 66
No, Emma isn't Jaeger's mother. It's just a manner of speaking.

St. Podkayne—Martian saint from R. A. Heinlein's *Podkayne of Mars*.

PAGE 67
Botanical gardens are very common in Anvard, closed off from fresh air as it is; they require expert attention to cultivate, cut off from natural sunlight as they are.

PAGE 68
Brain damage is a tricky thing, even for him.

PAGE 71
Lots of bipeds. Fewer quadrupeds than bipeds in this animal kingdom.

PAGE 72
Our first center-stage construct, a raccoon-faced animal keeper. He has four fingers and a thumb, which is commonly illegal for constructs unless they have a job-related need for the full complement of digits. Those that "have" can pass for nonconstructs, and are hotly resented by the "have-nots" and many nonconstructs. He was originally designed to be an accountant.

Notice the dogtags around his neck; no construct appears in public without these ID cards. Being an unconventional construct, his freedom is even more restricted than usual—he cannot leave the zoo grounds unescorted, not even into the parking lot.

PAGE 75
This guy's outfit and hairdo courtesy of my ex-Mormon pal Jason. The hair's bright blue and/or purple. The car is a Pontiac Mako prototype that was never produced.

PAGE 77
Songs on radio: "I Was Brought to My Senses," Sting; "Lady Noble," folk song, probably pure Ren Faire; "Rescue Me," Fontella Bass.

The little character in the window is Smut, mascot of the Comic Book Legal Defense Fund. Created and donated by Neil Gaiman.

PAGE 79
On the sign: Arabic, Miremai, and Laeske under the English. Miremai, the traders' language, is spoken more or less by most itinerants in this region. The root word, *miremne* means "unclean."

Anvard is a twenty-four-hour city, dividing the day into twelve double-length hours instead of twenty-four. People live on three different "shifts," the better to cut down on street traffic. It's as if there are three populations, three cities under one roof.

PAGE 81
This is the Painwright's "oracle." It doesn't predict the future except as suits its purposes. It's possible that it is not always nefarious.

People who can't talk to anybody else talk to the oracles in the cultural museums, many of which are far more benevolent.

PAGE 83
That is indeed Jaeger's mother on the panel behind him; no, he didn't see her.

PAGE 85
Emma's speech is partly inspired by Terry Gilliam's *12 Monkeys*. "Psychologically divergent" was at one time a popular PC euphemism within the mental-health community. I mean, the nuthouse.

PAGE 86
And this is Brigham Grosvenor. Ex-husband of Emma; father of Rachel, Lynne, and Marcie; ex-army officer; and root of the problem.

PAGE 87
These are nasty scenarios, "might-happens," presented by the oracle. Given its nature, it almost never presents a happy outcome. Like a nasty Magic 8 Ball.

PAGE 90
People with hyperactive immune systems are often prone to blinding headaches. Teeny, tiny character portraits. I'm not about to try to list them all.

PAGE 91
Unusual blond Medawar; his hair didn't darken in the usual way. People like him are accepted as variations only after a great deal of scrutiny. Clans are picky about what kind and how much variation is permitted in their members, but the exceptions are impossible to keep up with.

The patterns on their faces are "war paint," topically psychoactive mixtures applied to enhance various abilities in the wearer, such as concentration, fine motor control, patience, aggression, peripheral vision, *etc*. Different substances are identified by different colors; different patterns produce subtle effects.

The Brownways are the older, lower levels of the city, which are less clean, less safe, and less well lit the further down you go. The Brownways are mostly inhabited by "everybody else." The territory is subject to rolling power brownouts.

PAGE 92
The "First Families": the clans. Each clan has a distinctive look for all its members, not only distinctive dress but a physical look and temperament to which each member conforms. They are the ruling class. People who work for them compose the middle class, and "everybody else" makes up the poor.

PAGE 93
Poster on the front desk: constructs are usually identified by their hands. Any construct which has the bad luck to end up in a precinct house will need legal protection. Pete's a local organizer. Not quite a mob boss, more like a street boss. Layabouts like Jaeger appear and disappear, do jobs for him or men like him.

PAGE 97
This marks the first appearance and continuing ubiquity of the Finder symbol. Just one of those slippery cultural symbols. Doric, Ionic, and Corinthian columns are just bank architecture to us.

PAGE 98
Jaeger sometimes uses his tattoo as a timer. His body won't let him keep it; it fades away in time. The more stress he's under, the faster it fades. Jaeger lives on autopilot. When his tattoo starts to go, he starts wanting to go too.

PAGE 99
This is the first time we see Brigham in the flesh. Brig's looks are based on those of a friend of mine, but Brig is older and more portly.

"How not to be seen," Jaeger style. When he was younger, he was a little naive about his abilities. He thought everybody could simply not be noticed unless they wanted to be.

Out in West Texas, where the trees are sparse, hawks like to sit on lampposts. At dusk, when the lights are lit, you can't see them. Neither can the rabbits. It's quite something to watch them swooping between parked cars in hot pursuit of jackrabbits, which are often far too big to hide under the cars. Texas. It's a whole 'nother country.

PAGE 100
Jaeger didn't take these pictures—at least not with a camera. He heisted 'em from Emma's family albums.

PAGE 101
Both Lynne and Marcie have neurocranial jacks set into their skulls. Marcie's is far more complex than Lynne's, and was put in

specifically to combat her chronic illness by regulating her body right from the command center. Quite a few people in Anvard have these things, as it makes accessing information and "virtual real estate" much easier.

Kuai Hua brand vital signs monitor. *Kuai Hua* means "mallow blossom," and is symbolic of the power of magic against evil spirits. Chinese traditional medicine is very... orderly and complex.

The device itself is capable of monitoring and manipulating very subtle aspects of a patient's body through the cranial jack. In this case, it's meant to be running a series of simple programs designed to bring Marcie's hyperactive immune system into equilibrium long enough for her to get well.

Lynne, being too smart and wayward to keep her hands off the damn thing, is inserting her own program riders.

On dresser: King Henry doll. All that's left of the illustrious history of Henry VIII, once king of England, is this traditional child's toy.

PAGE 102
SGI IRIX, anyone? Nobody knows I'm a Luddite.

PAGE 103
Dad has no use for a photo of his middle child.

PAGES 104–107
I learned something important doing these pages. If you're writing a verbal fight, be *extra* careful to act the lines out yourself, out loud. If you feel dopey saying any part of it, it's badly written. Brig has a simple barcode-like tattoo; it's a prison thing. Many of the clans despise permanent marking.

PAGE 107
Panel 1. This is a very simplified way of describing the policy which built Imperial Rome.

PAGE 108
Emma is a rather exclusive landscaper/gardener. She doesn't advertise or solicit; she gets handed gingerly from patron to patron. Her calling cards are hard to come by. There are lots of parks and gardens, tucked into corners of the middle and upper levels. On rooftops, on terraces, alongside pedestrian bridges, strung between high-rises. Many people set aside space in their houses for "garden rooms." It takes skill, talent, and an advanced education to create these minibiospheres with only recycled air and artificial light. Notice the Finder pattern around the ornamental fish pool.

PAGE 109
Originally, I was going to run this page in full color, since it's our first brief glance into Emma's interior life. It didn't work out.

PAGE 110
Little Blythe Spirit! Given how disoriented and haphazard Emma's life is, she has to have somebody to order groceries, balance the books, answer the phone, and pay the bills. That somebody is Blythe, Emma's personal AI. She buffers Emma from the outside world. With her help, she can get through life and be thought of only as flaky, not actually crazy. The world needs its visionaries.

Villian Danceny. "Danceny" comes from the Callow Youth character in *Les Liaisons Dangereuses*, by Choderlos de Laclos. *Villian* is such a common misspelling of "villain" that I just had to give somebody that name. In feudal days, "villain" meant only "inhabitant of a village."

PAGE 111
Blythe's virtual conscience gives her headaches, but she and others like her are given entirely too much responsibility to have no ethical structure. Everybody gets the "one and zero" joke, right? Gooood.

"Don't Smoke in Bed," written by Willard Robinson. Sung by Peggy Lee, one of the sexiest singers of the big-band era.

Edith Piaf was a sweet canary-voiced French singer, who was very popular in the twenties and thirties.

PAGES 112–113
This is a British folk song, but I don't know much else about it. I first heard it in *The Wicker Man*, one of the best bad movies ever made; good trash as only the seventies can deliver.

The little spring ceremony the Medawar girls are enacting can also be seen in this cheesy flick. It still took place in rural areas of Britain in the early part of this century, but has pretty much died out now. The custom went back all the way to the Roman grain goddess Ceres. We've lost so many funky customs in this century! Where I'm living, the kids don't even trick-or-treat on Halloween anymore.

The purpose of this scene was to show how uniform the Medawars are, and how separate Rachel felt in the few years she was living only with her father's people.

PAGE 114
Lynne planted a bug on one of Jaeger's boots. She knows he only has one pair.

PAGE 116
"In the black" did not then, and does not now, refer to my bank account.

PAGE 119
More walking tours! Jaeger would say that Medina teaches valuable lessons in the perils of beaten paths. In truth, it's probably just the city dwellers' common hostility towards out-of-towners. Small cameo, bottom right corner: Shanda Bruin from *Shanda the Panda*.

PAGE 120
Although Jaeger does usually get his eight hours' sleep in a full day's time, he rarely gets more than a few hours at a time. His tendency to drop off wherever he happens to be can leave casual acquaintances with the impression that he's lazy as hell and sleeps constantly. He hates mattresses; they make his back hurt.

In the city of Javecek, commemorations are left on walls or nearby, wherever a person has died. It's considered grossly disrespectful to tamper with them or paint over them, so the casual walker may find them on the restroom floor at a fancy restaurant, by the sides of the road, on the walls of alleys, and surely all over the walls of hospitals.

PAGE 121
Is this a dream, a memory, or the future? The content of the vision is made up of voluntary euthanasia, the root meaning of the word "sacred," and the old idea of eating sin. A sin-eater cleanses the dying of all moral stains, taking them all on to himself, usually by the symbolic act of eating food laid out near or actually on the body of the dying. The Javeceki, with their obsession with disease, take this one step further. Sin-eating is a form of scapegoating. The sin-eaters themselves are encouraged to think of it as heroism.

PAGE 122
Whiskey Jack again—at least, for the moment.

PAGE 123
Jaeger has to be good and wired to stand up in front of a crowd and call attention to himself. He can draw someone to him if he needs to, and not flip out much, but if he were to walk out onto a stage with a crowd already there—oh, he'd bug. He'd dive off of the stage and start beating the crap out of whomever he could reach. Stage fright's funny that way.

PAGE 126
Yes, for years I dreamed of giving my VCR the same treatment, and in January '98 I finally did. I got a new VCR and an eight-pound maul for my birthday, and spent a happy half an hour beating the bejesus out of the cussed thing. The packaging on electronic equipment always warns the buyer to be careful, because the stuff's so fragile. They're right. But I still didn't have the nerve to do it until I had a new one.

PAGE 127
Pete, unhealthy gangster. He is a Medawar by birth, but a marginal one; full membership in a clan is not only determined by your pedigree. The further down the power scale of a clan you go, the more it resembles a street mob. Pete isn't a cop or a soldier, but he's still a Medawar, and that gives him certain authority in the streets. The very pregnant Medawar woman leaning on her walking stick? She's a mob boss. Not a heavy hitter, mind you; sort of a junior lieutenant.

There is no welfare or government assistance for the poor in Anvard. The clans do believe in helping the poor, but not necessarily in charity. In other words, they often expect favors, loyalty, that sort of thing, in exchange for their help.

The song is "The Obvious Child" by Paul Simon.

PAGE 128
Radio DJ is an AI, like Blythe.

First mention of the Pastwatch Institute, which is largely responsible for the presence of garbled renditions of today's consumer products in Anvard.

PAGE 129
Boot-camp flashback for Jaeger. The guy who told me this story is named "Lance."

So why doesn't Jaeger try to, ah, adjust himself? Anybody who's ever stood up in front of a drill sergeant can tell you about the rabbit-in-the-headlights paralysis that sets in. Whatever he did, he'd-a ended up doing pushups.

PAGE 130
Why is Brig watering the plants instead of using the facilities inside the house? Well, going in seems like an imposition on a woman who didn't invite him in.

PAGE 133
"Herod's Evil" is not usually a contagious disease, but in the city of Javecek, many normally nonvirulent diseases become so.

PAGE 134
Brigham is a Medawar. His clan dominates both the police force and the territorial army of Anvard. His particular family are traditionally police.

Brig, having lost status by marrying outside his clan, was shifted into the army. It's the closest these clans have to banishment for their own members. Now that he has no place in either force, his disgrace is complete.

Doing other people's dirty work comes naturally to a sin-eater, whether he likes it or not.

PAGE 134
In the eyes of the clans and society as a whole, Jaeger and Brigham are both untouchables. Brig still doesn't act as if he knows it.

PAGE 135
The men commemorate the place where Emma Hellena Davis died in the Javeceki way, alien to the people of Anvard. The custom is enjoying a brief fad; most Anvardians view such monuments as being in rather poor taste.

PAGE 136
All members of the Llaverac clan look female. This is not a sex-segregated school; you are looking at both boys and girls.

PAGE 139
The move begins! Yes, Jaeger did have something to do with Emma getting her dream house. That's what he got from Pete, for a series of favors. It suits him to keep Emma and her kids mobile.

PAGE 143
Some parts of Anvard are like caverns; others are more like the mall of the *Twilight Zone*, pastel rooms and painted girders and trees in pots for miles and miles. The vistas collect tourists.

PAGE 144
Lotta public TVs in this town. Most of the middle class don't keep TVs in their houses for several reasons: the TV stations are also the manufacturers of the sets, and market pressures have produced TVs that can't be turned off. Also, each station's set is engineered to receive only that station's programming, so you'd have to have a bank of multiple TVs in order to see the bewildering range of channels in any representative sample.

What most people do when they want to veg out is clodhop down to the neighborhood theater, which maintains several screens and shows everything you could expect to see on the boob tube. Each separate auditorium is usually dedicated to a specific channel.

The difference between a shop or restaurant in an alley and one inside a building is cleanliness and lighting.

The book being discussed is *The Killer Inside Me*, a frighteningly brilliant book by classic noir author Jim Thompson. In Anvard, the book was recovered by the Pastwatch Institute. The movie made from it is composed mostly of cobbled-together footage of real events. Filmmakers see it as the ultimate cinema vérité.

Panel 1. In traffic, a Laeske runner. The big lizards are true nomads and live almost entirely on the streets.

PAGE 145
Rachel's using a common device to tune into the soundtrack of a local TV station, not dissimilar to the one Emma used to "carry" her AI, Blythe. Anvardians live almost entirely in artificial light, from the dome (which they can't turn off) and the street lights, which they can. As I've said before, theirs is a truly twenty-four-hour civilization. Work, play, and school go in three four-hour shifts (eight hours, to us). This keeps street traffic and overcrowding down to what inhabitants consider a tolerable level.

A family may get up at what would be to us 8:00 a.m., get school and work over by

4:00 p.m., play and relax until midnight, sleep, and repeat. Or they may get up at four and run the cycle from there, or start from midnight.

Night and day are pretty much what you say they are, but the three time demarcations are pretty rigid for work and school, so people's circadian rhythms, once set, tend to keep them on that single schedule. So, if you're a kid in school, your grade will be divided into three separate classes based on time of day, and you may never meet the kids in the other two subclasses at all. And so on. The effects of the vast crowd of the hours are all around you.

PAGES 148–151
This is an obsessive daydream. This is running through Brig's head half of the time. He's only barely aware of it. It starts up when he feels thwarted or manipulated. It burns him into violent rages sometimes, and he doesn't know what's doing it to him.

The intractability of this fantasy animal is drawn from hounds.

Being a member of a clan, and marrying outside that clan, is romanticized by some people, but the culture shock of doing so is often insurmountable. In Brig's case, he just can't understand emotionally why his wife and kids don't "act right," although intellectually he knew they wouldn't. The very homogeneity that the clans prize creates a terrible craving in some of their members for "something different." Nonclan people are much more accustomed to variations in personality, physiology, and psychology, and handle the crossing of social lines with less distress.

Note Brig's hair: the police usually wear their hair short. The army's far more freewheeling and piratical.

PAGE 152
Marcie's dream bubble contains a butterfly. This was s'posed to refer to two things: the Greek symbol for the psyche was a butterfly, and also the classic solipsistic story about the Chinese philosopher who woke from a dream of being a butterfly, not knowing which was reality. Marcie looks much too babyish here. She's small for her age, but she shouldn't be that small.

"Rensie" was one of Will Eisner's pseudonyms.

PAGE 153
Mature Medawar women wear their hair in elaborate braids. Not all of it is their own. Some of it is the hair of their ancestresses, pinned on as braids or woven into their own hair. This is a defining custom of Medawar womanhood. After death, their heads are shaved, and their hair is partly distributed among their descendants, and partly braided into elaborate knot works that are not worn, but kept in the family shrines. It's a form of ancestor worship.

This is Lady Sethra, well placed in her clan and boss mare of her family, but not as powerful as she acts.

PAGE 154
Milady's family does know that Brig is out of jail. This is their oblique, resentful way of warning Emma that trouble is rumbling on the horizon. Were Emma not alienated from her own clan, the grapevine would take care of the rest.

PAGE 155
The centaur's face is reminiscent of another of my housemates'.

Skoptsy cabs—the Skoptsys were a bizarre Christian cult for whom the rejection of sexuality, evangelism, and the doctrine "If thy hand offend thee, cut it off" were a volatile mix. They violated other doctrines by practicing self-castration. All of the pink bits had to go, including women's breasts. Some believed in forced conversion, for which they were burned out, banned, and shunned by every other Christian cult. Some few still remain in modern Eastern European countries, bizarrely enough, as cab drivers.

Panel 5. Smudko's burger sign on cartop is from the remarkable *Akiko on the Planet Smoo* by Mark Crilley.

Bottom tier. Not all clan people live in neighborhoods dominated by their own clan, but most do. Such neighborhoods are naturally very insular.

PAGE 156
In spite of being the result of a cross-clan marriage, Rachel still has a chance to establish herself in her mother's clan. She fits a lot of the Llaverac criteria, and if she competes

successfully in what is like a cross between a beauty pageant and a cat show, she could find herself breaking into a world of privilege otherwise closed to nonclan people.

Of course, she thinks her mother's people are all crazy, and she is not attracted to male Llaveracs in the slightest.

PAGE 158

Emma, like many of her clan, engages in an intensive form of meditation. For some, it's just an excuse for histrionics. They behave like unbalanced actors. For others, it's a way of reeling in the hyperactive imagination and high-strung emotions common to their clan.

Emma's have come to dominate her life. She feels so out of control that she spends more and more time trying to get herself back together by meditating, and consequently is spending too much time in that strange, dreamlike, disorienting state to get herself straight between sessions. I have no idea who wrote the song she's singing. I used to hear it in older Warner Brothers cartoons, so it must've been a popular song of the thirties. Nobody in Anvard has ever heard of it, which is why Blythe is compelled to write it down. Information is currency to an AI, so she cannot simply record it without her mistress's permission. To her, that would be like stealing the silver.

PAGE 159

These are just random bums from another street crew, not Pete's but a member of Sylvan clan's. They're roustabouts like Jaeger, belonging to no particular clan. Alliances on the street are somewhat fluid, at least for people of no clan.

PAGE 160

The address on the card is a fake. Jaeger set Brig up with this fake place, filled with thrown-away stuff that belonged to his family. Painstakingly arranged to make it look like they really live there. His buddies in the street mobs helped him set it up.

PAGE 162

Brig's old leather jacket has a big patch on the back which shows his chapter affiliation. The military clan into which he was born begins the training of its young people very early. Prior to entry into the army or police, all boys are trained in like fashion, divided into troops called chapters, each roughly equivalent to a company. The chapters vary a lot in demeanor, from prep-school stuffy to good-ol'-boy biker club. The Red River is not entirely spit and polish.

PAGE 163

This city is home to many animals, some fairly large, who evade captors through the tangled-up alleyways but still sometimes get hit by cars. They're like those birds who fly into warehouse-style groceries and set up housekeeping there: building nests in the rafters, chowing down on the fresh produce, dropping what they will on the shoppers' heads, and resisting all attempts to eject them.

Emma's REAL apartment, which is busily being packed up, is a good few cubic miles and traffic headaches away. Even a crow can't fly a straight line in Anvard.

Panel 5. In the family portrait, Lynne's face is obscured by a smaller picture of Marcie. Brig arranged it that way while cleaning, but Lynne would've done the same.

Panel 6. This is a free-man license. It looks like a big, heavy ring, but it is in fact a neural plug. It fits into a jack at the base of the subject's skull. This is a regulatory device for parolees convicted of violent crime.

PAGE 165

This Medawar man is neither a cop nor a soldier, but a priest of a revived god named Huitzilopochtli, of Aztec origin. He was the state god of the Mexica, and like many such was believed to require regular human sacrifice to survive. He has been reinterpreted as the god of the public's lust for gory stories about murder, highway accidents, and other gruesome, violent things.

The priest's war paint is applied to enhance memory, attention span, and visual acuity.

The kid who shot this film was Ruth, who runs the streets with Brig's middle kid Lynne. She and her crew got a lot of money for it.

The white-haired guy with the patterns on his hands is named Eval. He's the only one of the lot who is a member of a clan—Sylvan clan, to be exact.

PAGE 166

The guys all know the address is fake. They helped

set it up and furnish it. Eval was there to make sure it looked lived in.

PAGE 167
All Llaveracs are viewed with some suspicion, since one never knows whether one is dealing with a male or a female until you get her pants off.

PAGE 168
Jaeger's hide is like leather. Rachel's got to scratch him rather hard if she wants him to feel it. She's known since she was a kid that he really likes having his back scratched; she just doesn't know it turns him on.

Jaeger's got the sniffles. For him, this means he's been taking it too easy, and his chronic illness is making a comeback. He needs a physical shock to throw it off.

PAGE 170
Eval, as a member of Sylvan clan, has a certain talent for objective magic. He can't do much besides manipulate smoke and mist into figures, but he's quite good at that.

Down at the bottom of the page, Marcie is holding a small wire-globe toy.

PAGE 172
These few impressions, along with intense anxiety, are all Marcie remembers of her family's escape from her father. The smell of hot chrome will bring it back sometimes, and her little wire toy both fascinates her and makes her a little queasy.

Ne kulturny is a Russian insult, meaning literally "uncultured." Equivalent to "ya ignorant slob." If you don't recognize this quote, go read your Thoreau, ya ignorant slob!

PAGE 173
The city, almost entirely enclosed by its dome, has troubles with fresh air. The dome does have a few big holes in it, but the city is so built up inside it that these aren't anywhere near enough to provide enough airflow. Air scrubbers keep the air clean and circulating—when they work. When they break down, out comes the fog squad. Medawar police, naturally. Every building, house, and car is supposed to be airtight and equipped with a backup air supply. The guys can't smoke because the truck's air supply isn't very sophisticated—just a couple of bottles of oxygen. Jaeger smokes a lot in town because his sense of smell is very acute. Outside cities, he depends on it far less.

The "ceiling" is not the roof of the dome. We are at the level of the river here, and the dome is far, far overhead. This semienclosed cavern is one of many such open spaces.

PAGES 174–177
Here's the physical shock he was needing.

In the center panel of page 174, you can just see the bug that Lynne put on the sole of his boot.

PAGE 177
Da-DAAAHHH! Enter Terry Ellis Lockhart, Emma's father, who is (sadly) just another character I don't have enough time to do very much with just yet. Terry Ellis is a very rich and powerful member of the Llaverac clan. Terry Ellis is male, though she'd slap my face off for saying so.

The little song Emma is singing is from Rodgers and Hammerstein's *The King and I*.

The semitoxic river water gives Jaeger the last of what he needs to shrug off his decline into sickness. He may lose his hair, his smokes, and his clothes (including the boot with the bug), but he'll be fine. If he didn't do this kind of thing, he'd just get sicker and sicker, never getting well until he did something heinous enough to himself to counteract it.

PAGE 178
Terry Ellis and his wife Marion look like they're years and years apart. This is partly custom, and partly vanity. Terry Ellis is, in fact, the elder by quite a bit, although of course asking about it is another slapping offense. Llaveracs favor at least ten years' difference in age between married people, and in this Terry Ellis and Marion are typical. Marion herself is unusual, in that she has not undergone any type of rejuvenation program.

So: Jaeger made his way to a fog-addled drop straight down to the river, which is hemmed in by bridges and buildings. He let the river carry him down a way, then climbed out and started climbing back up. He's done this before and he knew he was upstream of the fake apartment, already vacated by Brigham. Buildings are built every which way in Anvard, on top of each other and the lattice framework of the dome. He's got a long way to climb, but this keeps him healthy. Once in the apartment, he snatched Brig's free-man license.

A "fritillary" is a type of butterfly. The Golden Fritillary is a huge department store in a book by Joan Slonczewski, *Daughter of Elysium*.

PAGE 179
Fight Scene was originally published long after *Sin-Eater*, as issue #22 of the comic series. It has an additional nine pages of story that didn't fit into the twenty-four-page comic back in the day.

PAGE 182
My, my, Jaeger's hair is Shemplike throughout this chapter. Wonder what I was thinking of.

PAGE 183
The only account of a company town that I've read that isn't negative is in the semi-fictionalized memoirs of Homer Hickam. Sounds as if Coalwood was founded with the best of intentions.

PAGE 184
The cabin-shaped climbing gym looks a lot like one that stood in the playground of the grade school I attended. The boys had their show-downs in it from time to time. I don't think it took any instruction from the History Channel to recreate this innocent piece of playground equipment as the Roman Arena. It did afford some privacy from adult eyes.

PAGE 186
How could he know Martha wasn't his mother? I think it's just a matter of having no real bond with her.

PAGE 187
Fly fishing! For big, big dragonflies! If we can eat arthropods that come from the sea, surely we'd eat land-based bugs if they were big enough.

PAGE 188
Martha's son is named Royal; her daughter is Grace. In panel 6, the blurs recite a number of aliases Jaeger's father used, last names all beginning with the letter A.

PAGE 189
I hoped that the blur camouflage would look a little like fingerprints. The thing that always struck me about fingerprints is that they are individual enough to be the ultimate identifier of an individual, but our brains are not geared to recognize them the way we do faces. Even identical twins don't have the same finger-prints, but without training we can't glance at the whorls and swoops of a print and match it with another one. So these guys might even be wearing their own fingerprints on their faces as disguises.

PAGE 190
The Lorax, by Dr. Seuss.

PAGE 192
The company town does offer a fairly high standard of living in a beautiful setting, and protection from the large predators of the area.

PAGE 193
Jaeger did and does love mousy girls.

PAGE 194
The curly-haired kid to the left is the only child-hood friend Jaeger will retain after leaving home.

PAGE 195
The company decides which way you go, be it marriage and family and/or further education or training in a specialty. Only a few have real opportunities to buy their way out of the town.

PAGE 196
Jaeger is beating the guy with a pocketknife clenched in his fist. The company penalizes its citizens for getting hurt or sick. Jaeger did far more damage to this man and his family than just a beating.

PAGE 197
Martha's appearance is based on a cartoon girlie I was drawing back in college. I don't know why I used her here. Just to feel I was delving into something way in the back of my mind, I suppose.

PAGE 200
This is the first time Jaeger suffered from what he thinks of as his chronic condition.

Of course, many would say Jaeger has no real proof that his father is dead, or of how he died. More on that later. Way later.

PAGE 203
As nomads, Ascians can carry very large and elaborate households around with them simply because they have such enormous beasts of burden. The Laeske have done a lot of the work of domesticating the megafauna.

PAGE 206
Everybody knows about throwing a blanket over a guy the better to beat the hell out of him, right? Right. Onwards.

PAGE 208
This is the first of nine pages that weren't in the original version of *Fight Scene*.

PAGE 211
Jaeger wouldn't have had a digital clock in his bed in boot camp. But insomnia to me will always consist mostly of going nuts watching a clock drag along through the night.

PAGE 212
Medawars run on the twenty-four-hour clock, most Anvardians run on a twelve-hour clock, and everybody outside just looks at the sun.

PAGE 214
This training camp was "outside," not under a dome. Rachel was used to being "outside" when she was tiny, though city people think of it as dangerous and uncivilized. Solar radiation does burn your skin, after all. Llaveracs are mortified by their tendency to freckle.

PAGE 220
In retrospect I wish I'd drawn Jaeger in the same clothes (or at least with the same hair) as he appeared on page 216. You'll see him in these clothes at the very end of *Sin-Eater*.

Then again, he's probably told these stories a good few times in a dozen different places.

PAGE 227
This strange, changing face is something I sometimes see when I'm wide awake in a pitch-dark room long enough. It isn't scary; it's just weird. I can influence the way it changes, but only crudely. It definitely goes its own way.

The blue "eyes" are an optical illusion of some kind that I see when I look at a small, dim light, such as an LED, in darkness. I presume it's my eyes trying to use whatever light they can get, but I've never heard of this illusion described by anyone else.

One last oddity: I'll never forget the day I realized that a vague image I was used to seeing out of the corner of my eye was in fact my own eyeballs reflected on the inside of my glasses.

On pages of *Sin-Eater* Part 1, Jaeger dreams of doors and rooms with strange glyphs on the walls. He often dreams of mazes and twisty passages, as he does here on page 1 of part 2. For instance, the figure on the left upright of the door is a rebus. A favorite book of mine, in which I first saw this rebus, is Christopher Manson's *Maze*.

PAGE 228
"*Je Suis Désolé,*" lyrics by Mark Knopfler. It means, more or less, "I'm sorry (I am desolate), but I don't have a choice; I'm sorry, but my life demands it of me." Loosely, "That's just the way I am."

PAGE 229
"The Minstrel Boy" is a traditional Irish revolutionary folk song.

PAGE 231
Brigham, returning to the apartment he thinks belongs to his wife and three kids. He has his tattoos covered with athletic tape. The trigram designs might be recognized as prison markings.

PAGE 233
The hair is Jaeger's. He let the river carry him downstream to the point where he could climb straight up to this apartment, and the water is very caustic.

PAGE 236
Jaeger's eyes are yellow. He's a bit self-conscious about them, since they were considered ugly by the people who adopted him after his father's death.

PAGE 238
This city is a technological enclave, and very much an information culture. There are quite a few professions that deal solely in gathering and dispersing information. They're equal parts spy, gossip monger, and journalist, though they're despised by all three of those groups.

PAGE 240
This is a rather compressed account of (left side) Jaeger's time in the pokey, and (right side) Lynne's time in a Medawar colony after his father Brigham isolated him, his mother

Emma, and his sisters Rachel and Marcie from the rest of the group.

The composition of this page (a white rectangle enclosed by a black one) is something Lynne drew obsessively when he was younger. He still has a boxful of similar drawings at the bottom of his closet.

PAGE 242
Panel 3. Jaeger won't say no to Marcie when she asks him directly. She is unknowingly invoking an ancient code of ethics which he, as a Finder, can't help but honor.

Panel 6. Emma's "wedding ring scar" is still visible. Wear the same ring on the same finger for long enough, and it can mark your hand. Old wives' tales make much more of this, and that's just how it makes Emma feel: like an old wife.

Panel 7. When Lynne says, "they're all like that," he could mean all adults or all men.

PAGE 243
Jaeger overheard Emma singing *"Je Suis Désolé"* in his sleep, and it seeped into his dream. Where Emma got it is much less easy to explain.

Panel 6. Artificial intelligences like Blythe are programmed to pester their owners continually for new upgrade packages. They're depended on for too much to be designed to "break," so this is their makers' answer to planned obsolescence.

PAGE 244
The kids are used to their mother being "out" for set times of the day. Usually she can zone out during her meditations and thereby keep it from happening spontaneously. She is able to lead a relatively normal life, but, like lots of people with mental steeplechases to run, she has trouble keeping the day-to-day things straight. Blythe looks after the finances, and Rachel plays "little mom." All three kids display the self-sufficiency common to kids with "absent" parents.

PAGE 247
Tourists abound in summer, traveling slowly from city to city in luxurious zeppelins. Immigrants flood in during the winter, to escape the cold and sell to the rich folks, and celebrate Carnival. This tour group is a late one; it's winter outside.

Panel 2. Bobbi Ba Beer. Vietnam vets described the local beer as being flavored with formaldehyde. I'm guessing this is like putting antifreeze in grape juice so that it can be passed off as wine. This version of Bobbi Ba has a lot of other semitoxic substances in it as well—not for the squeamish.

PAGE 248
This bit with the kid wandering onto the train happened on my first trip to New York. The kid was maybe two or three, and when the train doors opened, she just wandered blithely onboard. The doors were just starting to close when her mom turned, saw her on the train, let out this tire-squealing shriek, and lunged for her kid; the door closed on her arm, and it seemed like a very long time before the doors opened again. The rest of the family was engaged in screeching and beating on the windows. I don't think any of them spoke English, and the thought of what could happen to a tiny kid in a foreign city stuck with me.

PAGE 249
Yes! The shaving cream song! Another childhood wasted on Dr. Demento.

PAGE 251
This is Brigham's internalized version of Jaeger speaking.

PAGE 252
What he sees is that the house is completely empty. He's in a terribly hyperreactive state of mind, and so his imagination supplies him with the worst possible image.

PAGE 253
That's our tour group, way down on the lower left corner.

PAGE 255
This is Swann. He's from Sylvan clan. He's a quiet, retiring mob boss. Whoops, make that clan official . . . The higher reaches of clan structure are basically familiar politicians and bureaucrats, but further down, closer to the street level, they more closely resemble the Mafia. Swann has a deep, gravelly, Max von Sydow kind of voice incongruous with his skinny, bird-boned frame.

PAGE 256
This is the palazzo of Llaverac clan, where the clanhead and the highest of the high live.

This family is headed by a queen (natch). It is common for a clanhead to be referred to as if he or she were the only member: "*the*" Llaverac, "*the*" Sylvan, *etc*.

The lion-women call themselves Nyima. The Nyima is one of the largest nonhuman civilizations. They live outside the domes, are very territorial, and extremely dangerous. Male Nyima are rarely seen by outsiders.

PAGES 257–258
This whole business with Swann and Jaeger was another story trying to be born. Swann had a problem: a Sylvan street-tough kid harassing a nonclan old lady. The Sylvans are a fastidious, orderly family. They don't like beating up their own, but they won't balk at hiring somebody else to do it, so Swann hired Jaeger. Now, Jaeger has no problem with doing people favors, but he has ethical problems with accepting payment or gifts.

Jaeger's life is a mass of contradictions. He keeps moving because he can't reconcile them for long. He's a warrior, and as such a leader can bestow wealth in the form of goods and weapons upon him. He's a Finder, and since Finders are supposed to act for the common good, they are not supposed to take rewards. He's a sin-eater, and though a sin-eater is supposed to take on the blame for another person's crimes, a sin-eater is never supposed to do this without being paid.

Jaeger, strangling on his own leash, should have been at the heart of this story. I can only say that, if this story was too ambitious for my skills as a writer, at least I learned quite a lot while blundering through it.

PAGE 259
This bathroom is inside Temple House, one of the classiest brothels in Anvard. Ice cream with alcohol on it was supposed to symbolize a desirable mix of innocence and experience.

PAGE 260
I first read this argument in Neil Gaiman's introduction to the fifth collection of *Omaha, the Cat Dancer.*

Jaeger lives by the mooch law. He does all kinds of things to stay fed and clothed, and never stints at mooching off his friends. Given that he'll do anything his friends want, and give them anything of his that they want, he doesn't see anything wrong with this. He usually doesn't steal. He occasionally Dumpster-dives, and ornamental ducks and koi are never safe around him. Barter, he understands. Money, not very well.

PAGE 262
This is a predominantly Llaverac neighborhood. Jaeger has set up a fake apartment here to distract Brigham from finding the one his estranged family is actually occupying.

Why? Jaeger thinks Brig is dangerous. He thinks Brig can't help but hurt his family, that he won't be able to control himself. Jaeger can't go to the cops for a multitude of reasons, but top of the list is the fact that cops can't do much about something that hasn't happened yet.

Jaeger set up the fake apartment with Swann's help—that was really all the help he wanted from Swann. He was hoping that if Brig was going to snap, he'd do it far away from fragile Emma, and in doing so maybe he'd realize what he is in danger of becoming. So Jaeger sent him into a neighborhood where Emma's face would be on every passerby.

PAGE 263
"Make a prayer." Jaeger knew that if Brig snapped, he'd probably attack someone who looked like Emma. Jaeger could only hope that whoever got caught in the blast would be better able to survive it than Emma. Of course, now he has a certain obligation to Brigham's victim. This is a small sacrifice, of leather rather than blood. It's a promise that he'll try to find her and make it up to her. Finders have complicated consciences.

PAGE 264
Long Tom was the name of the pirates' cannon in *Peter Pan*. As for fever cannons, they were placed all up and down the Mississippi in Louisiana. It was thought that firing these cannons dispersed the hot, damp air that was considered the cause of diseases such as yellow fever.

The old man's father probably was a Finder in the same way a griot and a minstrel are kind of the same thing but aren't thought of in exactly the same way. To the old man, a Finder is an ultimate adventurer and explorer. To Jaeger, it's a secret society. To others, it's more like being a forest ranger.

Blaue Engel. Marlene Dietrich's first movie was called *Der Blaue Engel*. The physical appearance of the Llaveracs is partly based on hers.

PAGE 269

Metapolis was an attempt to step back and incorporate more information about the various characters. It worked this one time. "Meta" means "between two states," or "the act of moving from one state to another."

PAGE 271

Dreams are very important to Jaeger's adoptive people. Developing the faculty for remembering everything that happens during sleep is considered one of the most important marks of adulthood. Personally, I think it sounds exhausting.

PAGE 272

The Hy-Brasil Theater is a typical neighborhood hangout. A lot of people don't keep TVs in their houses, because a TV with an off switch is not within everybody's price range. It's far easier just to go to the theater on the corner to see the news or their favorite show or a movie. Ticket prices are dirt cheap and shows run continuously. Most theaters are owned by a single station, and play only that station's programming, so each station competes to set up a theater on every corner.

Hy-Brasil was an old word for heaven.

Note the large, feathery dinosaur. This is a male Laeske in last year's breeding plumage. His long feathers mean he was successful in his courtship. All males who don't breed shed their fancy feathers at the end of breeding season.

PAGE 273

Most of this city's inhabitants have never seen any more of the sky than what is visible here. The Black Angel monument is a popular place to view the sky, although it is not considered as spectacular as nature footage on the big screen at the local theaters.

PAGE 274

Ivitye, as a goddess, is not so much an immaterial being who is believed to have influence over the lives and fates of living people as she is an anthropomorphized mnemonic. In other words, she was invented to explain what the dome does. Giving a thing a name and a vivid image makes a complicated lesson easier to remember. Devices like Ivitye are not to be taken literally.

What she stands for is well known. Anvardian scholars have been savaging each other for generations over who made her up, and whether she is a human or a Laeske invention.

PAGE 275

Seasonal immigration begins when the last harvest is in and the farmers start scurrying for winter jobs. Jaeger came in with the other itinerants—traders, road crews, truckers, nomads of all types and descriptions. He came in when things were still pretty quiet. He knows that anybody can get in before Carnival, but after Carnival ends, there will be a scouring of the streets, and any immigrant without a job and a fixed place to live will get hucked out the back door like yesterday's chicken necks.

Many of the jobs these immigrants get pay little more than the city's exit fee. Yep, they throw you out and make you pay for the privilege. Most know they won't get jobs, and won't be able to stay in the city through the worst of the winter. They don't waste their time. They do a whole year's worth of trading in six weeks or so, culminating in a frenzy of buying, selling, and stealing during Carnival.

Lynne's fear of puberty is nothing unusual. Every kid worries about how he or she will turn out when that god-awful biological machine grinds into gear. But Lynne has more reason than most to worry. The males of his mother's clan are extremely feminine. He knows they grow breasts as well as other curves. In his father's clan, the hair of boys his age has begun to change to the deep chestnut color of adulthood. Girls' hair stays light for quite a few more years. His own hair has not begun to change, so he's dyeing it.

PAGE 277

Rachel's friend Duryea is named after an actor from the forties and fifties, Dan Duryea. She doesn't look a thing like him, though.

Graves is a family that's part of the Labres clan. On the whole, Labres have a high degree of conformity of appearance, though they're one of those confusing clans that have different standards for males and females. Males are supposed to be tall, thin, and angular, while females are supposed to be under five feet four inches in height, small, and boyish. Those girls who inherit their fathers' height, or boys who favor their mothers: well, they're outta luck. They won't be accepted as full members, in spite of their pedigrees.

In contrast are the Llaveracs, who all conform to the same feminine ideal, and the Medawars, who emphasize differences between the sexes with sex-specific clothing and social roles. Lynne and Rachel are both a bit preoccupied with gender, being the offspring of two such different clans.

PAGE 278
Emma's ring scar again. In her case, that mark is partly a burn scar.

Panel 5. All of these people are members of Medawar clan, except Emma. Brigham thought he didn't want one of his own clan's solid, serious women. He was attracted to the clan his people dismiss as flighty idiots or perverts, the Llaveracs, because of their glamour and beauty.

He also wanted land. The Grosvenors are traditionally civic-army people, that is to say city cops. He was not entitled to settle outside the dome in a colony city. His defying custom in marrying outside his clan caused him to be shunted into a hardship position in the colonial army. This was, to his family, the best way for him to serve the common good, or get him killed young. Either would do as long as it got him out of the city and unable to influence the young people.

PAGE 279
The army often goes out with the stated intention of stopping small wars along trade routes and highways. They do this by taking over and settling there, sometimes displacing the residents. Calling for help from a city's standing army is asking for overlords.

"Mutt soldiers" are nonclan people like Jaeger, and once they're out in the middle of nowhere, they're not considered much above slave labor.

These large lizards are called rauo, plural rauos. As in falconry, rank determines what mount you're entitled to ride. The animal Jaeger is riding is a byelo: light, fast, and stupid as a sack of hammers. Brigham's loaning even this lowly riding animal to Jaeger is no small favor.

Rauos are easily tamed, but tend to over-bond with one rider. If they're not circulated regularly among several riders, they can become viciously possessive. They will attack anyone who comes near "their" rider.

City dwellers have very odd ideas about the outside. They tend to be hypochondriacal about the effects of unfiltered air, unscreened sunlight, *etc*. That's why they're so bundled up.

PAGE 280
Rachel remembers almost nothing of her life before coming to the ancient manor house in the new colony city of Tsarskoe. Her childhood memories are dominated by the big, dark, ornate house, and her mind is still laid out according to its architecture. It is so much a part of her personal cosmos that she had forgotten the name of the town, and was surprised to find it in a history book.

PAGE 281
Rachel and Lynne were very close as young kids, even though there is four years' difference between them. Their gender differences were less of a problem then.

PAGE 282
Jaeger's yellow eyes have always set him apart from the brown-eyed Ascians, the people who adopted him. He's so inured to the Ascian unease with light-colored irises that he himself is a little uncomfortable with blue- or gray-eyed people.

Byelos are mounts and carrying animals of the very lowest ranks. They're often given to young boys to train. In this way, the boys are also trained.

PAGE 283
Lynne cracks Rachel's skull for a number of reasons. He forgets she's a girl and doesn't like to be reminded. He doesn't want her to be disappointed because she isn't allowed to do boy things but doesn't want to show sympathy. He wouldn't be allowed to go with the boys himself, because of their mother, and he can't hit his mother. The other boys beat his ass regularly for being different, and for being attached to his sister. And so on, and so on . . . He knows she can beat the snot out of him, but he's just infuriated when she cries because he can't keep all this inside of him.

PAGE 284
Panel 1. In this panel, Rachel is in the present day. The rest is her memory. She's telling her story to the unseen oracle in the Painwright Gallery.

Panel 4 recalls the spring ceremony Rachel thought back to in part 1. After that event, she wasn't so eager to take part in this yearly celebration, which is dominated by prepubescent girls.

Panel 5. This is when Jaeger "hurt his head and was sent home," as related to Lynne on page 68 of part 1. He was sent back to Anvard in a coma. He's never told the whole story of how he was hurt.

Panel 6. Rachel is choking on her own shame because she thinks her father moved her family out of the manor house because he was ashamed of her, and didn't want the other Medawars to see his failed family anymore. Kids do overdramatize, but she wasn't far from the truth.

The worst thing was, the manor house was huge. It had plenty of room to run and play, even though the kids weren't allowed to go outside. The living space in this house's basement was less than fifteen by thirty feet.

PAGE 285

Paregoric is a narcotic stomach medicine. Marcie spent more of her childhood asleep than awake.

This "wet sheet" method of restraining a struggling human being was once commonly used in asylums and psychiatric hospitals. Cheaper than straitjackets and in some ways more effective, it gave the patient something to struggle against when emotions ran too high.

To this day, Emma has no idea what happened to the colony on Tsarskoe. She was far too out of it to put anything together, and was never recognized for what she was: a survivor and an eyewitness.

PAGE 286

Rachel went to the Painwright Gallery to speak to the oracle because she wanted answers, and doesn't realize that the oracles don't deal in plain talk.

PAGE 289

The Medawar man is a representative of the Church of Huitzilopochtli. They piece together video footage to make gruesome movies about death and bloodshed. These movies are intensely popular. Think of this guy as a movie producer more than a priest.

Huitzilopochtli himself was an Aztec deity. His worshipers believed the gods had to have blood sacrifices in order to delay the end of the world. This was all tied into acquisition of wealth, social mobility, and imperialism, but what it amounted to was an awful lot of war and an awful lot of human sacrifice. In Anvard, this church has coagulated around people's prurient fascination with murder, and named itself after an ancient blood god.

PAGE 290

Jaeger and the producer are each sitting in a shallow dish-shaped alcove, directly across from each other. Together these alcoves form a "whisper gallery." This phenomenon was first discovered in large churches and cathedrals with paired arches across a central nave. Each shallow dish reflects and receives sound, just as paired satellite dishes do. In such a gallery, a person positioned with his or her head at the focal point of each alcove can be plainly heard by a person at the focal point of the other alcove. The speaker's volume makes no difference. Other people standing nearby, but not in the focal point, may hear little or nothing. Traffic passing between the alcoves will not disturb the voices' transmission unless it's a truck tall enough to break the parabolic path of the arches.

PAGE 291

The producer records both sound and image of everything around him. He has risen to a position of prominence in his church because of his ability to capture vivid footage.

PAGE 294

The wendigo is a cannibal spirit among the Indians of the Northeast. It got into people and made them do hideous things.

Many medieval stories of werewolves were born in times of famine so severe that people mobbed gibbets to pull down the bodies of the hanged to eat their flesh before it even got cold. The resurrectors of Huitzilopochtli make much of things like this.

PAGE 297

There are a lot of people who cut themselves, bite themselves, scratch themselves, or do themselves other harm. Some call themselves "cutters." To oversimplify greatly, they do it because what's in their head hurts worse, and physical pain distracts them. It reminds them that they're still real and still inside their bodies. This behavior is not new to Brig. He's been gnawing his fingers since he was a kid; they're covered with calluses. He usually doesn't break the skin, unless his frustration is really overwhelming.

PAGE 298
The paint that runs down the steps of the Painwright Gallery is another reference to Huitzilopochtli, although the gallery is not run by the church. In the old days of the blood god's worship, blood ran halfway down the steps of his temples.

PAGE 299
This is the ballroom of the great manor house in Tsarskoe, in which Rachel spent so many years of her childhood. The staircase in which she and Lynne often hid is behind the "camera"—behind you, if you were there instead of simply looking at her now.

PAGE 301
What exactly is Rachel's fear? That there is no safe place anywhere, that no home is safe enough? That if it is strong enough to protect her, it is too small and confining for her to stay inside? That her desire to be safe can never be satisfied? That trying to escape from or take action against her vague, unnamed fears will be a hundred times worse than passively allowing them to roll over her?

PAGE 302
Jaeger has gone through a lot of changes in the back of my head. When I was young, he wasn't even human. In translation, he once looked not exactly like "John," but as if he were John's relative.

John is the oracle, temporarily displaced outside the auditorium. It really liked Rachel, and it's being very kind to her. It's volunteering information, and it means well. Frankly, the janitor guy is the oracle too, but it's done talking.

PAGE 305
Fantasies can become a deadly disease. Emma's do get ahold of her sometimes, just as Brig's do.

PAGE 307
SGM stands for sergeant major. The Medawar women, who begin medical training at an early age, have rank and order roughly equivalent to that of their militant menfolk. The markings on their faces are "war paint," psychoactive topical applications distinguished by color and location on the face and body. These enhance concentration and certain motor skills, and are mostly used by surgeons.

Medawar girls embarking upon a medical career do not gain their first rank until they reach the age of eighteen. Prior to that, they're in the Med Scouts, which they enter at age six. This is in addition to regular schooling, and gets more rigorous as they grow. Girls of ten are not uncommonly seen handling quite a few chores in a hospital setting, but more often they're seen doing routine medical duties in residential areas. Delivering prescriptions, helping with physical therapy, some day-nurse duties, some ambulance and paramedic work. Lynne is only thought of as slightly precocious.

PAGE 315
These representatives of Jaeger's tribal religious structure are here in Anvard as part of a circuit they travel. The Shrivers, as a body, do not belong strictly to Jaeger's tribe or even to the Ascians as a whole. They are racially mixed and move from place to place in a huge circle. The steeply peaked roof is their "nomad's cathedral," a very large and imposing tent. They can disassemble the whole thing and be on the road in a surprisingly short amount of time.

PAGE 316
These are memory traces in Lynne's mind. These voices are recorded in his mind and repeat themselves at the proper triggers. They will be with him always. The Shrivers never try to modify memories, though they may work to establish connections between them.

PAGE 317
Memory traces sum up larger and more extensive memories, which the Shrivers are causing Lynne to reexperience. This is very dangerous.

PAGE 319
Obviously this scene did not take place within Lynne's sight and hearing. This only happened once. In Lynne's mind, the event took on such great proportions that he remembers it as having happened several times a month. He has built false memories out of a real event. It appears far worse in his nightmares.

PAGE 321
Those marks on Lynne's right arm are the

result of his having taken a liberty with a hunting lizard the Medawar men captured wild and were trying to tame and train. They're old and faint, but in his mind they're battle scars to be proud of, and as such show up strongly in his mental self-image.

PAGE 322
The details of the trouble Brigham is counseling this young officer over aren't important. Brigham and many other officers see the Internal Affairs division, which investigates the behavior of officers and soldiers as something just shy of the Spanish Inquisition. Here in the boonies, in the debatable lands, it's pretty haphazard and unfair. Brig's not entirely wrong, but he *is* a weasel.

PAGE 323
Back to Anvard. Another winter, another Carnival. This is Lynne's Llaverac grandfather. The song is "I Need a Man" by Annie Lennox.

PAGE 324
Medawars and Llaveracs are inevitably going to view one another as vulgar and distasteful. Emma and Brigham, in marrying outside their clans, are really quite the rebels.

Seen briefly in panel 5 is Kalif, Lynne's half-horse street buddy. The centaurs, like the Nyima, are a force to be reckoned with outside the city, but are rarely seen inside it.

PAGE 325
Back to the old manor house, this time in Lynne's memory. The old house is much more fragmentary in Lynne's mind than in Rachel's. Older kids are better at the art of memory.

Rachel is reading Beatrice, from Shakespeare's *Much Ado About Nothing*. When Rachel began "turning into a girl," Lynne felt quite betrayed.

PAGE 327
Marcie was born in the manor house, and the family was moved out of it into the tiny house's basement within a few months afterward. Note that Marcie's had her dust bunny since before she can remember.

The doll in panel 5 is based on the trickster figure Pau-Henoa, from Rachel Hartman's *Amy Unbounded.*

PAGE 329
The staircase is on the south side of the ballroom of the manor house. The priest's hole under the stairs was one of the many hideouts they had to defend themselves from the other kids under ten years old. The presence of a heat register (floor grating intended to let heat travel upward from the floor below) is evidence that it really was meant for people to hide in—to spy in. The register allows fresh air and sound to enter along with heat.

PAGE 330
Kids hear things. Adults really are aliens, and they're up to no good.

PAGE 332
Lynne attempted to kill his father by injecting him with battery acid. He had access to all sorts of potent things in the hospital pharmacy, but only if he could get past the old ladies who guard them—old ladies accustomed to dealing with ten-year-olds. That's the practical reason for the gruesome nature of his choice of poison. The subjective reason was simply that he didn't believe anything less than a nuclear bomb would kill the old man. He used the most hideous substance he could think of, and it didn't work.

PAGE 333
This interrogation and subsequent trip down amnesia lane has all been taking place inside Lynne's head. The Shrivers' equipment gives the Shrivers a window into that perspective. The Shrivers are trying to exorcise the kid's demons while not robbing him of them. They are well aware that sometimes causing someone to reexperience their memories can be very damaging, but it's their belief that the only appropriate penance for some crimes is self-knowledge.

More "war paint." This pattern enhances memory and blunts dissociative tendencies.

PAGE 334
The Shrivers cannot absolve Lynne of his crimes. They can only try to help save his humanity. Jaeger's job as sin-eater is more along the lines of absolution.

PAGE 335
On the subway: the soccer stuff is a story unto itself. He's good at soccer. It's the only thing about school he likes. Having raised him

as a girl, Emma unthinkingly placed him in a girls' school. He was a soccer star until the headmistress found out he wasn't a girl, and everything's topsy-turvy now.

PAGE 336
Hospital administration again, Huitzilopochtli representative again. The church is incredibly wealthy, and supports a lot of financially risky ventures to get its material. They're parasites, sure—but trauma units are hard to keep running, especially in charity hospitals.

PAGE 337
Anything goes at Carnival. People complain about the chaos, but even that is considered a Carnival ritual.

Why did this idiot kid want to send his father's corpse home where his family could see it? Just to show them that it was all over, really. He just didn't count on the old man not being dead. Lynne certainly didn't count on being stolen from the hospital by some hairy-knuckled thug and delivered up to some psychological intrusion by itinerant holy men. Jaeger thinks that this has made some bond between them. He feels responsible for the boy now. He only half understands how much that makes Lynne hate him.

PAGE 339
Carnival may have begun, but that's no reason to cut back on pedantic TV shows. There's something about knowing that your face will be projected onto a screen three times bigger than God that really brings out the pompousness in Anvard's scholars.

Note that our current pedant is a member of Sylvan clan, like Swann and Eval. Sylvans are not albinos, but they're quite pale and tend to have light blue or gray eyes. The uniformity of their clan makes them unusually accepting of what few variations do turn up within their membership. Green eyes, or even brown, are highly prized, if they are sufficiently light in color as to cast no hint of non-Sylvan ancestry. Their pale eyes make Jaeger very uncomfortable.

PAGE 341
In retrospect, I wish I'd drawn Jaeger holding onto a huge rock as he falls, or maybe a lead weight with a handle, or something like that. He's eager to get where he's going.

PAGE 342
Downing Street is a "traffic well," enabling cars to move from higher to lower levels within the city. Anyone who's ever been in a traffic circle can tell you how well such things would work.

PAGES 343–345
The Lake of the Clouds is one of Anvard's most famous vistas. The city is so overgrown and built one-on-top-of-the-other that it's not uncommon for the residents of one level to have no idea what lies above or below them. To people looking down into the cistern, which contains part of the bay, it simply looks as if there are clouds drifting along the bottom of the lake, obscuring anything that might lie below. To residents below, it just looks like one of the many miniature weather patterns that often form in the larger caverns of the city. It is the only lake Jaeger knows of that really is bottomless.

The rooftop of this building is covered with small change and expensive cameras. Jaeger was shown this place by some Traveler kids who come up here regularly to collect money and anything not too broken. They don't care where the money comes from; it was he who figured out that he could get from high to low the same way people's wishing-well coins do.

PAGE 345
Panel 5. That's Buzz; he got the fuzz; he makes the elevator do what she does.

PAGE 346
These two women are teenaged Medawars. At this stage in their education, they are orderlies at a hospital. They're bringing Brigham to his family's house as per his kid Lynne's request. Since Lynne works at that hospital as well, nobody questioned this, but Brig was known to be unbalanced enough to require guards. Hence these two tough, well-trained girls . . . who are nonetheless still teenagers and subject to the stupidities of their age.

PAGES 347–348
All these things work. The number of destructive devices that can be made from ordinary household items is really appalling.

PAGE 349
Now we are in the Pastwatch Institute, place of garbled history. The Hopeless Diamond was engineered by scientists trying to create a principle by which planes with as little radar

signature as possible could be built. The planes of the diamond reflect radar signals every way except back toward the source, and a plane the size of a B-2 can have the radar signature the size of a pigeon. Of course, the Anvardians don't know that. They are like the scholars of the Renaissance, trying to recover the wisdom of older civilizations bit by bit.

The Nehi leg lamp was a newspaper-quiz prize back in the fifties. Nehi soda bottles used to have a shapely female leg printed on them. Knee-high, get it? That's the coveted major award won by Ralphie's dad in Jean Shepherd's *In God We Trust, All Others Pay Cash.* No, the Anvardians don't know that either.

Frida Kahlo's memory has been confused with that of Frito's corn chips. Makes for some vivid bag graphics, mind you; Anvardians enjoy nonsequiturs.

PAGE 350
Blythe may be an artificial intelligence, but she's equipped with just as thorny a set of rules to live by as any of us. Emma's vagueness makes her depend on Blythe too much, and this puts great stress on what is essentially an anthropomorphized answering machine and notepad.

I'm not going to list the real lyrics from these songs. Trust me—they're all wrong.

PAGE 351
Well, this one isn't wrong. This is "No One Lives Forever," by Danny Elfman, et al., in the good old days of Oingo Boingo.

Emma is a sort of reverse psychic, who hears the past instead of the future. The scientists in Anvard are forever searching for people with this talent. For her, it's just a byproduct. She hears songs from the past when she teeters into or out of her dreamscape.

PAGE 352
Here we see the Burning God. His image is reflected in many ways in Emma's dreamscape, as is Memwahr, the Lady of Smoke. No matter what shapes they assume, they have no true identity to Emma, but are wholly themselves.

PAGE 353
This mutual destruction is also a common theme in Emma's daymares. It is said of reflective people that they make terrible advocates, because they are too likely to see, and give weight to, the other side of an argument. The sad fact is, life isn't like the movies. Just assigning an identity, a real person's face under the char of the Burning God, doesn't free Emma of him.

PAGE 356
One thing you find out about New Orleans is that when Mardi Gras moves in, the locals move *out.* When the parades are in full swing, it seems like there are just as many people headed out as there are coming in. If you live there, it can be fairly hellish. The streets are jammed, you can't drive anywhere, and damn near anything can happen. Jaeger's getting around the only fast way there is.

Panel 3 is the first of many flash-forwards to come. Note how faded his tattoo is. Stress speeds up the dissolution.

PAGE 357
The problem with Brigham? Everybody has a different opinion of what that is. Jaeger's dilemma is a terrible one, well known to police today. What do you do to a man who hasn't done anything, but who you are certain will kill his target if he ever gets the chance?

PAGE 359
Brig is, in his corkscrew way, aware that Jaeger broke his legs to keep him from being a danger to his family. He's a little pissed that he still is potentially dangerous. In his mind, Jaeger didn't harm him any more than Lynne did. In his mind, if he's still able to hurt Emma, it's Jaeger's fault.

PAGE 360
I was listening to the old Gregory Peck version of *Moby Dick* while working on this page. The man in panel 6 is not exactly Queequeg, but I do love that Maori man. Many of the people in the streets are seasonal immigrants, like these tattooed spearmen.

PAGE 361
See, Marcie's spell was for a father. She thought it would make Jaeger stay. She's used to the idea that magic doesn't always do what you want it to.

PAGE 362
This is an electronic leash worn by some ex-convicts while still on parole. It does different things for different men; in Brig's case it's supposed to suppress adrenaline production,

a common therapy for shell-shocked soldiers. Brigham left it in the fake apartment. Its presence here in the real one is enough to tweak his paranoia in the sharpest way.

PAGE 364
Like the story Brig was telling himself about the boy with the bomb: sometimes there's no good place to throw it. Some sacrifice themselves; some say, "Aaah, fuck you!"

PAGE 365
Very cathartic, screaming. In high school, many of my classmates and I blew off steam by screaming our heads off in parking lots late at night. The local cops just loved us.

PAGE 366
Any kind of pyrotechnics will do for Carnival, and these folks don't know what a mushroom cloud is, anyway.

PAGE 367
These dice are white, black, red, green, blue, and yellow. The irregular object is a small ball of foil; it represents the seeker. This is the same divinatory set that Jaeger presented Miss Lennie with back in part 1.

PAGE 368
Panels 6 and 7. These are Jaeger's father and stepmother Martha. Jaeger did say that his father raised a hand to him. The truth is, what Jaeger considers a beating may not be what you or I would. The big fight never happened, so to him it's as if no fight between him and his father ever happened.

PAGE 369
Panel 1. These are the street kids from the early issues, revisited. These are the kids Lynne runs with.

Now, if the bomb had gone off, it might very well have killed Jaeger. He might possibly have been hurt only within his remarkable ability to heal himself, and walked out of the hospital on his own. Or he might have been so brain damaged he would have remained a vegetable. Or perhaps his instinct for self-preservation would have caused him to reflexively bat the bomb off to the right, where it could have killed Rachel at least, and he'd have had to live with that. It could always be worse, and often is.

PAGE 370
Jaeger thinks Brig just cracked, perhaps due to posttraumatic stress disorder. Lynne thinks he was a plain murderer camouflaged as a soldier. Emma blames it on cultural clash—that is to say, herself. Everybody's got a theory.

This is a series of flashbacks and flash-forwards. Jaeger is sitting in an outlands trading post, sort of like a saloon and a general store rolled together, telling yarns with the rest of the guys.

PAGE 372
Many of Emma's clan are inclined to be flaky. They prize it, even when it's not oriented around a meticulously structured dreamscape like hers.

PAGE 373
Guys like Jaeger don't talk about themselves much because they simply don't waste much time thinking about themselves. Girls like Rachel, however, spend entirely too much time both talking and thinking.

PAGE 374
Magic, faith, proof, belief...There are a lot of things Rachel would really like to believe in, but her common sense gets in the way, for good or ill.

Jaeger doesn't really have much faith in the oracles, except as a way of talking to himself. When Rachel needs to make a decision, she consults the telephone. She calls everybody she knows and talks their ears off, gets their advice, and then goes ahead and does... something. Call it peer-o-mancy. Jaeger talks to almost nobody, if he can help it, and so uses weird things like dice rolling to help him think.

PAGE 376
Jaeger has been trained from an early age to take blame onto himself. This is a trait much searched for in people of low enough rank to become sin-eaters. If the ability isn't present, it's instilled.

PAGES 377–378
This, then, is one of the things sin-eaters do. Jaeger followed this crowd of Ascians after his father died. They passed through his part of the world regularly. He was eventually adopted, but in the lowly role of sin-eater. He might have aspired to higher rank if anyone had taken a shine to him, but, until his remarkable

recuperative abilities showed themselves, nobody did.

The sin-eaters were the old man's last chance. If one of the Shakmah family had stood up and agreed to take the grandfather's punishment, that person would almost certainly not have had to take the beating. For his former offenses, fines were sufficient. But nobody stood up, so only the sin-eaters were left, and a sin-eater is never shown mercy. It is considered deeply wrong, disrespectful, to give a sin-eater an easy punishment.

Jaeger took the beating, and, having survived it, was adopted by a Finder to be taught that arcane knowledge. Since then he really believes that the only way out is through.

PAGE 379

Yes, the brochure is talking. Electronics are everywhere, and literacy is less depended on than it should be. Lynne has turned off the little holographic cartoon that normally accompanies this spiel.

The dark marks on the orderlies' cheeks are livid slap-marks. It's a ritualized reprimand. Usually when such things become customs, they become perfunctory and not very harsh, Sergeant Major Durga, however, has a palm like a brick and a slap that can rattle your teeth.

PAGE 381

Rachel doesn't know what's been going on, but she does know that there's no way that Brig could've gotten ahold of Marcie's toy without there being some connection between him and Jaeger.

PAGE 382

Blythe does have her own agenda. Her designers meant for her to be the perfect servant, but they also programmed her to be acquisitive of knowledge and control of her environment.

PAGE 383

The snake pit is yet another of the old medieval curatives. It was thought that if the mad were thrown into pits full of snakes that fear would drive the devils out and make them well. Of course, snake pits were also methods of execution, so perhaps they thought that the mad would either be made well or killed, and either way would no longer be a problem.

PAGE 384

Rachel finally hits the nail on the head. The thing she realizes in that split second is that it ain't likely to endear her to him.

PAGE 385

Medusa is either derived from *metis* (prudence) or *medon* (ruler). Medusa was one of three sisters, the Gorgons. *Gorgon* means monstrous, horrible, but the three sisters weren't horrible at all until Medusa dallied with Poseidon in a temple dedicated to Athena. Long an enemy of Poseidon, Athena put the mojo on Medusa and her sisters for defiling her holy ground. They became monsters with brass wings, brass claws, and snakes for hair, and any mortal who looked directly at their faces turned to stone. They lived on an island way out in the Western Sea.

It has been proposed that the story of Medusa, her killing by Perseus, and her body giving birth not only to Pegasus, but also to a great hero bearing a golden spear, is a huge and exceedingly complex political fable. If Pegasus, fathered by Poseidon (who was often associated with horses), was symbolic of a swift sailing ship, Medusa must have had quite a fleet. If her image became part of Athena's breastplate, she must have been associated with wisdom and warfare. Metis was the name of the goddess of wisdom, swallowed by Zeus, who gave birth to Athena inside the big man's skull. Untangling this kind of thing is the work of many lifetimes.

PAGE 388

This is the same trading post seen at the beginning of part 1.

KING OF THE CATS

PAGE 394
These four-legged creatures are called uluhaka by the Nyima, and are believed to be domesticated animals. The males run feral quite often. Females have never been observed in the wild.

PAGE 395
These women are third-tier wives of King Maroshezo, who rules over one of the few kingdoms that have acquired guns. The Nyima are eager to seize upon any new advantage, but they resist any new trade goods that they cannot make on their own. King Maro's highest-ranking daughters made it their duty to set up a small factory to make these guns and ammunition.

PAGE 396
It was speculated that the uluhaka are killed for food in lean times, but this has not been borne out by observation. The Nyiman women are typically very protective of their four-legged companions, and vice versa. Nyiman women rarely appear in cities without uluhaka escorts.

PAGES 399–401
This scene is a variation on the opening of *Sin-Eater,* the first *Finder* novel. The idea was suggested by my friend Boyce Kline, and Mike McNeil suggested the "snake eyes" line.

Poor Jaeger. Woe betide the favorites of gods who think they're funny.

PAGE 402
Dream over. Jaeger is riding in a small gun port on the side of an armored tour bus. Tourists often travel in huge, ponderous dirigibles—but not over the territories of Nyima who might or might not have guns with which to shoot them down. Jaeger got a job as a gunner on this line just to have a fast way of covering ground. He didn't know which way it was going and didn't much care.

This dad and his kids are Steinehans.

PAGE 403
First look at Munky. Up till now, Jaeger thought these people were making a religious pilgrimage, based on their awe and excitement. This is his first clue that there's something a bit more secular going on.

PAGES 404–405
A *buena vista*, indeed.

PAGE 406
I first saw drawings of the motor-sensory homunculi in Carl Sagan's *The Dragons of Eden*. The real ones are much uglier, and Munky's early incarnations were quite hideous. He's been cuted up.

THE HOURIS, FROM WHOSE NAME THE WORD "WHORE" IS DERIVED, WERE ORIGINALLY QUITE ANGELIC SPIRITS.

PAGE 407
Here we have one of the locals. This is Esveydy, a third-tier wife of Kokutsolado, the king whose territory overlaps Munkytown. She is a message runner and envoy. This ungulate she's riding is fast and strong and mean as an enraged hog.

Few tourists can resist the urge to film everything they see. For these tourists, it's a way of life. If you don't have a recording of what you did and saw, you can't sell it. Many cities' cultures are heavily biased toward the buying and selling of information.

PAGE 408
The driver and the crew have to get off here. They are not allowed to enter the promised land. A licensed driver can usually get a job on the next bus going out, but roustabouts like Jaeger might get a job or might not.

Jaeger can head for the hills on his own power if he doesn't like where he is. Most of the other people here think of wandering into the woods or down the road as being just as dangerous as being thrown overboard in the middle of the sea. This deep into Nyima lands, they're not far wrong.

There are two kinds of people living outside this dome. People from other cities who find themselves here with no money or prearranged job often aren't allowed in. The only way to get a job inside is to win one.

The other kind are citizens of the dome who have been sentenced to serve jail time. That jail is Shantytown. This city's system of criminal justice runs heavily to banishment and ostracism.

PAGE 410
Yes, the lottery numbers have fortune-cookie messages on the back. No weirder than fortune cookie messages with lottery numbers on them, is it?

Bottom tier. This explains Jaeger's odd haircut. He periodically hacks it off like this. He doesn't chop it off in the front because he's self-conscious about his yellow eyes.

PAGE 412
Panel 3. This is pretty standard company-town practice. Workers are never paid more than they have to spend on groceries and other necessities—and the company owns the shops, so they set the prices high. This guy is telling Jaeger this as if it isn't going to happen to all the people in this line anyway.

PAGE 413
Haurvatat is the name of a Zoroastrian spirit. He's a benevolent being associated with the water of the earth and the afterlife. His name means "wholeness" or "well-being." He may have been derived from a river deity. Given that river deltas give rise to cities, it seems reasonable that he'd have a city named for him.

Les Anges is a city far, far to the west.

PAGE 414
This is Shantytown. These people are given minimal supplies to keep themselves alive. The road people, who often have no supplies, are a constant threat to them.

PAGE 415
When the Nyima are on the road, they don't cluster all together. This is the traveling court of only one king. It's the center of a huge, slow-moving wheel of encampments full of secondary and tertiary wives and outliers who travel from the territory of one king to another.

PAGE 416
The current king's name is Kokutsolado. These three women are the last three wives of his predecessor, Jeikohsolado. They married Kokut when he was crowned, and edged out Eidi, who crowned Kokutsolado and was Jeikoh's chosen heir.

Jaeger could stay hidden from the Nyima for a long time, possibly long enough to clear out of their territory entirely. But he's curious about them, and so it's better to be polite and let them find him.

Bottom tier. For years, zoologists have debated the relationship between the largely female Nyima and the uluhaka, which were thought to be domesticated animals. Having concluded that the uluhaka were the males of the species, researchers then ignored all reports of bipedal kings for decades. The wives are very protective of their kings.

This woman's name is Tyi. She was very close to Eidi, and so is now rather low in rank among Kokut's first wives.

PAGE 417
The Nyima are much more territorial than the Ascians, Jaeger's people. They have been at war off and on for so long that nobody remembers peace. Asking to hunt with the Nyima is the kind of gray area that crops up between warriors that don't have a clue why they're

supposed to kill each other, and on occasion agree not to try.

"The dowagers" are the three old wives. A dowager is a woman who holds a title or property through her dead husband.

PAGE 418
I saw something like this happen. It wasn't a unicorn; it was a raccoon. I freaked out for days.

PAGE 419
The "*flarne, flarne, filth, and flarne*" bit is a Bill Cosbyism.

PAGE 420
These folks are Ascians, people of Jaeger's nation. They're nomads, traveling along huge circuits in the deserts and prairie. They're a bit like Plains Indians and a bit like Bedouins.

PAGE 421
This is the inside of a yurt, which is more or less a tipi parked on top of a round enclosure. The whole thing can be disassembled, packed up, and moved out with surprising speed.

Most nomads live in much simpler tents. The Ascians are able to live in bigger, more substantial houses because their pack animals can be trained to help strike camp, and can carry far heavier loads than horses, camels, yaks, or even elephants.

PAGE 425
Ascians travel in small groups of no more than forty or fifty. In the summertime, many groups will come together someplace where the hunting's good. But each small group has its chief, and the chiefs maintain a loose hierarchy, culminating in a high chief, or drum chief. There are many drum chiefs, and no real agreement among them as to who's in charge. Nomads need a lot of territory, and the drum chiefs rarely get together as they have here.

PAGE 426
The old guy doesn't know Jaeger is a Finder. He's just complimenting him.

PAGE 427
This is the other half of Jaeger's life. He was made a sin-eater, or ritual scapegoat, at an early age. It's part of the reason he wanders so much. He can't really reconcile being a member of a highly respected secret society with being an untouchable. He has to keep the one thing secret, and is duty bound to *reveal* the other. He has to tell them he's a sin-eater, even though he knows it'll kill the party.

Then there's the girl. She got what she wanted. Jaeger will sleep in her house, eat her food, and wear her finery. She's expected to sleep with him if he wants it. But instead of having a hero to show off, she has to look after a sin-eater. To her, it's like having to put a silk hat on a pig.

PAGE 428
Out go all the young blades who wanted to meet the new guy. Out goes all her new social status, and with it a lot of potential husbands. She can yell at him all she wants—nobody'll blame her—but there it is.

PAGE 429
Jaeger has traveled with other nomads very like Ascians and not felt obliged to tell them his social status among his own people. The custom of providing a guest with a "wife" is very common, and her sleeping with a stranger isn't taboo. It provides new genes for small families. So he's had the royal treatment before, but not without twinges of guilt.

PAGE 430
In tent societies, you're supposed to pretend you don't overhear anything said inside a house if you're outside. Ascians never, *never* call to each other from windows, or look through windows from the inside. Panes of one-way glass for yurt windows are highly prized... stealing a pie from a windowsill is one of the "dirtiest" pleasures an Ascian kid can find himself indulging in.

The fadh-felen is another weird British water monster (I've messed with the spelling a bit).

PAGE 431
This dome is different from almost all of the other domed cities. It has no internal lattice on which buildings may be mounted. In this dome, all buildings rise from the ground, rather than being built in multiple levels like in Anvard. The dome is just a covering, and a flimsy one by comparison.

PAGE 432
The dark background color behind the stars changes color to indicate day and night. There is a small "sun" which travels around the inside of the dome during daylight.

Since the folks who run this place would hate for the kids to miss out on the splendor of their pretty night sky with its luminous stars, there are roughly three "days" and "nights" in a twenty-four-hour period.

PAGE 433
Food vendors and other lowlies are stuck wearing unchanging uniforms that identify them clearly as park employees. Security guards and other more important folks do double duty in these showy costumes, which change from place to place to match the local environment's theme.

PAGE 434
So yes, these bims are all security guards. They try to get things done persuasively. If that doesn't work, the guys move in. The men's costumes are usually "boss" or "thug" themed.

PAGE 435
"Daggett" is Little Bill Daggett, masterfully played by Gene Hackman in *Unforgiven*.

PAGE 436
"Stereorealist" is the name of a company that made stereo cameras back in their heyday.

The security guards are now trying to find out who Jaeger is, and whether he's a legitimate guest. If he's a guest, they can't beat the shit out of him.

PAGE 437
"The Veldt" is the title of a Ray Bradbury short story that really knocked me sideways when I was ten.

Some of this stuff is authentic Nyima ornamentation; the rest is fabbed up for the sake of display. It was all made by Nyima artisans at the behest of the Munkymen. The Munkys are not terribly impressed, and are working on fancier items to make the whole thing look better.

PAGE 438
The uluhaka bumps against Jaeger's leg so that he will have a little of Jaeger's scent on his hide, a kind of chemical calling card.

These are unmarried females. When they marry, they cut off the long hair on their heads. Thanks to the chemical bonds of marriage, the hair doesn't grow back. Darker-haired girls will show a darker "cap" of hair on their scalps for a while, but this fades with time.

SHE'S NOT A BAD
KID REALLY.
JUST NOT VERY
SELF-POSSESSED.

PAGE 439
This is Maricch. She is King Kokutsolado's chosen, his heir. She will not become queen. Her job, as it was Eidi's job before her, is to choose the new king and give him his crown.

Only three of these girls are her sisters genetically. The rest are girls from other kingdoms, traded for the daughters of Kokut. Since the Nyima are so polygamous, it's very important for them to swap kids.

Jaeger is unknowingly quoting Bagheera, from Kipling's *The Jungle Book*. Nyima have very complicated social protocol.

This is the deal the dowagers made with Jaeger. They got him in the door to bring word to Maricch of the king's death. None of the other Nyima want to step foot into Munkyland, because the second they do, the Munkymen will hold them to a contract they signed and insist that they perform for an audience. The Nyima thought they were signing a treaty with another political entity. They wanted neutral ground to hear a proposal from the Ascian drum chiefs.

Once they start "performing," the Munkymen will work to get more hooks into them so they can't leave. That's what's happening with these daughters.

PAGE 441
Access tunnels run everywhere in the Munkydome. Out of the public eye, the guards can be as violent as they like, but that's okay with the daughters right now.

They're leaving the baubles because the stuff's cheap as ditch water to them. Maricch's necklace and what's in it are the family treasure.

PAGE 442
This four-legged female is what the daughters found so intolerable. They have been holding out against the Munkymen because they find the décor so deeply insulting.

PAGE 443
Another "day" dawns in Munkyland, but it's really only been a few hours.

IF YOU COULD LOOK CLOSELY ENOUGH, YOU'D SEE THAT EVEN THE SPARKLES HAVE TINY LITTLE GOONY SMILES.

PAGE 444
She's been making these beaded patches for years, ever since she was a little girl. Others she inherited from female relatives. They're kept in her hope chest, things she's been planning to give as love gifts to suitors. She's probably got a boxful of them, mind, but she's still pissed at having to waste them on Jaeger.

Hanging on the walls are the chiefs' drums. Sitting in front of the floor cushions are amulet bags and folded hides. On those hides are inscribed records of births, deaths, and marriages in their tribes. These items represent their souls, and the chiefs sent them in as stand-ins. Why? So they wouldn't have to sit socially with and give honor to a sin-eater.

PAGE 445
Ah, Chief Coward. He's got to be the most devious character who's ever introduced himself to me.

PAGE 446
Chief Coward is the one who pulled all this together. He convinced the other drum-chiefs to come together; he convinced Kokut to meet with them. Coward is a consummate politician, and now he's watching his plans fall apart due to the insanity of Munkyland and the death of the king. The other chiefs are starting to squabble. The young men are restless and wanting to start something. Coward is ready to add a new element of trouble into the mix—namely, Jaeger. Actually, he just wants to kick the other chiefs' butts a little. If he can't see his treaty through, he'll settle for counting coup.

PAGE 447
The other boot drops! Yes, Coward is a Finder. He probably suspects that Jaeger is one too, but for Coward's purposes it's really not important.

PAGE 449
Coward has been watching this town grow for many, many years.

PAGE 451
More female sphinxes. This one is partly inspired by Walter Crane's drawings of Buraq in his book *Sheba*.

These are the dad and kids from Chapter 1 again.

Security has a lot of strange ways of regulating guests' movements.

PAGE 452
Hoop dancing. A static medium can't show how amazing this looks.

All the young men of the different tribes were willing to put up with each other while the chiefs were in accord, but all that's falling down now. They want to steal the treasure from the Nyima pavilion, thinking that they can count coup on the Nyima that way.

PAGE 453
The other Ascians don't know that the Nyima have already cleared out. Only Jaeger knows. Thanks to Coward, Jaeger also knows what the other Ascians want to do—count coup on the Nyima by stealing their treasure. So Jaeger will sneak back over there and snatch it himself while the Ascians are fighting. This is how Coward gets his jollies.

PAGE 455
Coward's no slouch, even with stiff joints. Now he knows that the Nyima are gone, and that Jaeger got away with the stuff.

PAGE 456
Now that he's got it, what can he do with it? It's heavy as shit, and the guards will be watching for him.

Bottom of panel 1: Guadalupe and Casimira from Gilbert Hernandez's *Duck Feet*.

MOLLY GRUE:
POSTMODERN
MAID MARIAN.
AS PORTRAYED BY ADRINN FRIEDMANN, LLAVERAC METHOD ACTOR.

PAGE 457
On the screen is a scene from *The Last Unicorn* by Peter S. Beagle, as filmed by the Llaveracs. Llaverac clan is very involved with moviemaking the old-fashioned way: with actors. This woman resembles Emma because they are members of the same clan.

Jaeger loses track of time easily. He's been carrying this braid around for a good while now. The ball of hair in his left hand was what he chopped off at the gate.

PAGE 458
What kind of artisan inlays a corrosive metal into a noncorrosive one? One who's just going for looks.

PAGES 459–462
This scene with the log-flume ride is based on something that happened to my husband. Complete with the talking hat.

Lots of these goofy rides are designed to take your picture in order to sell it back to you. In our world, all you have to do to prevent this is go down the flume with both birds flyin'.

PAGE 463
Top of panel 1: Katharine Hepburn's character from *The Madwoman of Chaillot*, talking about her character from *The Rainmaker*.

PAGE 464
Sea monkeys! Yahoo!

PAGE 467
This is not the guard from the work-permit gate, just another guy from his same clan.

PAGE 468
The guards wouldn't have offered the free tickets if Jaeger had not stood his ground. Even he hasn't got the nerve to stand against that howling mob.

PAGE 469
This is all an elaborate ruse so the guards can chase him down like a dog without upsetting the guests. Most of the crowd of guests were guards all along.

PAGE 470
Can't leave anybody unhappy. Naturally, this kind of thing leads some guests to act like screaming three-year-olds.

PAGE 471
No, I wasn't trying to "erase" Jaeger's wobbly bits. Those are, uh, motion lines.

PAGE 473
This dome is mostly glass. This would never work in Anvard. The "happy cannonballs" are

balloons. When fired, they drift sappily out over the crowd, and then burst, releasing clouds of edible confetti. Awww. He's stretched out in the bowl just for yuks, really. That, and because he dimly remembers his dream from the gun port of the tour bus at the beginning of all this. He doesn't think they've really got the nerve to pull the lever and fire his ass out through the roof of the dome, and he's right.

PAGE 475
Talking heads, Munkyland style. These two guys do the voices of the moose and the bird, and control their movements. They're puppeteers. They're probably gonna end up in Shantytown.

PAGE 479
With any luck, these kids are scarred for life.

PAGE 480
The daughters hid in plain sight. Nobody questioned the uluhaka's presence as long as they were with the cute fur suits.

PAGE 481
Yes, the bipedal females do have sex with the quadrupedal males. Can't expect one king to keep up with *all* of them, can you? The uluhaka cannot impregnate the bipedal females, though. That's a job only the king can do.

PAGE 482
The Nyima are camped outside a different door.

PAGE 483
Mesnie Harlequin is a name used in France for the Wild Hunt. Some sources say "harlequin" or "hellequin" is derived from "hell king" and denotes a minor demon. Mesnie Harlequin is believed to be a portent of disaster, plague, and war, and was reported to have darkened the sun twice before the outbreak of the Revolution. The Wild Hunt is said to capture harmless and benevolent spirits, changing their natures to demonic ones and adding them to their ranks.

PAGES 484–485
Here's the pit trap again. The Ascians are far more used to commerce than the Nyima. A smart kid who can read foreign languages is definitely an asset.

PAGE 486
Now that the king is dead, his pheromone signature is fading. The Nyiman marriage bonds are chemical. The uluhaka are calm and manageable while all the females are bonded to a king. Now that he's dead, they're fiercely hungry for what they've been denied.

Kokut had a black mane. This is rare and much admired. The small votive statues at the bottom of the pyre represent Kokut's primary wives. Once they would have been driven a little crazy by the loss of his chemical signature, and would have thrown themselves onto his body. That's when the daughters started burning the corpses. Some women would still be addled enough to throw themselves onto the pyre, so the daughters keep watch at a discreet distance. The wives are standing as far away from the fire as they can.

PAGE 487
There are a lot of feral uluhaka. They stray off in their youth, sometimes traveling hundreds of miles, but always straggling into a place where they can smell Nyiman women. The farthest outposts of any kingdom are composed of groups of snarly unattached uluhaka who answer to nobody and challenge all comers. Some "fall in love" with some wandering outlier, some fall in with a family group, and some stay on the outskirts in bachelor bands. These are very, very dangerous, even to (or perhaps especially to) Nyiman women in the field.

Panel 8: The remains of the treasure bag. The one who stubs her toe on it is Tyi, who first brought Jaeger to the dowagers.

PAGE 488
The children. The kings keep their babies close by them. They're reared by the king's primary wives and by the king himself. There are five here: three girls, two boys.

The word *queen* has come to connote to the Nyima a female uluhaka, and is therefore appalling, debased, and vile. They have a hard time translating their terms of social status into other languages. The wives are like officers; they want a general. Maricch was born and raised to be a colonel under a general.

A Nyiman king's wives are addicted to him, in a very literal way. They can't do without a king. They can't just decide *not* to have one. The heir is always a daughter, because a daughter will not be knocked sideways by her hormones when her father dies. When she picks a new king, all the mature women not bonded to some other king will become the new king's wives. The wives of this first marriage always carry a certain status over wives married later in his life. They are the primary, first-tier wives, usually.

PAGE 489
The marking on Jaeger's coat is a type of predatory gull, also called a jaeger. It's a totemic animal associated with an Ascian clan, so it wasn't that much of a coincidence that Lele had a patch depicting one.

PAGE 490
Everybody's hung up on Jaeger's short hair. Cultural identity is a lot more fluid than people believe. Just because he doesn't look Ascian doesn't take away his nature.

PAGE 491
Most uluhaka can't speak this well. This one has a gift for it. Good voices and good hands are prized by Nyiman women. An uluhaka who's managed to retain his childhood dexterity with his front paws is usually provided with running gloves to prevent his calluses from getting too thick.

PAGE 492
He really can't help it. The women give off a pheromonal distress call, now that the king is gone.

PAGE 493
The kids with head hair are female. Note that they look just as animal-like as their brothers at this age.

PAGE 494
Maricch is in a very bad position for asserting her authority. Not only does she have that huge crowd of her father's wives still trying to run her, but she also still has the three dowagers—her grandmothers! She alone will choose their new husband. She will be one of the primary wives, but she has only this one piece of leverage. She'd hoped to find the right uluhaka on her travels, but she didn't. Now all the wild ones are whipped into a frenzy by their own chemistry.

PAGE 495
The wild ones won't flop helplessly at her feet. These have been partly tamed by the king's and his wives' scents.

Moro and Ebo's names come from Moro the Wolf God and Lady Eboshi, both from *Princess Mononoke*.

PAGE 496
The name "Rhun" I took from Joan Slonczewski's *Daughter of Elysium*.

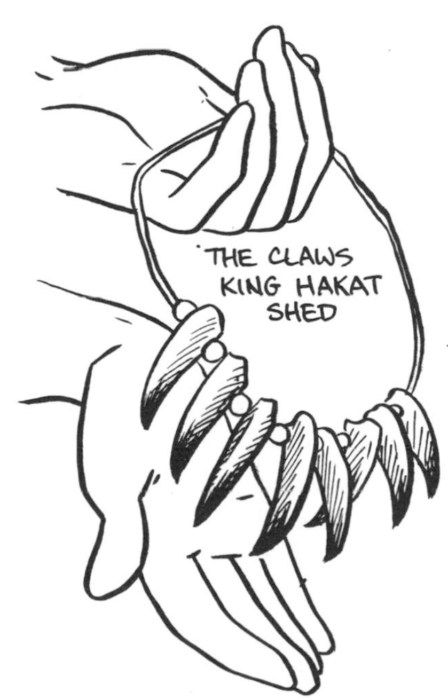

PAGE 497
Maricch's necklace contains a syringe. The syringe contains one good dose of a carrier virus produced in the body of the king. It carries his chemical signature, the signature of the Solado line. It is the "crown." With this substance (a disease to all others), he converts his daughters from their four-legged childhoods to bipedal adolescence. With it he "marries" his wives. With this substance his heir will transform from a four-legged male into a bipedal king. She has only the one dose. If her choice dies during the transformation, which is arduous, her kingdom will break apart and her family come to an end.

PAGES 498–499
She kills one; another runs away. The third she injects. Is this the same one that had Jaeger treed? Does he kill her in his frenzy or does she get away? She has to protect herself from him, and him from any other uluhaka who appear.

PAGE 500
Esveydy is the one who charged across the road in front of the tour bus in chapter 1. She gets around.

The Nyima riding animals are more like swine than those of the Ascians. The Ascian mounts are cattle. The Nyima animals can be trained to fight, but they're vicious. The Ascians prefer an animal that doesn't try to take a chunk out of you when your back is turned. The Nyima prefer an animal that can be fed meat, which they usually have in abundance.

PAGE 501
The king is still in the process of changing from quadruped to biped. This king chose to keep the children of his predecessor. Maybe he just likes kids; maybe he'd rather have someone else's kids than appear as a king with no offspring. It's a king thing.

PAGE 502
Why did Coward do all this? He wants land. The Ascians don't possess land the way the Nyima or the city people do. They're nomads; wherever they are is home. But he sees the Nyima prospering and spreading out. He sees this new city, the first built in his lifetime. The world is big; plenty of places for nomads to go. But it makes him wonder.

COVERS

PAGE 649
These people are all from clan Steinehan. True to all city clans, they aspire to a certain conformity. This clan has achieved a large part of its goal, and is fairly tolerant of odd clothing, hairstyles, tattooing, and other nongenetic modifications among its members. There are two facial shapes in this clan, two eye colors, three skin tones. Few clans have perfect uniformity, and the Steinehans are satisfied with their level of variability.

PAGE 650
These are Ascians of various types and extractions. In the crowd of Steinehans, Jaeger couldn't help but stand out. But even among his own, much more diverse people, his yellow eyes and hairy skin set him apart.

PAGE 658
King Hakatsolado. The Nyima are the most advanced of all the societies outside of the domed cities. They are highly acquisitive of any new technology that they believe will help preserve their autonomy among the nomadic hunters and somewhat settled herdsmen and farmers of their vast territories.

Those territories are ruled over by many Nyiman kings, who are rarely seen. Nyiman kings cannot tolerate each other's pheromones, so their wives are accustomed to being go-betweens and diplomats. There is no high king over all the Nyima land.

Part of what protects the less technologically advanced Nyima from invasion from the cities are the several virulent diseases they carry. The deleterious effects of these diseases upon the Nyima themselves have not been observed.

YAWL C'MON BACK NOW, Y'HEAR?

TALISMAN

PAGE 505
This is intentionally misquoted. The aphorism appears in *Bartlett's Familiar Quotations* as "My Book and Heart must *never* Part." The author of this quote is not known.

PAGE 507
Drawing based on a little girl I observed in the post office a few days before. Mom was shipping boxes, little sister was hanging on Mom's sweater, and this kid had her nose stuck in one of those Lemony Snicket books. She *never* looked up from it while trailing after her mother and sister without being called, and had no trouble opening the double doors.

PAGE 509
Lea Hernandez has named the cartoon version of her son, who appears in her online comic *Near-Life Experience*, Strangel. I coined the term while yakking on the phone with her, talking about her son. As far as I'm concerned, it's our word.

PAGE 511
I hadn't come up with an image for this story that really stood out, and I was getting a little nervous about it. The same day I saw the little kid in the post office, I was stuck in heavy traffic behind a car with what must have been two really small kids in the back seat. If one of them hadn't had this silly topknot I might never have known they were there at all.

All I could see was this little blond ponytail, set high on the crown of a head, held in place by either a really thick rubber band or a really compressed scrunchie. Since I couldn't see the actual kid's head, the effect was of a little puppet head, with a fluffy wig, bobbing about in the rear window.

That night I happened upon a Japanese website for customizable dolls. Their heads come off. The tops of their skulls come off as well, so their owners can a) change the color of their eyes, or the direction at which their eyes are looking, and b) tighten the elastic strings that hold the dolls' bodies together. All kids take their toys apart, and use them in their own inscrutable ways.

PAGE 512
In this world there is a measurable force that is described as magic. The Sylvan clan lay claim to a gift for it, and run well-funded schools to encourage talent for it. They test kids for certain abilities, and award scholarships or special training accordingly.

It's a rather quixotic gift. But that's all you need to know now.

PAGE 513
Ah—Marcie's doll, unlike the ones on that Web page, has those strange round eyeballs with eyelids painted on one side. They're weighted so that they "close"—roll to show the eyelid instead of the eye—when the doll's head is tilted. Many such dolls will "wink."

Those odd pegs on the sides of its head are fashion-doll-style earrings.

PAGES 515, 541, AND 565
These phrases are excerpted from a Lewis Carroll poem, which appears in my 1960 edition of *Through the Looking-Glass*, but also online at Project Gutenberg:

Child of the pure unclouded brow
And dreaming eyes of wonder!
Though time be fleet, and I and thou
Are half a life asunder,
Thy loving smile will surely hail
The love-gift of a fairy-tale.

FATHER &
DAUGHTER,
LEJEB CLAN
THIS CLAN
DOMINATES
MATHEMATICAL
BUSINESSES.

I have not seen thy sunny face
Nor heard thy silver laughter;
No thought of me shall find a place
In thy young life's hereafter—
Enough that now thou wilt not fail
To listen to my fairy-tale.

A tale begun in other days,
When summer suns were glowing—
A simple chime, that served to time
The rhythm of our rowing—
Whose echoes live in memory yet,
Though envious years would say "forget."

Come, hearken then, ere voice of dread,
With bitter tidings laden,
Shall summon to unwelcome bed
A melancholy maiden!
We are but older children, dear,
Who fret to find our bedtime near.

Without, the frost, the blinding snow,
The storm-wind's moody madness—
Within, the firelight's ruddy glow
And childhood's nest of gladness.
The magic words shall hold thee fast:
Thou shalt not heed the raving blast.

And though the shadow of a sigh
May tremble through the story,
For "happy summer days" gone by,
And vanish'd summer glory—
It shall not touch with breath of bale,
The pleasance of our fairy-tale.

PAGE 517
This is an open market, outside the dome, in what passes for sprawl around the big cities. In this case, however, sprawl doesn't consist of city people who want to live cheaply and own more land. These city people are convinced that life outside the domes is hazardous. The sprawl belt is made up of semi-settled people huddled around the trade routes leading into Anvard.

PAGE 518
The animal in the cage is a small quetzal. These flying lizards have feathers and claws on each of their four limbs.

Panel 2. Jaeger has on his belt two dark braids of equal length. These, plus the clocks in the background, are meant to indicate that he's going back to Anvard to check on Emma and her family, as he swore to do at the end of

Sin-Eater. Jaeger is a trash picker, a scavenger. He finds things to barter. When he comes back to visit people, he has to bring gifts. This is both his nature and his upbringing.

PAGE 519
The design on the cover of Marcie's gift was based partly on the caduceus and partly on the AURYN symbol in Michael Ende's *The Neverending Story* (a wonderful book and a dreadful movie). AURYN is, in turn, a clear reference to Ouroboros, the world serpent, and the common symbol of infinity.

Marcie hasn't progressed well in school in part because she was a very sickly kid, and has missed a lot, and in part because her mother is in constant dispute with her grandfather about how the kids should be educated. Granddad, you see, is Money. Marcie is not of an age to understand this—she just knows that if she expresses no opinion, Mom and Terry will fight to stalemate and Marcie won't be forced to go to school.

Panel 6. William Goldman says he asked his daughters what kind of story they liked. One said "princesses"; the other said, "brides." So there you have it.

PAGE 520
Quotes: "When suddenly"—Lewis Carroll, *Alice*

In Wonderland. "Henceforth"—J. M. Barrie, *Peter Pan*. "My own garden"—Oscar Wilde, *The Selfish Giant*. "It was fourteen"—Stephen King, *Rose Madder*. "The lamb said"—me myself, a mishmosh of Norse and English folktales. "I can't answer"—me myself again. Favorite fantasy stories of mine, all of them. The figure of Emma and her children on the lower right section comes from a remarkable sculptor, Thomas Blackshear. He makes lovely, sentimental resin figures, beautifully detailed and elegant. This one is from his Ebony Visions line.

PAGE 521
More quotes: "Until"—me again. "Bye, boys!"—William Goldman, *The Princess Bride*. "The bottom"—me. "Awake, awake"—C. S. Lewis, *The Magician's Nephew*. "In order"— Octavia Butler, *The Parable of the Sower*. "He saw her fall"—me again.

PAGE 522
Cosmic hangover. I live for it.

Panel 3. These tentacular strands emerging from Emma's head are complicated hardware, hookups for her profession. Details aren't really necessary—a lot goes on around Marcie that she doesn't think much about. A whole earth-shattering Jaeger Returns scene is taking place all around her, and it's just not making an impression on her.

PAGE 523
Brigham underwent a number of unpleasant therapies to correct a physical problem (two broken legs) and a psychological problem (an obsessiveness which led to his stalking his wife and family). These therapies don't draw the line between rehabilitation and revenge clearly at all.

PAGE 524
This is, I admit, all rather gothic, but the influence of the sickly relative on small children is something that fits Marcie well. This Cthulhoid figure lurking in some back bedroom—well, fear is the Philosopher's Stone of the imagination. It transmutes damn near anything into a story.

PAGE 525
Emma's "tentacles" are connected to these cables. The whole rig makes for a very high bandwidth connection between Emma's mind and the Pastwatch Institute's recording devices.

PAGE 526
If the thought of people not reading strikes you as implausible—well, it isn't. Literacy isn't really the issue. A staggering number of people who can read, don't. Of those who do, many read nothing but magazines, never actual books.

Metus is a merging of the names Medusa and Metis. Their names possibly derive from the same word, which means wisdom or prudence. *Mnemo* is an abbreviation of Mnemosyne, goddess of memory.

PAGE 527
Top left corner. This is Vince Sneed's character Stella Maris, the day-tripper. She has an enormous sheepdog named Digby. I'm not sure where he means to use them, but they fit.

Panels 2–4. Panel 2 is Jaeger's retelling of *The Night of the Hunter*. Panels 3 and 4 are actual dialogue.

PAGE 528
Panels 4–5. Here, Jaeger's kissing his fingers, then transferring the kiss to Marcie's cheek. Dunno if it comes across.

PAGE 529
Oh, the pain! I don't know how many times I just wanted somebody to read to me. Even though I could read—I can't remember a time far back enough that I couldn't—I just wanted to sit in a chair with somebody and have them read to me. But you know almost nobody reads a book well. Sigh.

Rachel's problem is she suffers from smarm. This excess of zeal really doesn't amuse small children. In fact, I have to wonder if it isn't a component of the common fear of clowns. All the adults are smiling—watching you to see what you do—and here comes this loud, brightly colored creepazoid, rushing at you, doing weird things. All the signals say that you are supposed to be pleased, encourage you to be excited—what you really want is, perhaps, an elephant gun to fend 'em off with.

PAGES 530–531
This is the kind of incredibly tedious, repetitive writing that characterizes the worst of children's fiction, much of which has never emerged from the Victorian period. This is all fake. In so many ways.

PAGE 532
What's in the book that Rachel flips out over? Probably an illustration. People freak out over visual stuff much more readily than they do over prose.

PAGE 533
"My birthday present"—No, it wasn't really; it wasn't Marcie's birthday. Like Smeagol, she tends to think of her most prized possession as her best present.

PAGE 534
This attitude is not really cruelty. Lynne's way of dealing with Marcie will get her up and out of her slough of despondence and into action faster than anything else.

PAGE 535
This school is dominated by the Llaveracs. Their curriculum is not as frivolous as it looks, but it isn't really what suits Marcie. Marcie's father was not Llaverac. Medawars are much earthier, more practical people.

PAGE 536
Marcie disabled and stole one of the roving cameras for Lynne. Lynne's been training her to do this kind of thing since she was able to walk. After all, small kids can smile innocently and get away with murder.

MARCIE, AGE EIGHT
THIS BLACK TURTLENECK-PLUS-TIGHTS THING SHE WEARS IS A COMMON UNIFORM FOR MEDAWAR CHILDREN.
IT'S USED BOTH AS OUTERWEAR AND AS A LINER FOR HEAVIER CLOTHING.
MANY CLANS HAVE UNIFORMS LIKE THIS.

PAGE 537
Bedridden people in nursing homes and "rest homes" often develop odd behaviors to get attention. Howling is one such. Some just keep up a constant low howl until somebody comes. Most of the howlers won't remember somebody came to check on them five minutes later, so they keep the howling up day and night.

There are kings asleep under hills or mountains in every system of folklore. The king who wakes up and ends the world, that's partly Brahma and partly *Through the Looking-Glass*.

PAGE 538–539
Yes, this is a horrible thing to do to a kid, and yes, it happens every day. I do think books are different, but some kids think the loss of a single Lego piece is as earthshattering as Marcie views the loss of her book. How's a parent in a heavily digital society to keep up?

PAGE 543
Now we are in the Midnight Library. Every book is in here, and there will be no fires that destroy. She can barely reach them, but she can read whatever she can pull down.

PAGE 544
Does anybody remember *The Nothing Book*? It was the first blank book I ever saw, way back in the seventies. Its slogan was, "Wanna make something of it?"

The importance of this dream is that she's rewarded for taking action. She's been given everything she ever wanted, but she has to do something for it. If it was given to her for nothing, it would be nothing.

PAGE 545
Most of her contemporaries simply don't understand why she has all these paper books, or indeed all this paper. It's a hands-on *craving*. I can't remember anything unless I write it down or draw it. Many of our words for cognition are tactile words. We speak of "handling" a problem, "turning it over" in our minds, "grasping" an idea. A keyboard just doesn't do it for all of us.

The malaise of this age can be terrible. You have nothing, no power, very little independence. Many of us fall under inertia. Marcie can't tolerate boredom—it keeps her moving.

PAGE 546
Any fourteen-year-old boy who can smoke at the kitchen table in front of his older sister and mother is the ruler of the roost, in nature if not in name.

The small tree growing in the center of the table bears fruits that may be used as condiments.

PAGE 547
Marcie is not me. But this sense of detachment from her feelings, as if they are things that happen to her—that comes from me. Also the ongoing daydream that fends off boredom.

The panel border (and puzzle) comes from Kit Williams's *Masquerade*. More quotes: "You are a little"—Orson Scott Card, *Songmaster*. "I ask for so little"—Jim Henson et al., *Labyrinth*. The Goblin King is one of my favorite not-all-there fantasy figures.

PAGE 548
Quotes: "Look, everyone"—Tanith Lee, *The Silver Metal Lover*. "He stared"—William F. Nolan, *Logan's Run*. "There were plenty"—Doris Piserchia, *Spaceling*. "Somehow, it was hotter"—Harper Lee, *To Kill a Mockingbird*. More favorite fantasies.

PAGE 549
Later in her life Marcie was transferred to a school run by and populated with Medawars. Medawars believe in sex segregation. Llaveracs don't.

Marcie may suffer the slings and arrows of her teachers, who disapprove of her mixed heritage, but Medawar girls are pretty self-willed. Marcie will have friends, even though they think she's bats.

PAGE 550
Marcie's hookup is very simple. Just a crude connection that allows her to manipulate the computer display, and receive and transmit simple information, including simple sensations.

PAGE 551
Panel 6 touches briefly on the source of Lynne's fortune, and the focus of his obsession. Many people in this society are forever running after compelling footage to sell to TV and movie companies, such as the one run by Marcie and Lynne's grandfather. He may be a viciously opportunistic voyeur, but in his society, that's easy money.

PAGE 552
This "footage" may be seen in *Finder* #11. Any bets on how Lynne got it away from the Huitzi priest who originally shot it?

PAGE 553
There are so many tiny studios... Like garage bands, everybody tries to come up with a weird name; anything memorable will do. This would work if they didn't change their names so often.

Panel 4—Lynne shot this image in issue #5, while Jaeger was sleeping in the tub.

PAGE 554
This idea of having direct control of an audience's emotions came from Hitchcock. I shudder to think what would have become of that man if he'd had access to this imaginary technology. Nothing good, I think.

PAGE 555
The name of this bookstore is another reference

to Michael Ende's *The Neverending Story*. I urge you not to judge that book by its movie.

PAGE 556
The pipe smoke comes from Attic Books, a used-and-rare shop close to me. The owner's got a replica of the Maltese Falcon on his desk. The stuff that dreams are made of.

PAGE 557
I am not Marcie. I didn't have the guts to break the window.

PAGES 558–559
Well . . . since I can think of nothing to elaborate on these pages, I suppose I might call them successful.

MARCIE TAKES AFTER HER MEDAWAR FATHER, EXCEPT FOR HER HAIR (WHICH ISN'T TURNING DARK BROWN WITH MATURITY) AND HER NEARSIGHTEDNESS (COMMON AMONG HER MOTHER'S CLAN).

PAGE 562
I had one of these stupid books as a kid. It wasn't cool, though; it was horrible. Big, crude, line-printer type, so obviously fake. It was illustrated with classic images from Maurice Sendak, Dr. Seuss, all the greats—badly reprinted, entirely without context, and almost certainly used without permission. The story left no impression on me whatever, but the surrealism of these familiar pictures thrown in for no reason both appealed to and appalled me. I have no idea where that book went. No doubt my mother threw it out.

One other thing. I did to one of my small cousins what Jaeger did to Marcie. Y'know how a kid will bring you the same book over and over and over again. They just want to sit with you, more than anything else. Fine for the kid; death for the adult. So I would just make stuff up. I'd blather and she'd turn the pages whenever she felt like it, and I'd just blabber on until she decided the book was over. I don't know if she really knew I wasn't reading, but she always brought me that same book, and wouldn't ask anyone else to read that particular one. I used to worry about what would happen when she got old enough to learn to read. I needn't have worried. She's ten now, and has no recollection of my doing this at all.

PAGE 563
Lynne's a good Vulcan. Vulcan thinking cuts through a lot of troublesome melodrama.

PAGE 567
Now I've got people pestering me to write the story Marcie's writing. I can barely keep track of what goes on in my own head! How can I know more about what goes on in hers?

The three small panels are meant to look like sticky notes. This is what my notebooks look like—messes of sketches and gibberish covered with phone numbers and sticky notes.

On the sticky notes: such things as "martinene 144-bv-273" are "narnebers." That's a phone ID number that follows you wherever you go. It's not always a bad idea, except when it's a terrible idea.

PAGE 568
This bookstore scene is taken directly from life, with me as Marcie. Poor kid! I knew just how she felt. When you're that age, you lose track of the Right Book easily—you don't remember titles or think to write down authors' names. I loved this one odd little book when I was in the third grade, had no idea what it was called or who wrote it (Wrote it?? Nobody *wrote* it! It's just, y'know, like, a *book* I like!), and couldn't find it again. Not until I was twenty-six years old did I spot it again—riding under the elbow of a customer in the bookstore I was

working in. I pounced on her, I can tell you; I'd recognized the cover and I *had* to have a better look at it. Thank God, she understood completely. She was One of Us, fellow book freak. *No Flying in the House* by Betty Brock, wonderfully illustrated by Wallace Tripp. I felt so strongly about that book when I was seven, I rewrote the ending on the two blank pages at the back of the book. In grubby pencil. That little hardcover may still be out there, with my first attempt at script doctoring penciled in. Who can say?

PAGE 569
Smoke the Magnificent and his Lovely Assistant are both members of Sylvan clan. Sylvans have odd talents for what they call magic. This is smoke sculpture, a mostly useless form of psychokinesis. Smoke particles drifting in the air are easy to manipulate.

Many of the references—light making a statue blink, the library book—these are references to a Studio Ghibli movie called *Whisper of the Heart*. Japanese anime. A beautifully plotted exercise in serendipity and "real" magic. If you can get past the John Denver song that serves as a theme, it's amazing.

PAGE 570
"Scepticism is the chastity of the intellect, and it is shameful to surrender it too soon or to the first comer: there is nobility in preserving it coolly and proudly through a long youth, until at last, in the ripeness of instinct and discretion, it can be safely exchanged for fidelity and happiness." George Santayana, *Scepticism and Animal Faith, IX.*

Why is Lynne, of all people, applying lipstick? Over a five o'clock shadow? Well . . . he's a complicated person. He imagines this is something Jaeger would never do in a million years.

PAGE 571
Marcie's Medawar side comes out. Medawars are really solid, practical, rolled-up-sleeves kind of people. If she can't have "magic," which, since it exists on a shaky foundation of mood, must be delicately danced around, she'll pitch in and learn the hands-on stuff.

PAGE 572
See? Screech owl. I'd had this job in mind for her for a long time. Marcella Grosvenor, queen of the Silver Scream. The kind of person who's just a footnote on movie history, known only to serious collectors of trivia.

PAGE 573
Panel 3. Yes, the lady in leopard skins is actually Marcie's grandfather, Terry Ellis Lockhart. Llaveracs love female fashion, in clothing and in skin.

PAGE 574
"Daughter-of-war" is a literal translation of Marcella, Marcie's full name.

A tarn is an alpine lake formed by glaciation. They're usually round. Bronze Age people would throw in weapons, jewelry, bones, bodies, whatever tribute or libation seemed fitting. Like fountains in malls, I suppose; people can't resist throwing in a penny and making a wish.

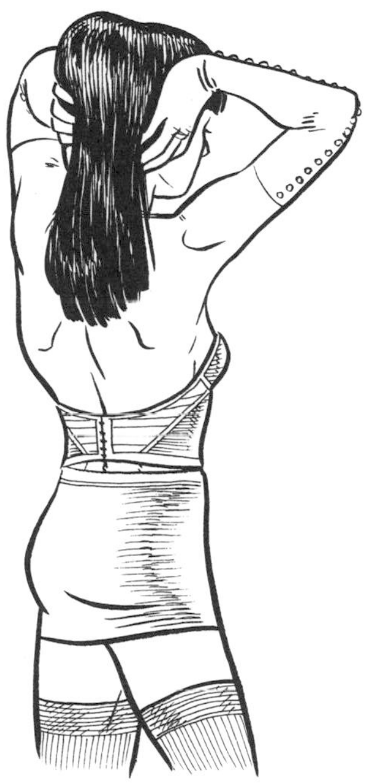

Yes, okay, fine; the warrior goddess at the deep end of the pool did come from youthful late-night viewings of *Heavy Metal* on HBO. So kill me.

PAGE 576
This armor is fetishistic and rather impractical, but hey, it's her fantasy. Let the kid have some fun.

PAGE 577
Note that Marcie has removed her glasses for

her bounce down these dark stairs. For those who are not nearsighted, this increases a feeling of... dissociation, a sensation of floating. You can't quite see where you're going, so you'd better know the territory intimately.

Panel 3. This frustration—mood broken, story gone—was described by a pen pal as the GODDAMNFUCKSHITS. Yep. That's basically it. It's the bitch slap of the muse.

PAGE 578
Go read *The Color of Light* by William Goldman. Then I'll discuss this page.

PAGE 579
That hideous drawing is one of mine, circa age five. No, you may not look at it. Ever.

Panel 7. This is a teenaged Medawar orderly. They don't all become full-fledged doctors or nurses, but they all receive a lot of medical training. They're all expected to learn from their mistakes. This girl made a pretty dumb mistake.

PAGE 580
Then the Medawar girl compounded it by freaking out. She could easily have done what Marcie does to get Brigham off of her. She'll have quite a lecture waiting for her when she has to explain the condition of her arm back at the hospital.

PAGE 581
The sphinxes come from *The Neverending Story*, and from the New York Public Library (since I couldn't use their lovely lions). The Palace of Memory is *not* a public library. It's the private property of a very aristocratic family, the Ambersons, whose name is a tribute to Orson Welles.

PAGE 582
Practicality and fantasy fistfight in Heaven. You can't do good work without making a balance between them. Not a balance so much as an engine.

PAGE 583
Bottom left—an eBook is a file. That object is an eBook Reader™ (as well as a day planner and heaven knows what all). It happens to come with new books already loaded. On the bottom right are the small chips containing more books that can be loaded into the reader. The object in panel 2 is a cardboard dust jacket for an eBook Reader™, originally designed to protect such things from scratches, but sold in the zillions as accessories.

PAGES 584–585
Okay, yes, I actually did this. I blew a *day* doing this. But mine was still there when I went back for it.

PAGE 587
The cut-open-to-reveal-deeper-self also comes from *The Voyage of the Dawn Treader*. Inside the dragon thing is Marcie's loony Cthulhoid father. Inside the loony father is Brigham back when he wasn't apparently loony. When you can't really have him back... he's worse than the dragon.

PAGE 588
He quiets when she picks him up. Just as he used to do when she was the child.

PAGE 589
Yes, my book is still empty.

PAGE 590
I have two lamps in my studio. I see this double shadow when I work. The idea of using this image, the moment before creation, came directly from Oscar in Dave Sim's *Jaka's Story*.

COVER GALLERY

FINDER

FINDER
EL-M
L'AS
EL-MELAK L'ASWADH
R. TROPHY BOOKS
FINDER
2
$2.95 U.S.
$4.15 CAN

FINDER

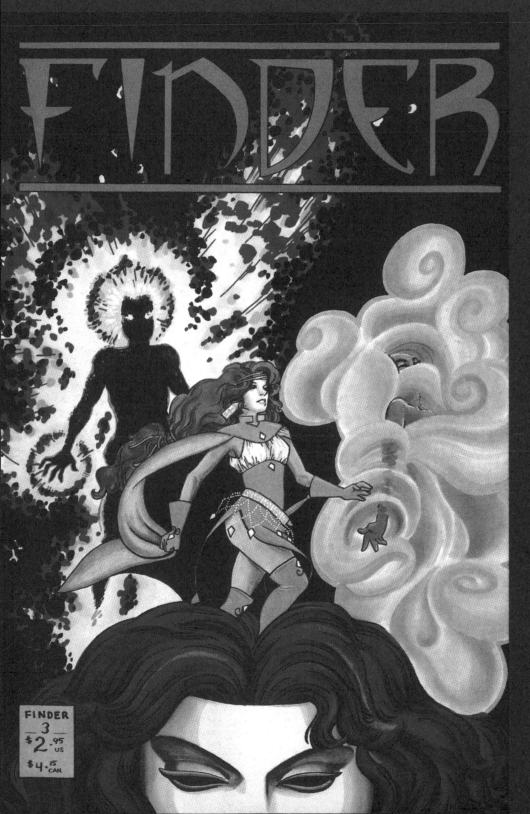

FINDER

SHMONAT HAKHEREVIM.
MAVET.
MALKAT HAKOSIM.
FINDER
4
$2.95 US
$4.15 CAN

FINDER

5
2.95
3.15 CAN

LOCKHART

SPEED
'97

LIGHT
SPEED
PRESS

FINDER

GRAVUS GERMANIC LXVIII
LIGHT SPEED PRESS
SPEED 97
6
2.95
3.15 CAN

FINDER

FINDER

CSM98

FINDER
CSM '98

FINDER

LIGHT
SPEED
PRESS

11

2.95

CSM
'98

FINDER

TALISMAN

19

2.95

©SM2000

LIGHT SPEED PRESS

1 OF 2

CSM
2001!

"COMPLETELY FASCINATING" - WARREN ELLIS, CO-CREATOR AND WRITER OF PLANETARY & TRANSMETROPOLITAN

FINDER

SIN-EATER, VOLUME TWO BY CARLA SPEED MCNEIL

MIDNIGHT LIBRARY
STACK PASS